& LETTERING BIBLE

a comprehensive guide to the design, construction and usage of alphabets, letters and symbols

Leslie Cabarga

David & Charles

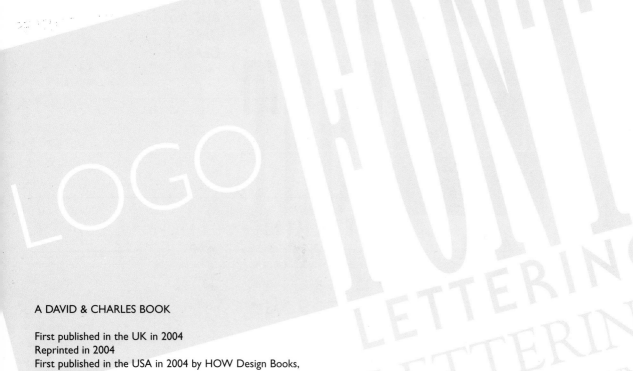

A DAVID & CHARLES BOOK

First published in the UK in 2004
Reprinted in 2004
First published in the USA in 2004 by HOW Design Books,
Cincinnati, Ohio

A catalogue record for this book is available from the British Library.

ISBN 0 7153 1699 0

Printed in China by Leefung-Asco
for David & Charles
Brunel House Newton Abbot Devon

Visit our website at www.davidandcharles.co.uk

David & Charles books are available from all good bookshops; alternatively you can contact our Orderline on (0)1626 334555 or write to us at FREEPOST EX2 110, David & Charles Direct, Newton Abbot, TQ12 4ZZ (no stamp required UK mainland).

DEDICATION & ACKNOWLEDGEMENTS

To my father, Ted Cabaraga, who taught me discernment

Lots of help is required in writing a bible...and not just from the Spirits of Lettering Past. Thanks to Clare Warmke, editor in chief of HOW Design Books, for her wise shepherding of this project, and to the other Good Samaritans at F&W: Lisa Buchanon, Clare Finney, Ruth Preston and Lisa Collins. I am also indebted to my late friends, the letterers and typophiles Clarence P. Hornung, J.J. Herman, Joe Weiler, and Don Sturdivant for sharing their memories and their collections. Thanks also to the following for their friendship, their words of advice, and myriad other contributions: Michael Doret, Jill Bell, Stuart Sandler, Allan Haley, Tom Nikosey, Gerard Huerta, Roger Black, Rick Cusick, Danny Pelavin, David Berlow, Harry Parker, Sam Berlow, Cyrus Highsmith, Mark Record, Ken Barber, Tal Leming, Laura Smith, John Gowling, Seymour Chwast, Tony DiSpigna, Jonathan Hoefler, Jonathan Macagba, Ted Harrison, and John Homs. And finally, to my wife Marga Kasper and our children Anna and Kodo, and my daughter Casey Robbins, for your love and encouragement.

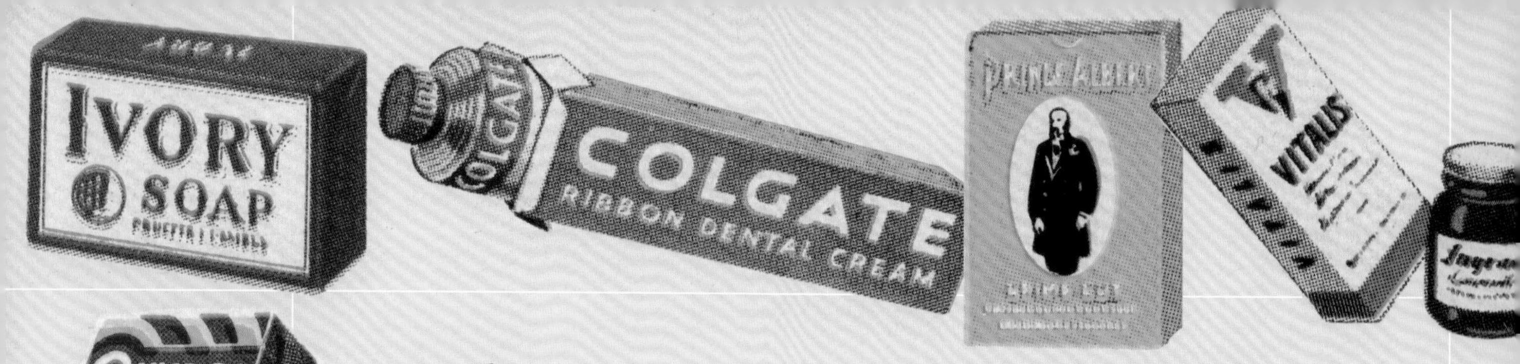
IVORY
SOAP
COLGATE
RIBBON DENTAL CREAM
PRINCE ALBERT
VITALIS

OXYDOL
PURINA
MILLS
SKELLY

Contents

CRISCO
CAMAY
DUZ
JOHNSON'S
WAX
PALMOLIVE

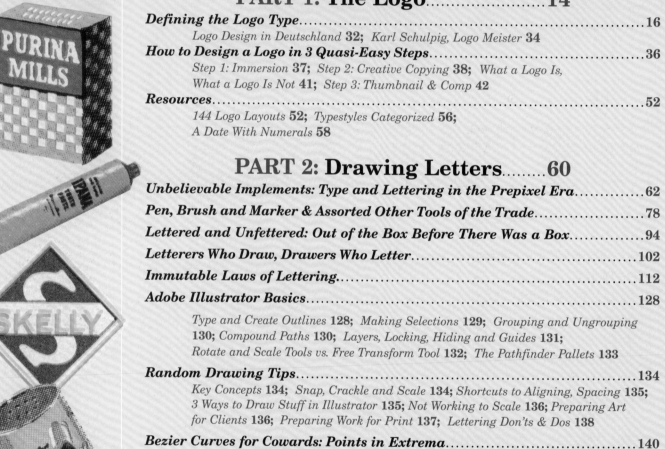

Fine logos and lettering are ubiquitous as even these common, everyday household products remind us.

drene
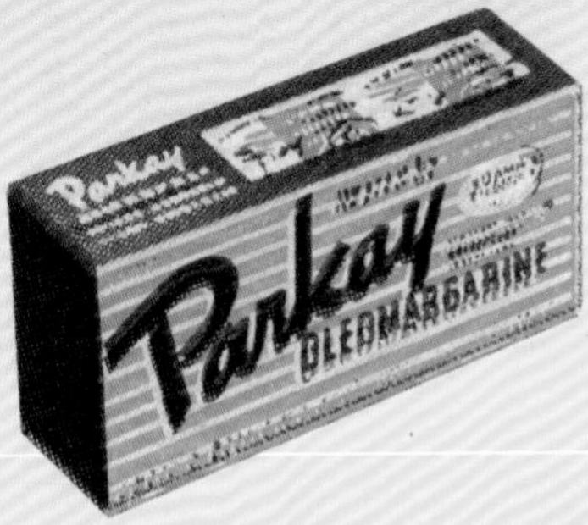
Parkay
OLEOMARGARINE

Betty Crocker
SOFTASILK
CAKE FLOUR

SPEEDBALL
PENS
for Drawing and Lettering

Instant
POSTUM

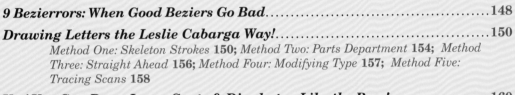

PART 3: Fonts—The Art of Making Faces...198

MAXWELL
HOUSE

Skrip
SHEAFFER'S

PART 4: Business Section...........228

KRAFT

Cheerioats

HEINZ
CREAM OF
TOMATO
SOUP
57

Post's 40%
Bran
Flakes

dreft

INTRODUCTION

Once upon a time, all lettering was hand-lettering. By the nineteenth and twentieth centuries, when type had become cheap and accessible to all, the indicator of a quality job was that the logo, the main display headline or the embellished initial cap had been hand lettered, rather than set in standard fonts that any competitor could obtain for a few dollars.

ENTER TYPE, EXIT LETTERING

Up until about the mid-1960s—the dividing line between the crew-cut conformist age and the new age of inquiry—the majority of logos and display headlines in magazines and ads were hand lettered with brush or pen. The changeover to a preference for type over lettering undoubtedly had something to do with the emergence of huge photolettering type catalogs by that time. But even Photo-Lettering, Inc., maintained an active studio of hand letterers to tweak fonts for custom jobs.

As late as 1989, some agency hired me to hand letter three words for a newspaper circular ad. I thought they were nuts, since the style they specified was almost identical to an existing font. But they didn't want type, they wanted unique, custom lettering exclusively theirs.

The tradition lives on today in the upper echelons of publication design. You might look at a logo and say, "But it's just Helvetica." No, it's $20,000 worth of hand-lettered Helvetica with a slight upturn added to the crossbar of the lowercase *e* that justified the expenditure and gladdened the heart of some CEO.

To this day, despite the computer revolution that has loosed the font industry from its pig-iron age moorings, type has yet to match the limitlessness and flexibility of letters drawn by hand where each letter shape can be nipped and tucked to accommodate the surrounding ones and every word or phrase can benefit from the designer's maximal interpretation.

Because of the continuing glut of computer fonts—the greater percentage of which are embarrassingly amateurish—the idea of custom lettering has lately been discarded along with the 1.5MB floppy disk. This is fine for the many and for those who don't mind using OPF (other people's fonts) as the basis of their logos. After all, the amazing number of fonts now in existence, and the hundreds more that shall emerge between the time of this writing and its publication, might be said to provide a measure of exclusivity to our work since most people will never even be able to identify the fonts we use.

But if you are designing an exclusive logo for a company or a magazine masthead, would you really want to use a font that anybody can purchase for a few bucks or download for free?

Certainly, the owners of font foundries, myself included, hope designers will continue to buy our fonts for making logos. However, in my other job, as a book writer, I'm the embodiment of the noble Chinese saying: "The extract of the indigo plant is bluer than the plant itself," which means, *May the student surpass the teacher*. Of course, I hope you don't surpass me, because I need to earn a living, too.

DESIGNERS DO IT WITH STYLE

The difference between a designer and an actual artist is, a designer can indicate preferences and arrange preexisting graphic elements but cannot draw well enough to bring his best visions to fruition by his own hand. A designer's inability to draw may also unconsciously limit his ability to conceptualize.

Of course, lots of designers create incredible pieces that make us all go, "Wow!" and want to copy them. And since the end result is all that matters, who cares if assistants do our creative grunt work? The trendsetting designer Herb Lubalin had letterers such as Tony DiSpigna and Tom Carnase to bring his wonderful conceptions to fruition. Seymour Chwast, on the other hand, despite the many designers he's employed, has always kept his hand, literally, in the work he produces.

"Today's designers," says letterer Gerard Huerta, "are assemblers of stock images and fonts. They learn how to assemble from source books and put it all together, and they never have to hire a photographer or illustrator, because it's just a matter of assembling ready made pieces."

It wasn't always this way. Many of the art directors of old who hired the Norman Rockwells and F.G. Coopers of those times had prodigious drawing and lettering skills. But standards have fallen. Few of us today can design, draw and letter the way guys like Will Dwiggins, Walter Dorwin Teague, Clarence P. Hornung and C.B. Falls did. (See "Letterers Who Draw" on page 102.)

Throughout this book, I will try to create that breakthrough for you, from being a designer who specs type and pushes it around, to one who creates type and *then* pushes it around. You, too, can be like Frank Lloyd Wright, who wrote, "Were architecture bricks, my hands were in the mud of which bricks were made."

I will attempt to do this merely by convincing you that you can do it—you've just been afraid to try. Another reason you've relied on OPF is that nobody ever told you the little secret that I was privileged to have revealed to me by the late, legendary cartoonist Wally Wood: "Never draw what you can copy; never copy what you can trace; never trace what you can photostat and paste down." Nowadays, we'd say, "Never trace what you can scan into Adobe Photoshop." And there you have it; the secret to becoming the logo designer you've always wanted to be is: "Research."

THE PURPOSE OF THIS BOOK

I wrote this book to enable you to expand your creativity and end your reliance upon the logos and fonts of other designers to become a logo and font designer yourself. Of course, there's nothing wrong with using OPF, especially if you like them. I do it myself—constantly, as we all do at times—but won't you feel proud when you can point to a logo or font and say, "Look, Ma, I drew that... *by hand!*"

At this point I should define the terms *hand-drawn* or *hand-lettered* not just as letters we create with drawing tools on paper, but also letters we create on computer, because the hand still guides the digital tablet, mouse or trackball. But the important distinction as far as this book is concerned, as to whether a logo or

Paul Whiteman

OBEY

The logo, font and lettering samples in this book have been liberally selected from the past as well as from the present. The basic principles of typography never become outdated, they just reappear dressed up in contemporary garb. Case in point: In the past there was the iconic bandleader, Paul "Pops" Whiteman, and at present we have Shepard Fairey's ubiquitous Andre the Giant logo, about which he says, "The concept behind 'Obey' is to provoke people who typically complain about life's circumstances but follow the path of least resistance, to have to confront their own obedience. 'Obey' is very sarcastic, a form of reverse psychology."
Paul and Andre: two icons separated by over seventy years, and both leaders in their fields. That's what I'm talking about!

Who are these individuals?

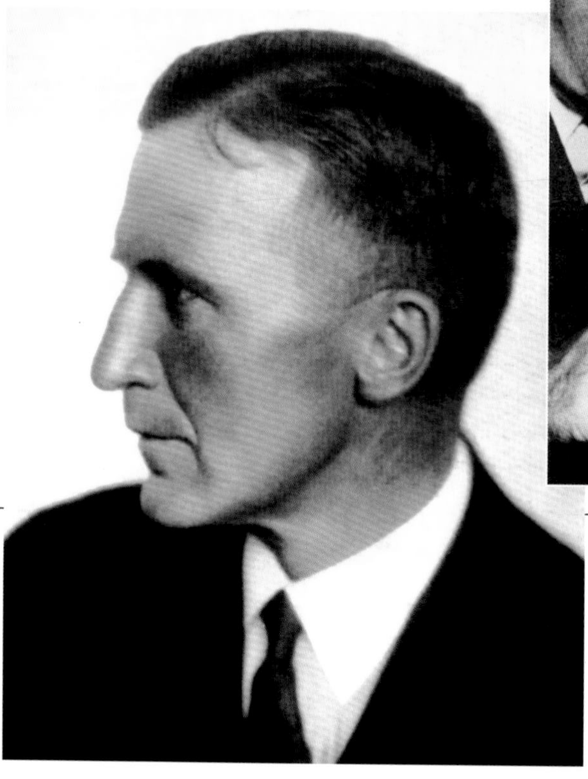

ANSWERS: Clockwise from top, William Caslon, English type designer; Edward Johnston, wrote influential treatise *Writing & Illuminating & Lettering*; Frederic Goudy, dean of American type designers; Paul Renner, designer of *Futura*; Linn Boyd Benton, creator of *Century*, *Century Oldstyle* and Morris Fuller Benton; Morris Fuller Benton, creator of *Franklin Gothic*, and many other important fonts for ATF.

a font can be called "hand lettered," is whether or not *you* drew it. Which begs the question...

DO YOU HAVE WHAT IT TAKES TO BE A REAL LETTERING ARTIST?

Take a moment to answer the following questions in this simple quiz:

- Do you fill pages with doodles of weird letterforms and potential fonts?
- Can you tell the difference between Garamond and Cheltenham; Times Roman and Century Schoolbook?
- Have you ever found yourself studying the type on a poster or ad, assessing its letterforms and kerning only to realize afterwards that you never even read what it said?
- Do you collect clippings of ads, rave cards, and other material containing great, unusual and beautiful logos and lettering?
- Can you identify any of the individuals on the opposite page?
- Do you bitterly resent Arial as the cheap ripoff of Helvetica that it is?
- Have you ever tried to contact by mail or email—or made a pilgrimage to the studio of—an accomplished, older letterer or type designer whose work you admire?
- Do you hang around for hours in large chain bookstores reading all the design magazines for free?

If you answered "Yes" to any or all of the above, you may be a born lettering designer and you may continue to read this book.

THE HISTORY OF TYPE DESIGN

The subject of type history has been thoroughly and passionately covered in countless books and articles through the years and to this day. This book is mainly interested in how to draw letters, so the subject of history is only touched upon in passing, insofar as the work of various historic figures in the world of type and lettering offers lessons to be emulated. I have included, however, a concise and sarcastic history of how it was in the old days called Unbelievable Implements: Type and Lettering in the Pre-pixel Era to be found on page 62.

YES, WE SPEAK MACINTOSH

This book is written for Mac users because most of us agree that Macintosh computers are more designer friendly. It seems that nine out of ten contributors to this book, who use computers, choose the Macintosh over the leading brand. There's a rumor that most web designers are PC-based. If that is true, it's because many web designers come by the title, not through prior experience with graphic design, but through the HTML programming back door. This book offers an opportunity for web designers to get up to speed—and we're not talkin' 56K—on real world type and lettering.

PC users with basic knowledge of drawing programs including Macromedia Flash will find that the many demonstrations and tutorials in this book involve mostly basic commands like Cut, Copy, and Paste that should pose no real translation problems.

TABLE OF EQUIVALENTS:

MAC	PC
⌘ Command	Control
⌥ Option	Alt
⇧ Shift	Shift

A MANUAL FOR IMPATIENT DESIGNERS

I hate most computer manuals because I don't want to read a book, I just want to immediately use the program. So I have tried to streamline the verbiage of the instructions in this book to avoid the problem of most computer books, written by professional writers, not professional users, containing dense columns of pictureless text that do nothing more than rephrase the programs' own user manuals.

It is impossible to present tutorials without using examples, but my hope is that you won't actually follow them verbatim. What good will it do you to recreate *my* logos? The same drop shadow I apply to a certain letter in my example can be applied by you to any letter you prefer. My own personal policy is to work only on actual jobs, rather than on practice pieces that

What Is Wrong With These Logos?

(Answers on opposite page)

SUGARPLUM SCENTS

ACTION PLUMBING

Painless

Argenta

TECKNOR

are useless afterwards. So I suggest that you read this book in bed, to absorb the strategies and concepts, rather than reading it at a computer, slavishly following the instructions step-by-step.

Drawing letters and fonts in Adobe Illustrator and Macromedia Fontographer is the heart of this book, and it is assumed the reader already has a middling knowledge of these programs. Refresher sections, covering some pertinent aspects, have been provided to make the techniques demonstrated here more comprehensible and to help you catch up if you lied on your résumé and don't really know the programs.

In addition to discussing correct letter forms, this book will attempt to teach strategies for drawing letters with rapidity, efficiency and consistency (you'll read the word *consistency* many times before we're done). In Illustrator there are more ways to approach almost every drawing problem than there are ways to skin a cat (and they are more humane and far less disgusting). By approaching one problem—such as how to make a block drop shadow (see "Incredible Type Trix," page 166)—from several angles, I demonstrate various strategies as well as help you to retain the lessons through repeating key procedures.

Your particular version of Illustrator is not too important since the basic functions used are so intrinsic to the program that they have not been (and probably will not be) radically changed between older and yet-to-come versions. I was surprised to discover how many of my illustrious contributors are still using Illustrator 6.0 or 8.0, which just goes to show that most of the features developers add to new program versions are gimmicks

Answers to WHAT IS WRONG WITH THESE LOGOS?

(Don't cheat. First, write down your own thoughts, then compare them to my answers below. All these examples were created by the author so as not to get sued by anybody.)

SUGARPLUM SCENTS: The designer has gone crazy with swash and "expert" characters that are best used judiciously. Overuse of special characters has caused legibility problems and also some difficulties with color massing and spacing. This logo was a perfect opportunity for hand-lettering. Then each letter might have been better fitted to the others, but the designer, lacking manual skills and a knowledge of bezier curves, was limited to the fonts in his library.

ACTION PLUMBING: Aside from being bland—a very boring font was used—the icon not only doesn't tickle or intrigue or inform, but it tells us nothing about the nature of the company. The inner and outer rounded-corner boxes surrounding the icon have different corner radii, which really looks awful. The one-point stroke underline perhaps serves to unify the type and icon, but its light weight is incongruous with the heavy title font.

PAINLESS: This logo is painful because it appears to be comprised of several fonts, though probably only one free web font was used. The interesting and distinctive flaring hood of lowercase *a*—my favorite letter of the motley batch—is not followed through on the *e* or *P*. The concave base of *i* is another distinctive feature not applied to the other letters. The circular counter in *e* is different from the ones in *P* and *a*. Worst of all, the two letters *s* have serifs, yet none of the other letters do. In hand-lettering, you'd never have two of the same letter next to each other with the identical shape; you'd always enlarge or somehow tweak one of them. I'm aware that the designer's intent was to create something bouncy and fun, yet this is a prime example of a complete lack of consistency that often marks amateur work.

ARGENTA: The apparent intent of this lettering style was to make a classic, bottom-weighted cola script, which originally would have been the product of a lettering brush. Yet no single brush formed such letters. They are the result of a pencil attempting to draw this script in outline without the faintest idea how a real brush, held at a consistent angle, would have distributed the thicks and thins in a natural manner. Specifically, the weight of the top flourish on cap *A* doesn't match the rest, and it curves in a clumsy, inorganic way. The descender loop of *g* isn't bottom-weighted to match the rest of the style, and the connecting stroke creates too large a gap between it and the next letter. The *e* is top-weighted as well as bottom-weighted and is placed too close to *n*, whose curving right stem is awkwardly drawn. The stem of *t* flares wide toward the top, which breaks style and it is angled more than the rest of the letters. The bowl of *a* is not bottom-weighted like the other letters, and its right stem tapers toward the top. (See also page 118.)

TECKNOR: The outline and drop shadow obscure a multitude of sins, but fail to mitigate the myriad mistakes of this logo. Basically, everything is wrong with it. Almost every stem is a different width and angle than the others. If it's a monoweight style, why do some stems taper or flair? The angles of corners and stroke terminals vary widely. Letter spacing is bad, and the widths of individual letters have not been considered. There is no follow-through in the stem of *K* or the leg of *R*. See how they begin one width and end up another? Tecknor is what happens when you draw a logo straight ahead instead of building each letter from standard parts.

These are examples of the ways in which professionals scrutinize their work.

Need to Know

IMPORTANT TERMS for the DESIGNER

LOGO: A specific design with unique characteristics made as a corporate "signature." A logo is pretty much the same as a trademark, which when legally registered, will bear the familiar R-in-a-circle symbol. A logo can be a nameplate or a monogram, emblem, symbol or signet. The wealthier the corporation, it seems, the simpler the logo. A logo should be: (1) Intelligible: Never confuse a potential customer. (2) Unique: Make it different from other logos, avoid trendiness. (3) Compelling: The design should provoke further investigation. It should "Say the commonplace in an uncommon way"(Paul Rand).

FONT: Before computers, a font was called a *typeface* or *face. Font* or *fount* originally referred to the product of a foundry where hot metal is poured into molds, and *type font* referred to the complete character set in one specific point size and style of type within a type family. Now *font* has become revived as the term for any computer typeface sold, traded, pirated or offered for free.

LETTERING: Also called *hand-lettering* to differentiate it from machine-made type. All lettering emerges from the hand, even when it's a hand on a mouse. Lettering is any sequence of letters forming words that come from the pencil, pen, brush, marker, spray can, computer and so on, as opposed to having come from a preexisting type font. Of course, all type started as lettering. At some point, someone drew it before it was cast or digitized.

TYPE: Around 1982, a client called me up and said, "I need some type." I almost said, "So call a typesetter, I'm a *hand-letterer,"* but I'm always polite to anyone who might potentially pay me. It turned out that one fine day, *Type* became the hip term for hand-lettering. Type, as we know, comes as the result of setting words in a font. *Type* is not synonymous with *hand-lettering.*

CALLIGRAPHY: Literally means "beautiful writing." In calligraphy we find many of the foundations of modern type, yet it has always held the Rodney Dangerfield position in the world of lettering. Calligraphy mainly suggests a style of flourishy, chisel-point-pen lettering, rather than letters that are first drawn and measured, then slowly inked according to the drawing. It really annoys hand-letterers to have their work referred to as calligraphy. Good calligraphy has finally gained respect, though. It's become a legitimate means by which certain ideas and emotions may be vividly expressed in commercial lettering.

like ugly background patterns, crazy gradients, and weird distortion tools that are mostly shunned and ignored by professional designers. As for Fontographer, the latest version is still six years old. At this writing Macromedia has no plans to upgrade for compatibility with Mac OS X. Meanwhile, FontLab, a new and very high-tech font creation program, has come on the scene. We compare the three programs on page 224. (For those wanting to learn more about FontLab, check out my book called *Learn FontLab Fast, a Simplified Guide.*)

VECTOR vs. BITMAP

Creating pixel lettering in Adobe Photoshop is not covered in this book. It can be done, but the limited and incomplete vector-drawing tools found in Photoshop would make it unnecessarily difficult, so why bother? Also, absolute edges are not clearly defined in Photoshop files. Enlarged, you always see those light/dark double pixel edges—so accuracy in rendering lettering would always be a problem. Everything we create in Illustrator can be imported into Photoshop, but because Photoshop is bound by our choice of resolution, our logo work becomes trapped at 72 or 300 dpi and cannot be enlarged indefinitely as vector art can, and it cannot easily be tweaked after it is rasterized (made into a bitmap). I've seen company logos, done for the web at 72 dpi, that were thereby completely lost and unusable for print, or for the poster or billboard that the company later envisioned.

A TANGLED WEB OF TYPE

Ten years from now, we'll realize that the Internet of 2004 was as much a dinosaur as our early computers now seem. In ten years the resolution of our monitors will presumably have increased substantially, and issues of creating special fonts for the web that are more easily read will have become moot.

At the present time, however, many font designers endeavor to design attractive, yet legible text fonts for screen and Internet use. They try to improve the hinting of their fonts, making minute decisions as to whether a pixel should be turned on or off here or there, and they strive for letterforms with optimal legibility in low-resolution environments. Certain fonts, like Verdana, have certainly achieved this.

I am one who sees all media roads leading eventually to the Internet, but those designers who want to see nice typography should instead look to print media and not split pixels trying to fine-tune HTML text type. This book, therefore, doesn't cover web-specific fonts. However, on page 212, we do have David Berlow's insights on how he created a family of fonts designed for e-mail communication.

ALL STYLES WELCOME

I like every style of type and lettering—from the most ancient letterforms chiseled in stone to the latest graffiti sprayed on stucco—as long as it's well done. I also like funky fonts, rave fonts, and grunge fonts, although for me, the novelty wore off by 1996.

This book, however, was not written for grunge font designers—you're doing great at it already! Just be sure, if you're making quickie grunge and careless free web fonts, that these are really your goal and that you're not just settling for less because you don't know how to draw letters.

Grunge fonts certainly have their place in our vast design spectrum. They carry a distinct message and communicate as effectively in an appropriate context as any other font. It's just that there is much less "craft" to making distressed fonts than in creating by hand a beautiful, matching suite of abstract letterforms that are unlike any others ever seen before in the history of the world, yet still manage to remain comprehensible.

This is the exhilaration and challenge of lettering, whether of the logo or font, that goes beyond just impressing a few friends when they pass by it in their cars or see it on the Internet. It's something more like a magnificent obsession, that perhaps—if you don't already have it—this book will help to instill in you.

ICON: Traditionally, a sacred picture or an important and enduring symbol. Today's icons are those tiny, hard-to-see pictograms on our desktops and programs that require computer manuals to decipher. Well-done, intuitive icons serve important navigational functions, like the male/female icons on lavatory doors. At best they are everything a logo should be, but even more compact.

RETRO: Short for *retrospective*, this became the hip term for any evocation of a period style prior to ours. I dislike this word, which entered the parlance in 1974, my editor says, but I use it because we all agree on what it means and it's less off-putting than the word *nostalgic*. And, the user of the term isn't required to know the difference between Nouveau or Deco—which many people don't know—it can all be just "retro."

GLYPH: This is the latest cool term for a drawing of a letter, especially in the character slot of a font creation program. God only knows what the cool people will be calling letters next season.

COOL: As in "cool fonts," *cool* is the highest possible accolade; the best a thing can be. But *cool*, as in "cool on a subject," also means disinterested, aloof. Cool, actually, is a protective mask worn by the fearful. Cool is disenfranchised, dispassionate, alienated and frightened. Cool is noncommittal for fear that to commit to an unpopular idea might make one uncool. Cool defined is cool dissipated. Like Dracula, cool can't know the light lest it wither. Cool is uncreative. It follows, but does not lead. True *cool*—if that term can still be used—is being true to thine own self. As Martin Luther King Jr. said, "Our lives begin to end the day we become silent about things that matter." Snobbery is so often a characteristic of young graphic designers—I was a snot at twenty-five, too—it helps to remember that no matter how fine, elegant or cool our design may be, it is usually being used to con people into buying mundane commodities, most of which lack quality and integrity, are unhealthful and bad for the environment, and in many cases, nobody really needs them, anyway.

EDGY: When clients say they want "edgy" they really mean for us to make our work slightly obscure and a tad grungy in that safe, nonthreatening edgy style that everybody else does, but not so edgy as to actually make a statement that might upset Mr. Murdoch, Mr. Turner, Mr. Eisner or Mr. Ashcroft. *Edgy* comes from *cutting edge*, like a design that initiates a trend, or *on the edge* which refers to coffee nerves, or the state between sanity and insanity. It indicates anger and defiance, not compliance. *Edgy*, as it is used, really means to pander to the youth demographic. Amusingly, the youth "market" never recognizes the ploy; instead it embraces the commodity as a symbol of its own culture and generation, even coming to define itself through mere ownership of the product.

Part 1

The

*"In the future everyone
will be world-famous
for fifteen minutes."*
—Andy Warhol

*"In the future everyone in the
world will have a new logo
every fifteen minutes."*
—Leslie Cabarga

TIME TO RE-TIRE
"GET A FISK"

DEFINING THE LOGOTYPE

U*ntil about the 1930s*, the majority of logos in America tended to be of the pictorial or literal kinds. Trademark characters such as the Dutch Boy, the White Rock girl and the Fisk Tire boy, often reproduced from large oil paintings, were common in more innocent days. Nowadays, the friendly company trademark has matured into the hard-edged icon, a "shorthand" version of the "formal script" that was the complex, old-fashioned logo.

Above, the Fisk Tire boy used a clever pun to induce sales. Below, Psyche, the goddess of purity, watches over White Rock Beverages just as she has done since this painting was first presented at the World's Fair of 1893.

Logo design of today includes a limitless variety of styles. As in fashion, a broader range of styles is acceptable than was ever the case historically. That's because today's logos are more often concept-driven, which means that the idea we wish to convey often dictates the style we choose to express it in. In this section I've attempted to show examples of various logo categories. The "literal" logo is often just a nameplate (pages 18–21). Monogrammatic logos are an ancient tradition, reaching back to the first time Glug scratched his initial on his club (pages 22–23). Abstract logos, when well designed, succeed just like modern art (pages 24–25). Retro logos are taken seriously by some who emulate the best aspects of the Victorian or Art Deco styles in their logos, while others delight in purposely aping the naïveté found in much period work (pages 26–31).

White Rock

Of all the styles of logo design, I am most intrigued—and sometimes amazed—by logos that pull double and triple duty. These kind not only present the company name or its initials, but convert them into graphics that identify the company's product. The viewer of such a logo becomes a participant in an interactive project to decipher the riddle of the image. Of course, if the design is too clever or difficult to decipher, the logo would have to be considered a failure.

Ending this section is a showcase of German designers who pioneered this conceptual form and influenced the style of today's logo design (pages 32–35).

EXERCISE: Design a logo (find someone—even if it's yourself—for whom to make a real logo, rather than wasting time on a useless, hypothetical project) and produce rough comps based on the various categories demonstrated in this section.

Dutch Boy paint has been used in American homes since 1907. The image has been kept alive, below, with updated type and design to keep it fresh.

CASH MUST BE SENT WITH ALL ORDERS. NO GOODS SHIPPED C. O. D.

A 4025

SEARS, ROEBUCK AND CO.

CHEAPEST SUPPLY HOUSE ON EARTH

OUR TRADE REACHES AROUND THE WORLD

INCORPORATED UNDER THE LAWS OF ILLINOIS, WITH A CASH CAPITAL OF OVER TWO MILLION DOLLARS. PAID IN FULL.

REFERENCE BY SPECIAL PERMISSION
NATIONAL CITY BANK, NEW YORK
METROPOLITAN NATL BANK
CORN EXCHANGE NAT'L BANK, CHICAGO.

OUR MAMMOTH CATALOGUE CONTAINS OVER 100,000 ILLUSTRATIONS AND QUOTATIONS, MAILED TO ANY ADDRESS ON RECEIPT OF 50 CENTS.

WE SELL EVERYTHING BY MAIL ORDER ONLY, TO OUR TWO MILLION CUSTOMERS ALL OVER THE WORLD.

68-96 FULTON, ST.
73-87 N. DESPLAINES, ST.
1-31 WAYMAN, ST
74-88 N. JEFFERSON, ST.

CABLE ADDRESS: "SUPPLY."
DIRECT WIRE WITH WESTERN UNION AND POSTAL TELEGRAPH COS.
LONG DISTANCE PHONE: MONROE 24

CHICAGO, May 3, 1902, 9

The Sears company has come a long way since the 1902 letterhead, above, and so has its logo. The current version, right, is a good example of the current trend in corporate identity. Basic and legible as its letterforms are, the unusual inline treatment, suggesting strokes overlapping one another, brings a unique dimension that makes this logo unlike any other currently in use.

SEARS

Once upon a time, as this letterhead reminds us, a logo was only as good as the local printer's supply of fancy wood and metal fonts. Surprisingly, design has lately come full circle, with many designers offering little more than "font selection" as their creative contribution to logo design.

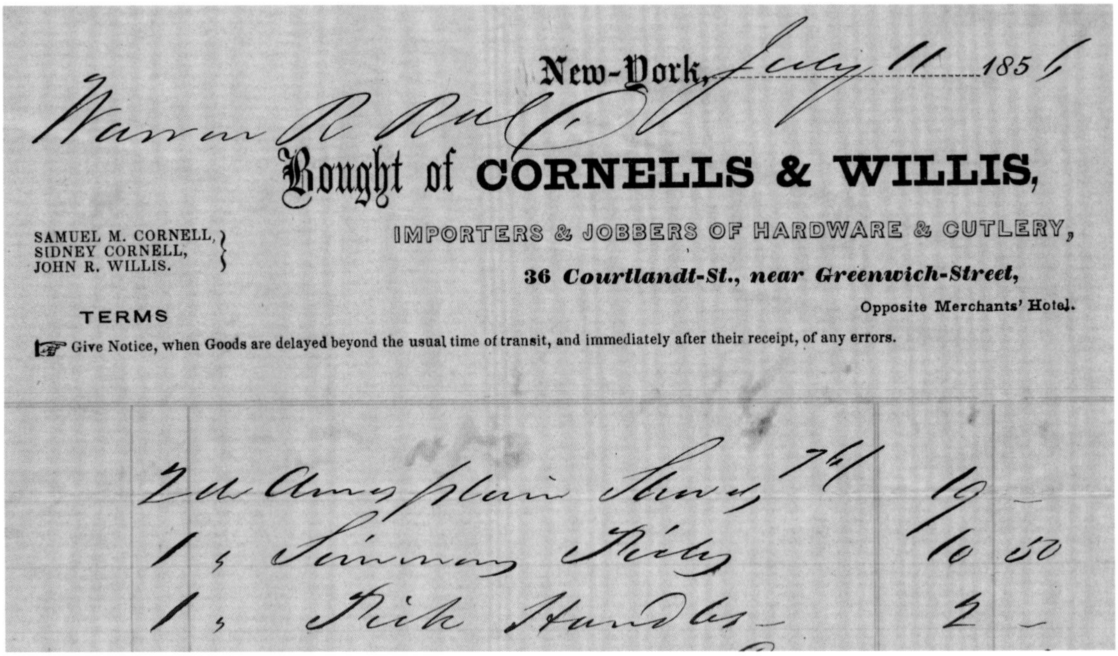
New-York, July 11 1856

Bought of CORNELLS & WILLIS,

SAMUEL M. CORNELL,
SIDNEY CORNELL,
JOHN R. WILLIS.

IMPORTERS & JOBBERS OF HARDWARE & CUTLERY,

36 Courtlandt-St., near Greenwich-Street,

Opposite Merchants' Hotel.

TERMS

Give Notice, when Goods are delayed beyond the usual time of transit, and immediately after their receipt, of any errors.

The logo below, designed by JHI with Lizette Gicel, utilizes the font Copperplate as its basis. Yet the simple design for a real estate company rises above the commonplace by the elegant and ingenious device of the overlapping double *D*s that draw the eyes to this fulcrum of interest.

UNITED DOMINION™

W. L. DOUGLAS
$3 SHOE. FOR GENTLEMEN.

Above, the owner of the W. L. Douglas Shoe Company was his own logo. His face became a "media" fixture at the turn of the nineteenth century. Although it lacked any decent sense of typography, no one would argue with this logo's attention-grabbing appeal.

Below is the American eagle in a design of classic symmetry and elegance. Though it was originally used as a self-stamped envelope design (unfortunately the envelope of choice in the recent Fort Detrick anthrax mail scare), this piece by Michael Doret for the U.S. Postal Service has all the dynamic qualities of a good logo.

USA
34

The Post and Courier

Before

The Post and Courier

After

Jim Parkinson specializes in the design and redesign of publication mastheads, like that above for Charleston's *Post and Courier*, seen both in its pre- and post-Parkinson incarnations. This is as literal a logo as one can get—it's just a nameplate—with a concept having mainly to do with the "Old English" lettering suggesting decorum and a lengthy heritage. Parkinson's revision exemplifies those qualities one considers in improving lettering designs. Most noticeably, letter weights have been evened up by eliminating too-light and too-heavy strokes, creating consistent angles and stem weights, and making all letters appear to be of the same family. Such details may go unnoticed by 95 percent of readers, yet I believe such improvements elevate a publication's overall status and credibility for that discerning 5 percent (which may include advertisers). And I do think, on some subconscious levels, the masses generally recognize quality.

The logo for TreePeople, designed by Ray Wood, functions on two levels: It is both literal and inferential. We recognize the leaf motif at once, but the design also cleverly suggests an earth where the gift of greenery is universally celebrated.

At first glance, we view the name Katz Radio Group and see the rules merely as decorative architecture. Only then do we recognize the radio dial in Jonathan Macagba's literal concept.

Use of the American eagle as a trademark image for the American National Bank might be considered literally obvious. But designer Chris Costello's excellent and powerful rendering picks up in the decorative department where any small lack of concept left off.

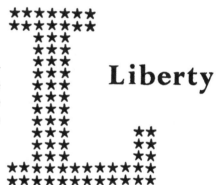

The name of the company is Liberty and if the viewer is still unsure, the concept is spelled out in a monogram of stars.

Punchstock's punchy font is totally unique. That's because it's actually custom lettering by Jennifer Katcha with Kevin Wade for Planet Propaganda.

Left, so obvious yet long overlooked was this concept behind Nate Lambdin's logo for JHI. I've never before seen the simple, ubiquitous market sandwich sign being used as a logo. Above, the clever hole and tag string added to this otherwise simple logo by Keith Campbell is just enough graphic context to indicate the company's purpose—it sells advertising on airline luggage name/address tags—and to capture the viewer's curiosity.

Far left, a simple logo for Bell, a butcher. I'm not sure if the image is supposed to be some handheld bell or just a fortuitous arrangement of black lettering, but it's so damned beautiful. Left, another simple, literal logo so nicely arranged, we don't mind the lack of any tricky design.

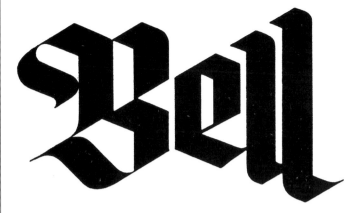

Far left, this logo by Mark Fox literally portrays the red herring but then throws us one in the nifty treatment of *R-R,* which becomes the concept of the piece. Left, this logo by the author for Kitchen Sink Press, lacking any real concept, derives its charm from the literal image of the antique kitchen faucet.

Cat's Paw, a logo designed by Lucian Bernhard, is such a classic, it had to be included here. The concept is, again, literal: There's the cat, and there's his paw. But through sheer strength of the stark composition, the logo grips us like a pair of rubber heels.

The name is Golden Barrel, and here we have a...golden oak barrel, appropriately rendered in imitation woodcut style by Russ Cox of Smiling Otis Studio. Originally inked with a brush, the logo was meticulously redrawn in Adobe Illustrator and quite gracefully so, which is not an easy task! As with many of the examples on this page, the literal approach, lacking cleverness or concept, has been justified by virtue of a really swell illustration.

Right, *iconoclast* literally means the smashing of images, and that's why I made this frame-breaking logo for Iconoclassics Publishing Co. Middle right, Jonathan Macagba's chemical table logo is a great solution for Future Beta, Inc. Far right, another Macagba logo. The *M* is for Mercury.

Large in center, *pd* stands for Paper Doll, a very happening clothing company with a happening logo to match. Below right, the *VA* is for Vinyl Avenger, a DJ in Dirk Uhlenbrock's neck of the woods.

Below, I love the simple logo for JHI, the Richmond, Virginia–based design firm. The dotted *i* reads "lightbulb" as if to illustrate the firm's web site name: www.jhigoodidea.com.

Above, find the monogram in this logo by the author for Very Important Planet, a gift shop located in the Virgin Islands.

Left, variations on a theme for Seth Bernstein's Form, Function & Finesse studio. I always like to introduce alternate versions of a single logo, and I trust the public at least to the degree that they'll still recognize the basic image. Apparently, Bernstein feels the same.

Find the monograms: Above left, an amazing double monogram in the logo for Mel Whitson Stationers, designed by Robert Overby (1962). Above center, logo for Westcoast Landscape by Conrad Angone (1962). Above right, Mike Samuel's design for Small Craft manages to included both initial letters into the logo.

Left, the *KM* stands for Konrad Mathieu, an IT-solutions company in Köln. Logo by Dirk Uhlenbrock. The backwards *K* also functions as an arrow.

Above, a rebus mark by Dirk Uhlenbrock for a design firm. In his words, "This area is called Revier. The first syllable sounds similar to *Reh*, the German word for *deer*, and the second syllable, *vier*, could also be the number *vier*, which is four." Pretty cool, Dirk! (*.de* is the suffix for *Deutscher* web sites.)

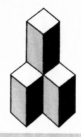

INTERNATIONAL SERVICE OF ART TO INDUSTRY

CONTEMPORA · INC ·

BRUNO PAUL · ROCKWELL KENT · PAUL POIRET · LUCIAN BERNHARD

PAUL LESTER WIENER · BUSINESS DIRECTOR

MODERN ART FOR INDUSTRY

PRONOVA

ASSOCIATED ARTISTS

Top, with the emergence of the field of industrial design, which came about in the 1930s, four artists, hoping to capitalize on their combined international appeal, formed Contempora, Inc. The logo is abstract, but certainly evokes contemporaneousness to me.

Above, another set of three artists formed Pronova. Their abstract logo at least implies a triumvirate—of something. Their stamp, right, reverses the logo's color sequence, which today's clients are often afraid to do.

DESIGNED BY

FOR YOUR APPROVAL

PROPERTY OF

PRONOVA

MODERN ART FOR INDUSTRY

114 E 47TH ST N Y

WICKERSHAM 7359

DESIGN NO

Above left, this delicate abstraction may have been meant to suggest the three stars of the Von Der Lancken, Lundquist and Sorenson Agency (1955).

Left, the Museum Books logo by John Ciampi is a beauty. It evokes Picasso's *Guernica* with an added initial *M* in a skewed warm gray rectangle that just reeks (in a positive way) of the 1950s.

Above, a copper-engraved logo from 1802 with a literal depiction of folds for this fancy cloth goods merchant. Many years later, the (possible) fabric bolt in the Chase Manhattan Bank logo takes on a note of abstraction through its stylization.

Top, Tom Geismar's famous abstract Chase Manhattan Bank logo suggests continuity, stability, possibly an ancient coin design. And maybe an indication of a *C* can be found in the folds of such a classic commodity as dry goods, or perhaps ticker tape? Above, designer Stan Endo swears his GuerillaOne.com logo is no guerrilla parody of Chase. Any resemblance between Chase and this logo for a dance party organizer is purely coincidental.

Gerard Huerta tackles any style of logo or lettering with the same consummate skill. Design is design, only styles change while the underlying principles remain. Maybe that's why Huerta's Caroline St. Railroad, DeRosa's and *Cigar* logos are all so different in style, yet all so finely rendered.

Above, Gerard Huerta must have been born out of time. His intricate lettering for the Hand Made Cigar Collector's Guide & Journal would have landed him a job at any nineteenth century print shop.

For this tractor logo, right, *Deutscher* designer Dirk Uhlenbrock retained the symmetrical layout, the bursted seal and Sütterlin-style antiquated German handscript as his links to tradition. But his simplified treatment of these elements is strictly *now*—and totally Uhlenbrock.

Right, and above right, if intended as examples of classic label design, these First Colony Coffee & Tea logos by Nate Lambdin for JHI could be said to have missed the mark. But as examples of modern design that add some new verbiage to the classic label lexicon, they work smashingly well.

Louise Fili's logos for the Pink Door, Malama and Delamar reveal her penchant for retro styling. Yet Fili manages to imbue her work with all the elegance and romantic flavor of classic European Deco design without ever letting it become cloyingly "nostalgic."

The
P·I·N·K
Door
PINK DOOR

M Ā L A M A

DELAMAR
· GREENWICH · HARBOR ·

FERRY
BUILDING

ELMA
GARCIA
FILMS

SUNDANCE

THE MOTHERSHIP

Michael Schwab is one of those designers whose every piece carries his unmistakable stylistic signature. Although Schwab's work takes its cues from retro reference, his dynamic and spartan compositions have a timeless appeal.

Right, Mercury must have had better things to do than to flit around Manhattan delivering photostats, but this naïve period image, accompanied by really nice lettering, would barely have raised a snicker in 1945.

RAPID
COPY
SERVICE
RAPID COPY SERVICE CO.

Right, some logos try to seriously achieve a retro look. This design by the author for a silk-screen T-shirt printer mocks the gravity of much Art Deco imagery that some 1930s companies used in all seriousness.

ANDERS
Manufacturing

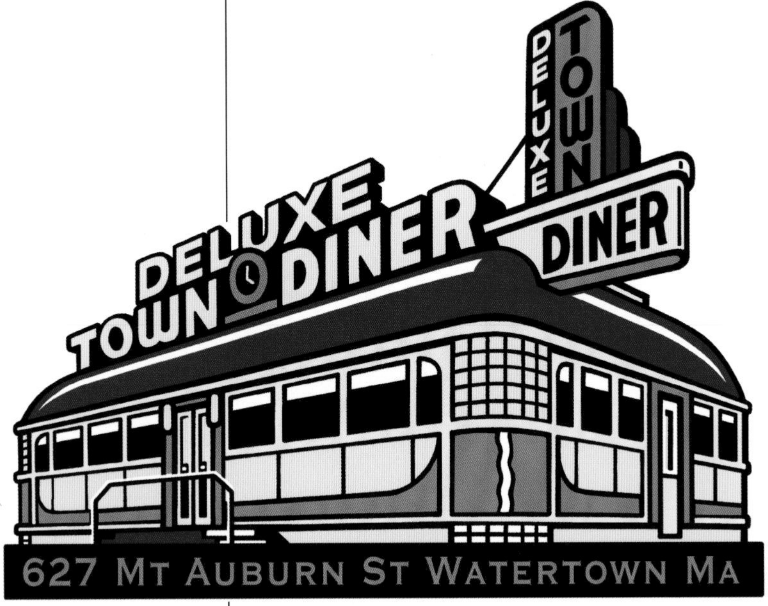
DELUXE TOWN DINER
DELUXE TOWN
DINER
627 MT AUBURN ST WATERTOWN MA

COSMO
ICECREAMO

Above, this gorgeously designed, inked and colored logo by Mark Fisher conjures up all the alluring nostalgia of an old matchbook cover. Above right, Fisher brings the naïveté of the 1950s to this logo for Cosmo Icecreamo. But it's too over the top to be truly of the period and becomes instead a delicious parody. Bless the client that lets us get away with designing something this much fun.

The logos of Seymour Chwast and his current Pushpin Group associates are noted for their strong design and gentle humor. In pointing out the references to the 1920s and 1930s in his work, it should be noted that in the 1960s, Chwast became one of the first retro revivalists and gets a lot of the credit (or blame?) for pointing the rest of us in this direction. Above, Solo, designed with Greg Simpson, for a publishing group; right, Lörke, a German clothing concern; below, for the Museum of Comic and Cartoon Art.

Above, the original logo for Seymour Chwast and Milton Glaser's Push Pin Studios, c. 1959. The name itself is gently self-parodying and certainly indicative of the style and attitude that put this highly influential, and trend-setting studio on the map.

Right, Brave World is a film production company whose logo giddily parodies old self-important RKO Pictures movie titles. The brave design—nicely executed!—is by Dan Ibarra and Jamie Karlin of Planet Propaganda.

Michael Doret has made his fame by illustrating with letters. His logos, like U Mogul, Coolsville and Bedlam Ballroom, above and right, reveal his total unreliance upon stock fonts. Instead, each letter is drawn from scratch, according to the design concept. Doret revels in retro and has long been a trendsetter in the style.

Planet Propaganda's Jamie Karlin and Dana Lytle created the logo above for an E-business consulting company. Dog collar and sunrays are cleverly combined into one image.

Right, a double-take Mark Fox logo for a proposed production of the rock opera *Jesus Christ Superstar*. The cross on Golgotha can be seen in the face of Jesus.

Far right, logo for a textile manufacturer by Ross, Culbert and Lavery, Inc. in the old German style. The letterforms are unusual, especially the *X*.

Left, there can be no better expression of the word *Triumphant!* than in Jill Bell's exuberant logo for a point-of-purchase display. Below, Bell's treatment of the Seahorses is an interesting brush treatment that breaks step with traditional calligraphy style.

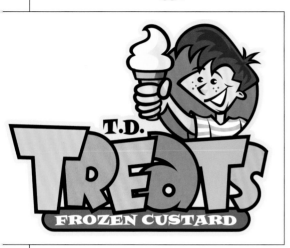

Left, this logo by Russ Cox maintains a consistent feeling from the casual, cartoony lettering to the cartoony kid. Right, Carol Chu created this logo for a group working with children who lost a parent in the 9-11 disaster. This design, with its unassuming type and optimistic graphic, reminds us of how a logo can be used to convey the most subtle concepts.

Below, a delightful calligraphic logo by Chris Costello in "Turklish." Adding to the intrigue is the two-tone blended watercolor treatment.

Above left, a proposed logo by the author for a restaurant. The name alone put me in a Mediterranean mood, which inspired the mosaic tiles. Drawn in Illustrator, in strokes, outlines were created, then the whole was united. Releasing Compound Paths allowed me to fill each tile differently from a pallet of alike tones.

Above, Mark Simonson says of his logo for the Lake Wobegon baseball team, "The Whippets were perennial losers, so I did the mandatory baseball script running downhill rather than up."

LOGO DESIGN IN Deutschland

Many old German printers' logos incorporate the griffon. Klingspor's griffon takes the form of initial *K.*

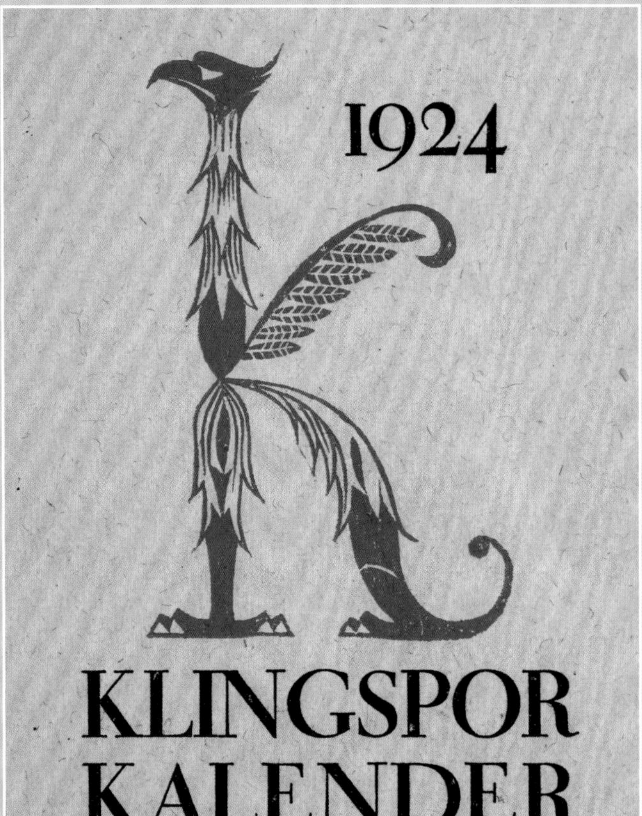
1924
KLINGSPOR
KALENDER

The Germans are responsible for inventing the modern iconic trademark as an outgrowth of the heavy gothic, black-letter *schrift,* or script, that evolved as their unique adaptation of the roman alphabetic forms. They started playing with simplified design as far back as 1905 when America had just renounced the excesses of Victoriana for an only slightly less fussy Colonial Revival. I always say that if it weren't for African Americans' influence upon music, the rest of us might still be waltzing in powdered wigs. To that I might add, but for the Germans, all our logos might still be kitschy oil paintings of cows, kids and mythical figures. But they did more, the Germans: They added the concept of *concept* to their stripped-down trademark symbols, many of which were no longer arcane abstractions as old tradesmen's marks had been, but became endowed with wit and meaning.

Trademarks for German printing firms: Top, Saladruck by Karl Prinz, and above, Erasmus Druck, designer unknown.

Plakate
Packungen
Schutzmarken
Kataloge
Prospekte
ZIĘTARA
MÜNCHEN
TENGSTR.
5

DEUTSCHE OSTMESSE
KÖNIGSBERG

Above, in Weimar Germany, designers were masters of all media, but trademark design was an area of specialty. Today, Zietara would add web design to his list, although it'd cause a symmetry problem.

Charal was another trademark designer, who placed the ad above in a 1926 directory listing hundreds of other designers. His logo samples are nice, but the lettering of his name is exquisite.

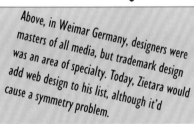

From top: Manoli (tobacco) by Wilhelmwerk, 1916. Thüringer Mützenfabrik (hats) by Konrad Jochheim, 1913. Hausleben (insurance) by O.H.W. Hadank. R. Oldenbourg (publisher) by Peter Behrens.

BENZ

Trademark for Benz automobiles by the eminent F.H. Ehmke.

Trademark by Hermann Virl for an unknown company.

Karl Schulpig
LOGO MEISTER

Very little is known about Karl Schulpig (1884–1948), who has emerged as the quintessential German logo designer. Schulpig's bold style and clever visual puns, widely emulated after the publication of the author's *A Treasury of German Trademarks* (1982), might even qualify him as the father of the modern icon. German designers appear to have been so well respected, and printing so accessible, that Schulpig could issue a yearly booklet displaying his accomplishments, something unheard of in America at the time. The marks on these pages were created from 1922 to 1928.

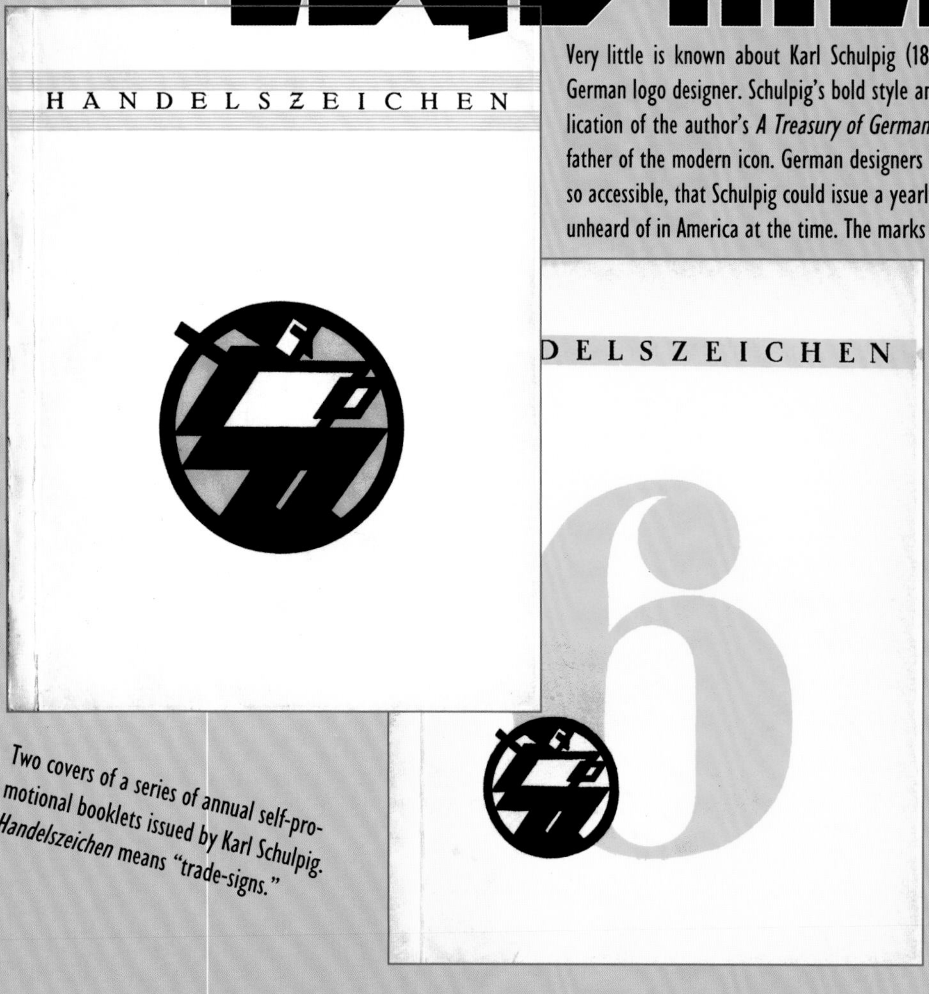
HANDELSZEICHEN
DELSZEICHEN
6

Two covers of a series of annual self-promotional booklets issued by Karl Schulpig. Handelszeichen means "trade-signs."

VOGT JUNIOR

W. Vogt, Jr. Geschaftbucher, a publisher of account books. The company's product has been arranged as initial V.

Top, a classic mask made of initials for the German Theatre Austellung Magdeburg. Middle, an abstract motif for an unknown firm. Bottom, design for Milchwerk, a dairy farm.

Far left, logo for Messeamt Köln am Rhein, an organizer of industrial trade shows for the city. The letter *M* echoes the spires of the Köln cathedral, and a simple squiggle indicates the Rhein. Wow!

Left, putting a friendly face on the chemical preparations of the Robert Nikutowsky company.

Below left, a leg has apparently been added to the *S* from Karl Saborsky's Quanto, a railroad supplies company, indicating a figure lifting a stylized cross section of a railroad track.

Left, I've seen musical symbols arranged to form pictures before, but never so cleverly and concisely as in this logo for Crescendo Verlag, a music publisher.

Right, a ship cutting through the waves is immediately seen in this logo, but so are the *F* and—*it seems to me*—the *W* for Frerichswerft, shipbuilders.

How to Design a LOGO in 3 Quasi-Easy Steps

STEP 1
IMMERSION

STEP 2
CREATIVE COPYING

STEP 3
THUMBNAIL & COMP

SEE PAGE 60 (for further instructions!)

STEP 1 IMMERSION

The first step in tackling a logo design is immersing yourself in the mentality of the product and the client company. As advertising legend Jerry Della Femina once wrote of this process, "I can tell you how to be a route salesman for a product called Moxie.... I know more about the feminine-hygiene business than I should legally know."

That's right, dive into it! Start buying books and magazines on the subject, drink the cola, wear the shoes, study the web site, interview company employees, arrange focus groups, and so on. If it's a restaurant logo, eat at the restaurant, then check out competing restaurants and their logos. One very important aspect of the immersion stage—which is really about doing your homework—is that you'll be able to speak knowledgeably to your client about his or her product or company, and this will give them confidence in you.

On the other hand, immersion is sometimes completely unnecessary. All that's required is just some hip-looking lettering that relates more to current fashion than to anything about the client company. A mystique gets attached to the logo creation process, because a design firm likes to make clients think that there is some magical logo solution only it can provide. And companies, wanting to feel that they've hired the hottest designer on the planet, come to assume that a logo by any less a talent than you would spell doom for their enterprise.

I believe that if one thousand halfway decent designers each presented logos to Exxon, Sony and Nike and each of those companies picked one logo out of their respective hats and used them, there would be no measurable effect upon these companies' year-end financial statements. Unless a logo is really terrible—which can indeed do damage to a company's image and thus affect sales—the choice of this logo vs. that logo just isn't *so* important; it's more about the context in which the logo is used.

Usually, the logo version that gets chosen is never the best one—if such a criteria as "best" even exists. It's the logo that the CEO's spouse or drinking buddies preferred. Several times I found myself sitting with presidents and vice presidents of large companies, discussing ads or logos. I realized that these guys were not really smarter than anybody else, mainly they just had bigger inferiority complexes, which caused them to become more unconscionably avaricious than other men.

But anyway, immersion can also involve coming to understand a client's needs. Lou Dorfsman said, "I do my best work when I perceive the need, the solution to the need, and sell that perception to management." Herbert Bayer said, "[When making a presentation to a client] I concentrate on the purpose of a project, or meaning and content. I use the word *art* as little as possible. By explaining the nature of the solution, I have few difficulties getting ideas accepted."

And according to Bill Golden, "My solutions do not spring from aesthetic considerations but from a business or marketing position. The aesthetics will take care of itself."

So that's why we immerse ourselves in research (then end up doing whatever it was we wanted to do in the first place).

STEP 2 CREATIVE COPYING

Often, logo inspiration will result automatically from the first step, immersion. But then there comes the point where we set to work to design a logo in a wide range of styles to insure that nothing possible has been overlooked. This is where the second step, creative copying, comes in. Almost any source will do. Your local yellow pages—though most of its contents will be junk—is brimming over with inspiration. Other good sources are graphic design magazines (especially the annual compendiums of the year's best) or any magazine with ads. Depending on your taste, old lettering books and type catalogs are great sources for ideas…but they've gotta be old old. You will depress everybody and become a walking anachronism if you copy from "old" 1980s sources. Currently, 1950s, 1960s and early 1970s are "in." The 1920s are out, and the 1930s have peaked.

Copying, or using "reference" material, should be done as an aid, not a crutch. Try never to copy anything verbatim. Besides being plagiaristic, it's just dirty pool. But if we are truly focused upon finding solutions for our own logo problem, any color, border, picture, type effect that we see in a magazine may be the key to that alchemical reaction turning our design into gold. Sure, any one of us can create visual ideas straight from our imaginations, at times, but I have often found the results to be needlessly limiting: One becomes trapped in circular thinking. Like when you're trying to figure out how to get away from your wife, and again and again, all you can think of is poison, then your friend suggests divorce and you suddenly realize you'd been stuck in one mind-set and neglected other options.

More to the point, I may be sketching a series of logo comps, all of them with a sans-serif lettering style. Then I look through a magazine and realize I'd completely forgotten to try serif styles…or scripts. Often, we use various reference materials and combine different elements. As the saying goes, "S/he who copies from the most sources is most original." To paraphrase an old saying, usually reserved for describing another indoor sport, "The designer who says he doesn't copy is either a liar or a fool." After all, that cool billboard you passed the other day, or the commercial you saw on TV last night, are both in your mind and may come out on your sketch pad tomorrow.

EXERCISE Open your yellow pages, or any magazine, to any random page containing ads. Make a set of logo comps based on ideas you find on these pages. Adapt! Don't copy verbatim.

Bezier Store
1000s of Points!
All kinds in stock!
Handle Matching!
Since 1952
• VANISHING
• EXCLAMATION
• DECIMALS
• BEZIERS
• ETC. ETC.
Serving POINT PLEASANT & HUNTERS POINT

Our Points Are Well Taken!
BEZIER STORE
• VANISHING
• EXCLAMATION
• DECIMALS
• BEZIERS
• ETC. ETC.
WE MAKE A POINT OF OFFERING QUALITY SERVICE

Bezier STORE
BAD CREDIT? NO HASSLES!
POINTS DELIVERED FREE OF CHARGE. SHARP, DULL, CUSTOM and ORIGINAL FRENCH BEZIER POINTS!
MADE IN THE U.S.A.
POINTCRAFT

Bezier Store
HOT POINTS
NOrthrop 7 -555

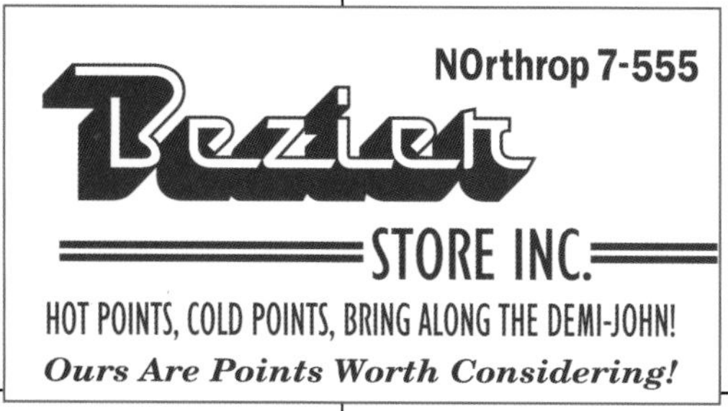
NOrthrop 7-555
Bezier
STORE INC.
HOT POINTS, COLD POINTS, BRING ALONG THE DEMI-JOHN!
Ours Are Points Worth Considering!

RAY POINTER
PIERRE DUPONT
MAJOR CREDIT CARDS ACCEPTED
Bezier Store
Architects' Vanishing Points
POINTILLISM EMPORIUM
Read Our: "All-Points Bulletin"
"We Give Points for Accuracy"

Left, I made this set of rough comps for a hypothetical logo and advertising design job based on the ads in a 1952 yellow pages, opposite page. I don't particularly love the designs I came up with, but I did them to prove my contention that virtually anything can be used as a copy source. Hey, here's a question: If you were to select a sign shop from these yellow pages ads, whose ad would inspire more confidence, Adcraft Studio or Cappy's Signs?

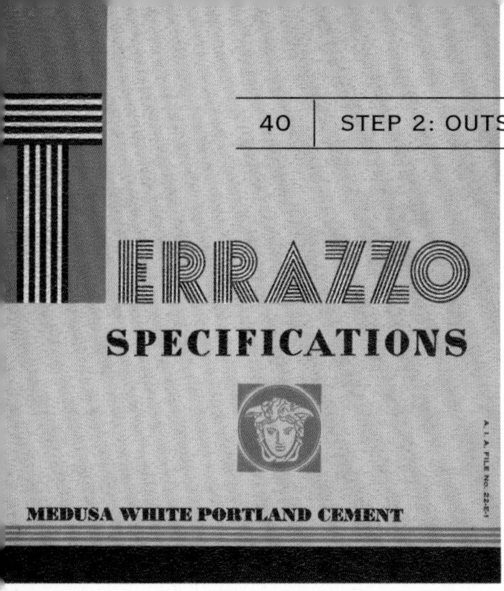
TERRAZZO
SPECIFICATIONS
MEDUSA WHITE PORTLAND CEMENT

IT PICKS YOU UP
Minimum Contents 12 fl. ozs.
Dr. Wells
A DELICIOUS CARBONATED BEVERAGE
REG. US. PAT. OFF.
MAKES A NICKEL THIRSTY
Hy's Better Beverage Co. - Oakland, California

CORN
ALAMEDA SWEET
F. LAGOMARSINO & SONS
SACRAMENTO, CALIFORNIA

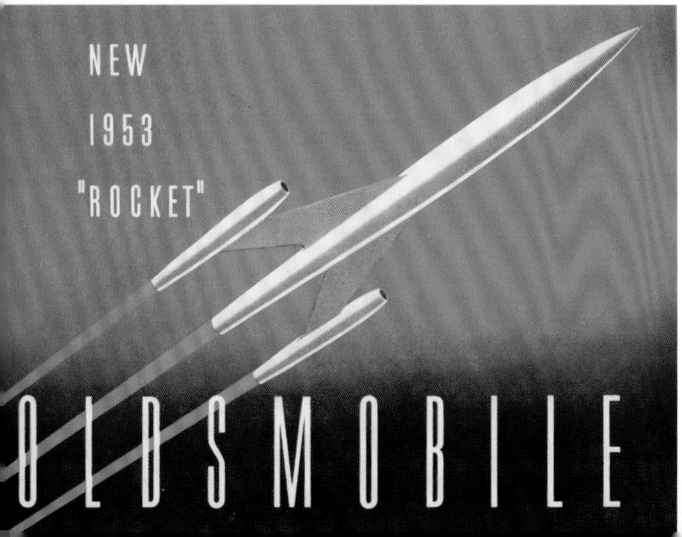
NEW
1953
"ROCKET"
OLDSMOBILE

CREATIVE COPYING

The retro reference pieces at left were selected randomly to demonstrate how almost anything can be used for logo inspiration. I've used old pieces that are in the public domain because I doubt any of you designers out there would want me showing how I adapt from your work. The logo I created for a company called Century Loofah, below, contains elements from all these sources, yet so obliquely referenced that no one could accuse me of being a rip-off. This is creative copying.

Century
LOOFAH

To create the piece above, I copied the green block and enlarged initial capital letter from the Terrazzo brochure. I liked the lettering on the Dr. Wells beverage label—even though it's really badly designed—as well as its outline and drop-shadow treatment. But I was torn because I also liked the open-spaced Oldsmobile lettering, below left. So I copied the latter but gave it the drop-shadow effect of the former and made the letterforms slightly clunky. You'd never know that I started drawing my new letters by working off the husks of the font Mekanik. I also borrowed the ever popular subtitle lettering-in-the-tail-emerging-from-the-last-letter treatment of the Dr. Wells logo. From the corn seed package, I took the color scheme. See my books *The Designer's Guide to Color Combinations* and *The Designer's Guide to Global Color Combinations* for more on deriving color schemes from reference. I wasn't sure what a loofah looked like so I typed the word into a search engine and found tons of pictures of loofahs to copy. I got the shading treament for my loofah from the Oldsmobile rocket illustration, and also borrowed the up-fading background idea.

WHAT A LOGO IS, WHAT A LOGO IS NOT

Before we go any further, let's define some terms. Visual communications consists mainly of pictures and words—letters often having their origins in pictures. Today, the world is divided up into picture people and word people, the latter being usually jealous of the former. Since pictures usually accompany words, it is the job of the picture people not merely to illustrate those words in a literal sense, but to help enhance comprehension and even enjoyment by adding comment, innuendo, criticism, humor or an intriguing invitation to read or purchase. If we didn't do this, we would be mere decorators.

I believe that, whether we create an illustration, logo or icon, it is our job to add concept—that is, some sort of really cool idea—to the piece. Admittedly, sometimes the designer's concept is not really required, and sometimes it is resented (remember those sullen word people I mentioned?).

So, what is a logo? On this page we will attempt to explain the distinctions between an illustration, a picture, a design, plain type, a logo and an icon.

DUCK COMICS
#1
ALLSTAR COMIX
A

Popular
COMICS
JOKE BOOK
FAMOUS FUNNIES
10 CENTS
The Nation's Comic Monthly
BALL ONE! INSIDE!
B

#@?!
FUNNY BOOK
COMIX
C

Example A is not a logo, because it's too complex in technique and in concept to communicate its message instantly at a glance. This is an ILLUSTRATION by the author for a Rolling Stone article about comic-book conventions. My approach was to satirize the big business of comic cons and the ardent young fans whom I'd observed at cons. Example B is not an illustration. It has no concept. It's just a literal PICTURE of comic books about which one could say, "So what?" Example C is a DESIGN. It has a sense of composition, but no concept, though the enlarged speech balloon kind of makes an intriguing statement, albeit an ambiguous one. Example D is not a logo, it's TYPE. The two words aren't unified and there is nothing unique about them. A border enclosing the words or enlarged initial caps might have saved the arrangement. And—while not always necessary in a logo—there's no concept here, except perhaps the comic-book-style font. Example E is a LOGO. All the elements were designed as a unit and form a distinctive overall shape. The concept is the dollar sign $ and splashy comic-book-style hand-lettering. As shown in the beginning of this section, logos come in endless stylistic variations, and this is only one approach. In example F, a super familiar emblem made into a dollar sign communicates the concept of this purely graphic, or perhaps monogrammatic LOGO. Example G, a simplified version of the same logo, with bold strokes to "read" when severely reduced, is one style of ICON.

SUPER SALES

D

Comics R Big Business

SUPER$ALES

E

F

G

Cable Address: LIBWEEKLY

Liberty

A Weekly for the Whole Family

STEP

Harvey Deuell
Executive Editor

Pivot comfortably.
Full Backhand left ~~fully~~.
Hit against left side.

Pivot
Left ~~hand~~ backhand
Left side

E[...]IA[...]CE
247 [...]ENUE
at 46th Street
Telephone Ashland 4160

New York, N.Y.

August 26, 1926.

F.G. COOPER

Mr. F. G. Cooper,
Broad Street,
Westfield, N. J.

Dear Mr. Cooper:

Will you illustrate this poem with some of your little "funnies". The pictures to take up about the same space as your editorial page cartoonettes in LIFE.

Please quote me a price before going ahead provided you will take this on.

Sincerely yours,

M. B. Aleshire

M. B. ALESHIRE

Art Director

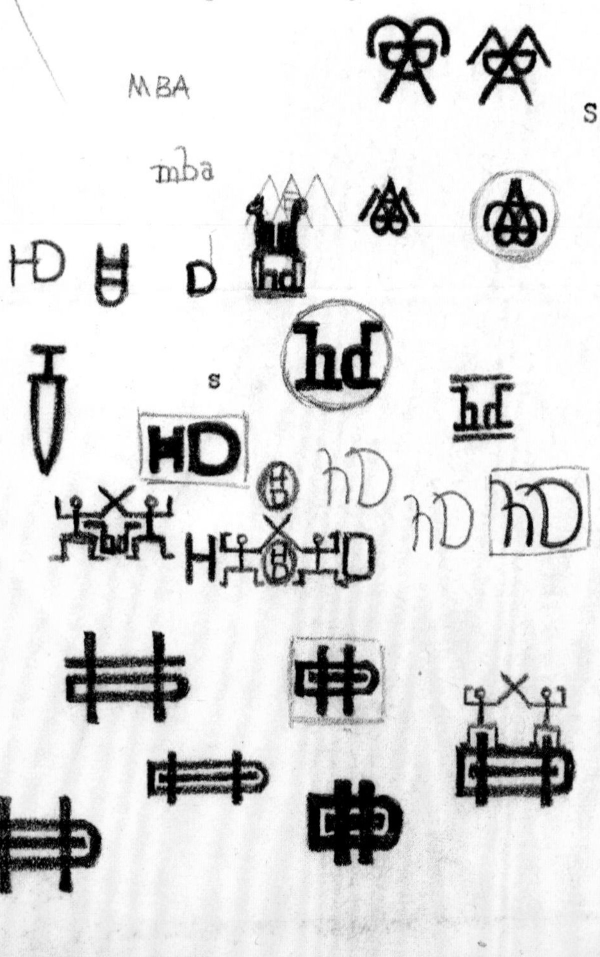
MBA
mba
HD
hd
s

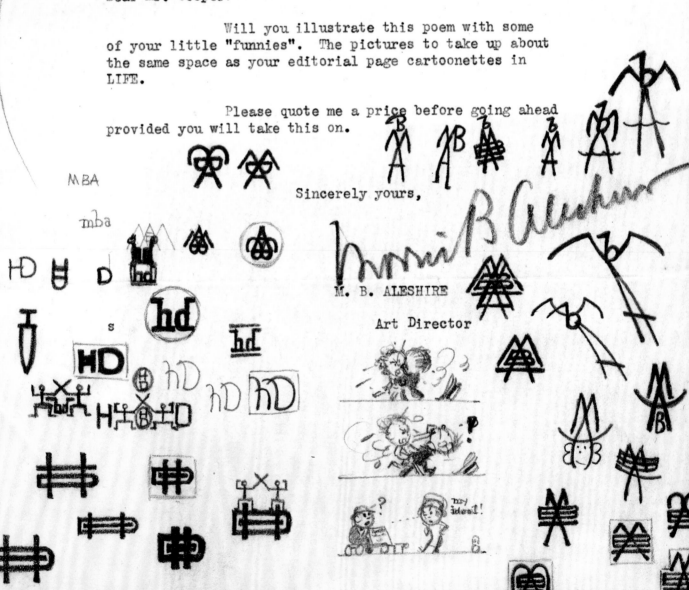

THUMBNAIL & COMP

Opposite page, the restless mind at work: Fred Cooper (1883–1961) emblazoned this letter from a national magazine with rough monogram designs for the editor and art director. Watch as Cooper's ideas take flight, sequencing from one concept to the next. (This page was reprinted from the author's book *The Lettering and Graphic Design of F.G. Cooper,* 1996, Art Direction Book Co.)

After the research and reference phases, the next step is thumbnail sketches, so called because they are done about the size and shape of those 1950s-style spatulate-type thumbnails that Jack Kirby always drew on Sergeant Fury. Thumbnails, leading to larger roughs and "comps" (the almost-finished sketches the client will see), are an important step in logo design because concepts can magically emerge as we sketch.

No less ingenious is Daniel Pelavin, who creates his thumbnails in marker, below, scans, then auto-traces them to e-mail to clients. This method has its merits. The client understands that these are roughs and doesn't take anything too literally at this point, leaving the artist lots of leeway to embellish later. Yet, despite the sketchiness of these roughs, little doubt is left as to the direction the artist is heading. Note that while color is not yet indicated at this stage, the all-important interplay of light and dark contrasts is already fully developed in Pelavin's mind. He adds letters beside each sketch so the client can say, "I like F, it's perfect! But could you just make one little change…" Bear in mind that a less accomplished designer than Pelavin might not get away with such sketchy comps. The finished artwork, right, was done in Adobe Illustrator.

PLAY
20
Questions

DANIEL PELAVIN

A)

PLAY
20
Questions

B)

20
PLAY
QUESTIONS

C)

PLAY
20
QUESTIONS

D)

20
Play
QUESTIONS

E)

PLAY
20
QUESTIONS

F)

PLAY
20
QUESTIONS

G)

PLAY
20
QUESTIONS

H)

PLAY
20
QUESTIONS

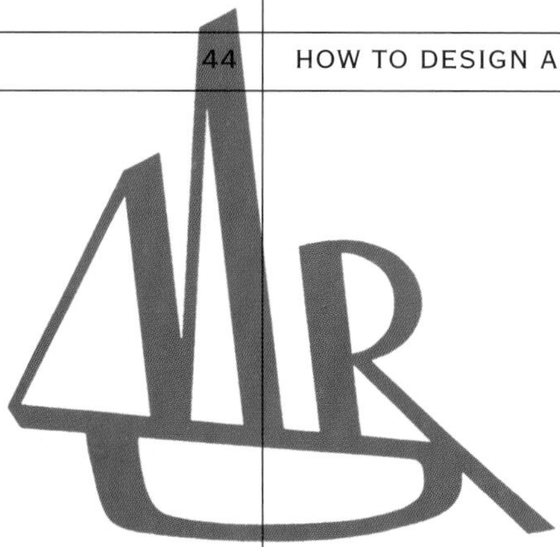

F.G. COOPER

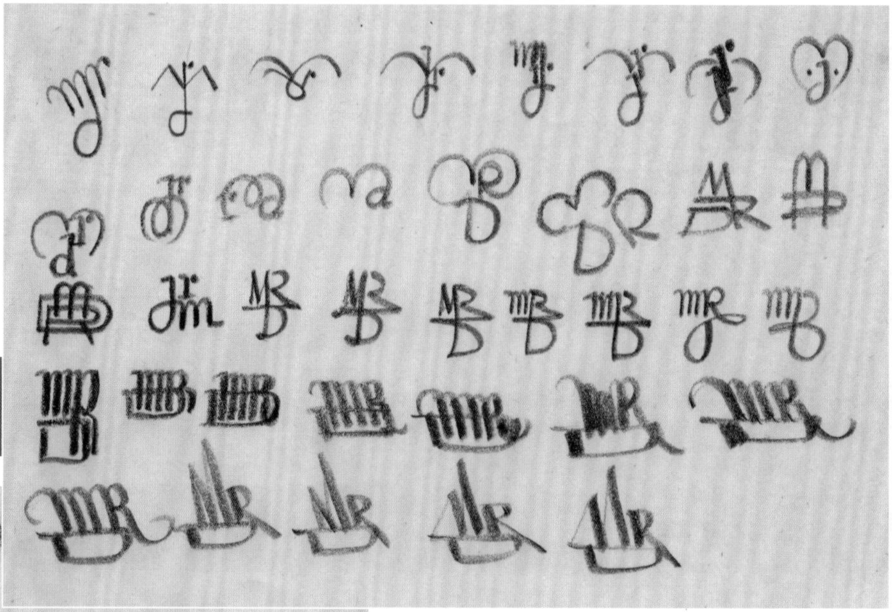

Here are more Cooper monogram sketches. Designing monograms became one of his hobbies, something he offered free to friends like Marione R. Derrickson, above.

The very name "Rube Goldberg" has become synonymous with any contrivance that brings about by complicated means what could have been accomplished simply. Left, the "Goldberg Variations," as I like to call Cooper's page of roughs for the legendary cartoonist, may seem Goldbergian as they inexorably wend their way to a finished design that is a caricature and monogram in one.

CLARENCE P. HORNUNG

RICHFIELD
Gasoline

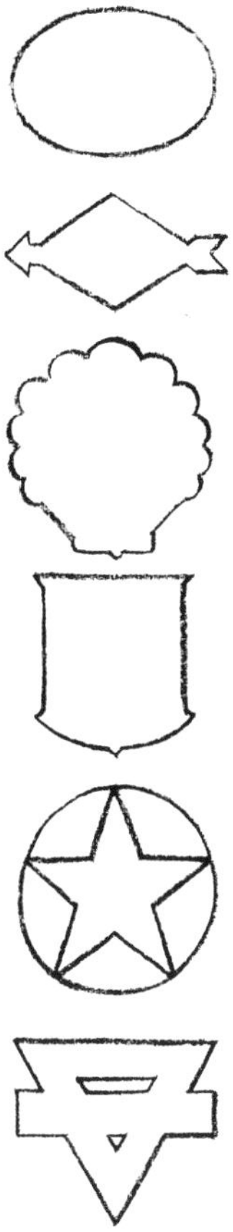

Far left, Clarence Hornung brandishes a grease pencil (Magic Markers didn't exist in 1940) as he refines a series of rough sketches for the Richfield Oil Company's corporate identity program. In the immersion stage of his process, Hornung took inventory of the competition's logo shapes, left, to ensure that Richfield's would be unique and distinctive. The final result appeared on all the company's products and on its service station signage, bottom left. Below, from the 1920s, one of Hornung's pencil roughs for an elaborate border design. Interestingly, he preferred to rough-in masses first, and later get specific about the ornamentation.

RICHFIELD

PHILIPP SEITZ

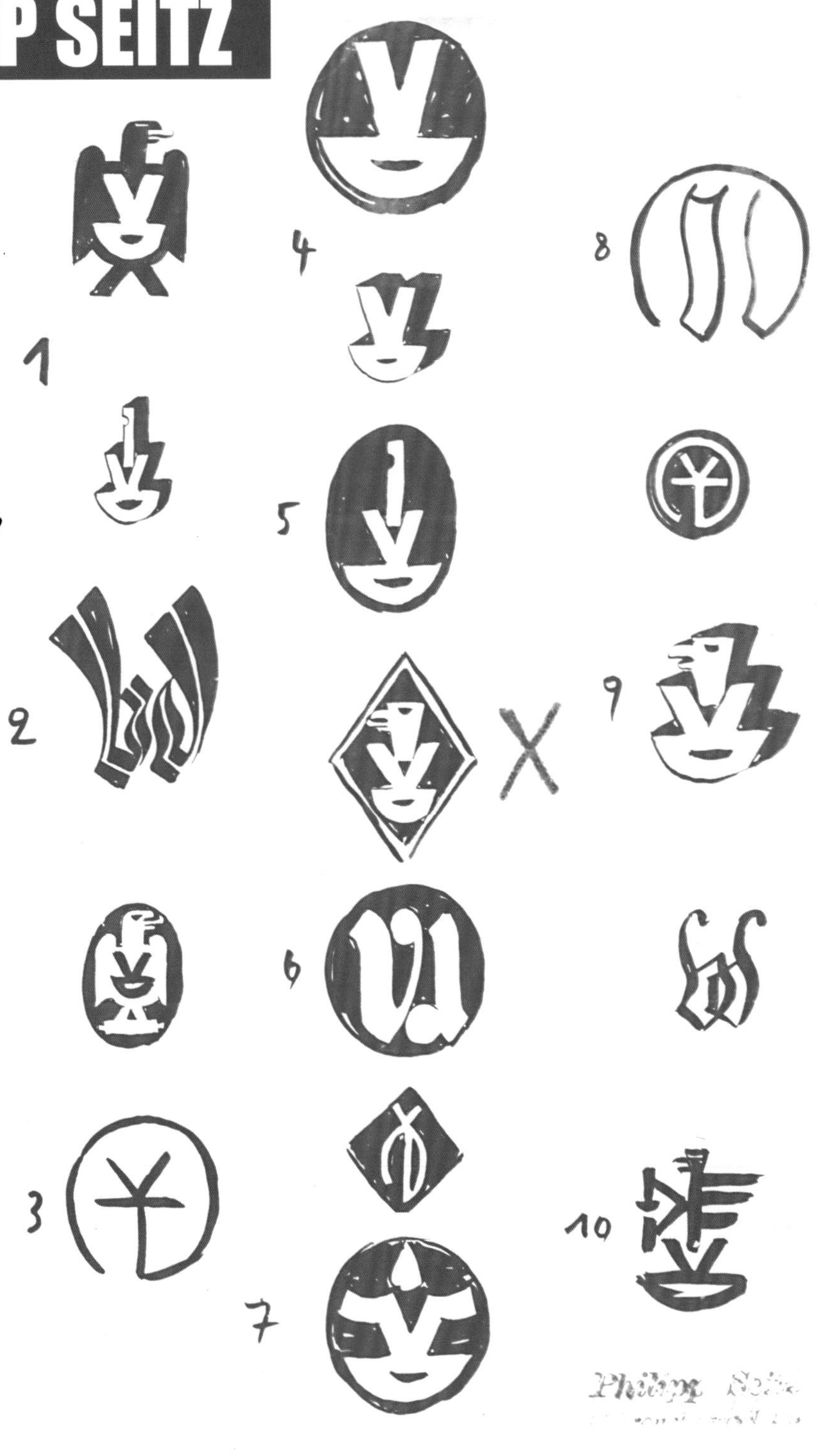
1
2
3
4
5
6
7
8
9
10

The thumbnail is nothing new. Even the great old German designers utilized *daumennagel skizze,* just as we do today. These pencil sketches from 1929 were done by the phenomenally prolific trademark designer Philipp Seitz for the Volksfreund Druckerei, a printing firm. The final mark is shown above. Interestingly, it is quite crude by today's standards, and not so far advanced from the rough version.

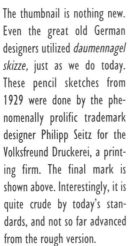

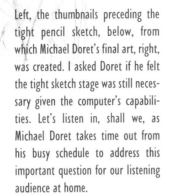

Left, the thumbnails preceding the tight pencil sketch, below, from which Michael Doret's final art, right, was created. I asked Doret if he felt the tight sketch stage was still necessary given the computer's capabilities. Let's listen in, shall we, as Michael Doret takes time out from his busy schedule to address this important question for our listening audience at home.

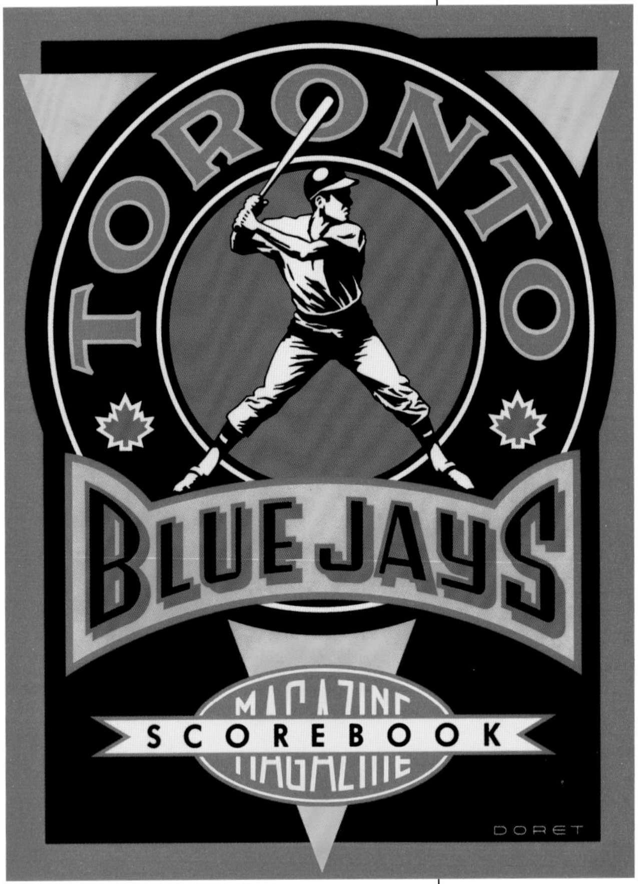
TORONTO
BLUEJAYS
SCOREBOOK
DORET

MICHAEL DORET

DORET

"I prefer to make a tight pencil sketch for whatever I'm designing," he says. "Otherwise, I feel as though I'm working in the dark; I have no sense of scale working directly in Illustrator. I think going straight to computer and not making a tight pencil sketch would determine the direction of one's work. A design often evolves from the capabilities of the medium you're using." I agree. It would be difficult, although not impossible, to create the complex Bluejays lettering shown in the tight sketch at left, without first drawing it out. So, I asked myself: Does my own work suffer by my preference to go from thumbnail right to computer? Am I wasting my eyesight staring at the screen while endlessly moving points back and forth instead of first working out my designs in pencil? This might be a question all of us should ponder.

I usually start designing a logo by making a page or two of thumbnails while looking through any design book or magazine. Then I move to the computer, where, just as on paper, one logo flows into the next until I've got a page of Illustrator "roughs." Usually, we have no idea what the client will go for, so we make stabs in very different directions.

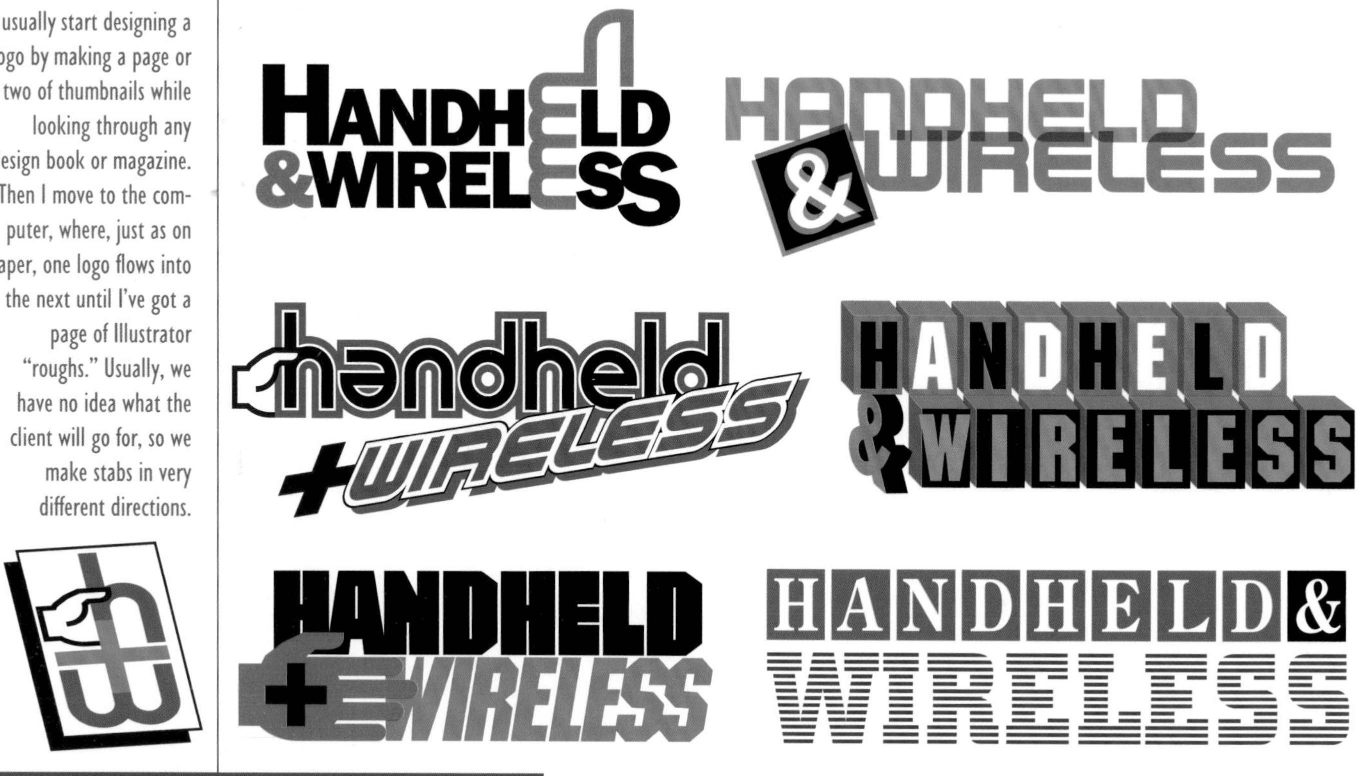
HANDHELD &WIRELESS
HANDHELD &WIRELESS
handheld +WIRELESS
HANDHELD &WIRELESS
HANDHELD +WIRELESS
HANDHELD& WIRELESS

LESLIE CABARGA

Logo comps for Winning Directions, a firm specializing in political direct mail. These comps were "sketched" directly in Illustrator without any pencil thumbnails. Concepts of these logos include the directional arrow; the checkmark and ballot box; red, white and blue colors; map of America; and folding paper, indicating direct-mail brochures. WD selected as their logo the version at bottom right.

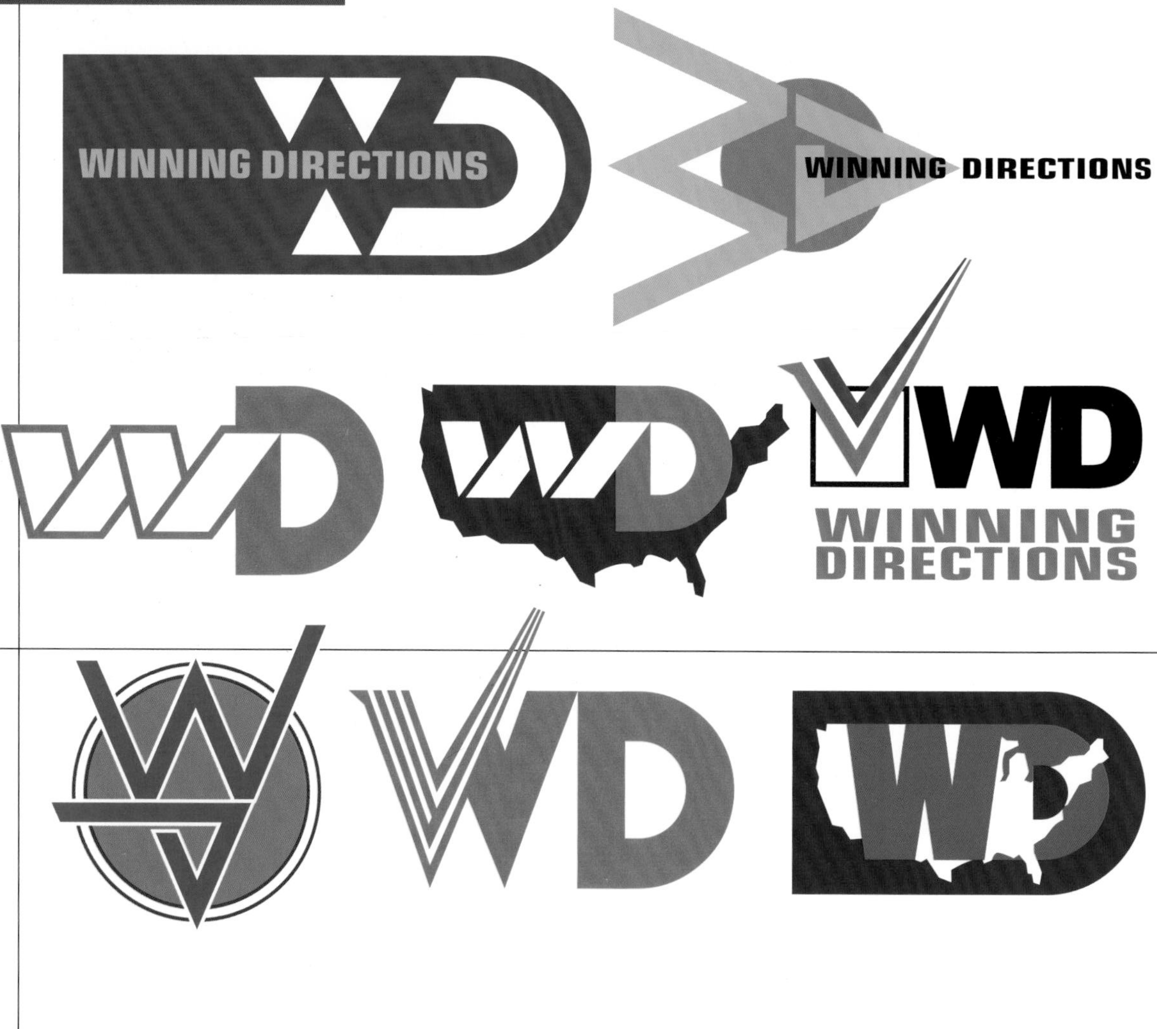
WINNING DIRECTIONS
WINNING DIRECTIONS
WD
WD
WD
WINNING DIRECTIONS
WD
WD

SHAKE, RATTLE
and
Roller
Derby
BYLINE HERE?

Shake, Rattle
AND
ROLLER
DERBY

SHAKE,
RATTLE
AND
ROLLER
DERBY

SHAKE,
RATTLE
and
ROLLER
DERBY

Shake,
Rattle
and
ROLLER
DERBY

Shake,
Rattle
AND
ROLLER
DERBY

Shake,
Rattle
AND
ROLLER
DERBY

Here's a good idea from David Coulson: He makes pencil sketches of various rough ideas, then scans them into the computer and adds tone or color for presentation to the client. It's important not to leave gaps in the pencil outlines so that discrete areas can be completely selected with Photoshop's Magic Wand tool. Precomputer, I used to Xerox my pencil sketches, then try out different color combos with marker. Above are examples of Coulson's comping technique and the tight pencil drawing (bottom row, right) he used to create the final color piece, right. These sketches are larger than thumbnails. Call them "palm prints"?

DAVID COULSON

For every movie logo on a Broadway marquee, there are a half-dozen broken-hearted designers. These unchosen logos by the author were done with Mike Salisbury Communications, a design firm whose logo "hits" include *Jurassic Park*, *The Shadow* and hundreds more. The examples here show how key elements can be treated with various effects, and in different combinations, to supply the client a wide variety of possibilities as well as to puff up the presentation package. (Keep this between us designers, OK?) The ease with which variations on a theme are created is one thing we love about computers. Years ago, when I worked for him, Mike Salisbury told me not to use flush-right, ragged-left type columns, because it makes the type hard to read. I didn't listen—most likely to my detriment as a designer.

MOULIN ROUGE

MOULIN ROUGE

MOULIN ROUGE
MOULIN ROUGE

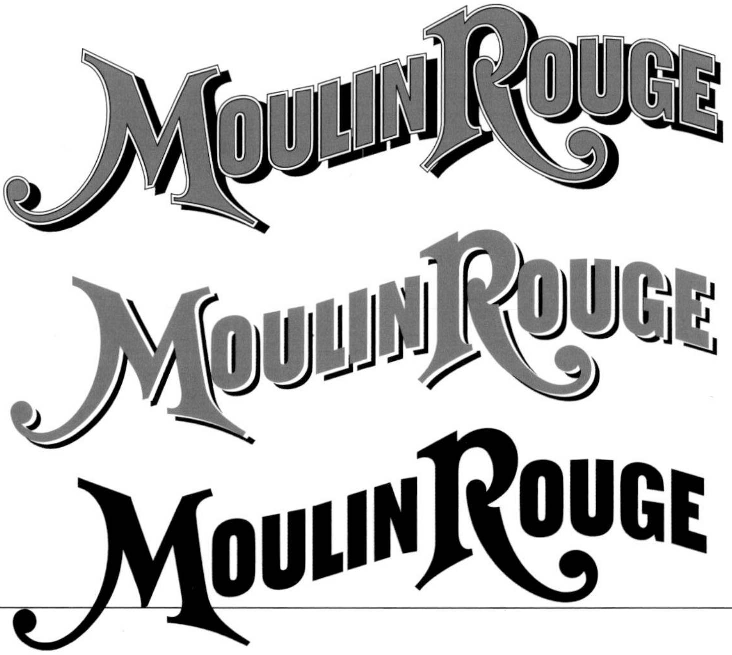
MOULIN ROUGE
MOULIN ROUGE
MOULIN ROUGE

LESLIE CABARGA

TONY DISPIGNA

There are a number of letterers who wish their finished work looked as good as Tony DiSpigna's rough sketches. Below, for an infamous motion picture, a series of rough logo designs utilizing several versions of Spencerian script. All were rejected. See, what'd I tell you about the movies breaking designers' hearts? (I suppose DiSpigna's flourishes didn't look enough like wire hangers!) Left, most Spencerian scripts exult in extravagant decoration for decoration's sake alone. Here, in the rough penciling, left, and the finished penciling, below left, for a logo to emblazon the side of a yacht, the embellishments evoke the feeling of waves, wind and sea—perhaps the first time Spencerian decorations became the logo concept! Below left, a section of DiSpigna's unbelievable final inks with the most uncannily careful whiting-out I've ever seen.

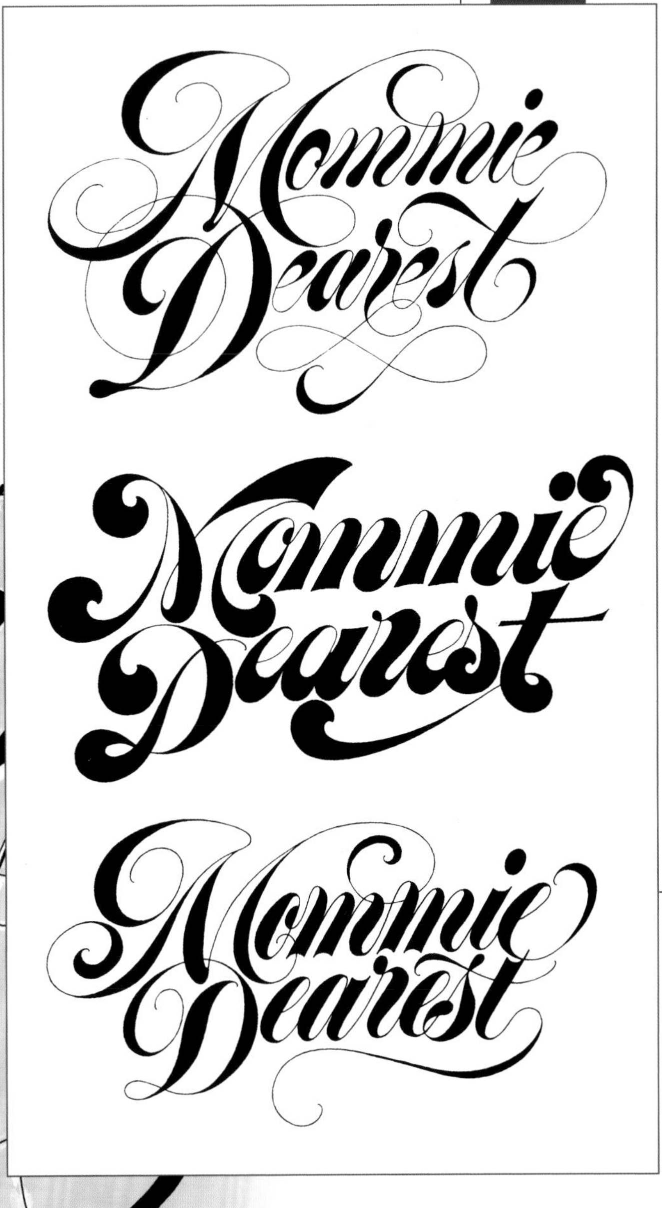
Mommie Dearest
Mommie Dearest
Mommie Dearest

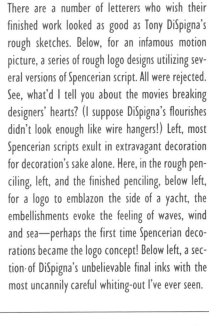

Resources: 144 LOGO LAYOUTS

Here is a selection of common logo arrangements of the present and past. You can refer to these in designing your own logos. Although specific fonts and graphics are used with hypothetical company names, none of this is meant to be copied literally. Draw your own lettering and icons to replace the ones shown. Below, three levels of interpretation.

When I design logos, I always worry that I'm overlooking layout possibilities. So I researched old and new logos to come up with this survey. As I suspected, today's hippest logo layouts differ very little from their old-time counterparts. Right, seventy years separate these two logos. Lettering and graphic rendering styles have changed, but the layout is essentially identical. It would be nice if we designers could really come up with something new in logos, but it seems that most of the differences are only superficial.

Blue Bonnet
VINK

FLUOROSIS
PERMANENT
SF
MOTTLING
FIREBALL
TABASCO
HOT AS
FT
HADES
FIREBALL
TABASCO
HOT AS
FT
HADES
FIREBALL
TOBASCO
HOT AS HADES
FT

(Original Inspiration) 1. Literal Adaptation 2. Creative Interpretation 3. Free Association

FLUORIDE
SF FLUORIDE
FLUORIDE RAT POISON
SF FLUORIDE SODIUM RAT POISON
FLUORIDE
SF FLUORIDE
FLUORIDE SODIUM RAT POISON
SF FLUORIDE SODIUM RAT POISON
SODIUM FLUORIDE
SODIUM Destroys Plumbing Kills Rats Dead FLUORIDE
Destroys Plumbing FLUORIDE SF
FLUORIDE
FLUORIDE
SF FLUORIDE
SF FLUORIDE
FLUORIDE SODIUM RAT POISON
FLUORIDE
FLUORIDE SODIUM RAT POISON
CALCIUM FLUORIDE, SI
FLUORIDE
SODIUM FLUORIDE, NO
FLUORIDE
FLUORIDE
Original Rat Poison
FLUORIDE
Destroys Plumbing
SODIUM
FLUORIDE
SF

FLUORIDE

Fluoride

FLUORIDE
SODIUM RAT POISON

FLUORIDE
SODIUM RAT POISON

Industrial Aluminum Waste
FLUOROSIS
Permanent Enamel Mottling

SODIUM FLUORIDE

Fluoride

POISON
FLUORIDE
DENTAL

FLUOROSIS

FLUORIDE

SODIUM FLUORIDE

FLUOROSIS
HIP FRACTURES

FLUORIDE
DENTAL POISON

FLUORIDE

FLUORIDE

FLUORIDE

FLUORIDE
ALUMINUM BIPRODUCT

Enamel
FLUORIDE
Mottling

FLUORIDE
DENTAL POISON

FLUORIDE

RATTE
FLUORIDE
POISON

FLUORIDE

FLUORIDE
ALUMINUM BIPRODUCT

RATTE
ALUMINUM BIPRODUCT
POISON

PERPETRATED
SF
UNWITTING PUBLIC

FLUOROSIS
ALUMINUM
BIPRODUCT

DF

FLUOROSIS
HIP
FRACTURES

SF
FLUOROSIS

SF

SF
FLUORIDE

F

FLUO
RIDE

FLUO
RIDE

DF

FLUOROSIS
PERMANENT SF MOTTLING

DENTAL FLUOROSIS
POISONS TEETH

FLUORIDE

DENTAL
FLUOROSIS

FLUORIDE

MERCURY AMALGAM
Systemic Poisoning

MERCURY AMALGAM
Long Term Systemic Poison

MERCURY
Long Term Systemic Poison

MERCURY
AMALGAM

MERCURY
• AMALGAM •

DENTAL
Mercury
AMALGAM

MERCURY
AMALGAM

MA
MERCURY
AMALGAM

MERCURY

MA

MERCURY
EPA TOXIN

AMALGAM

MERCURY
AMALGAM

MERCURY

MERCURY

MERCURY

FILLINGS?
MERCURY

AMALGAM

AMALGAM

MERCURY

Mercury
MOST TOXIC METAL

NO
Hg

AMALGAM
Guaranteed 50% Mercury

MERCURY VAPOR INHALATION
DENTAL AMALGAM

MERCURY TOXIC

NO
Hg

NO Hg
MERCURY
Silver Is Mercury

Mercury
"SILVER" AMALGAM
WORLD THREAT

MERCURY

Mercury
AMALGAM

TIME
AMALGAM
BOMB

MERCURY

SYSTEMIC TOXICITY
50%
MERCURY
AMALGAM

MERCURY

MERCURY
TOXIC OVERLOAD
AMALGAM

TIME
BOMB

MA
TOXIC OVERLOAD

SYSTEMIC DENTAL
MERCURY
AMALGAM SYNDROME

SYSTEMIC DENTAL
MERCURY
AMALGAM SYNDROME

MERCURY
50%
Guaranteed
AMALGAM

(Notice redundancy setting in? I think there are really only about seven logo layouts, the rest are stylistic variations...but OK, I'll press on.)

TYPESTYLES CATEGORIZED

(If your views are not colored by fear or greed, then the words of the following you should read.)

The importance of selecting the right type for a logo or design cannot be overstated. If, as the saying goes, clothes make the man, then type makes the design. Here is a meager outline of available fonts, to help provide awareness of options when designing. It's not meant to advertise specific fonts. For each style shown, there are hundreds more in that category. This chart provides a point of departure to lead you to the most appropriate styles for your design.

SERIF ROMANS

BEN FRANKLIN
Classic: **Trajan**, Adobe.com

A.S. Neill
Basic: **New Century Schoolbook**, Adobe.com

Jerome I. RODALE
Calligraphic: **Zapf Chancery**, Adobe.com

Peggy O'MARA
Round serif: **Cooper Black**, Adobe.com

Paul M. FLEISS
Extreme contrast: **MT Bodoni Ultra Bold**, Fonts.com

Alice WALKER
Old-style: **Garamond**, Adobe.com

Jiddu KRISHNAMURTI
Hand-tooled: **Cloister Open Face**, Fonts.com

Noam CHOMSKY
Modern (after Electra): **Electric**, Jim Parkinson / *San Francisco Chronicle*

Robert S. MENDELSOHN
Distressed italic: **Letterpress Text**, Costelloart.com

JOHN LENNON
Spurred gothic: **Copperplate Gothic 29BC**, Adobe.com

SANS-SERIF

Viera SCHEIBNER
Romanized thick/thin: **Optima**, Adobe.com

Herbert M. SHELTON
Classic geometric mono weight sans: **Futura Book**, Adobe.com

Josiah WOOLFOLK
Basic modern: **Helvetica Bold**, Adobe.com

CHRISTINE MAGGIORE
Heavy miter corner: **Machine**, Fonts.com

MAHATMA GANDHI
Comic book: **Astro City**, Comicraft.com

Napolean HILL
Squared mono weight: **Eurostile**, Adobe.com

SANS-SERIF

John H. TILDEN
Standard heavy: **Franklin Gothic Heavy**, Adobe.com

John HOLT
Deco poster: **Kobalt Bold**, FlashFonts.com/Font Bureau.com

Ina Mae GASKIN
Round stroke-end: **VAG Rounded**, Adobe.com

Nikola TESLA
Calligraphic heavy: **Hombre**, Font Bank

POST ANCIENT

ARUNDHATI ROY
Early roman: **Pompeijana Roman**, Fonts.com

LANGSTON HUGHES
Early roman: **Rusticana Roman**, Fonts.com

NELSON MANDELA
Early roman: **Beata**, LetterPerfect.com

BLACK LETTER & GOTHIC

KAHLIL GIBRAN
Modified gothic: **Aureus Uncial**, Fonts.com

FREDERICK LEBOYER
Modified gothic: **MASON**, Emigre.com

Maya Angelou
Free gothic: **Saber**, FlashFonts.com/Font Bureau.com

Helen CALDICOTT
Formalized gothic: **MT Engravers Old English**, Fonts.com

Sojourner Truth
German black letter: **Fette Fraktur**, Adobe.com

IVAN ILLICH
German gothic: **Angle Inline**, FlashFonts.com/Fonts.com

STENCIL

Rachel CARSON
Art Nouveau: **Auriol**, Fonts.com

MALCOLM X
Classic: **Stencil**, Adobe.com

SCRIPTS

Barbara Marciniak
Formal script: **Kuenstler Script,** Adobe.com

Thomas Jefferson
Formal handscript: **Snell Roundhand,** Adobe.com

Aldous Huxley
Streamlined script: **Streamline Light Extended,** FlashFonts.com/Fonts.com

Royal Rife
Streamlined heavy script: **Magneto Bold Extended,** Flashfonts/Font Bureau

Barbara Ehrenreich
Classic heavy script : **Casey Ultrabold,** Flashfonts.com/Font Bureau.com

Dennis Kucinich
Casual brush script : **Brush Script,** Adobe.com

CALLIGRAPHIC & HANDWRITTEN

Vance PACKARD
Calligraphic : **Blackstone Italic,** Costelloart.com

FLORENCE SCOVELL SHINN
Faux foreign : **Ginko,** Fonts.com

Bob Marley
Brush italic : **Rapier,** Myfonts.com

Martin Luther KING
Pen grunge : **Smack,** Myfonts.com

Otto Messmer
Fancy pen italic : **Swank Bold,** Fonts.com

Helen KELLER
Casual : **Handwriting,** Sam Wang

CURRENT

Albert EINSTEIN
Bastard composite : **Dead History,** Emigre

César CHÁVEZ
Grunge typewriter : **Crud Font,** Scott Yoshinaga

JACK HERER
Techesque : **Computer,** Fonts.com

[illegible]
Current free geometric : **BillDing,** Büro Destruct

Helen SCHUCMAN
Current free geometric : **Generik,** FlashFonts.com

PERIOD STYLE FONTS

BERNARD MAYBECK
Art Nouveau : **Kolo Regular,** Fonts.com

Sergio ARAGONÉS
Art Nouveau : **Arnold Boecklin,** Fonts.com

THOMAS NAST
Victorian fancy : **Pepperwood,** Fonts.com

Howard ZINN
Victorian heavy slab serif : **Giza Nine Three,** Font Bureau.com

Suzanne ARMS
Art Deco decorative : **Futura Black,** Fonts.com

Julia BUTTERFLY HILL
Art Deco fat poster : **Kobalt Black,** Flashfonts.com / Fonts.com

Paramahansa YOGANANDA
Art Deco thin line : **Ojaio Light,** Flashfonts.com / Fonts.com

Jessie JACKSON
Art Deco monoweight sans : **ITC Bauhaus Light,** Adobe.com

Edgar Cayce
Fifties script : **Rocket Regular,** Flashfonts.com/Font Bureau.com

THEODOR GEISEL
Fifties bouncy : **Volcano King,** Fontdiner.com

Harvey W. Wiley
Sixties bouncy : **HiBrow,** Flashfonts.com/Font Bureau.com

GEORGE BERNARD SHAW
Sixties Psychedelic : **Peace Outline,** Flashfonts.com/Font Bureau.com

Walene JAMES
Seventies : **Bellbottom Flair,** Flashfonts.com

GERALD JAMPOLSKY
Seventies : **Chromium One,** Fonts.com

Gore Vidal
Seventies : **Harlow Regular,** Fonts.com

NOVELTY

Linus PAULING
Effect : **Shatter,** Fonts.com

ralph nader
Object : **Pushtab,** Regleszero.com

AMY GOODMAN
Auto trace : **Rubber Duck,** Girlswhowearglasses.com

Resources: A DATE WITH NUMERALS

Here are numerals spanning 570 years. Sources include mason's marks, old manuscripts, iron work, gravestones, wood and copper engravings, wood and metal types, and present-day digital fonts. At least one hundred potential font ideas (not counting the existing fonts) reside on these pages. I made current this collection of numerals from an old German book.

Opposite: A. Luscious old-style numerals by Fred Cooper from *Lettering*, 1926. **B.** Oswald Cooper's sleek sans-serif old-style numerals, from *American Alphabets*, 1930. **C.** Typical 1930s poster numerals from Kobalt Bold by Leslie Cabarga. **D.** Art Nouveau numerals by J.M. Bergling from his book *Art Alphabets and Lettering*, 1918. **E.** Engraved gothic numerals, also by J.M. Bergling. **F.** Old-style numerals from Matthew Carter's Big Caslon. **G.** Modern cap-height numerals from Richard Lipton's Detroit Bodoni. **H.** Unique set of numerals from Paul Renner's Futura Black.

1234567890

234567890

C 0123456789

D 0123456789

E 0123456789

F 0123456789

G 0123456789

H 0123456789

1734	1798	1855	1922	1954
1738	1804	1857	1925	1956
1740	1812	1862	1928	1957
1742.	1813	1868	1929	1961
1748	1818	1883	1932	1967
1756	1824	1884	1933	1972
1760	1827	1887	1934	1984
1768.	1835	1894	1937	1990
1781	1837	1897	1939	1992
1789	1840.	1905	1942	1995
1792.	1843	1908	1945	2001
1795	1852	1913	1947	2003

ABC
DRAWING

A–F Initials: Leonardo da Vinci; G,S: Frederic Goudy; Hell: Leslie Cabarga; A,B,C,E: Egon Weiss; Mouse: Apple; q: Will Dwiggins; Symbol diagram: Anonymous

Part 2

LETTERS

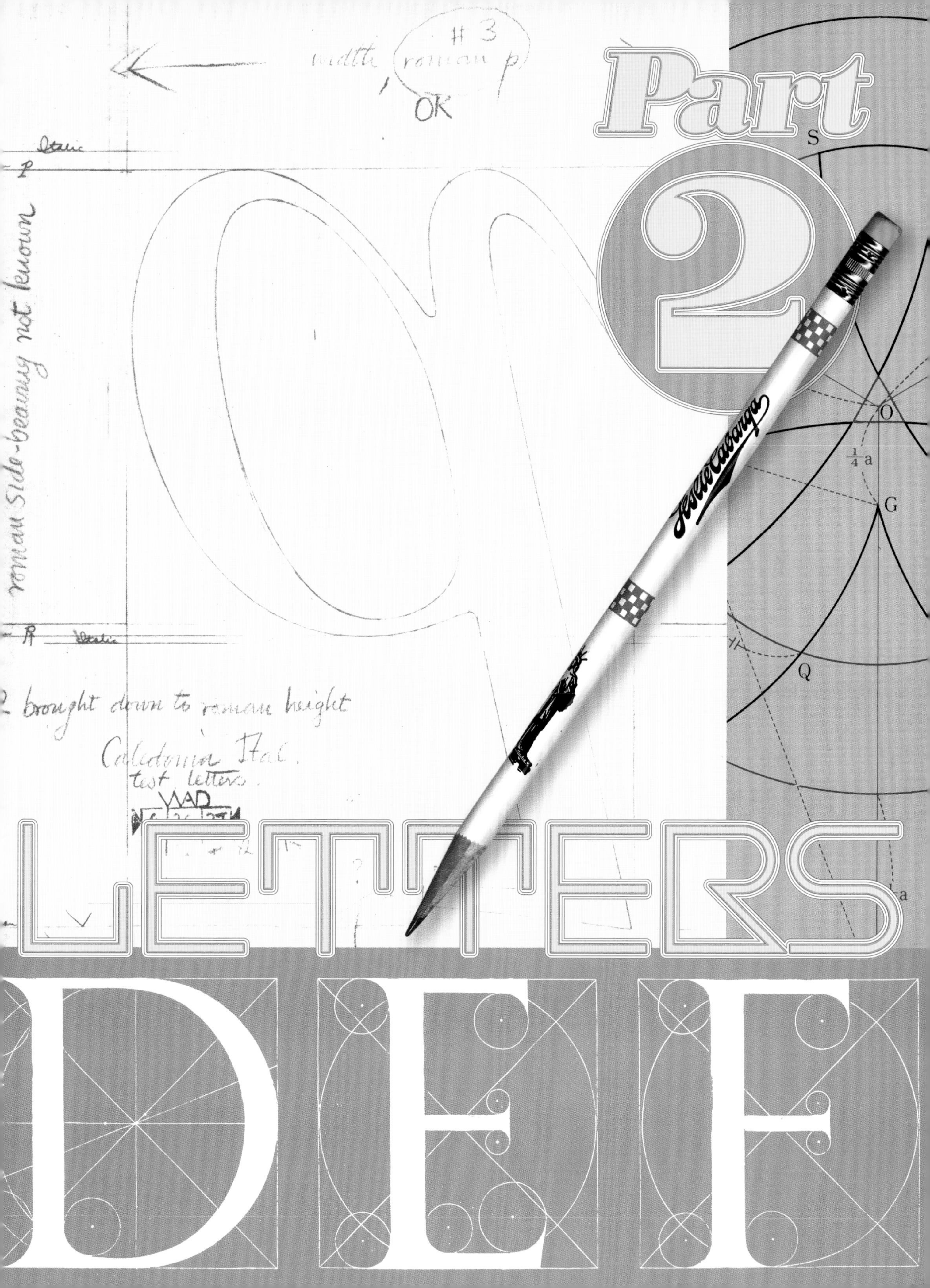

width
roman p
OK
roman side-bearing not known
brought down to roman height
Caledonia Ital.
test letters
S
O
G
Q

UNBELIEVABLE IMPLEMENTS

Type and Lettering in the Prepixel Era

Evolution is the process of matter becoming ever more intangible as it moves toward the ephemeral, eventually reaching the realm of pure information. Take type, for example. It started out as hunks of metal and wood. Today, it's anybody's guess as to whether the computer fonts we design actually exist at all.

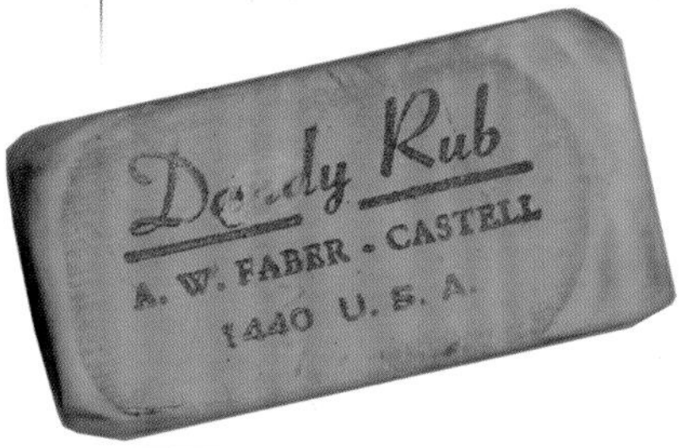
Dandy Rub
A. W. FABER - CASTELL
1440 U. S. A.

Primitive "COMMAND-Z" DEVICE. Apparently dubbed the "Dandy Rub" (a *dandy* was the forerunner to the *dude*), the device, a monolithic slab of malleable rubberoid material containing no moving parts, was used to efface the markings caused by the pen-cil; for instance, if one erred. But instead of simply pressing Command-Z or Delete as we now do, the "eraser," held firmly between thumb and forefinger, required a repetitious and vigorous rubbing motion, which soon became tiresome. This device—which never truly erased, but left ghostly remnants along with gougelike pen-cil impressions in the paper—was also available in classic pink, like the smaller version typically appended to the posterior region of the pen-cil.

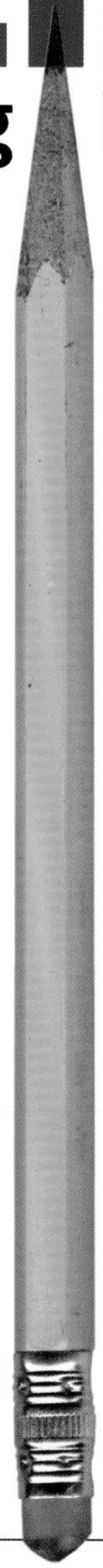

PEN-CIL. An intriguing manual input device of the twentieth century. With one hand firmly grasping the faceted amber shaft, the user of this lead-impregnated wooden implement would impress the pointed end upon a sheet of paper and draw it in any direction, producing a series of smudged lines that came to be called a "drawing." Often these "drawings" were executed in such a manner as to describe the contours of a person or object or even to delineate alphabetic characters.

The machines that "proved" type's existence were massive handpresses built of iron and wood. The output devices we use today for the same effect can weigh as little as a few ounces and will not degrade in soil. Ever. Now that's progress!

The day fast approaches when all the world's knowledge, the memory of every single event that ever occurred and ever will, all the great works of music, art and literature throughout history, and every cool font on the Internet will be storable on media so minuscule that it'll make the Akashic records seem like an 8-track tape.

So it kinda makes you chuckle to take a look back at some of the unbelievable and cumbersome implements devised by ever resourceful early lettering man (homo-speedballus) of the nineteenth and twentieth

MEASURING STICK. Used for judging relative intervals in an arbitrarily devised system of measures. Made obsolete with the adoption of standardized paper and print formats, and the invention of Step and Repeat, Copy and Paste, and Duplicate functions. This stainless steel model includes the "Inch," the "Point," and something called the "Pica," which the dictionary defines, curiously, as a syndrome involving the abnormal desire to eat unusual substances, such as dirt, june bugs or household cleanser, like my little brother used to do. Not surprisingly, he's also become a graphic designer.

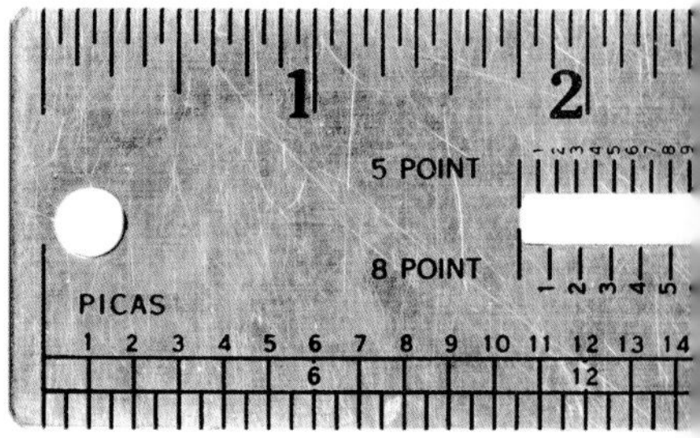
1
2
5 POINT
8 POINT
PICAS
1 2 3 4 5 6 7 8 9 10 11 12 13 14
6
12

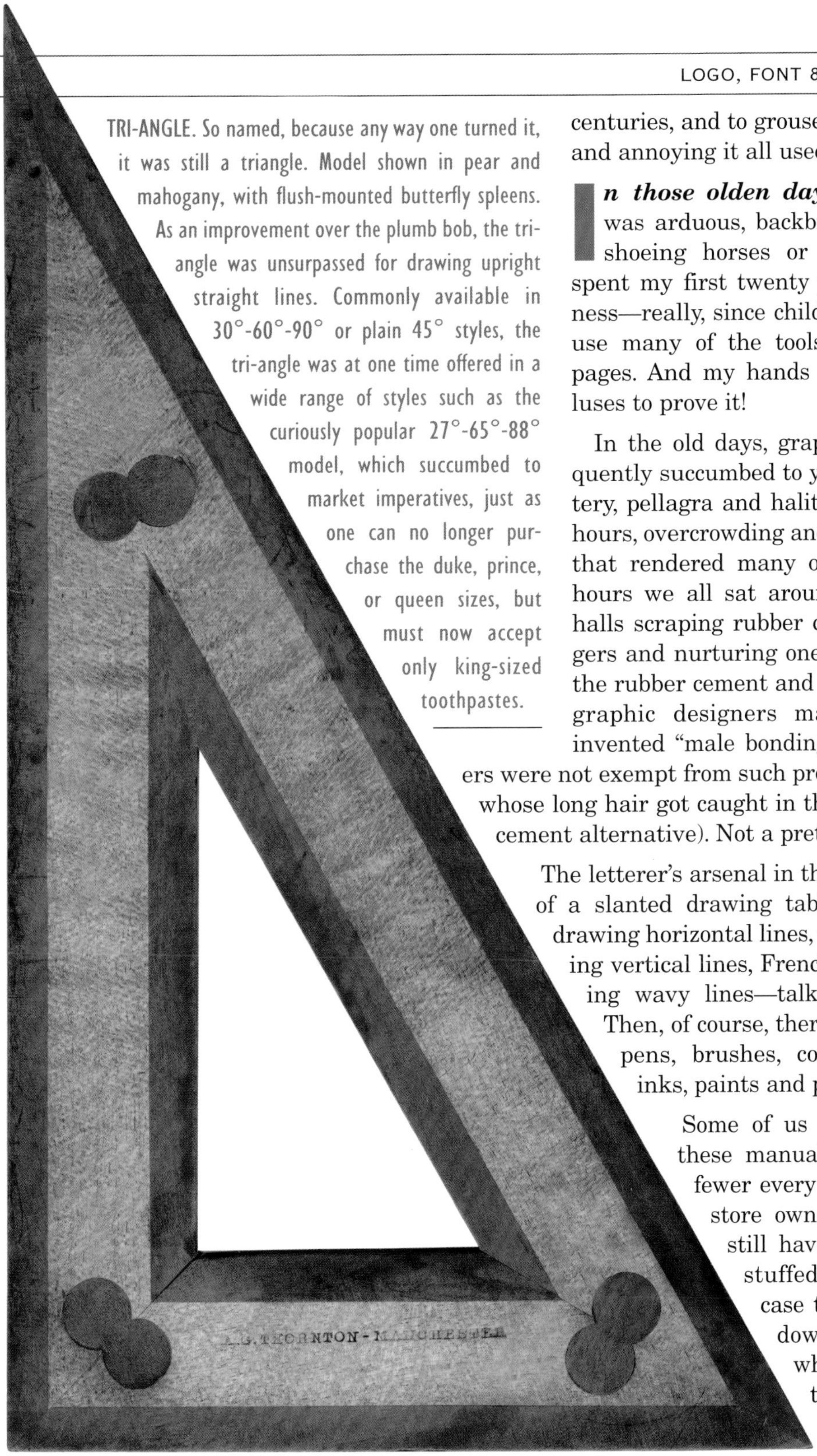

TRI-ANGLE. So named, because any way one turned it, it was still a triangle. Model shown in pear and mahogany, with flush-mounted butterfly spleens. As an improvement over the plumb bob, the tri-angle was unsurpassed for drawing upright straight lines. Commonly available in 30°-60°-90° or plain 45° styles, the tri-angle was at one time offered in a wide range of styles such as the curiously popular 27°-65°-88° model, which succumbed to market imperatives, just as one can no longer purchase the duke, prince, or queen sizes, but must now accept only king-sized toothpastes.

centuries, and to grouse over how difficult and annoying it all used to be.

I*n those olden days,* graphic design was arduous, backbreaking labor, like shoeing horses or shoveling coal. I spent my first twenty years in the business—really, since childhood—learning to use many of the tools shown on these pages. And my hands still bear the calluses to prove it!

In the old days, graphic designers frequently succumbed to yellow fever, dysentery, pellagra and halitosis from the long hours, overcrowding and tight underpants that rendered many of us sterile. After hours we all sat around in murky beer halls scraping rubber cement off our fingers and nurturing one another. Between the rubber cement and the fraternization, graphic designers may actually have invented "male bonding." Female designers were not exempt from such problems. I knew one whose long hair got caught in the waxer (a rubber cement alternative). Not a pretty sight!

The letterer's arsenal in those days consisted of a slanted drawing table, a T-square for drawing horizontal lines, triangles for drawing vertical lines, French curves for drawing wavy lines—talk about confusing! Then, of course, there were the pencils, pens, brushes, compasses, erasers, inks, paints and palettes.

Some of us still use many of these manual implements, but fewer every day, as art supply store owners will lament. I still have all my old tools stuffed in drawers (in case the electricity goes down), which meanwhile provide entertainment for my young daughter.

6 & 12 PT. AGATE INCHES
TURTLE'S STANDARD GAUGE NEW YORK

DECORATIVE BACK SCRATCHER. Numerals indicate it may also have served some secondary function relating to the gauging of type.

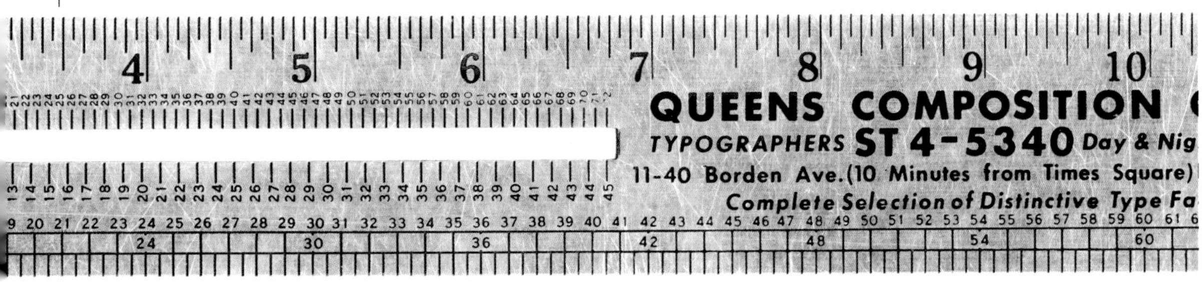
QUEENS COMPOSITION
TYPOGRAPHERS ST 4-5340 Day & Nig
11-40 Borden Ave.(10 Minutes from Times Square)
Complete Selection of Distinctive Type Fa

Left, the Queens Composition Corp. was one of many such typesetting operations that flourished before the advent of the personal computer. Now, you and I get to do the design as well as set the type!

GALLERY of PRIMITIVE INK-DELIVERY DEVICES. Don't laugh, but the following arcane instruments were all that were available to ancient lettering man. (A.) PEN. For freehand ink rendering only. Came in a huge variety of point styles and sizes. Required continuous dipping to refresh ink supply. (B. and C.) PAYZANT PENS. For freehand use when maintaining a specific stroke width was desired. Came in a variety of point sizes and had a large ink reservoir, requiring less frequent dipping. (D.) DOUBLE-STROKE RULING PEN. For those times when drawing lines, one at a time, seemed far too time-consuming. Was useful for mapmaking when a consistent relationship between two differently colored and sized strokes was required. (E.) RULING PEN. The specimen is a fancy version of the classic ruling pen used for all technical ink renderings before the invention of the technical fountain pen. Delivered an ink stroke of consistent width for about eleven inches before the ink ran out. (F.) RAPIDOGRAPH PEN. Still available in antique and artist supply shops, Rapidographs come in a variety of point sizes. Although they clog constantly, leak frequently, skip and blob repeatedly, they represented a huge step forward compared with the other tools shown here.

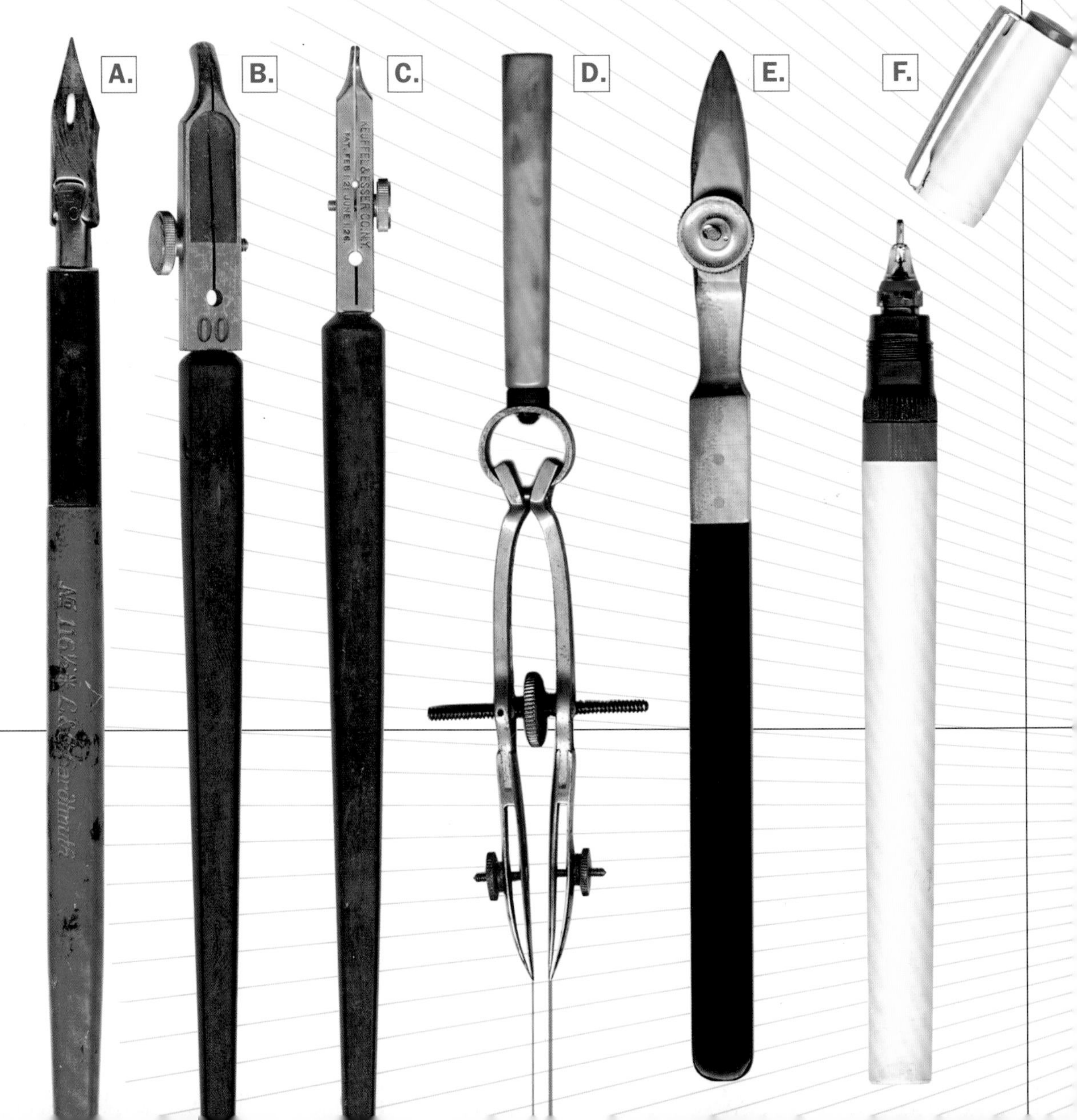
A.
B.
C.
D.
E.
F.

ACME PARALLEL LINE DRAWING MACHINE. Had I a nickel for every closely spaced parallel line I've drawn in my life. . . well, suffice it to say, I wouldn't have to write books for a living. This contraption was de rigueur in its day, and no well-appointed graphics studio was without one. Simple adjustments allowed variable spacing between lines. It was also useful for propping up casement windows that wouldn't stay open.

In days gone by, the handmade and imperfect qualities produced by these tools (with our help) were viewed as "artistic" and were accepted in the design field. Not now. Today, perfectly sharp corners and machinelike accuracy are expected and demanded, and these qualities the computer provides to even the least adroit of us.

By the time I began learning the trade, the revolutionary Rapidograph technical pen came along, obviating the ruling pen for inking lines of consistent width. Rapidographs constantly clogged, and dried up if you didn't use them for a month, necessitating taking them apart for cleaning. The Rapidograph was still better than the ruling pen, which held only a small amount of ink at a time and frequently blobbed up at the beginning of a stroke, or wouldn't "lower" the ink to start at all.

I messed around with Speedball lettering pens but found them frustrating. For lettering I preferred Rapidographs and for illustration, only the Winsor & Newton, Series 7, no. 2 sable brush would do. Only one in twenty of these Winsor & Newton brushes were made correctly, but I remember one especially good one that I used for ten years, until falling hair made its line weight too narrow.

Inking a circle was accomplished with an instrument called a compass, whose fulcrum point left a hole in the middle of your paper. Yes, we actually did our inking on paper then (rather than just *printing it out on paper* with a laser printer). Circles and ellipses could also be inked with various plastic "ellipse templates." If you weren't careful, the ink from your Rapidograph would usually bleed under the edge of the template, leaving a smudge that would then have to be whited out with white paint.

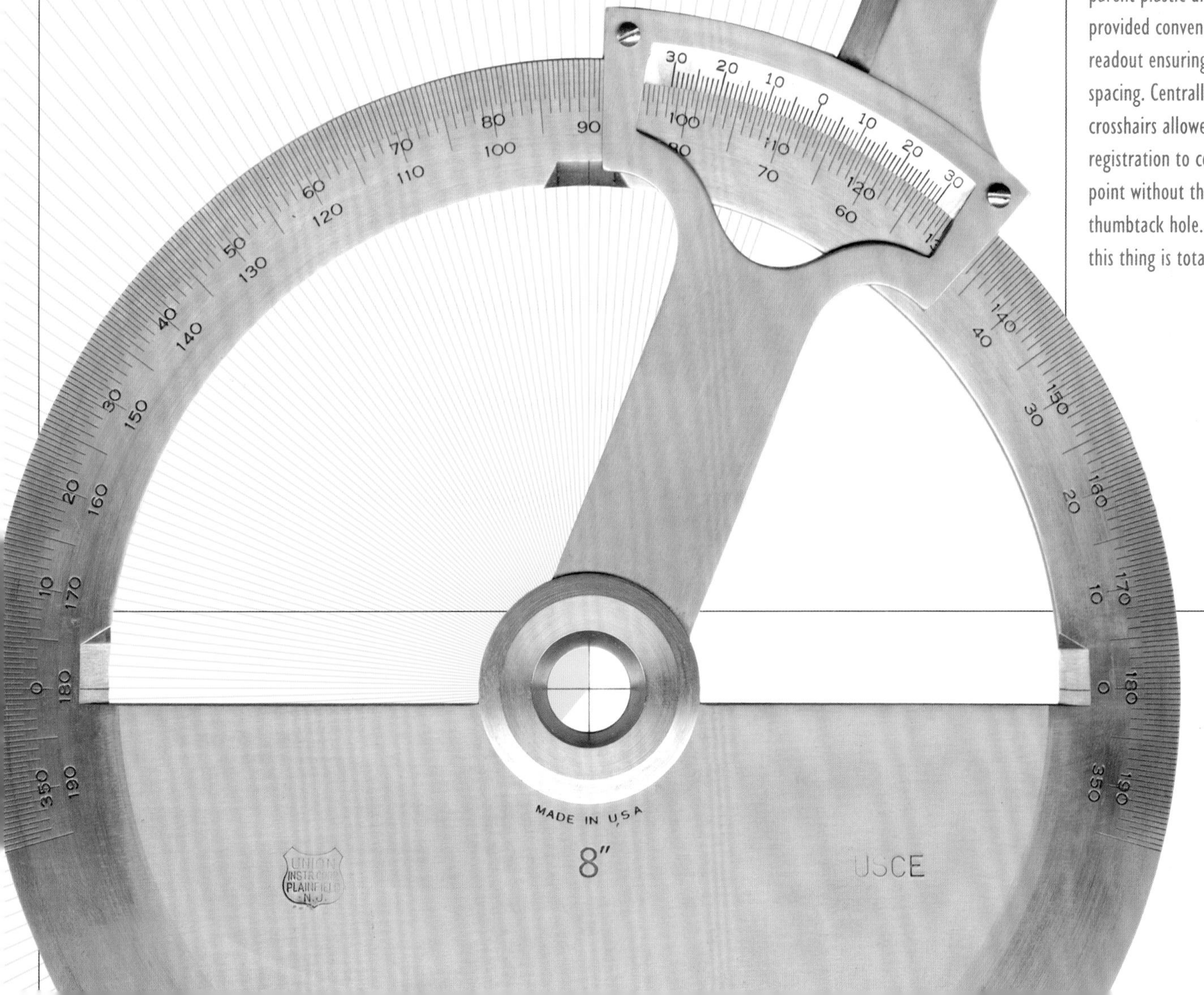
MADE IN USA
8"
USCE

RADIATING LINE DRAWING MACHINE. Rays emanating from a central point are a good way to jazz up a logo and there was never a better way to accomplish the task—in the stupid old days, that is—than with this gizmo. Transparent plastic display provided convenient ocular readout ensuring accurate spacing. Centrally placed crosshairs allowed perfect registration to center point without that telltale thumbtack hole. Today, this thing is totally useless.

AUTHENTIC
LAYOUTS
LETTERING
BORDERS
1920 ◆◆ 1940
AUTHENTIC
LAYOUTS
LETTERING
BORDERS
1920 ◆◆ 1940

INKING WITH TECHNICAL PEN AND TEMPLATES. Above left, finished inking, drawn on frosted Mylar by the author. I scanned this from the reverse side of the sheet (then flopped it above to be right-reading) to show the white paint used to make corrections. Note how the corner strokes of each character were extended so that they could be trimmed back leaving sharp corners. Above right, the final result. Inking is not mechanically perfect; some of the strokes have a charming, if unintentional, flair to them. But, I am so glad I'll never have to do that again!

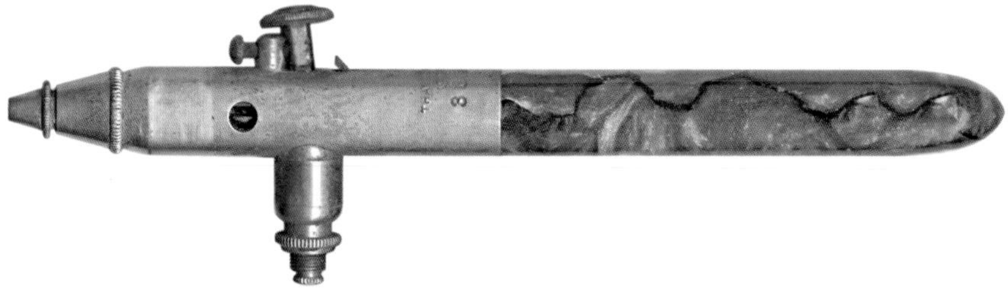

AIRBRUSH. A paint delivery device utilizing air by which ancient man of the early *Esquire* period created calendar pinups to adorn dorm walls and later to customize "hot rods." Current "airbrush tool" in programs like Photoshop represents 1000 percent improvement over performance of manual variety, except that the artist is left without a tangible piece of original art to sell later when he really needs the money.

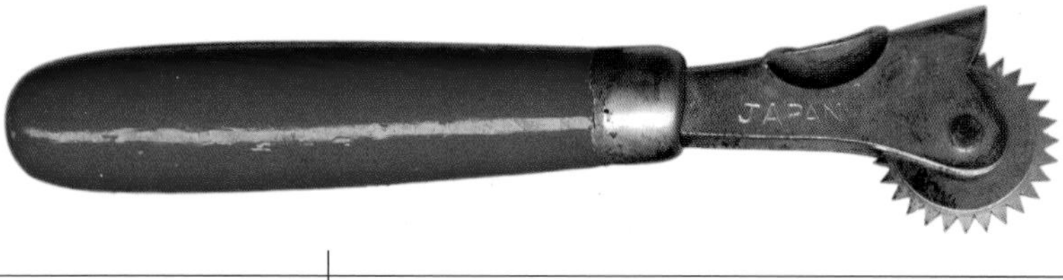
JAPAN

PRICKER. A device for stimulating certain sensitive parts of the anatomy during bizarre sexual rites involving satin cords and clothespins. May also have been used to effect a transfer of a pencil or charcoal sketch to the final media for inking.

DIVIDERS. At least use of this medieval-looking device, at right, for checking stem widths and letter spacing, obviated the even more barbaric use of numbers and measurement.

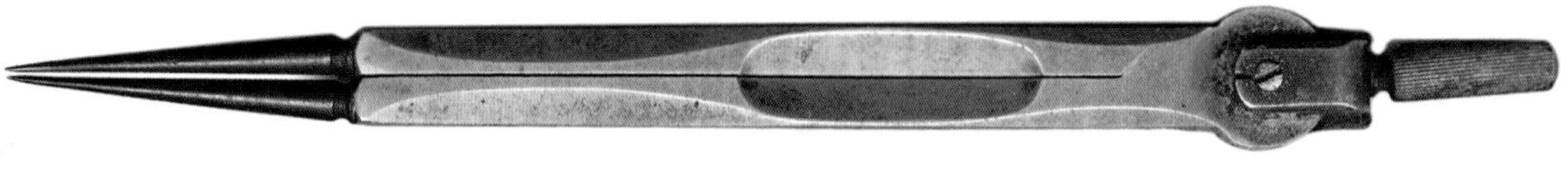

LETTERING BRUSH. At right, a man tickles paper with horsehair attached to a stick. What's that all about? This is yet another example of the sorts of indignities the early hand-letterer suffered simply to be able to ply his humble trade and maybe get to spend the weekend tooling around town in a Pierce-Arrow with a sluttish-looking flapper riding shotgun.

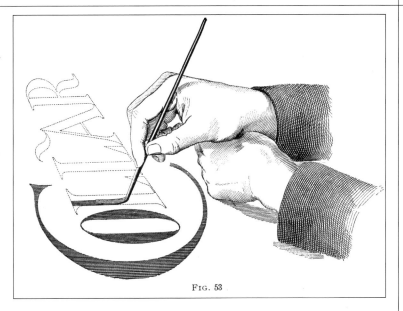

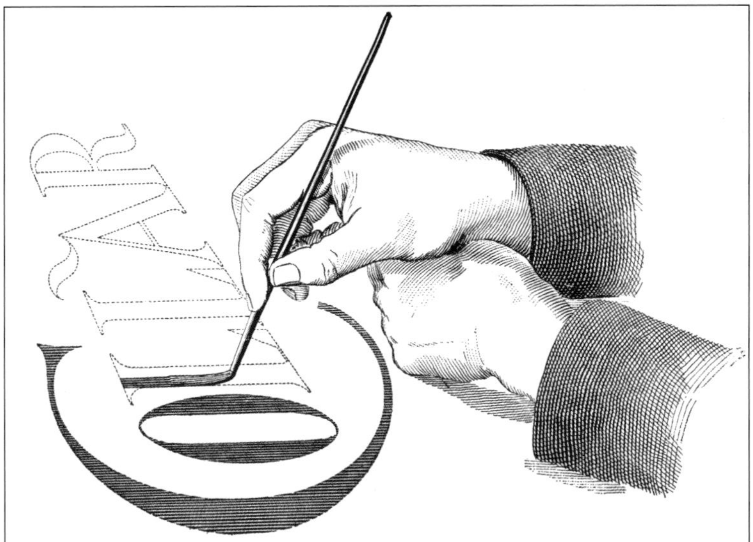

FIG. 53

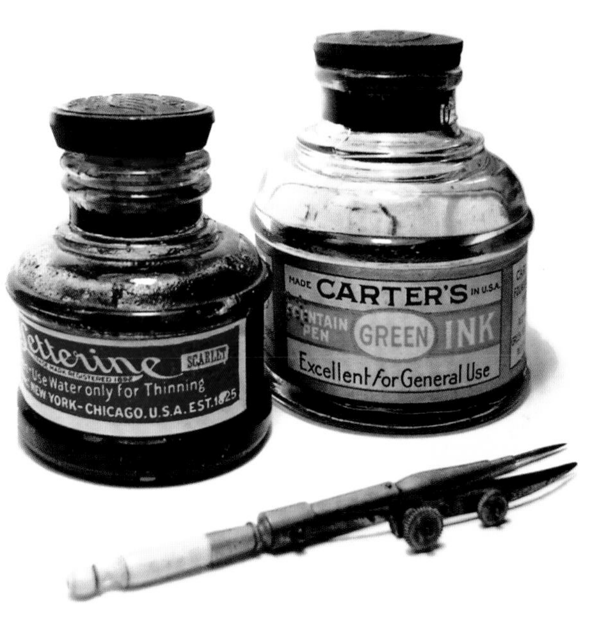
CARTER'S
GREEN INK
Excellent for General Use
SCARLET
Use Water only for Thinning
NEW YORK-CHICAGO.U.S.A.EST.1825

INK. Without ink there could not have been writing, lettering or reproduction and the world as we know it might never have existed. In fact, ink, not oil, may be the world's most important substance. The plastic-handled, ink-bearing implement (at bottom of photo above) could run circles—at least, small circles—around any of the single-shafted ink-delivery devices shown on the previous pages.

I spent years learning to perfect the rounded-corner rectangle by matching up the inking of straight sides to the quarter circles in the corners. Since stopping the Rapidograph stroke just at the start of the circle, then continuing again with a compass or ellipse template was sure to produce blobs and smudges at the beginnings or ends of any of these strokes, this procedure was as difficult as rendering a hog or tilling forty acres...without a mule. Nowadays, of course, any child can select the rounded-corner box tool and easily accomplish in seconds this essential task that formerly brought tears to the eyes of the manliest of letterers.

In 1971, I walked into a musty little type shop just off Park Avenue South and saw my first Linotype typesetting machine. I thought I'd stepped back into the 1920s. The incredibly complex contraption, standing taller than I, made Rube Goldberg's most outlandish mechanical fantasy seem mundane by comparison.

The miracle of this Linotype machine was that it brought five hundred years of hand composition to an end. It actually pulled indi-

text continues on page 70

6 FINE EDGE series 865 ARTSIGN U.S.A.

BRUSH. This fine specimen belonged to theater sign man Don Sturdivant, who told me, "When you get ahold of a good brush, you treat it like gold."

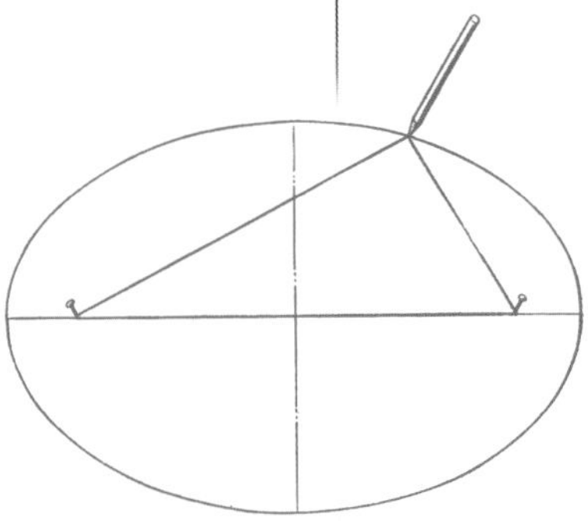

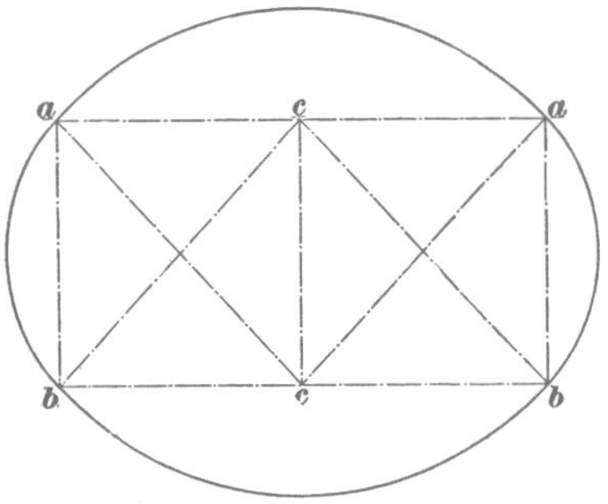
a
c
a
b
c
b

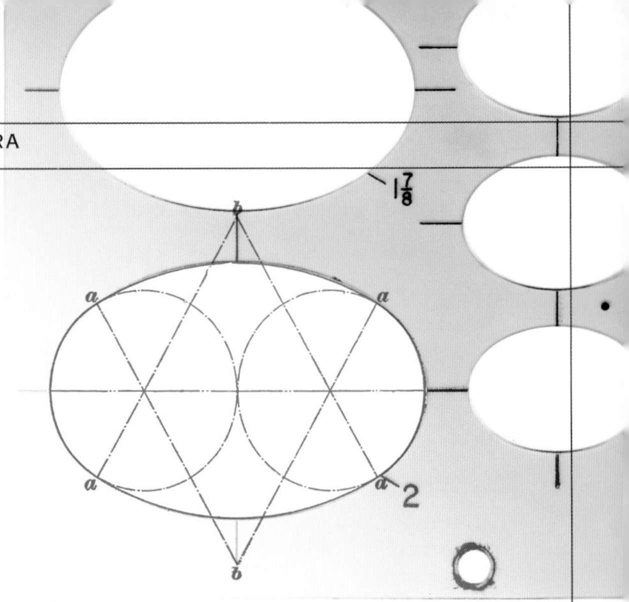
$1\frac{7}{8}$
b
a
a
a
a
2
b

ELLIPSE-MAKING. "Describing" an ellipse, as they used to say, was simple providing one had a hammer, two nails and a piece of string! Above right, two additional ellipse-drawing methods involved matching up portions of compass-drawn perfect circles. Creating perfect matchups of line segments is indeed difficult, especially if the final result is to be inked, but it can be done. After designers spent years struggling to draw ellipses, any child can now instantly draw a flawless ellipse in a computer drawing program. What a pity that within today's design aesthetic, ellipses, now so easy to "describe," are totally passé.

THE ELLIPSE TEMPLATE. Purchased singly or in a set, the stamped plastic "guides" came in a wide range of convenient dimensions from extremely anemic to positively rotund, comprising every imaginable ovoid contour—except the exact one you needed at the moment! To avoid having ink from a technical pen bleed under the edge of the template, I often would select a second template and use one of its larger-size ellipses to place under the ellipse I wanted, thereby raising it off the surface. Bleeding and smearing the ink was still usually inevitable.

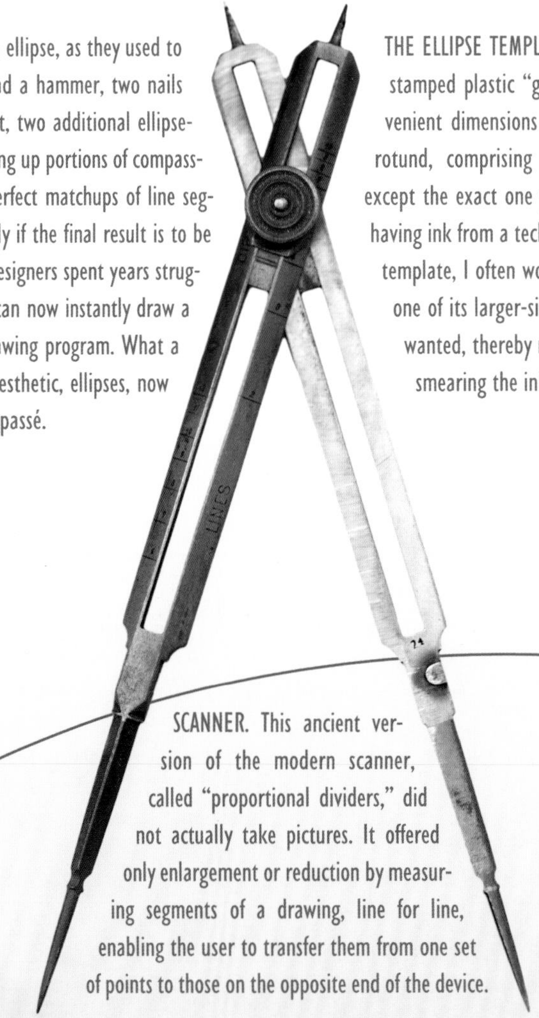
LINES

SCANNER. This ancient version of the modern scanner, called "proportional dividers," did not actually take pictures. It offered only enlargement or reduction by measuring segments of a drawing, line for line, enabling the user to transfer them from one set of points to those on the opposite end of the device.

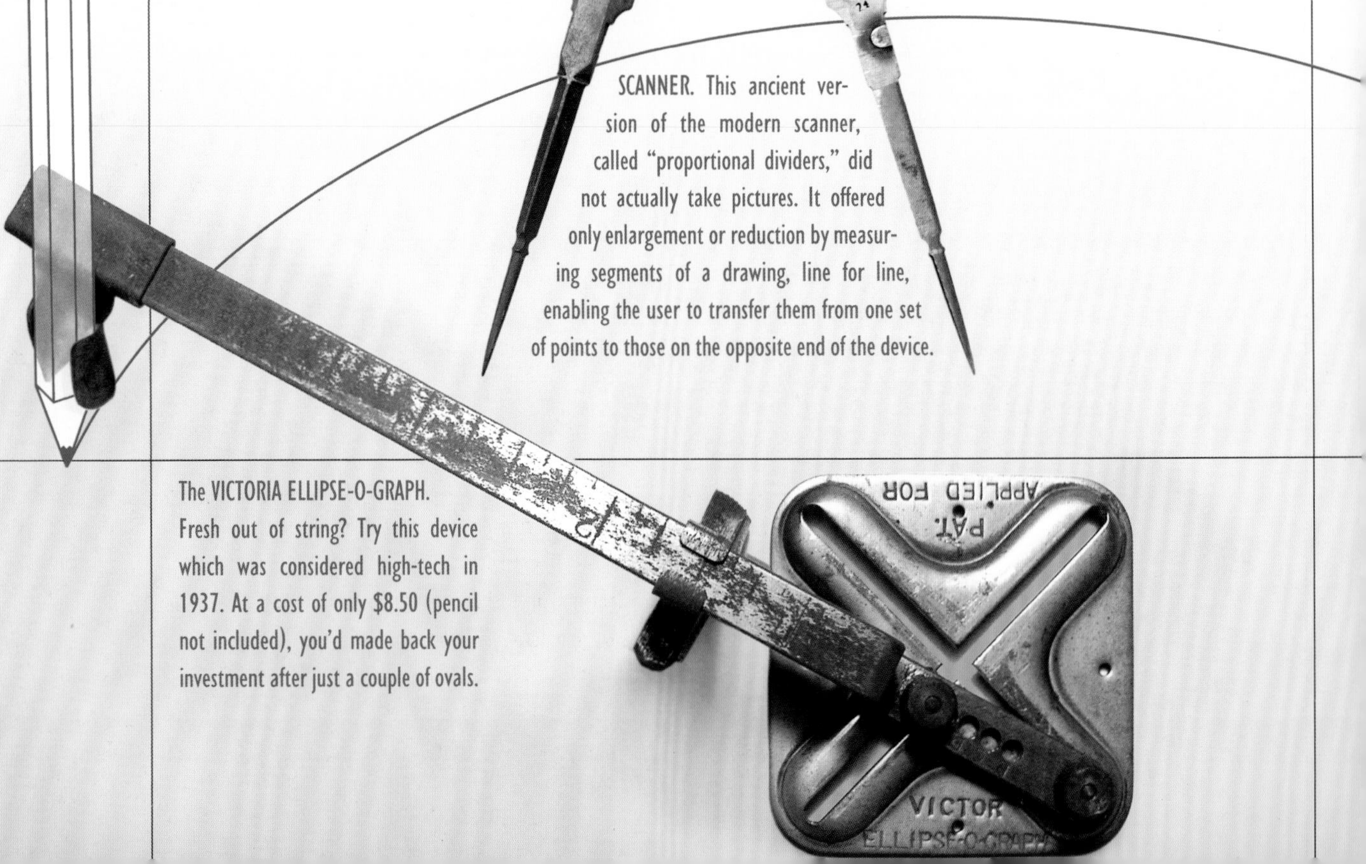
PAT.
APPLIED FOR
VICTOR

The VICTORIA ELLIPSE-O-GRAPH. Fresh out of string? Try this device which was considered high-tech in 1937. At a cost of only $8.50 (pencil not included), you'd made back your investment after just a couple of ovals.

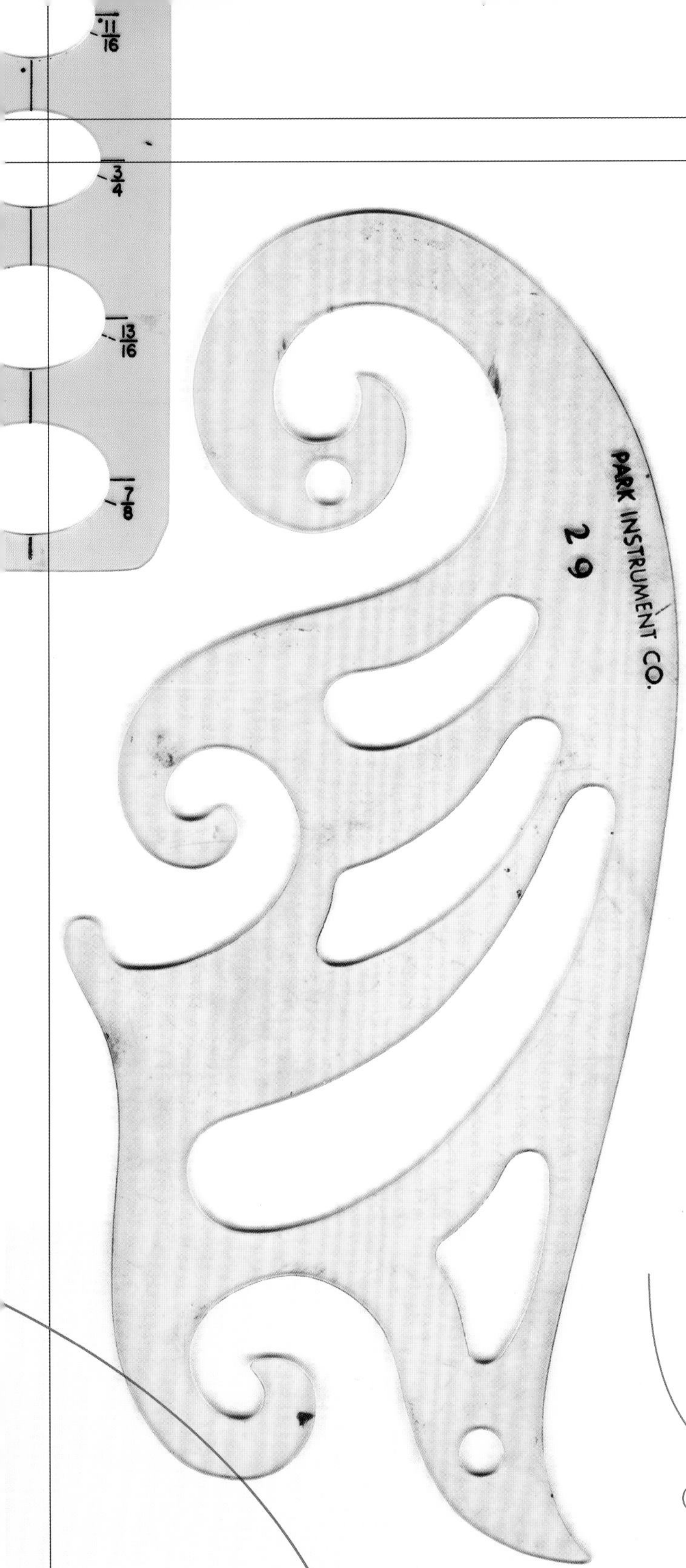
11/16
3/4
13/16
7/8
PARK INSTRUMENT CO.
29

The French "Curvier," Pierre Bézier

Modern designers can hardly imagine the squareness and humdrumnity of a world without curves. And such a world it was ere a young Pierre Bézier (pronounced "Pea-air Bez-zee-ay"), discoverer of curvature, wandered into a Paris music hall one afternoon and, inspired by a lusty cancan performance, promptly hailed a cab back to his atelier and thereupon commenced to discover the mathematical formula ("pie are round, cake are square"); that is the foundational basis of modern-day curvalineature and which made *Bézier curve* a household word, like Bibendum and beesknees. *(In actuality, Pierre Etienne Bezier [1910–1999] was a brilliant electrical and mechanical engineer with a degree in mathematics. He enrolled to study mechanical engineering at the Ecole des Arts et Métiers and received his degree in 1930. In the same year, he entered the Ecole Supérieure d'Electricité and earned a second degree in electrical engineering in 1931. In 1977, forty-six years later, he received his DSc degree in mathematics from the University of Paris. His research in CAD/CAM [design/computer-aided manufacturing] for the Renault firm in France led to his most famous innovation, the means by which curves are defined in today's computer drawing programs.)*

(True story from *Computer-Aided Design*, Vol. 22, No. 9.)

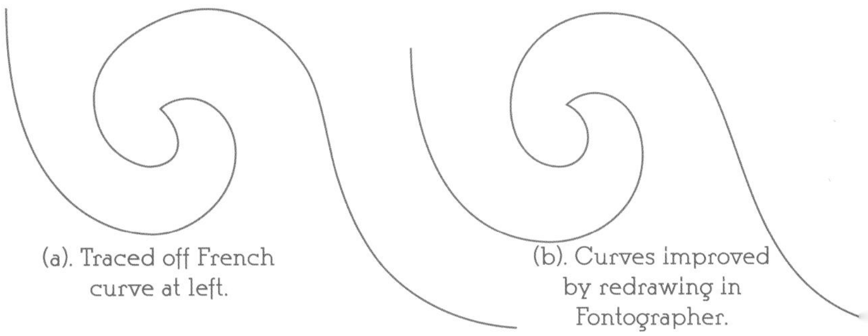

(a). Traced off French curve at left.

(b). Curves improved by redrawing in Fontographer.

THE FRENCH CURVE. Matching French curves, segment by segment, to similar hand-drawn pencil curves was how letterers of yore attempted to achieve smooth inking of complex, curving characters. French curves came in a variety of styles comprising every conceivable arc and ogee—except the exact curve you needed at the moment! Incredibly, many of these templates, stamped from translucent plastic, were often quite flawed, as my analysis, above right, demonstrates. But how did the manufacturers originally design the curves for a French curve prototype? Maybe they used French curves.

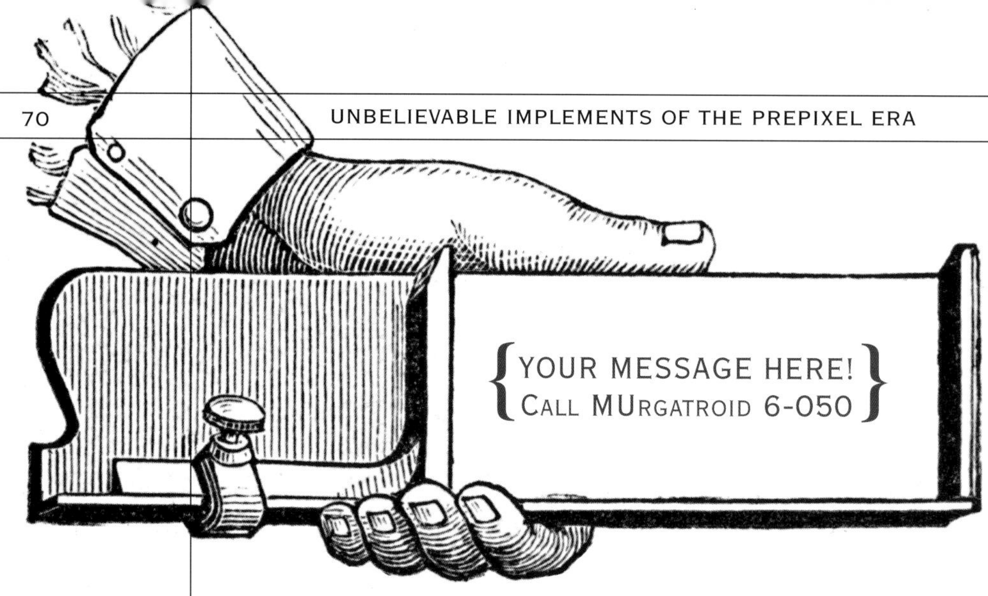
YOUR MESSAGE HERE!
CALL MURGATROID 6-050

TYPESETTER'S COMPOSING STICK. Taken from the cases, type was arranged on the composing stick, left, adjusted to the desired column measure, and justified with blank type spaces.

Opposite page, "cuts" or illustrative engravings were nailed onto wood blocks or cast in metal "type-high," then locked up with the type matter to form a printed page. What a total pain!

TYPE CABINET, 1867. Its wide, flat, segmented drawers were filled with type of different kinds. The companies that sold such cases tended to be the type foundries themselves. Drawers filled with type were mounted on top when in use. This model displays only a single, top-mounted type case.

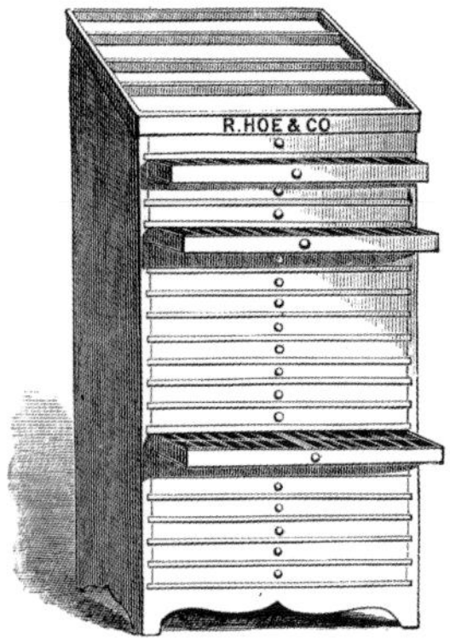
R. HOE & CO

vidual type matrices, letter by letter, down a series of channels, aligned them into columns, justified the columns and finally poured hot metal over them to form a "slug" from which a proof could be taken.

When one ordered typesetting, the results came back from the typesetting shop as "galleys": long, printed strips of clay-coated white paper along with several extra copies on newsprint and a gelatinlike paper for roughing in the type. Since the galleys were really prints on slick paper, by the time one's layouts were printed, the type was already second generation.

The galleys would have to be trimmed close to the edge of the type column, then the type rubber-cemented down to the layout board. The type would easily smudge, so care had to be taken to avoid abrading the surface. This was really hard, since at the same time you had to rub along the close-cut galley edges with a rubber cement "pickup" to remove excess cement.

By the 1970s, the Phototypositer from VGC came into widespread use. It revolutionized the way headline type could be set. The advent of photolettering allowed designers themselves to manipulate type as it was being set, controlling aspects like kerning,

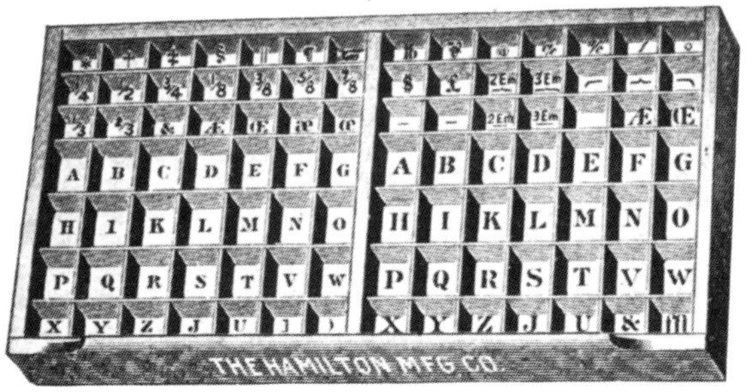
THE HAMILTON MFG. CO.

News Cap Case, $0 80
A new Cap Case that meets all requirements and one that is exceptionally popular with all compositors.

THE HAMILTON MFG. CO.

News Lower Case, $0 80
The universal layout as put into the regular Lower Case from which every printer has learned his a-b-c's.

U&LC. There's a reason we refer to letters as being uppercase and lowercase and it's not just because—as I used to assume—capital letters stand taller than most of the small letters. Fonts used to come separated into cases that were placed on top of the type cabinet one above the other. Today these delightful drawers are still used by elderly ladies to display miniature bric-a-brac that they buy on eBay.

SHELL

the size, or changed your mind, it was back to the stat house or make do. Using a Proportion Wheel, you'd determine the desired size of enlargement or reduction and mark the type, say, 20 percent. That seemed to be clear enough to most stat guys, except to the one who called me up and asked, "You mean, you want it 20 percent smaller than it is now?" (That would have yielded only a reduction to 80 percent.) I said, "Set the damn camera gauge *at 20 percent* like everybody else does!" Sheesh! Of course, many publishers and ad agencies had their own in-house stat cameras. One of these was a little self-standing camera/darkroom unit that looked like a Bauhaus version of a fairy-tale cottage. I remember the tall operator at one company had to hunch way over to enter the unit.

Hassles with Rapidographs, photostats, metal type and pasteups were only part of the tribulations designers faced daily.

Printing used to be a great art. It may still be now, as well. But in between then and now—roughly between 1960 and 1990—printing fell into the dark ages. What happened, as I see it, is that everybody inter-

TYPESETTER, 1888. At his cases, in his cups, plucking out letters one by one, day in and day out (and the worst part: later he'd have to put 'em all back in again). Plaintively, he wonders when the heck Ottmar will finish tinkering around with that prototype of his so a hardworking compositor can get in a bit of fishing now and then.

spacing, point size and overlapping. Photolettering also created a revolution in type design since it became cheaper and easier to draw a font and output it as a simple strip of film negative than to cut it in metal. I know, because when I was seventeen, I made a Phototypositer font myself by splicing together negatives of an alphabet I'd drawn. I didn't align the baselines of the negs carefully enough so the type came out a little bouncy, but otherwise the font worked fine.

The "Typositer" output a strip of developed, positive film that looked like a photostat. The photographic paper was trimmed close to the edges of the type and rubber cemented or waxed down to the layout board. (A quick method was to use Scotch Magic Tape with its matte finish for pasteup. It looked sloppy but the tape disappeared under the camera.) Resizing Typositer type still required sending out to the stat house to have photostats made at a few dollars per shot. Once you got your stats back, if you didn't like

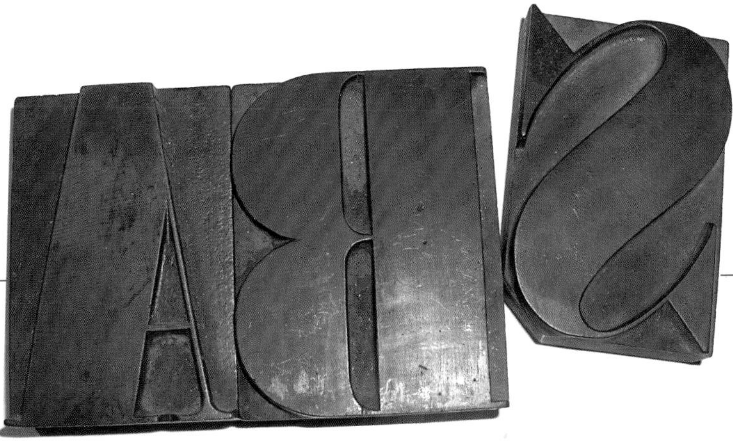

WOOD TYPE. Display type (the larger types used for headlines, posters and display advertising) was often made of wood. Entire catalogs specialized in oversize types like those at right, which continued to be set by hand, even after the advent of the Linotype.

OAKLAND ENQUIRER.

NUMBER 86.

OAKLAND ENQUIRER, FRIDAY EVENING, OCTOBER 12, 1894.

VOLUME XXV.

WHAT WOULD GUTENBERG SAY?

Machines That Will Set Type

Are Now at Work For the Enquirer.

The Greatest Invention of The Age.

LINOTYPE

TYPE IN THE NEWS. In 1894, as probably three hundred hand typesetters were given pink slips, newspaper management had something to crow about. Sixty years later, newsboys might have shouted, "Extra! Extra! *Enquirer* gets set of Rapidographs. . . will revolutionize drafting department."

esting in art and design was born between 1880 and 1910. By 1965 they were mostly all dead. The great printing firms, run by men who had learned the art of printing from the ground up and who cared about it passionately, were, by the early 1960s, left to the care of the sons: These coddled rich kids graduated from Eastern colleges—an advantage their fathers never had—and now these brats, having discovered that you can't really earn a living as a second-string tennis pro, reluctantly took over their fathers' printing firms. Things started to go downhill fast from

Looking Forward
We do know that the most stupendous task of all
time lies ahead, during the period of reconstruc-
tion, and we must be thinking of this as we now
work to win the greatest of all wars.

PULLING PROOF. Unidentified hand, above, pulls a "proof," or an inked sample copy, from a solid metal block of text that would have been the end product of the Linotype or similar typesetting machine. For more than seventy years, heavy metal reigned in the world of type.

there. Exact color registration became a thing of the past. I mean, how annoying is it to have to tweak a press for registration?! The sons couldn't care less. They were not concerned with art, just profit, and were sure their fathers had done it all wrong.

The actual guys running the presses, I always assumed, must have been the ones with those bumper stickers on their pickups that read, "I'd rather be sailing." Printers became uncannily expert at making excuses for their sloth. The problem was always "ghosting," or "offset," or "too much ink coverage on the left side screwing up the right," or "Kodalith always goes too red. . . ."

Color separations and halftones were photographed once, never corrected. I know it was possible to have a halftone made correctly because when I could stand there and make a guy do it—using a brief secondary "flash" exposure to blow out the highlights—my halftones came out gloriously. But most of the time, halftones turned out like mud with little tonal range.

It was completely beyond the ken of printers to retain middle gray tones in a halftone of a wash painting while still keeping the white parts of the drawing absolutely white. In the days of metal plates there were guys with routers and engraving tools who'd expertly cut out or etch white highlights into halftones that were muddy, but by the time offset lithography moved to flexible metal plates, there was no one willing to pay the costs of etching, and hardly anyone left who knew how to do it.

Many of the criticisms I've leveled at the printing industry never applied to the most expensive printing firms, which always turned out quality work, and of course, they never applied to European and Asian printers, who never lost the work ethic that many American printers scoffed at.

A*ll this has turned around.* Thanks to the Macintosh computer, we designers have now taken over the jobs of the typesetters, photoengravers and film strippers. We can now make our scans of art and photography as they should always have been, and we can "dot etch" and "opaque" and strip photos into hairline rules (that used to require double burning) and do all the other things printers used to complain about and overcharge for.

text continues on page 77

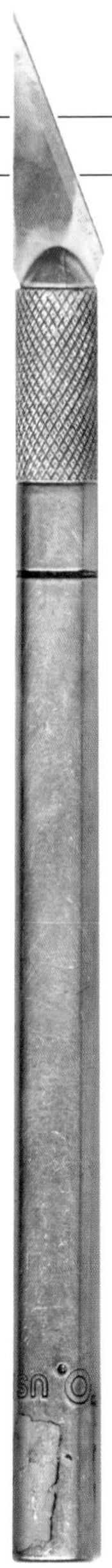

X-ACTO KNIFE. Jim had the Bowie, Lizzie had the axe, and we designers have the X-Acto with which we would paste up our mechanical layouts. The X-Acto is also a dangerous weapon, as many designers have inadvertently discovered. Once, one rolled off my desk and stood straight up in my big toe. X-Acto Rx: When I plunged this very X-Acto knife, right, into my thigh the other day (I was cutting a paint roller in half), I was able to quell the bleeding instantly by shaking cayenne pepper liberally into the gash. Try cayenne yourself!

Oxidized area of blade indicates depth of my most recent X-Acto wound.

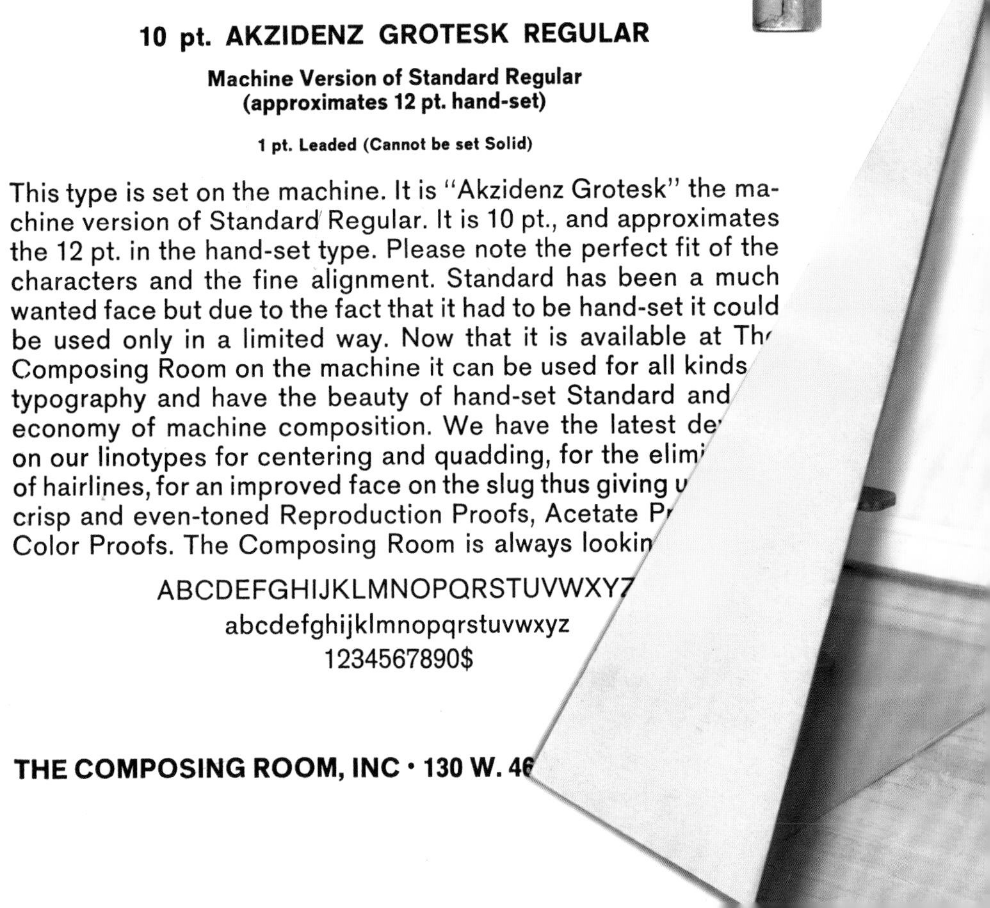

10 pt. AKZIDENZ GROTESK REGULAR

Machine Version of Standard Regular (approximates 12 pt. hand-set)

1 pt. Leaded (Cannot be set Solid)

This type is set on the machine. It is "Akzidenz Grotesk" the machine version of Standard Regular. It is 10 pt., and approximates the 12 pt. in the hand-set type. Please note the perfect fit of the characters and the fine alignment. Standard has been a much wanted face but due to the fact that it had to be hand-set it could be used only in a limited way. Now that it is available at Th Composing Room on the machine it can be used for all kinds typography and have the beauty of hand-set Standard and economy of machine composition. We have the latest de on our linotypes for centering and quadding, for the elimi of hairlines, for an improved face on the slug thus giving u crisp and even-toned Reproduction Proofs, Acetate P Color Proofs. The Composing Room is always lookin

ABCDEFGHIJKLMNOPQRSTUVWXYZ
abcdefghijklmnopqrstuvwxyz
1234567890$

THE COMPOSING ROOM, INC · 130 W. 46

PRINTED PROOF. Right, a showing of a new type specimen on green-backed galley paper from Robert L. Leslie's famous Manhattan typesetting shop, the Composing Room.

A FEW MILESTONES IN MACHINE COMPOSITION

1888: THE ROGERS TYPOGRAPH, above, used a set of matrices (master type characters) that slid into position when the keys were pressed and were automatically justified. After a single line of type was cast in hot metal, the back of the machine tilted downward, allowing the matrices to slide back to their original positions, ready for reuse. With this arrangement, yet another hand operation, the refilling of type "magazines," was obviated.

1872: THE EMPIRE COMPOSING MACHINE, above, was the first American typesetting machine to come into common use. A three-section keyboard, corresponding to three type cases above, released individual type through converging channels to form a line. A second operator was required to manually place type spaces where necessary to justify the line. The only mechanized aspect was a small motor that advanced the assembled line of type to make way for the next character. When the type cases became empty, hand-filled cases replaced the empty ones. The value of this arrangement, though far from perfect, was that it eliminated handpicking of type from cases.

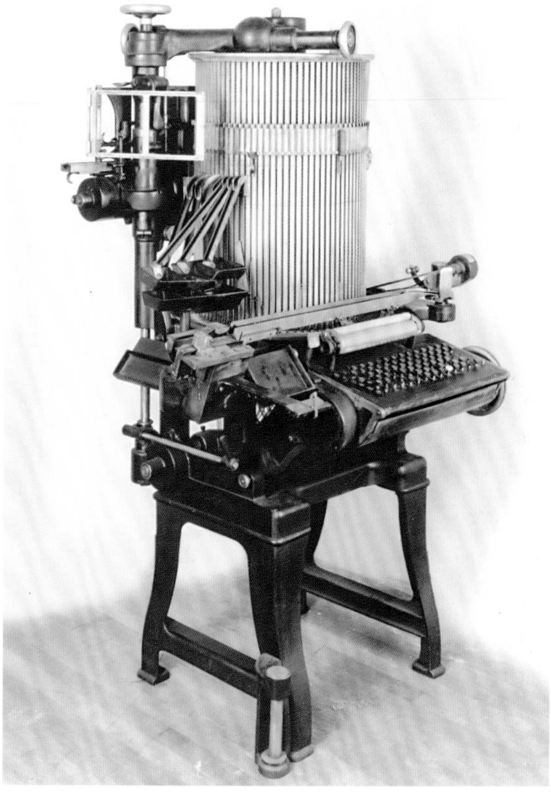

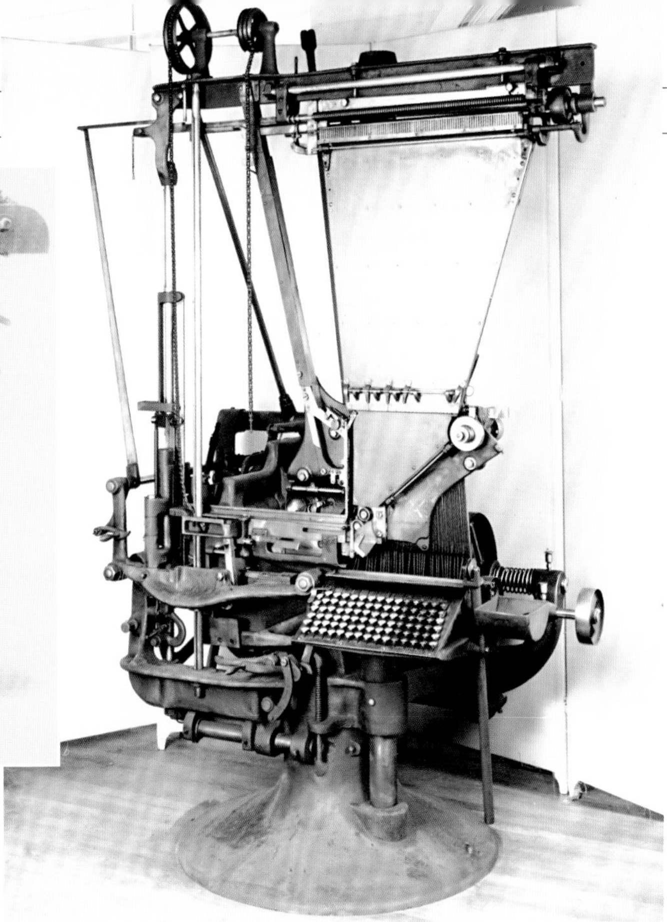

1898: MERGENTHALER ROUND-BASE LINOTYPE. This model offered several technical improvements over earlier machines, but since the user experience was unchanged (no new bells and whistles were offered), it was not widely adopted by industry. And tech support was rumored to have been lousy.

1886: THE BLOWER LINOTYPE. Inventor Ottmar Mergenthaler's first commercial success, the Blower Linotype, above, was the dream machine of its age. It automatically justified the line, pressed molten metal into the indented matrices to cast one "line o' type" at a time, and returned the matrices to their holding positions, ready for reuse. Operators then locked up the individual lines to create galleys ready for the press.

1898: THE UNITYPE ONE-MAN TYPESETTER. Opposite page left, specially designed type characters were released upon key depression. Although the operator was required to manually justify the lines, this machine, invented by J. Thorne, was at least able to automatically keep type chambers continually refilled, and it appears as if it may also have doubled as an ice cream maker.

LATE 1930s: LINOTYPE. Right, this elaborate model featured multiple type magazines for a wider range of styles at the touch of a switch. Typesetter "Murgatroid" demonstrates proper ergonomic seating arrangement with arms in ideal position for comfort and natural lumbar support. Two other companies, Monotype and Intertype, marketed competing machines, but these great photos of Linotypes were all I had.

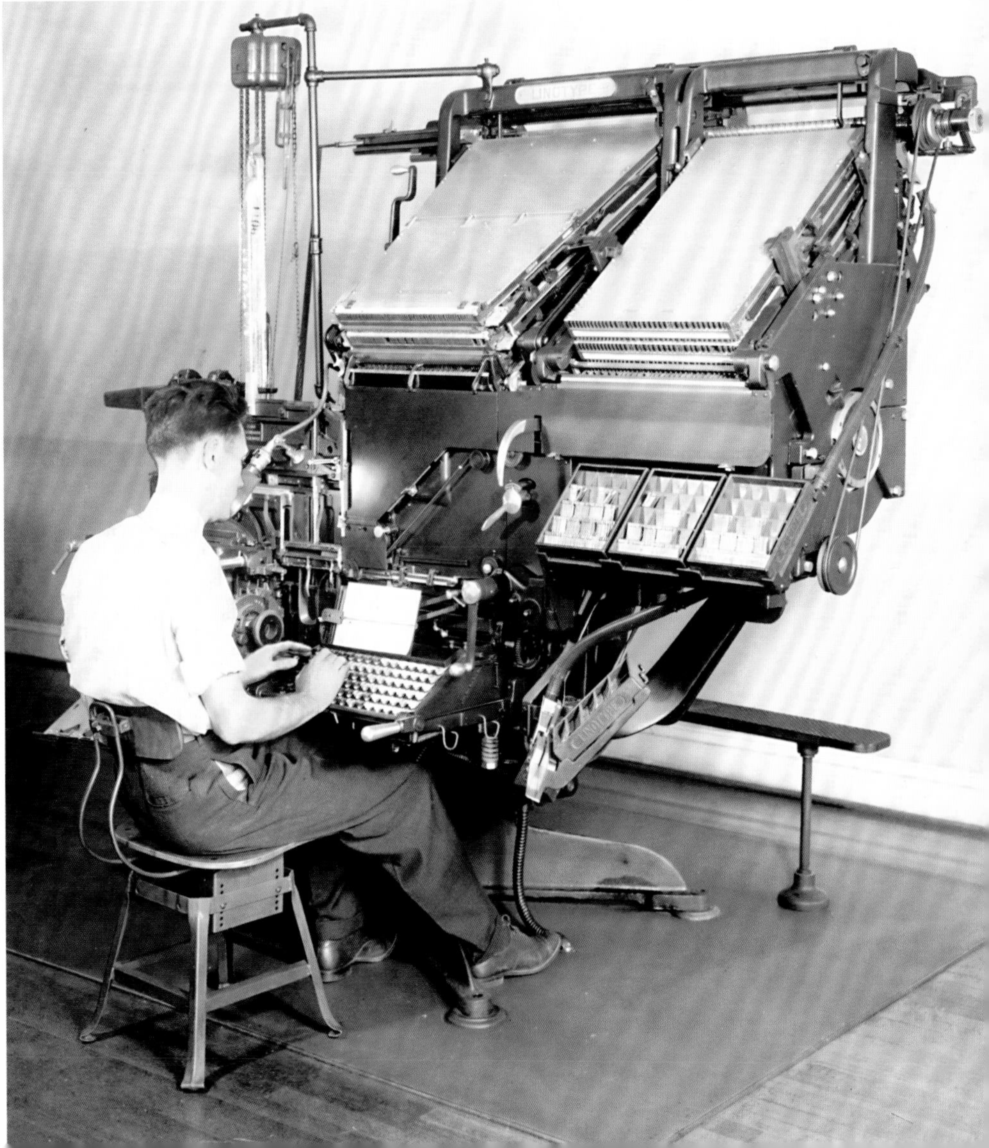

PRINTER'S FRIEND: THE OXYMORONIC "HIGHLIGHT DOT." The photo, above left, is how most photography appeared in print until the 1990s, when the chore of making halftones was lifted by interested designers from the shoulders of the printer. In order to save themselves the extra work of making a good halftone, printers invented the myth of the "highlight dot," which maintained that due to dot gain and dot loss on the press, a halftone must start out as middle gray so that when printed, the darkest grays would become black and the lightest highlight dot areas would drop out. It never worked that way. What happened was that the highlight dots became darker still, and the darkest areas of the halftone never really gained so much ink to exceed about 77% gray. In my experience there has never been a class of workers more adept at devising client-confounding excuses than the printer, unless it would be home remodeling contractors. The photo, above right, shows how completely thrilling a halftone can look when processed correctly.

PRINTER'S FOLLY: THE CRUSTY EDGE. In the old days of letterpress printing, a halftone that graduated from gray to 0%, or paper white, would often develop, after repeated imprints, a dirty edge from the metal plate bumping against the paper. In offset printing the problem was never so acute, although fear of the edge remains. I argue that even if a noticeable 3% dot separates ink from paper white, it is better than intentionally creating a highlight dot of 3% that always dot gains to 7%, producing a highlight that is no highlight at all.

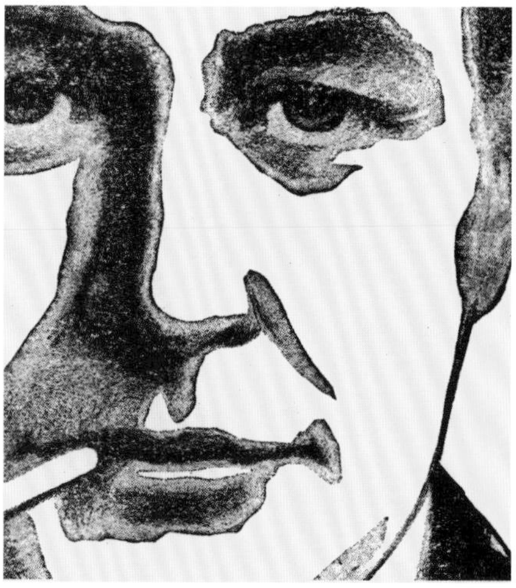

AUDETTE
LBERT
FRED
MURRAY

CRUSTY EDGES. Left, enlarged movie ad originally printed on newsprint shows an ink-engorged halo at the rim where the halftone stops. I actually like these slightly darkened edges, which seem to outline the shape, unless they're ridiculous, as above right. This overambitious example of routing of the metal plate is one of the many ways, including manually scratching highlights into halftones, that printers attempted to make up for murky halftone camera work.

Three phenomena have revolutionized the world of printing. First, German printing presses have become so foolproof and automatic that perfect registration has become the rule, not the exception.

Second, Asian printing firms (with German presses) have taken color book printing away from American printing houses. I suppose it's true that many of the employees are not paid commensurate with any ethical standard, but lemme tell ya…! If you are foolish enough to have a four-color book printed in the USA, you'll get "color proofs" to check that are dye subs, "color keys" or just high-quality laser prints. If any of these don't look right, they'll tell you the problem is "only in the proof." Asian printers think nothing of firing up the presses to actually run off several dozen copies of the book on the actual paper stock! Then they gladly make any requested changes!

Third, gang-run print shops have demystified high-quality, short-run, four-color printing, making it available to the masses at popular prices, too.

I laugh when printers tell me they need a "match print" proof as a guide to "get the colors right." First of all, they *never* get the colors right. In thirty years of having my work printed in newspapers, magazines and books, they never got it right, except perhaps 10 percent of the time. Secondly, all they have to do to get the colors right is to ink the presses right, check their color bars on the sides of the press sheet to make sure 50% magenta is 50% magenta and 100% cyan is 100% cyan, and so on. Then the job will be right. Gang-run print shops have proven this.

The point that I am trying to make in concluding this little swing down memory lane is that every day I feel thankful for all that I can do, all by myself, on my own little Macintosh, the capabilities of which easily exceed $300,000 worth of graphic arts equipment and encompass the labors of perhaps two dozen people, a little less than twenty years ago. ■

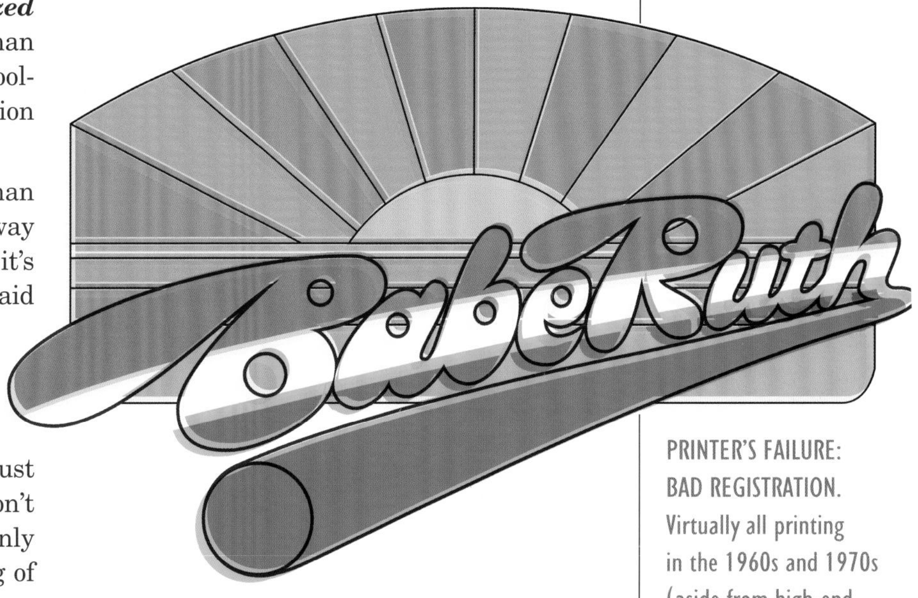
BabeRuth

PRINTER'S FAILURE: BAD REGISTRATION. Virtually all printing in the 1960s and 1970s (aside from high-end printing) was off-register for at least part of the press run. Maybe not as badly, however, as in the mock example above. Nowadays, even high-speed web-printed newspapers—increasingly going toward full-color—tend to have excellent registration. What a great time to be alive!

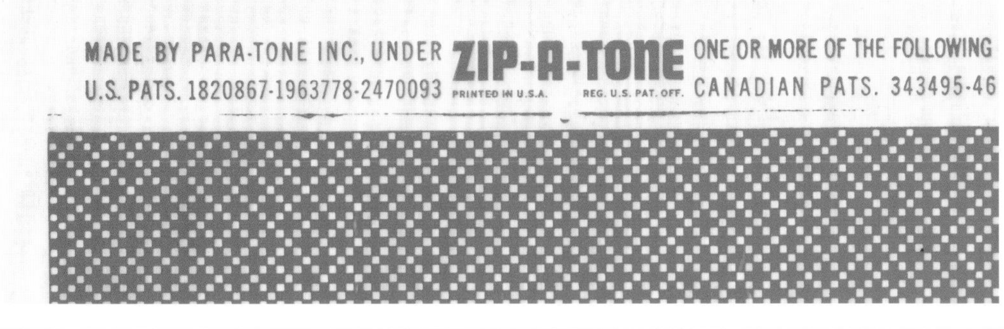
MADE BY PARA-TONE INC., UNDER
U.S. PATS. 1820867-1963778-2470093
ZIP-A-TONE
PRINTED IN U.S.A.
REG. U.S. PAT. OFF.
ONE OR MORE OF THE FOLLOWING
CANADIAN PATS. 343495-46

ZIP-A-TONE: Printers used to charge an arm and a leg for stripping halftones, or flat shaded areas, into a specified part of a layout. And they'd complain about it, too. The answer? Do it yourself with easy to use Zip-A-Tone. Just cut out a section of this self-adhering plastic film and trim to fit. Benday shading films are still available in a wide variety of patterns, from typical halftone dot to wacky patterns of every description. But avoid carelessly overlapping two pieces of Zip-A-Tone, or a moiré might result. To paraphrase an old song, "When-a two halftone screens, They-a cross in between, That's a moiré. . . ."

PEN, BRUSH AND MARKER

& Assorted Other Tools of the Trade

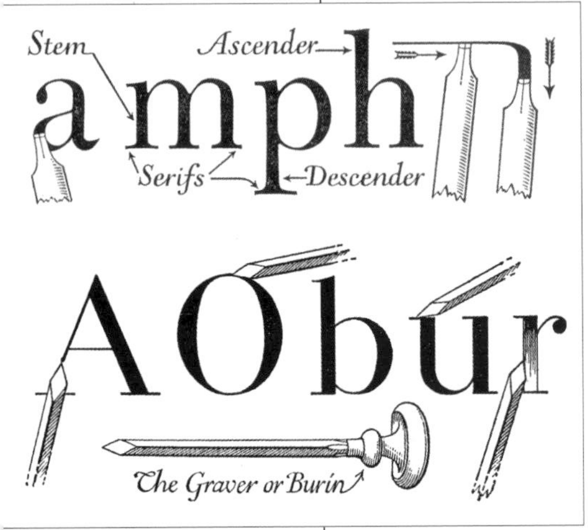
Stem
Ascender
amph
Serifs
Descender
AObur
The Graver or Burin

Thomas Cleland drew this little diagram comparing the flexible pen and the nonyielding graver to show how the tool affects the form of the letter.

Very few designers today are adept at wielding brush or pen. Most have never even attempted to do so. Abundant and accessible fonts have largely obviated lettering, and most of us who endeavor to create original fonts and logos generally favor logically geometric styles that are so readily constructed in computer drawing programs. Lettering historian Oscar Ogg observed that at a point, type became its own animal, unconcerned with how the old tools, like the chisel, pen and brush, might have affected its forms. Still, many of us admire these earlier lettering styles deftly drawn by steadier hands than ours. We try to replicate them in outline drawings and with our bezier curves, expanding an entire alphabet from an old logo. Naturally, the result is clumsy, but we are reluctant to get out a brush to discover what the strokes of the missing letters might really look like, partly because we are arrogant, partly lazy and probably mostly because we fear we won't do it well.

Calligrapher Rick Cusick laughed when I admitted I never could stand calligraphy. "Yeah," he said, "there's always been a division between the 'built-up' lettering guys and the calligraphers—with exceptions, of course. I never did understand it. They both design with letters." To me, built-up (mechanically drawn, not single-stroke) lettering is like a carefully honed studio recording. Calligraphy, however, can seem like a live concert recording with a shallow, raw sound and awkward "accidentals." But calligraphy has grown on me, and a distinction must be made between the calligraphy of high school diplomas and that of experts whose work is often breathtakingly beautiful. To look at the work of old masters like Rudolf Koch and Warren Chappell, or newer ones like Rick Cusick, Jill Bell, Michael Clark or Paul Shaw, is to admire a skill, confidence and coordination comparable to champion gymnasts.

This section looks at traditional lettering tools, as well as some unusual ones, to understand how each informs the outcome of our letters. Ogg explains, "The reason that the letterforms of many early designers are superior to their modern counterparts is that the modern letterers have attempted to arrive at the conclusions of the early designers without first having become acquainted with the sources of their results."

EXERCISE From an art supply store, purchase a few Speedball "C" series flat-edged pen points and/or a sign-painting brush. Practice drawing letters without a mouse. Try not to judge your results harshly; the point is not to do perfect brush lettering, but to gain an understanding of why, for instance, roman lettering naturally alternates between thick and thin strokes.

XVIe Siècle. École Allemande. — Albert Dürer. Pl. 7.

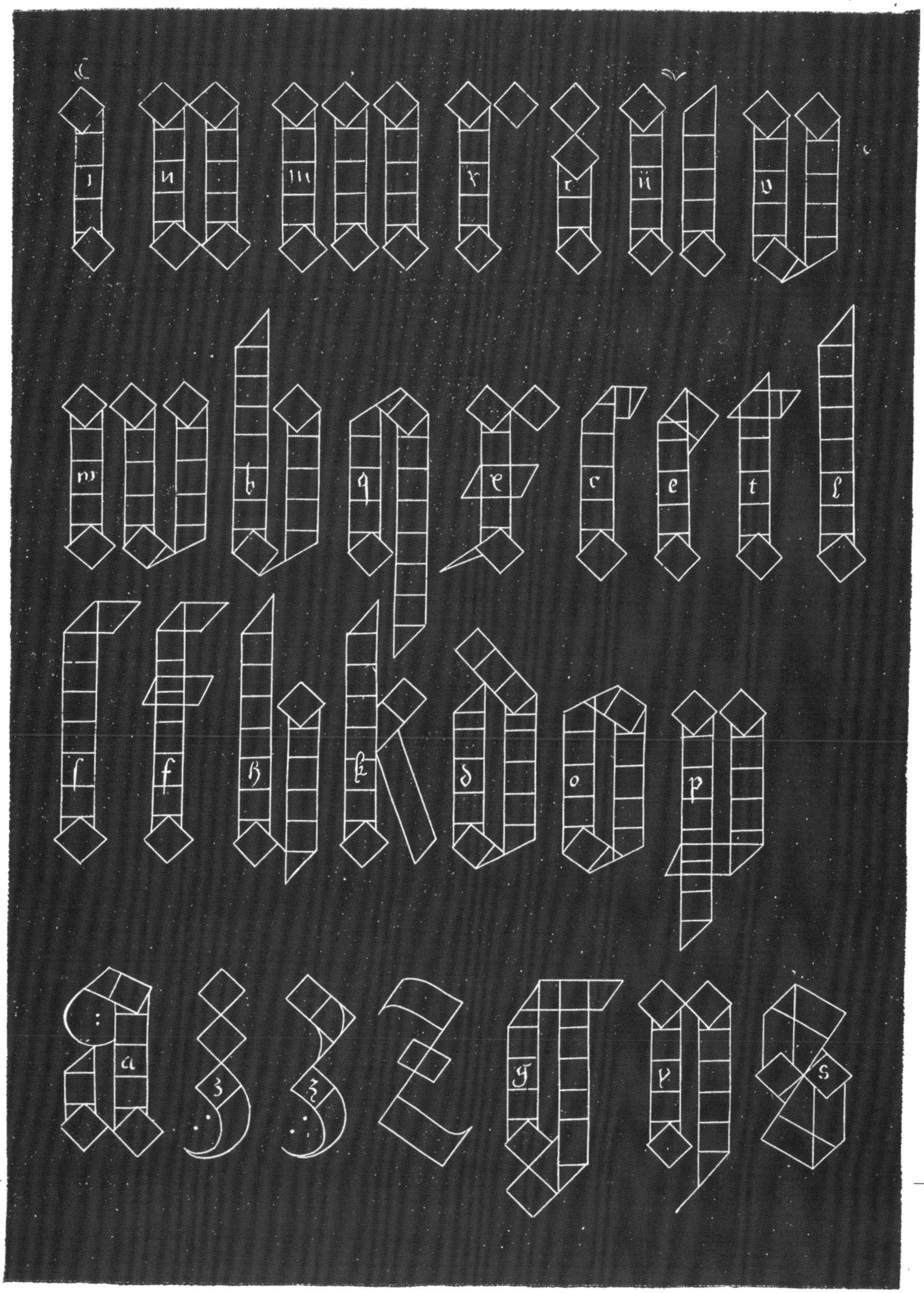

Albrecht Dürer knew a thing or two about drawing and also drawing letters. He left us this proportional guide to the pen-drawn black-letter schrifts of the "German school." Illustration from *Types de Lettres*, published in Paris, 1895.

Examples of Proportions, Distances, &c.

(See the Rules in pages 42 & 43.)

1 mn 2 mute 3 lvia 4 hy

5 oo ve 6 cn ea 7 ru is ly 8

9 to the 10 nhy 11 hints

12 tnf 13 nod Elm 14 Elm

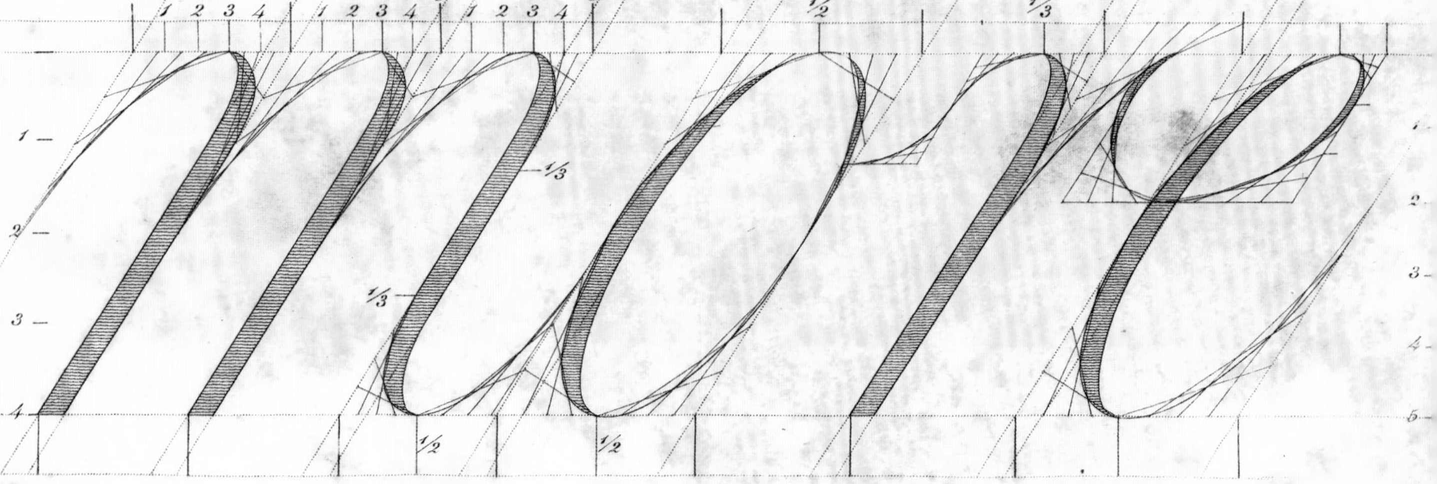

Opposite page, *Dean's Analytical Guide to the Art of Penmanship,* 1808, was printed from copper engravings. One needed to know calculus to follow Henry Dean's instructions. Above, pencil sketch and inking by Clarence Hornung for an obviously unfinished set of initial caps. Hornung favored the flexible Gillot 290 pen point. Right, a logo by Tony DiSpigna, who says 80 percent of the job is the tight pencil sketch because "You don't want to have to draw and ink at the same time." He inks fairly rapidly, "like those quick figure sketches in life class," using a Gillot 291 point. He works at 200 percent so the pen lines will reduce cleanly and always uses reference for his Spencerian work but expresses wonderment at how the old guys did it: "What did *they* have to look at?" Below, F.G. Cooper used a Gillot 850 pen to ink the built-up lettering job. *Built-up* means, of course, that instead of using a thick pen or brush and making a single stroke to accomplish a letter, many strokes are used, or the shape may be outlined and filled in—whatever it takes. Hey, guess what: All the pen points mentioned above are still available!

COSTELLO
McCullam
Whitley
Inc.

simple adjustment!
special adjusting knob available

And in the sixth
month the angel Gabriel was
sent from God unto a city of Gali-
lee, named Nazareth, to a virgin
espoused to a man whose name was
Joseph, of the house of David; and
the virgin's name was Mary.
And the angel came in unto her:
and said, Hail, thou that art highly
favoured, the Lord is with thee:

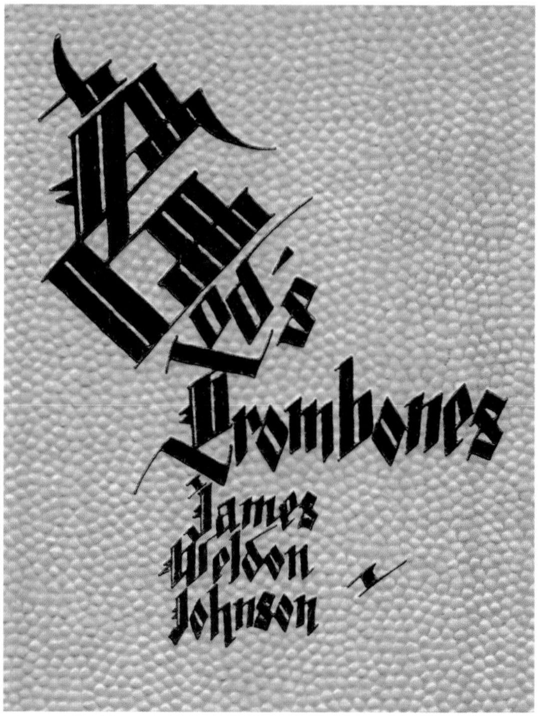
God's
Trombones
James
Weldon
Johnson

Charles Buckles Falls was another letterer-illustrator equally renowned in both fields. Above left and below right, there can be no better example of harmony between lettering and art than Falls's *The Story of the Birth of Jesus Christ*, 1929. Top right, *God's Trombones*, 1927, was illustrated by Aaron Douglas, with incredibly eccentric gothic black-letter *schrift* by Falls that went further even than his amazingly free, calligraphic lettering for *Jesus*. Below, the *ABC Book*, 1925, was produced entirely by woodcut. Falls's signature, an *F* within a funky square (under the elephant), became so well known, he eventually dropped the *F*.

Fear not,
Mary: for
thou hast
found favor
with God.

ABC
BOOK
by C·B·FALLS

PAUL SHAW / LETTER DESIGN 785 WEST END AVENUE NEW YORK CITY 10025 TEL 212 / 666·3738 FAX 212 / 666·2163

Paul Shaw made this amazing alphabet soup (he calls it his "Arabic carpet") as a promotional postcard. How do calligraphers get their work to look so even, I wondered? "That's the easy part—*that's the pen!*" Shaw explains. The piece started out as a doodle, "…just fitting letters into spaces." He then cut it all up into pieces, respaced it more tightly, then traced it over clean. And I just assumed he'd done it perfectly the first time!

Below, part of a 1932 letter from Rudolf Koch to Warren Chappell, who had spent a year's "apprenticeship" with Koch in Germany. This letter, reproduced as a keepsake by the Composing Room, is as dynamic an example of calligraphy as any.

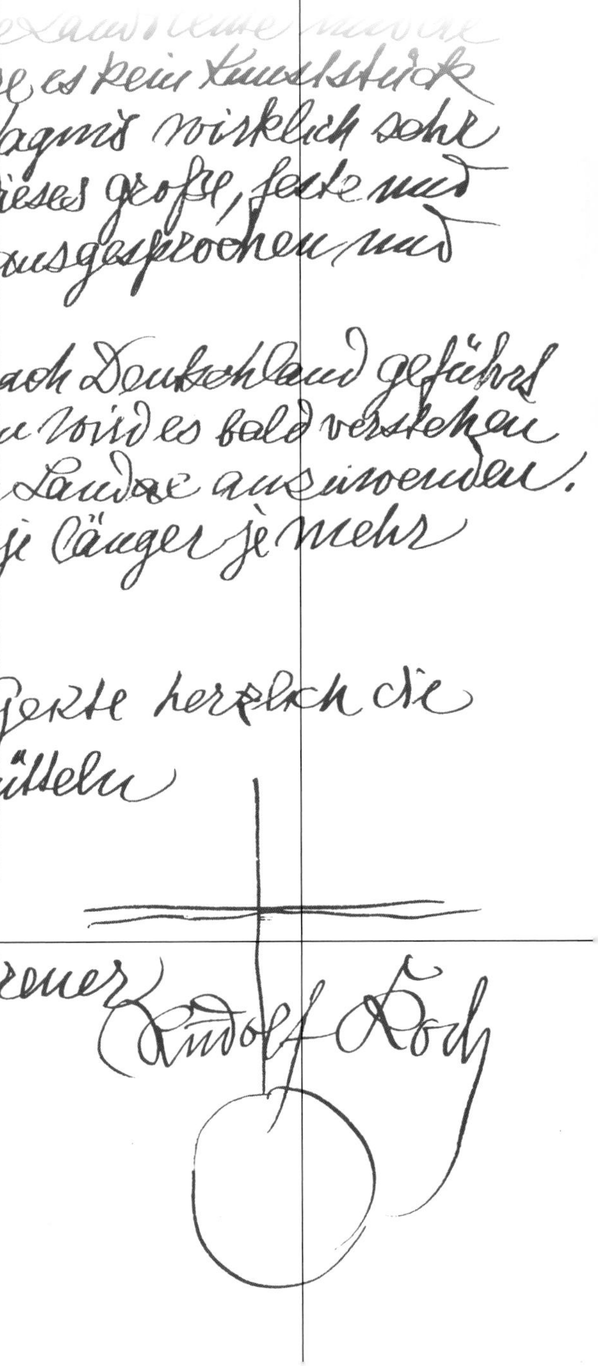

Calligraphy

Even for calligraphy, this piece by Rick Cusick, right, is especially freewheeling. Notice how the thickest strokes have been distributed evenly to balance the piece. Far right, an analysis of Cusick's logo, traced at its optical extremes to test for balance and coherence, proves that its asymmetric logic is at least as sublime as its letterforms.

12
1
2
3
4
5
6
7
8
9
10
11

Right, brush lettering by logo and font designer Doyald Young from his magnificent book *Logotypes & Letterforms.* He explains, "The cartouche is composed of four separate overlapping designs and is contrived to bisect the cipher precisely at the baseline and dead center of the counter." Young's numerals are based on the Fat Faces of the nineteenth century, which are derived from Bodoni. Each line is actually two strokes, done freehand, drawn in outline, then filled in with a Windsor & Newton Series 7, no. 2 brush.

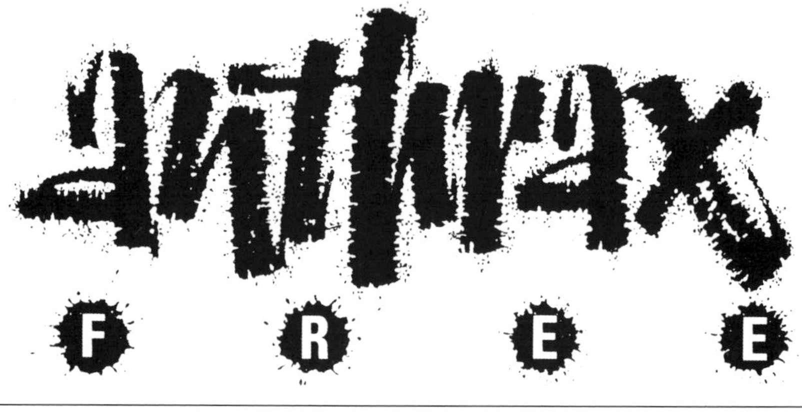
anthrax
F R E E

Michael Clark is known for sensuously undulating calligraphic letterforms as seen in this logo for a T-shirt, right. It was commissioned by some intrepid letter carriers in his area during the anthrax cozenage. The piece was done with a ruling pen on rough paper, causing the pen to "spit" with each stroke.

When you think of Jill Bell, you think of graceful curves (in her work, I mean). But there's also a philosophical side to her. Left, Bell's interpretation of the "Vahm" stands for "the supreme Buddha of esoteric Buddhism," the spiritual sun center of Buddhism. There are also the historical Buddha, Siddhartha Gautama, and many other aspects. Siddham is how Chinese and Japanese Buddhists interpret Devanagari for religious purposes (glad you asked?). Bell's sensuous brushwork in pearlescent paint further deifies the character's iconic qualities.

ROTAS
OPERA
TENET
AREPO
SATOR

The
Alphabet
AND ELEMENTS OF LETTERING

Above, lavish hand-lettering by Frederic Goudy for the title page of his book, *The Alphabet.* Goudy apparently preferred the brush to the pen, even for small lettering. I was curious about that so I compared the *E*s and *T*s above to discover whether the subtitle was type or lettering. I conclude it's the latter. Left, some way-out calligraphy by Ernst Bunz, c. 1955. I automatically think of old guys as having been conservative, but there's nothing at all stodgy about the roman *N* stuck in the middle of this kooky piece.

Right, the proper order of brush strokes, from light to dark, by Chas. J. Strong (inset), author of the classic *Strong's Book of Designs,* 1908. He writes, "Always make brush-strokes continuous. Avoid short, choppy strokes. Begin by executing the vertical strokes, and finally add the spurs or other peculiarities. Don't work with the point of the brush, use the side instead, and keep the hair spread. Begin a new stroke back of [or within] the preceding one."

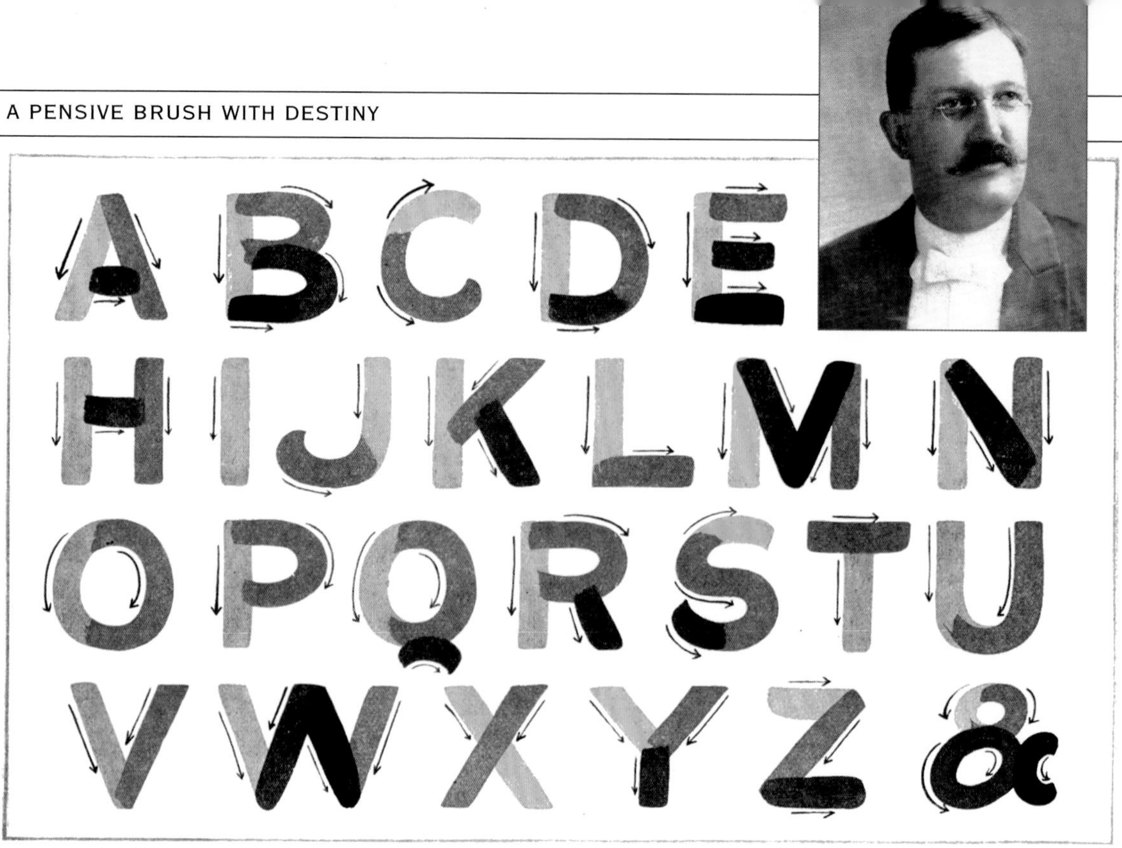

Right, Tommy Thompson, author of another classic, *The Script Letter,* 1939, shows us how our letterforms benefit from the underlying structure of perfect circles. He writes that no matter the style of script, or how condensed it may be, "It must be clearly understood that the turns must be round." And I want to tell you that I am in complete accord with this principle. When unhappy with a particular curved shape, I often draw circles and ellipses as guides to help reestablish the integrity of the shape.

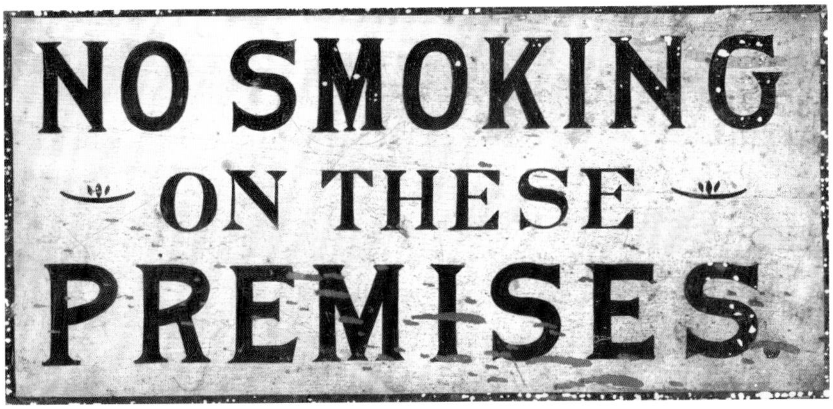
NO SMOKING
ON THESE
PREMISES.

Left, a classic, brush-lettered sign, c. 1910, complete with a period at the end. It's not the best example of well-drawn letters—the *S*s stink, except for the final one, and the *M*s are too narrow—but it's the real thing! I do like the spur serifs added to the bottom points of the middle strokes on the letters *M*.

NEW FOLLIES
16th. ST. at MISSION
BURLESK
The ONE and ONLY
LIVE
The GOLDEN GODDESS of BURLESK
PAGAN JONES
TALL... TEASIN' & TERRIFIC!
onSTAGE In Person
TAMMY LEE
JOAN MARLOWE
KARAMENEH
Faye Raymond
and... for Laffs... Manny King TONY LOCICERO Bill London
On Screen DREAM GIRL
Adults Only
BACK by Popular Demand
AVA "Legs" Rey
4 STAGE SHOWS DAILY
1:30 4:00 7:45 10:30
CONTINUOUS 12 Noon to MIDNITE
Midnite Show Every SAT. NEW SHOW FRI.

Long after type had supplanted most hand-lettering, some classy theater owners still valued the *Zing!* that a brush could impart to an ad like this one at left. I *had to* find out who was still doing ads like this—in the 1970s!—and finally met Don Sturdivant, the author of *Modern Show Card and Theatrical Poster Lettering*, 1948. I once asked him why the white-out he had used to touch up one letter had been allowed to carelessly cut into another. "Y' know, Les," he replied, "Frank Lloyd Wright once said, 'Let the nails show.'" Which I thought was surely one of the most brilliant excuses for sloppiness I'd ever heard. Who would dare argue with Frank Lloyd Wright?

Nail head
THEORY
Oiliness
PRIMER

Right, free brush lettering by Warren Chappell. Above, sample of Chappell's Lydian type showing strong calligraphic influences yet great restraint as required of a font designed for text as well as display headline purposes.

Graffiti writers are the scribes of our day. They are counterculture calligraphers with a can instead of a quill. I love graffiti, as long as it's not on *my* garage. I see it as symptomatic of a culture that, at the leadership level, has little use for art or artists and relegates those of us with the most meager means to virtual outlaw status. Such an attitude extends to all that is creative or provocative of thought. In 1671, Sir William Berkeley, Virginia's colonial governor, candidly discussed the dumbing-down of Americans that today would find little disagreement in the uppermost echelons of government: "I thank God we have not free schools nor printing, and I hope we shall not have these hundred years. For learning has brought disobedience and heresy and sects in the world, and printing has divulged them and libels against the government." Top right, LM (Little-Man) from Philadelphia posed in front of his piece painted on a wall in Tijuana, 2002. Left, calligraphy, 1955, from *A* to *M* by Arnold Bank, an expert in historic "handstyles," looks amazingly like graffiti. Right and below, photos by the author of artistic vandalism in his *'hood.*

THE

BRAZE
HANDSTYLES

Philadelphia-born aerosol artist Braze came over and tagged this page. Like many graffiti writers, he claims extensive knowledge of regional "handstyles" as demonstrated here. Far left, his own signature in typical old-school Philly tallprint. Above left, the Philly "print hand," popular in all boroughs, became a universal style. Left, a Braze masterpiece coming soon to a wall near you. Center left in green, new-school script evolved as writers entered the game after all the stylistic innovations of the 1990s had been introduced. West coast writers took the New York script and added "the new lunacy," their version of the psychedelic graffiti styles of the time.

"The world of graffiti has its superstars and sages, who won't be kept inside any cages. Graffiti writing evolved through many stages, but some early styles are lost to the ages."
—Braze

Graffiti gangs challenge each other with skills and art, and many artists have said that if it hadn't been for graffiti, there would have been a lot more violence. Every city has its "wall of fame" to showcase all the top talents. If you have a good reputation, you'll be invited to join all the top crews.

HANDSTYLES

CHOLOSTYLE

BRAZE

Above, Cholostyle, typical of Mexican gang graffiti, seen from Mexico to San Francisco, tends to have left-leaning letters. Right, another Braze signature in a New York script derivative.

Jill Bell says, "With most of my work, I begin with pen and ink, or brush and ink...but seldom with pencil sketches." Right, a fax from the client containing rough ideas. Though sometimes stifling, it usually saves us time fishing when a client is able to indicate what he's looking for.

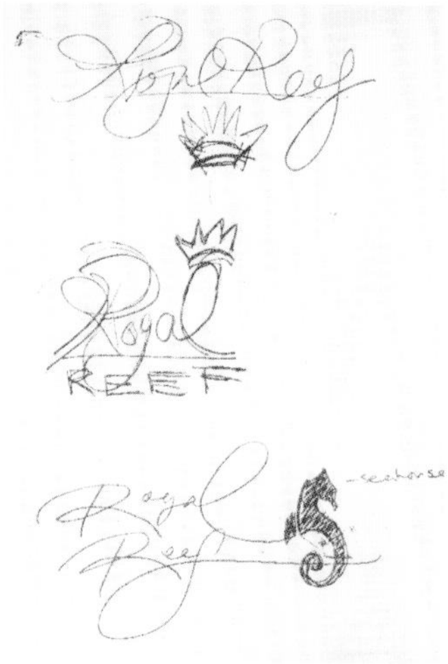

Royal

Royal Reef

Right, Bell's embellishments on the client's concepts. These are just a few of the roughs she produced for the job that involved designing a logo for a resort. Such sketches are then refined by cutting apart and pasting together the best letters and images. Then Bell "scans 'em, auto traces 'em, and fixes 'em, ad infinitum—well, at least until the deadline comes—in Illustrator." She often decides to smooth the logo's contours, "because you may not know what the client's size range may be, so creating a smooth logo is more versatile, though the textured ones are really my favorites." Bottom, the final result showing some of the bezier points.

Royal Reef
Royal Reef
Royal Reef
Royal Reef
Royal Reef
Royal Reef

Royal Reef

a
b
c
d
e

Above, a sappy logo by the author done with the Calligraphic Brush tool using the settings shown at right. The stars are just outlined objects. Each of the strokes shown above, a, have fills of 0% and strokes of 0.3 points. With no scan to trace, I drew this on my Wacom tablet, freehand. That is, with my digital pen in my right hand, I posed my free hand as a model and drew it from life. *TOGETHER* was also drawn live, with lots of point editing afterwards. At b, the actual strokes shown in VIEW>Outline mode. At c, OBJECT>Expand Appearance was used to release "brush" strokes, leaving superfluous center strokes, d, and overlaps that were cleaned up, e, with the Merge tool in the Pathfinder pallet.

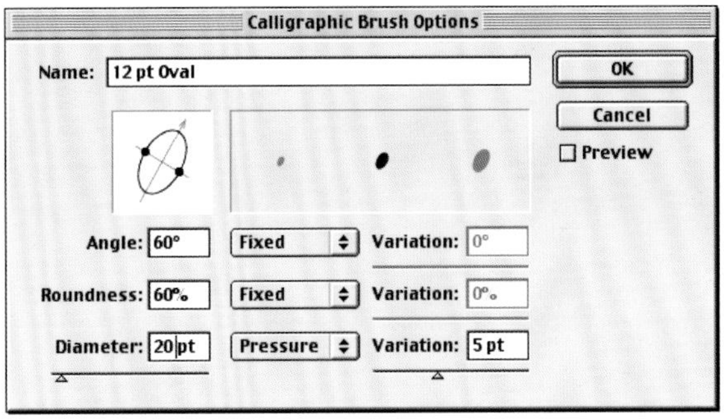
Calligraphic Brush Options
Name: 12 pt Oval
OK
Cancel
Preview
Angle: 60°
Fixed
Variation: 0°
Roundness: 60%
Fixed
Variation: 0%
Diameter: 20 pt
Pressure
Variation: 5 pt

a
b

Left, ugly, aren't they, these first practice samples I made with the Calligraphic Brush tool? I've never been an accomplished brush letterer—I'm the built-up guy, remember. I use only brush, digital pen and. . . lipstick, to educate myself as to what the natural strokes of the tool should look like, then I begin the hard, patient work of assembling pieces and editing points until you think, "Wow, he's a calligrapher, too!" At b, this was the point that I Expanded Appearance of my strokes to begin tweaking. For example, I thinned down the *ing* in *Going* and thickened *G* and *C*. At c, I flopped the logo with the Reflect tool, which gave me objective eyes with which to check the logo's color massing, and I added diagonal lines to check for consistent slant. The finished logo is seen at d.

c
d

The problem with calligraphy in the digital age is that once our brush or pen masterpiece is completed, it must be scanned into the computer, there to become bound by whatever resolution it was scanned at. This is usually limiting for logos, which should be able to work at any size up to that of a billboard. We can autotrace the scan and work on the bezier points to perfect them, as Jill Bell does, or we can use a digital pen tablet with Illustrator's Calligraphic Brush option and do our calligraphy live, on-screen, as shown in the examples on this page. This is not a perfect solution, nor applicable to every job, by any means. Digital pens are really clumsy to use. Illustrator translates our digital pen strokes fairly poorly, and worst of all, we can never really achieve the rough-edged, dry-brush and grainy effects of real calligraphy.

What could be more appropriate for the cover of a book called *Tender Murderers* (far right) than lipstick lettering? I got out my wife's lipstick (Oh, they really *hate* that!) and wrote a few samples, right, which I scanned into Photoshop, then cut and pasted. The letters a through f show which parts were chosen for the final composite at bottom. Almost all the rough letters, especially d and f, were cleaned up and tweaked in one way or another. Although this was meant to look rapidly handwritten, I still aimed for consistency, balance and rhythm just as with any lettering. For the cover art, I was given a 1940s book cover as a direction. I flopped the legs and made other changes to more or less make the art mine.

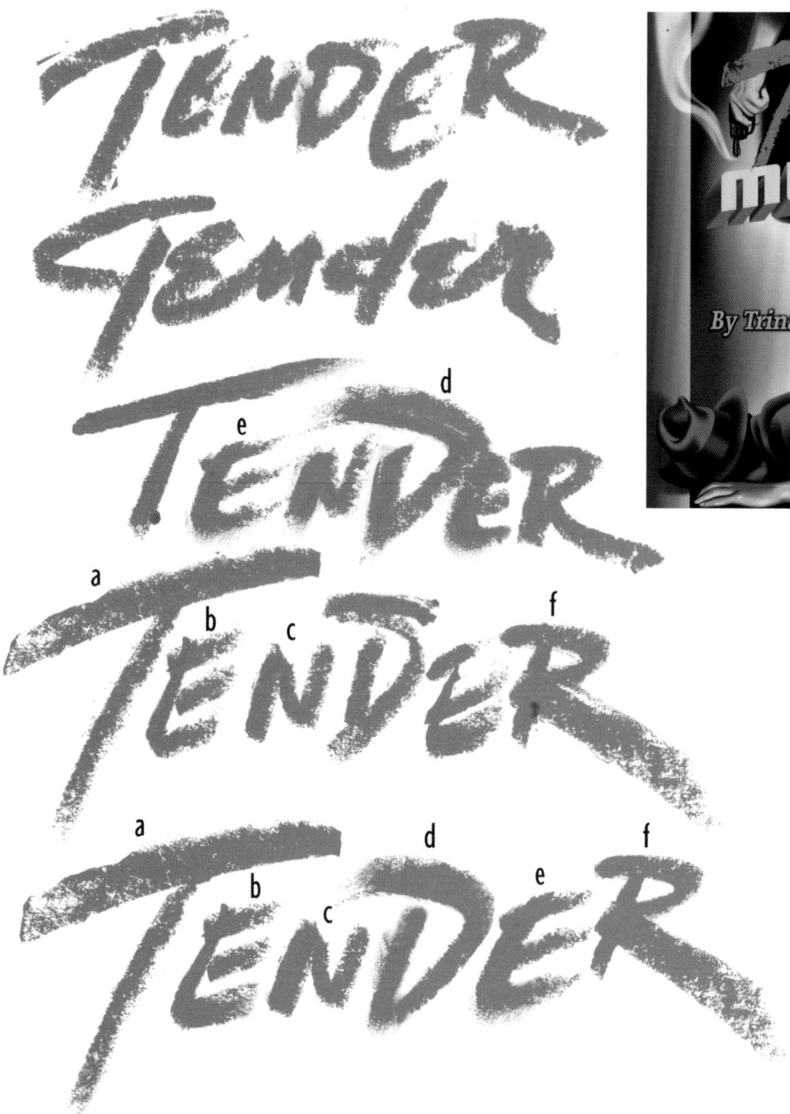
TENDER
Tender
TENDER
TENDER
TENDER
a
b
c
d
e
f

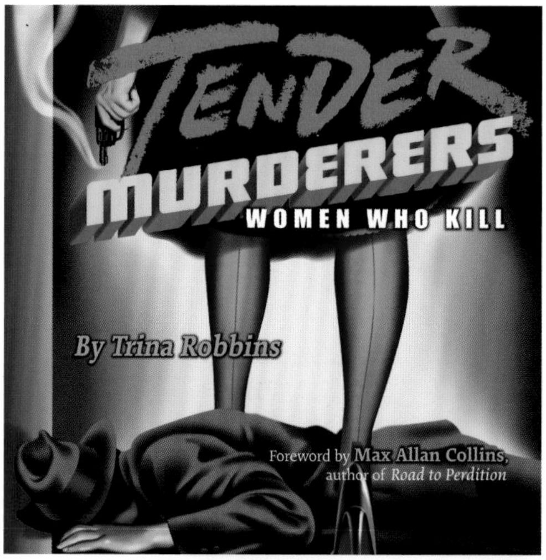
TENDER
MURDERERS
WOMEN WHO KILL
By Trina Robbins
Foreword by Max Allan Collins,
author of Road to Perdition

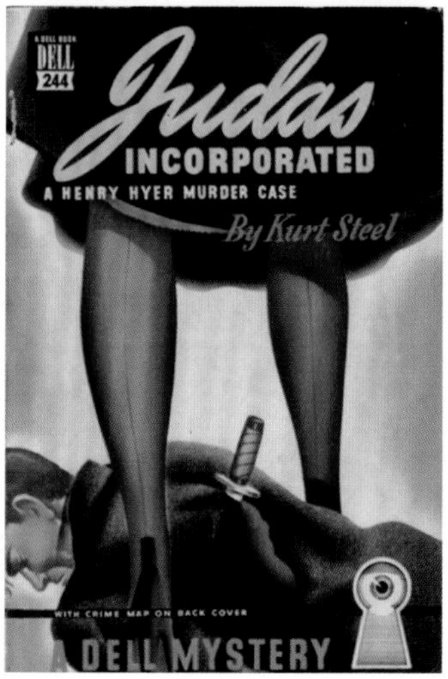
DELL
244
Judas
INCORPORATED
A HENRY HYER MURDER CASE
By Kurt Steel
WITH CRIME MAP ON BACK COVER
A DELL MYSTERY

Those UPTOWN GALS & BOOTLEG WHISKEY! Swingin' Haarlem Nights

I had a chisel-edge marker that was so new it bled on tracing paper at the end of strokes, suggesting serifs. The marker sketch at left became the guide for my fonts Haarlem White and Haarlem Black, above. Later, when I'd decided to add the lowercase, the marker had dried out enough so that I couldn't get that fleeting bleeding effect and had to sort of figure out what the strokes would have looked like based on the shapes of the capital letters. By the way, Harlem was originally spelled *Haarlem,* which was the original name of New York.

What was the most memorable scene in the original 1968 *Planet of the Apes* film? For me it was the one in which Charlton Heston comes across the Statue of Liberty buried in the sand. So when I was hired to come up with title lettering for the remake of *Planet of the Apes*, I went to the beach at Santa Monica and tried writing in the wet sand with a wooden tool usually used for clay modeling. One example, right, shows the unexpected, evenly spaced curls of sand left in the tool's wake, which I incorporated into the capital letters. For the lowercase letters, I dipped the same clay tool into paint to produce an alphabet and a set of numerals (examples below). A wooden stick has no ink repository like a pen, nor the capacity for absorbency like a brush. The hard, flat end of the stick and the necessity of constant redipping when the paint played out certainly influenced the letters. I call the font Djungl. It shows how the implement can inspire the lettering and how almost any weird tool can be tried. My apes lettering wasn't used in the film, but I got a check and a half-done font out of it—not bad for a day at the beach.

456
789

Below is a sample of the font Djungl. I still don't quite like all of it, but I'm not sure why. I've often said that the difference between a free font and one you have to pay for is about six weeks. And it might take me almost that long to thoroughly go over this font and fix everything about it until it looks right to me. This process will mainly involve trying to make every stroke of every letter consistent in weight, style and "feel" with every other letter. I may even go back to the beach to make sure my letter shapes, and the angles of my strokes, are consistently true to life, and to get a tan.

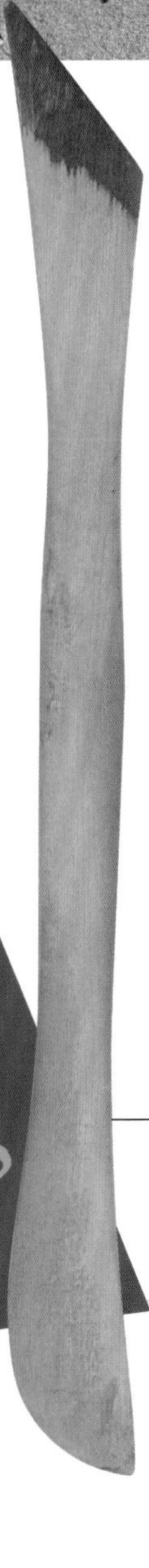

569 Sand Based
Monkey Letters

LETTERED & UNFETTERED

Out of the Box Before There Was a Box

BY ***the time several thousand years*** have come and gone, there's pretty much nothing left to try that hasn't already been tried by somebody. That goes for spearhead designs as well as alphabets.

But cultural boxes develop that stifle creativity through nonverbal agreement and millennial myopia that says, "Here's a style we all accept and if you don't follow it, nobody'll buy your stuff." So we all go from A to B, and maybe to C, but access to D is denied because our minds seem to be capable of taking only baby steps toward the future. That's why computers go from 300MHz to 466MHz to 700MHz instead of leaping from 300MHz to 1GHz. Those who do dare to leap ahead may be stoned (either connotation works).

Then, too, styles of design, like styles of thought, are subject to whether the moon is in Pisces this millennium or if Mercury is casting a dark cloud over everything relating to communication, publishing and clip art. That's why in the 1980s everybody went red-and-black "Eurostyle," sniffed coke and bought real estate. Here, in any event, is a gallery of letters and designs that, if not quite representing leaps from A to D, still surprised me when first I came across them.

As everybody knows, life through reincarnation is an everlasting continuum. I've noticed that a little bell seems to go off in my mind every time I do something that perhaps I've never done before in all my past incarnations. It's the same feeling I get the first time I see something new in lettering. Some of you may not get the same kick I got from these examples; you may have seen them before. Nevertheless, they are presented here with captions describing just what I found unique about each one.

Here's a *B* that is about as inside the box as you can get, because it's inside a box. And though there will be many who would claim that the way the stroke of the top bowl narrows as it hits the bottom bowl is just the way the brush or chisel naturally forms the stroke, in my opinion this aspect of the Trajan Column *B*, as interpreted by Frederic Goudy in a woodcut from his 1936 book, *Capitals from the Trajan Column at Rome*, is just sublime.

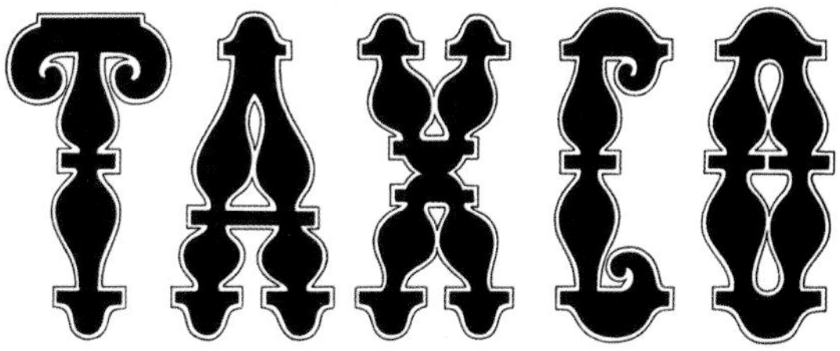
TAXCO

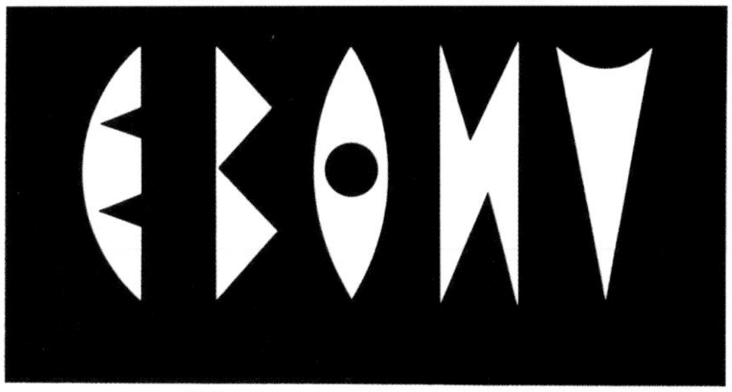
EBONY

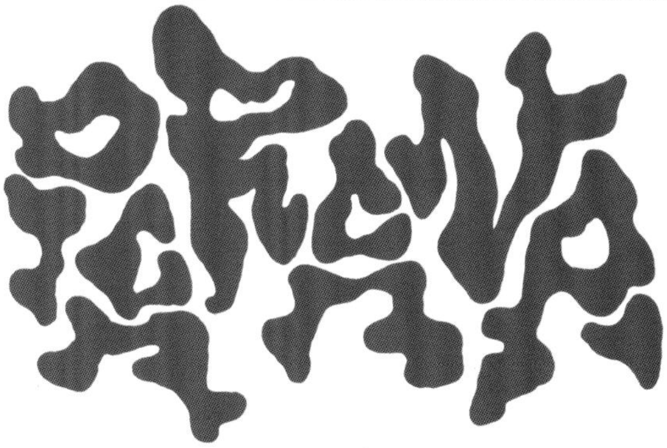

THE BLUES

FOTO

boutique fantasque

The lettering above came from the book *Lettera* by Armin Haab and Alex Stocker. It was published in Switzerland in 1954, yet it contains some of the most exciting, unusual and creative lettering I've seen. Did the authors presage the psychedelic and 1960s type revolution by twelve years, or was the book simply used by later designers to steal from? Both suppositions are undoubtedly true. In any event, these and other amazing examples in the book were definitely cutting-edge.

the
fgc
book
pages from Life
by Fred G. Cooper
with a foreword by
Hal Marchbanks
and a preface by
Robt. E. Sherwood
The Soandso Company
New York
1930

Fred Cooper claimed that he wasn't into sloppy lettering: "The crudeness in my work is not intentional. I make every effort to be as perfect as possible, within the time limit I impose on its making." It was natural then that happy accidentals, such as the stem of *b* looping up and around to form the bowl, would result from this speedy execution. Other characters, such as the lowercase *o* in *book* also show what happens when you play, innovate and constantly reinterpret as you go along.

M

This top left serif surprised me. It's unorthodox, but why not? I can see the logical thought process behind the idea of opening up the lower left counter to match the right one by allowing the serif above to match the one below without having to compromise its shape in order to meet up with the diagonal stroke.

The treatment of the *M*s in this 1898 French lettering breaks all the rules. You're not really supposed to double the width of the joining strokes as they meet at top, because that adds a huge width to the stem. However, by joining the center diagonal stems at almost cap height, there is no accumulation of excess weight and so it works.

BULLETIN DE
COMMANDE

A
F

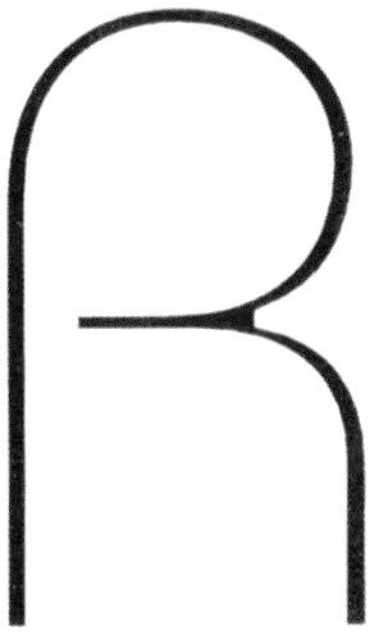
R

This cap *R* and the words below were set in some thin variant of the Bauhaus font family. I'm fascinated by the on-purpose "clog" at the junction of the bowl and leg, which adds a spot of weight, but becomes a decorative feature. I also like the rounded tops and bottoms of *N* and *V* and the unconnected horizontal *A* and *D* strokes.

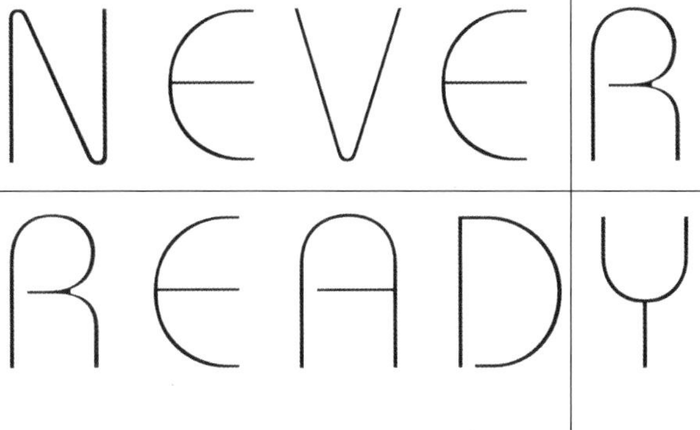
NEVER
READY

There are many ornate, decorative initials around, but perhaps few quite so neatly executed as these by Christophe Weyle of the Ecole Allemande (eighteenth century). The heavier strokes defining the central part of the letters, and the embellishing strokes appear to have been drawn with two widths of pen nibs, but both of the chisel-edge kind.

There are many aspects of this never-published type prototype by J.J. Herman that break the mold, even by today's standards. Note how the bowls of *B* and *R* join fat in the center; the unusual epsilon shape of *E*; the graceful swelling stroke of *K*; the funny top of *T*; the serifs on the bottom points of *W*, *V*; and the cool *S* and hourglass *X*. In his heyday (1920s–1950s), Herman was just one of a battery of artists supplying advertisers with lines of lettering, frequently indistinguishable from type, but offering that extra punch that metal type could not provide. Typical pay in those days was around $2.50 for a short headline. I'm so pleased to present Herman's work here. He was in his eighties when I met him and purchased much of his amazing lettering book collection. He cried as I carried out armloads of his babies. I felt awful and could only consolingly suggest, "Well, they're going to a good home."

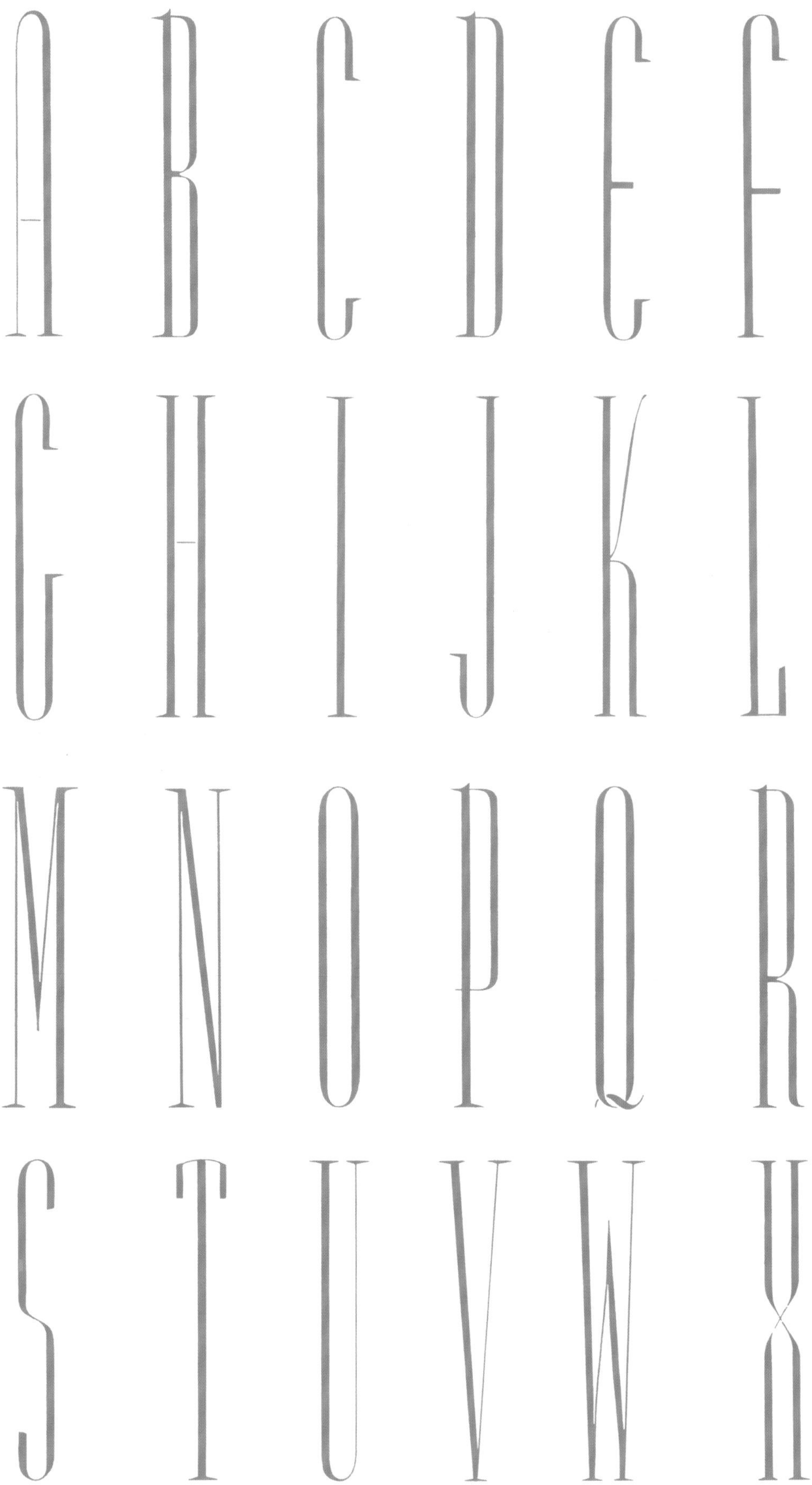

"Bluebird" Curtain Rods

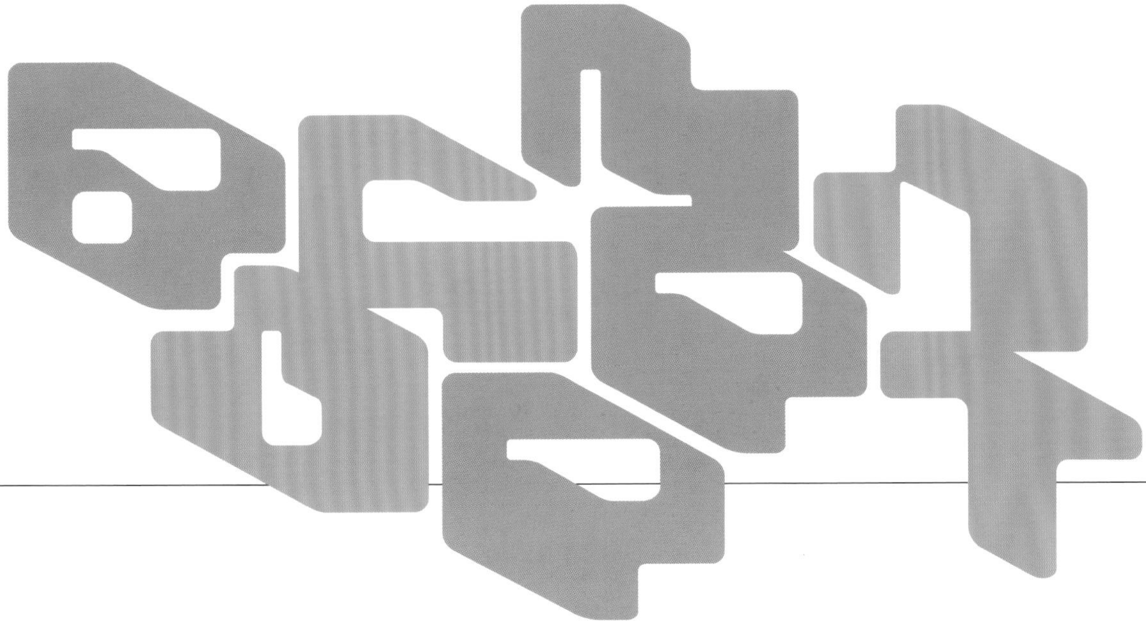

Above, early twentieth century initials by Marcel Lenoir with fascinating sculptural strokes in the Art Nouveau style.

The lowercase *b* in this 1920s Bluebird logo, center left, caught my eye. The initial cap *B* follows the quirk through, though less thrillingly, but the last letter *d* should have, also.

A gold star to anyone who can decipher Stan Endo's logo, left. It's a dimensional puzzle that reminds me of Montreal's Habitat 67.
OK, the letters in this logo for a fashion outfit spell *Basement*.

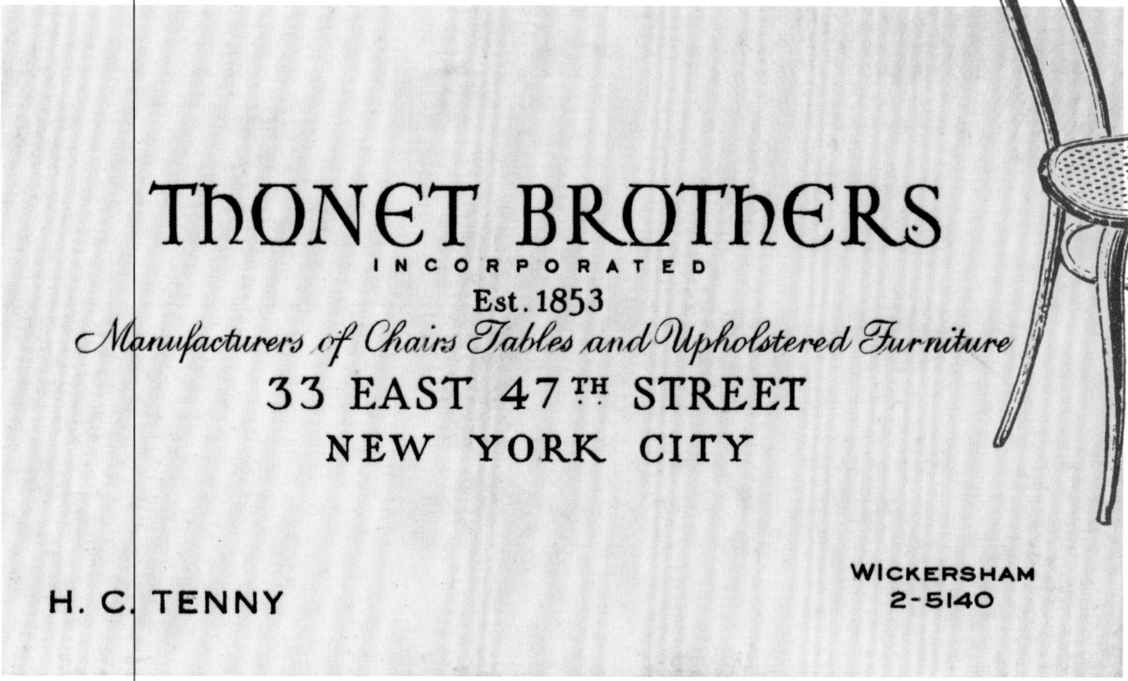
THONET BROTHERS
INCORPORATED
Est. 1853
Manufacturers of Chairs Tables and Upholstered Furniture
33 EAST 47TH STREET
NEW YORK CITY
H. C. TENNY
WICKERSHAM
2-5140

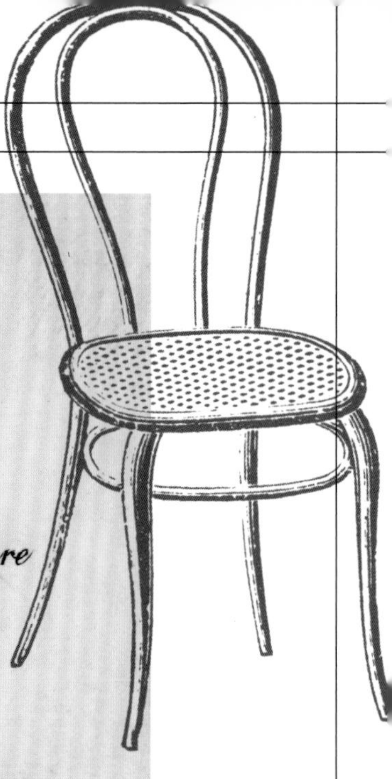

THE FOREST
CRAFT
GUILD

Above, you know those classic dark, bentwood café chairs with the caned seats? Those were originated by Thonet in France (later of New York). Although less expertly executed than their chairs, the Thonet Brothers lettering has some unique and unexpected touches, like the uncial-style *H* and serifed Greekesque *O*.

The *Forest Craft Guild* lettering, being utterly inconsistent, is not technically any good. But the designer has devised some wonderfully unorthodox letterforms, such as *E, F, S* in the top row, and *R, A, G* at bottom. I look at something like this and ask myself, "Wouldn't such characters look great lettered better?" (In other words, if I ripped them off to make a font.) This is also a perfect example of "accommodation," as the designer has fit *F-O* together on top, exaggerated the bowl of *R,* below, to fill the gap left by slanting *A,* lowered *F* into the hollow of *L* below, and—preposterously—swung the right side of *G* into the middle of *U*. I love that!

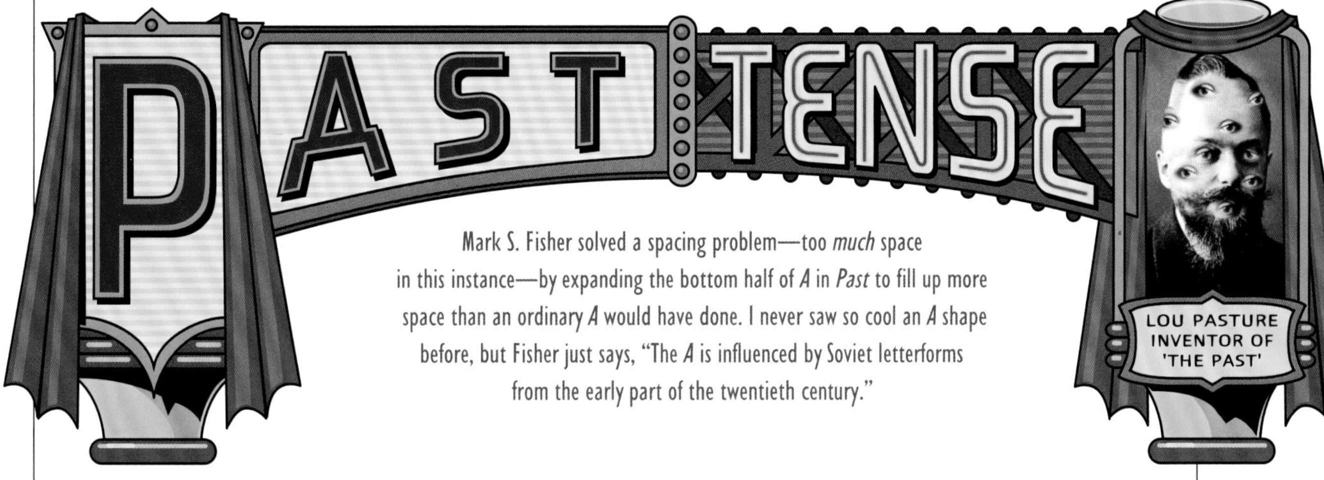
PAST TENSE
LOU PASTURE
INVENTOR OF
'THE PAST'

Mark S. Fisher solved a spacing problem—too *much* space in this instance—by expanding the bottom half of *A* in *Past* to fill up more space than an ordinary *A* would have done. I never saw so cool an *A* shape before, but Fisher just says, "The *A* is influenced by Soviet letterforms from the early part of the twentieth century."

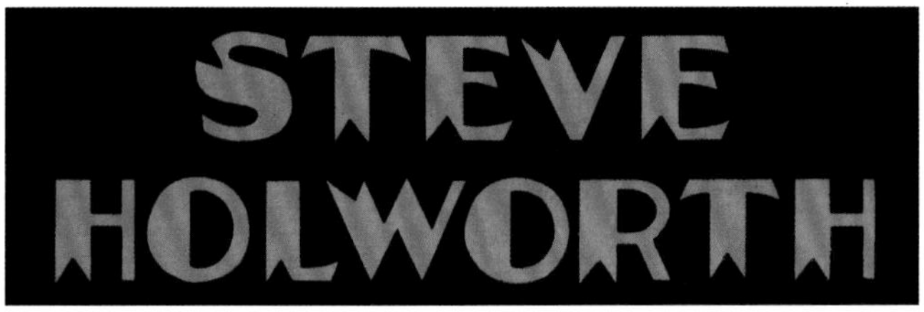
STEVE
HOLWORTH

It has always amused me how some artists of the period could never quite "get" the angular Art Deco style when it exploded full strength in America by 1929. Though well executed, this off-target ziggurat book title design is some of the most preposterous lettering I've seen.

OPTICAL DELUSION?

Rian Hughes's eye-confounding font, Lusta, example left, is "based on an idea that started with the lowercase *s*—a kind of 'inline/outline' hybrid," Hughes says. "The variants derive from mechanical operations applied to the basic font."

Right, a classic example of newspaper movie-ad brush lettering, circa 1930. I've placed it here to point out the unusual flourish hanging off the first *R* in the word *Warner*. Obviously, it was done—and elegantly so—to fill the visual hole between *A* and *R*. Then the designer added a second flourish to the leg of the last *R* to balance and rationally justify the placing of the first one.

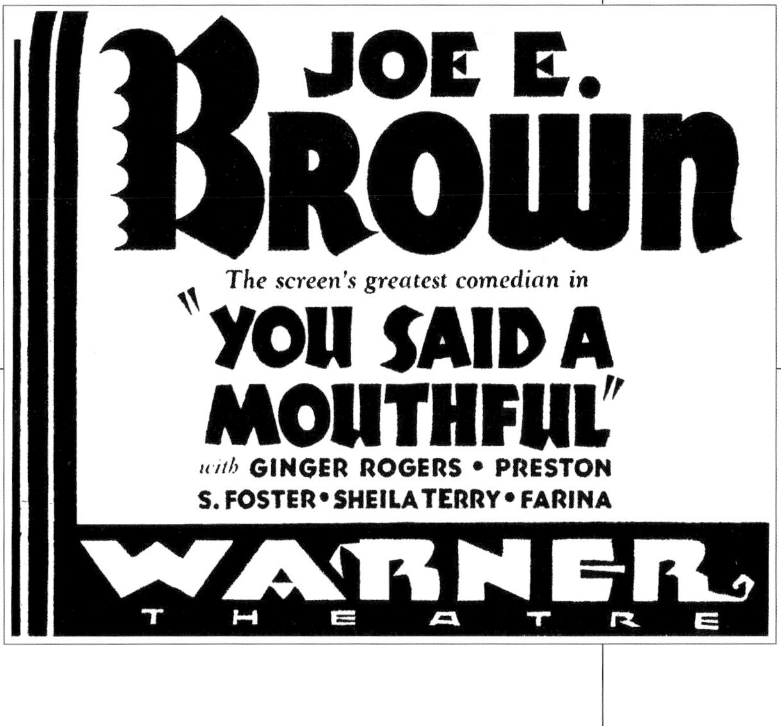
JOE E.
BROWN
The screen's greatest comedian in
"YOU SAID A
MOUTHFUL"
with GINGER ROGERS • PRESTON
S. FOSTER • SHEILA TERRY • FARINA
WARNER
THEATRE

LETTERERS WHO DRAW and DRAWERS WHO LETTER

Anyone who can draw will naturally be able to draw letters. And I believe those who draw better will letter better, too. Gerard Huerta says, "Good drawing is the only basis for good lettering." But not always. Some artists have more of the designer in them, and these kind tend to consider every dot they commit to paper, which makes their lettering more adept, even if they can't sketch for beans.

An artist's signature can be a telling indicator of the quality of his or her work. Famous illustrator J.C. Leyendecker's signature, above, was as carefully considered as was every stroke of his brush, but the grace and rhythm of this design is something you can't fake by measuring really careful. The guy just drew like crazy!

Perhaps lettering requires a different mind-set than drawing. Lettering is, in most cases, simpler than drawing human anatomy, for example, because many aspects of lettering seem obvious, repeatable and mechanical. But some letter styles, like certain scripts, italics or even classic roman, are anything but simple and mechanical. The shaping of each curve and serif benefits from an artist's touch.

Don't get depressed if you feel you can't draw. Instead, pick up a pencil and start to copy the world around you. The more able and intrepid you become at this, the better you will be at designing interesting, complex, subtle and beautiful letters. Keep at it! Remember: *Ars longa, vita brevis est!*

The following pages contain examples of work by artists whose ability to draw well carries over into their being multicreative in a variety of graphic and dimensional milieu.

THE EDISON MAN PUTS HIS BEST FOOT FORWARD

F.G. Cooper's monogram, left, was one of the most widely recognized artist's signatures of its time. His work was ubiquitous and his imitators legion. Above, from 1906 onward, Cooper supplied virtually all the posters and advertising art for the New York Edison Company.

EXERCISE Take turns with your friends sketching each other naked, every Wednesday night at 7: Also, go out and sketch trees and flowers. See if then you don't approach lettering with less trepidation and an increased sense of proportion, balance and rhythm.

Fred Goss Cooper was an illustrator before he started lettering. His World War I posters, example right, earned him the moniker "F.G. Cooper, the lowercase letterer." He often applied his restless mind to anthropomorphic monogram design, such as those for friends Ervine Metzl, below, and Lillian R. Givner, below right. Though he was lightning fast on the "draw," he lovingly crafted each letter with a pen point honed to his custom. Cooper preferred lettering over type that he called "frozen in tradition" and "lacking in spontaneity." His celebrity was enough that he could appreciate the lettering of Oswald Cooper (no relation), who designed the Cooper Black fonts, though they were said to have been based on F.G.'s lettering. However, it's been recorded that Caslon Oldstyle 471 was the favorite font of both men, and its influence may account for their uncannily similar styles. Although F.G. Cooper chose to stylize his figures, the anatomy behind his drawing is solid, and his skill at rendering enabled him to take on many different stylistic suits during a prolific career lasting from 1906 to 1960.

Save a loaf
a week
—
help win
the war

there is more
leisure
for the housekeeper
in
electrical
housekeeping

Left, another of Cooper's elegant "lowercase" posters for New York Edison, 1913. Right, a monogram for his friend, Frederic W. Goudy, after the style of classic printers' marks.

QUOD SI DEFICIANT VIRES, AUDACIA CERTE LAUS ERIT
FREDERIC W. GOUDY

When he was eighty-four years old, Clarence P. Hornung's wife died suddenly. I was visiting him when, in a morose mood, he tearfully lamented, "Look at me, I'm a has-been!" I had to stifle an incredulous chortle as I considered the man's output: over four hundred logo designs, dozens of books, as well as industrial designs, patented inventions, several fonts of decorative initials for American Type Founders, and the meticulous pen-and-ink advertising illustrations, like the portrait of Goudy, opposite, that started his career off with a bang. When he passed away at eighty-nine, Clarence still had projects in the works.

NET CONTENTS 6 OUNCES
SLIM
MODERN HEALTH PRODUCTS
A DELICIOUS NON-HABIT FORMING BEVERAGE
MODERN HEALTH PRODUCTS

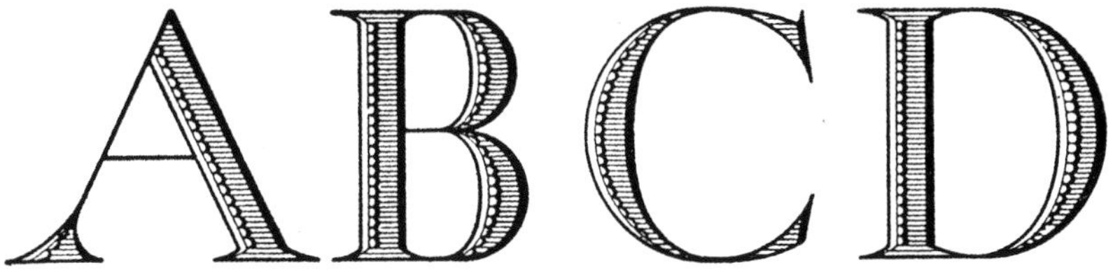
ABCD

The Liquid Olive
A Scalp Oil Concentrate
OLIVESTEROL
Each Olive a Complete Oil Treatment
ODORLESS — ANTISEPTIC — GREASELESS — QUICKLY ABSORBED

A smattering of Clarence Hornung's work from the 1930s: A doughnut company trademark; one of a suite of product designs that included the Swiss Kriss packaging still available in health food stores today; Georgian initials for American Type Founders; Liquid Olive packaging; Mainline Mysteries and Farrar & Rinehart publishing logos; Boys Clubs of America logo.

HOW THIS BOOK ALMOST CONTAINED ORIGINAL GOUDY SKETCHES: Visiting his friend Fred Goudy one day, Clarence Horning noticed some sketches lying about and asked if he could have them. Just as Goudy handed him the drawings, his daughter-in-law stuck her head into the studio, saying, "Now, Fred, remember our agreement, you promised to give all your sketches to me." "Yeah, I guess that's right," replied Goudy resignedly. Since this author acquired much of the Hornung collection before he died, those Goudy sketches might have become part of this book.

Schaut hin! Der Name Jahwes kommt von fern
JESAJA
brennend sein Atem, eine schwer aufsteigende Wolke! Seine Lippen sind voll Grimm seine Zunge wie fressendes Feuer!

The results of German calligrapher and type designer Rudolph Koch's Sunday nature-sketching expeditions were published as *Das Blumenbuch*. Delicate woodcuts, example right, by his Offenbacher Werkstatt associate, Fritz Kredel, reproduced Koch's sensitive linework. The *unbefangenheit*, or free abandon, of the flower drawings began to influence Koch's alphabets, allowing him to overcome some of the rigidity associated with classic German black-letter scripts. Koch's woodcut illustration, above, and his font Neuland, below, designed directly in the freehand woodcut, may be examples of this *unbefangenheit*.

ICH HÖRTE DIE STERB-
LICHEN STAUNEN AM
MEISTEN + DASS ERDE

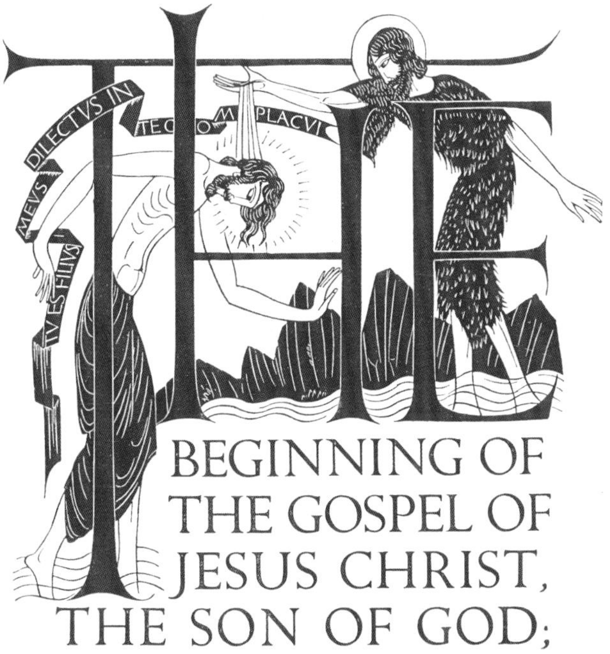
TV ES FILIVS MEVS DILECTVS IN TE CO M PLACVI
THE
BEGINNING OF
THE GOSPEL OF
JESUS CHRIST,
THE SON OF GOD;

REGISTERED MONOTYPE TRADE MARK

GILL SANS

THE HISTORY OF A FAMOUS TYPE FACE:

"MONOTYPE" GILL SANS

FROM ITS INCEPTION IN 1928 AS TITLING CAPITALS 231

TO THE END OF 1935, WHEN IT COMPRISED

THE LARGEST RELATED SERIES GROUP

FOR MODERN COMPOSITION AND DISPLAY

EVER BASED ON A SINGLE DESIGN

WITH THE CHIEF REASONS WHY IT WAS FOUND NECESSARY

TO CUT SUCH A WEALTH OF RELATED FACES

SET FORTH AS A SUMMARY SPECIMEN

OF THE VARIOUS SERIES OF THE DESIGN

ABOVE: 231 BELOW: 262

★

In June, 1928, "Monotype" GILL SANS made its first appearance before the printing industry. The occasion, an important meeting of executive printers, was worthy of the *début* of a design which can well be called "important" for its effect on commercial printing.

The programme of the Publicity and Selling Session of the F.M.P.A. Conference at Blackpool was the first public use of Gill Sans for any purpose; and its first published specimen appeared simultaneously. There were vehement protests against its use in the programme, not because it was a *bad* sans-serif, but because it *was* a sans-serif, then known as a "grot", and as such to be shunned. The contrasts drawn with another programme, which had a renaissance-style initial, were in favour of the more artistic job. The word *art* was freely, and reproachfully, used by most of the critics.

It is worth recording the emotions with which Gill Sans was greeted on its first public appearance, because the incident showed what a different attitude was then taken towards what we now call the *functional job*, as against what was called the "art job". Unless that difference is recognized, it is impossible to understand why "Monotype" Gill Sans has destroyed so much that lay in its path: so many imitation woodcut initials, so many "art borders", so many leaden leavings from the past. Gill Sans did not enter as "another candidate" for the crowded display frames. It certainly did not win its way as "another grot" (grotesque). It came as a live destroyer of dead metal and dead categories—such as "artistic job", or "mere commercial printing". But in 1928 those two phrases were still used to challenge the newcomer to the type book.

231 42 pt.

CONSPECTUS

Everybody knows the name Gill of Gill Sans fame, but fewer know of the Eric Gill whose illustrated works ran the gamut from *Hamlet* to *The Jungle Book*. I discovered this by searching Gill on www.abebooks.com. The two pieces above are from *The Four Gospels*, 1931 (the original woodcut was only seven inches wide), and *The Passion*, 1927. The clean lines and orderly composition of these woodcuts reveal a talent equally suited to type as to drawing. This ode to Gill Sans, left, was published in *The Monotype Recorder*, 1931. According to Dictionary.com, *conspectus* means "a general survey of a subject; a synopsis." That can be our word for the day!

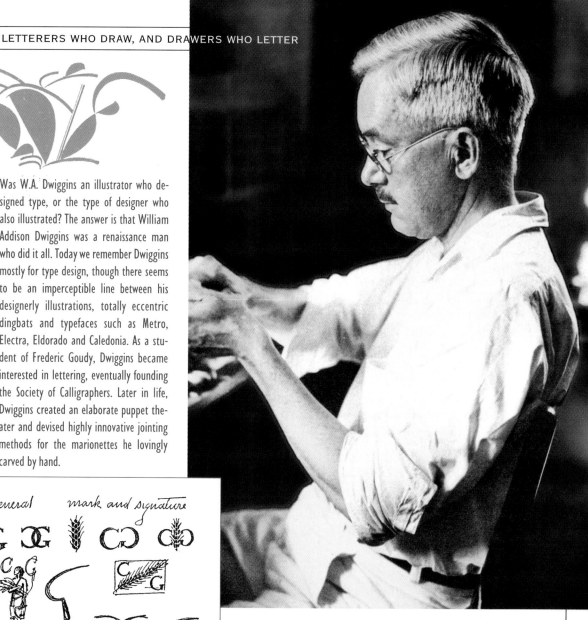

Was W.A. Dwiggins an illustrator who designed type, or the type of designer who also illustrated? The answer is that William Addison Dwiggins was a renaissance man who did it all. Today we remember Dwiggins mostly for type design, though there seems to be an imperceptible line between his designerly illustrations, totally eccentric dingbats and typefaces such as Metro, Electra, Eldorado and Caledonia. As a student of Frederic Goudy, Dwiggins became interested in lettering, eventually founding the Society of Calligraphers. Later in life, Dwiggins created an elaborate puppet theater and devised highly innovative jointing methods for the marionettes he lovingly carved by hand.

Cereals General
mark and signature
CEREALS GENERAL
CEREALS GENERAL
Cereals General

Above, a touching portrait from the 1930s shows WAD engrossed creatively. Left, a page of logo sketches from Dwiggins's book *Layout in Advertising,* 1928, clearly demonstrates how the ability to draw expands a designer's conceptual horizons. Nowadays, it might be uncool to use a Greek deity in a logo, but it'd be nice to be able to draw one as perfectly proportioned as Dwiggins's if we wanted to. Below, a sample of Dwiggins's font, Metro Black No. 2 shows the exquisite subtleties for which this designer was so acclaimed.

ABCDEFSTUVWX
abcdefghijklmwxy

Illustrations by Dwiggins from the 1920s and 1930s show his versatility and terrific compositional sense. He could draw the figure well and used shading to define contours, also quite decoratively. The crowd scene at right seems to be made up of almost alphabetically constructed characters.

Type ornament, with landscape attached
WAD

RAGS

WAD
SINBAD'S TROPHIES

Opposite page top, one of WAD's eccentric dingbats and a colophon, right. Above, hand lettering drawn with a pen, 1930, for *Rags*, a paper industry brochure that he also designed.

H

Mitch O'Connell is not afraid to draw. He delights in juxtaposing more retro references into each piece than would seem possible. His grasp of anatomy and general skill at drawing mean there's no way he could fail to draw excellent lettering that abides all the rules of consistency, balance, spacing and so on—whether or not he's made a conscious study of these qualities.

IRONHEAD

NOTHING
PERSONAL

O'Connell has taken the style and imagery of classic tattoo art and given it his own unique spin. I doubt there's any better examples than the collection found on his web site, www.mitchoconnell.com. Tattoo designs, especially those with banners and lettering, are really body logos, and every well-designed stroke in O'Connell's work is a masterpiece unto itself. His inking style, falling somewhere between graffiti and calligraphy, remains consistent whether applied to the art or the lettering. O'Connell's is a 1950s stroke, because his brush is always cocked at about the same angle as Elvis Presley's signature smile.

MITCH
O'CONNELL
TATTOO
FLASH

Paul's
Garage

Rian Hughes is a prolific designer-illustrator as well as a font designer. Many of his fonts were expanded from original lettering done for his stunning posters and ad work, like that for *Yellow Boots*, left, and *Partners in Crime*, below. Hughes is another artist whose lettering is in complete harmony with his drawing style, and whose fonts seem to benefit from his fine sense of proportion and the apparent ease with which he wrangles his beziers.

Yellow Boots

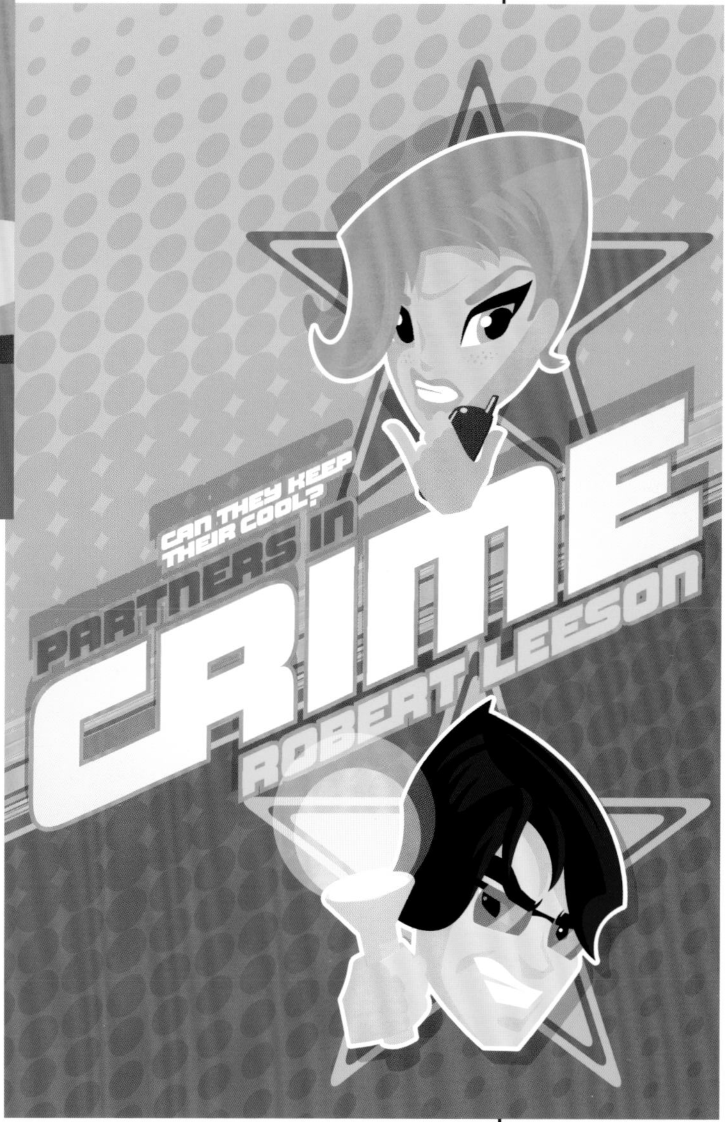
Can they keep their cool?
Partners in
Crime
Robert Leeson

PSYCHO
ZEALOT
wacky

Above, legibility is such a boring and cumbersome quality in fonts! Rian Hughes's cuddly digifont Mastertext Plain, top rows, and his high-tech-Aztec Terrazzo, middle row, show a maniacal fascination with resolving tricky spacial conundrums. Blackcurrant Squash, bottom row, and its derivative sister, Blackcurrant Cameo, right, have, I'd say, as much verve and honesty of form as anything Zapf ever did.

SIMPLY
BUXOM

IMMUTABLE LAWS OF LETTERING IMMUTABLE LAWS OF LETTERING

...and the myriad exceptions thereto

1. **LETTER HEIGHTS MUST BE ADJUSTED OPTICALLY**
The heights of curved letters like *C-G-O-Q* and pointy letters like *A-V-W* should be drawn slightly beyond the top and bottom guides or these letters will appear shorter than the rest. Here's why: Letters like *K-B-L-T* ride along the top and baseline guides for a good while, but *O* and the point of *A* come in contact with them for only seconds.

KOBALT

Optical adjustments properly made. Letters appear optically equal in height.

KOBALT

Here, all letters are exactly equal in height, but *O and A* appear diminutive.

KOBALT

Keep it subtle! Exaggerated enlargement of *O and A* is as bad as none at all.

The rule regarding height adjustments applies to all curved and pointed characters in all fonts and to lowercase as well as uppercase.

tivoli

Above, bottoms of *t-v-o* and tops of *i-o* optically adjusted. All letters appear virtually equal in height.

tivoli

Here, with no adjustment, *i-v-o-i* appear shorter than *v-t*, whose flat tops establish the visual (and actual) x-height.

But... Here's a dilemma I've had with some monoweight styles: At right, I've optically adjusted *O* so it looks right with *E*. Ideally, the bowls of *C-D-O* should have the same diameter, but they can't since the bowl of *D* must connect at proper vertical stem height to match *E*. Thus, *D* may appear shorter than *E* and too small next to *O*. The only solution may be to ignore the problem.

EODEC

2. **STEM WIDTHS SHOULD APPEAR CONSISTENT**
A vertical stem rotated or sheared may appear heavier or lighter than it did in upright position. This is proved by comparing the horizontal strokes of the *E* (in the previous example, just above) with its vertical stem. All strokes in *E* are exactly the same, yet the horizontals appear thicker. To counter this problem, designers of monoweight letterforms make adjustments as needed to keep all strokes looking optically identical.

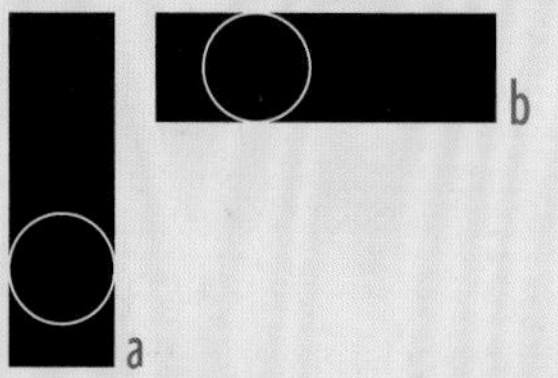

b
a

The vertical stem, a, was copied and rotated 90°. Your eyes do deceive you! The copy, b, now horizontal, appears to have become slightly thicker than the original, but the identical circles prove that both shapes are the same thickness.

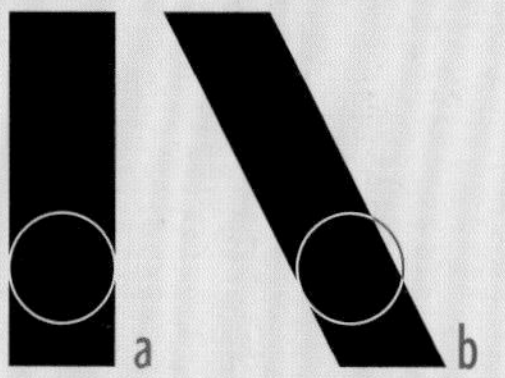

a
b

The vertical stem, a, was copied and sheared (sometimes called "skewed"), b, as we might do to make the diagonal strokes in *A-N-V-W-X,* and so on. Shearing causes the stem to be *actually*—not just optically—narrower than it started out.

a
b

A better way to maintain stem weight is to rotate, not shear, the vertical stem, a, which technically maintains width although there may be a slight illusion of weight gain, b, that would need to be manually adjusted. The illusion becomes more acute when stroke ends are squared off, c.

3. INCREASE STEM WIDTHS ON CURVES TO OPTICALLY MATCH STRAIGHTS

In roman styles, the width of thick vertical stems as in *M-D-E-R,* below, should always remain consistent. But at the maximum stress points of the bowls of *O-D-R,* strokes must be drawn slightly wider than the standard straight vertical width or they will appear to be too narrow. This is because the widest points of curved bowls achieve that full width for only a second, while straight vertical strokes establish full width for a good while.

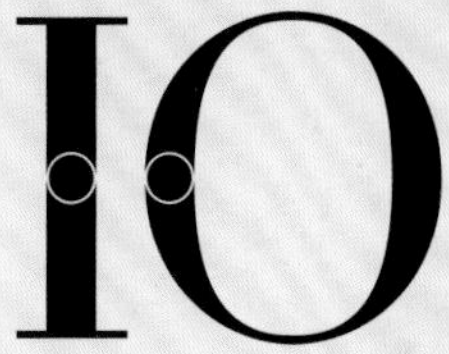
IO

Here, the widest parts of all upright strokes are equal, but *O* appears more slender than *I,* wouldn't you agree?

MODERN

H2Oak

Richard Lipton's Detroit Bodoni, based on Morris Fuller Benton's revival of Bodoni for ATF, is used in the examples above. Note the flawlessness of the rendering, the perfection of weight distribution and the complex logic behind serifs that alternate between square and curved-approach. The *N* at top right is fascinating because the designer brought the diagonal stroke straight past the thin left stem into a square serif without feeling the need to curve the junction.

In designing lettering we usually establish six horizontal guidelines: baseline, cap height, x-height, optical (sometimes called "overshoot") baseline, optical cap height, and optical x-height line. So you're asking, "These optical overshoot guidelines are, what, like 1percent or 2 percent of cap height?" I can't help you. Establishing these tolerances is something one does by eye and by trial and error. We draw *H-O-H* and adjust the height of *O* until it looks the same as *H.* We then base the height of *C-G-Q* and applicable numerals on *O.* We do the same with lowercase letters, establishing first the height that lowercase *o* looks right compared with flat at midheight letters like *i, k,* or *w.*

4. CROSSBARS MUST BE ADJUSTED FOR OPTICAL CENTERING

Standard theory is that a crossbar, such as would appear in *H* or *E,* must be placed slightly above center lest it appear to be drooping below center. Check out most traditional fonts and you will see that this rule has been applied: The crossbars have been placed on or slightly above dead center. The same law usually applies to other letters, like *B-G-K-R-S-X-Y-f-k-t,* depending upon style.

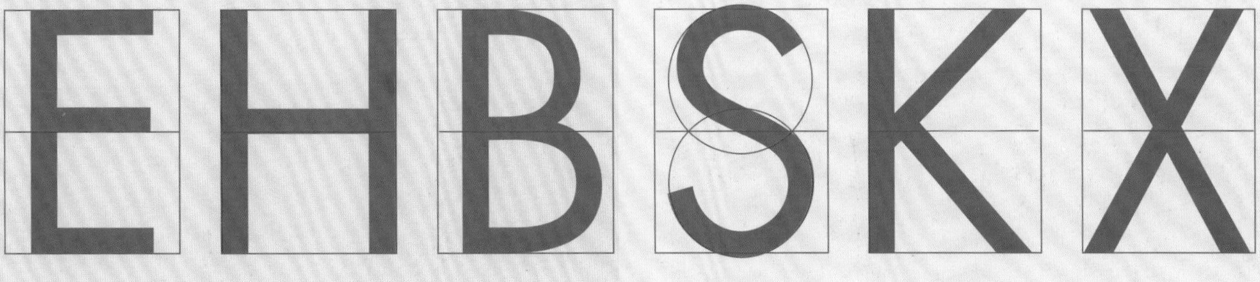
EHBSKX

Above, analysis of letters from the font Futura Book reveals that the optical balance is in all cases above dead cente r. Right, in these letters drawn as examples, the centered crossbar, a, appears too low. When it's placed above center, b, it looks right. Crossbars too high or too low, c and d, look weird. But exceptions to this crossbar rule follow on the next page.

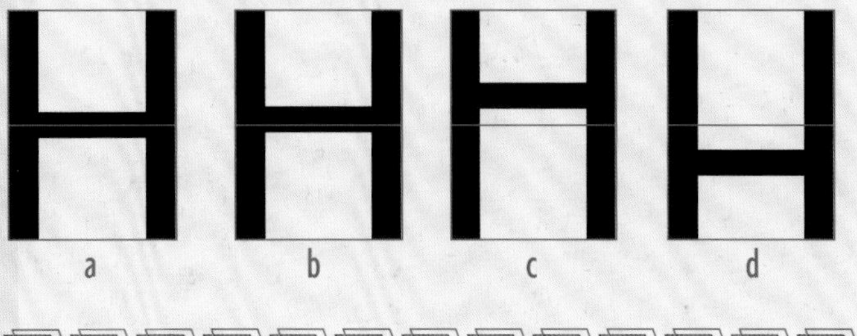
HHHH
a b c d

REVLON PRODUCTS CORPORATION
125 WEST 45th STREET
NEW YORK, N. Y.

But...

The heights of crossbars or horizontal strokes may be purposely drawn higher or lower to achieve a certain effect. A lowered crossbar is often indicative of Art Deco fonts from the 1930s, such as the 1939 Revlon letterhead, above. This hand-drawn and -lettered design is a good example of illustration in harmony with the "color" of the type.

1926 BAKE CHRONICLE

Above, a sample of the font Anna by Daniel Pelavin perfectly captures the essence of the Art Deco style. This very successful typeface marketed by ITC is noted for crossbars lowered to about one-quarter of cap height that reemerge on the left for a streamlined effect. Note how the diagonal stroke of *N* joins the vertical stem only halfway down, in keeping with the crossbars.

SCHRIFTEN ATLAS

Right, typical Art Nouveau lettering adapted from the 1898 *Schriften Atlas* of Julius Hoffmann Verlag. Here, the crossbars have been raised to two-thirds of cap height. This is high enough to leave no mistake that there has been a design decision here, not just an overcompensation for optical droop. The raising of the crossbars has given strong stylistic definition to the entire alphabet. The bowl of *R* and the top of *S* have been raised to match *H-F-E-N,* and *A*. Like the font Anna, this is a monoweight style of letter that doesn't slavishly remain mono. Both styles exhibit subtle variations in line weight, like the flairing stems above, that are typical of their brush- or pen-drawn origins. I don't really like the *S*, above, because the abrupt angle breaks style with the rest.

5. DRAW LETTERS CORRECTLY

DRAW LETTERS CORRECTLY Amateur letterers so often make the following mistakes that I included some of them in BadTyp, right, my font that is a virtual library of commonly misdrawn letterforms. Below, the center strokes of *M* and diagonal stroke of *N* should always extend to the baseline. The center of *W* must reach full cap height, unless all other letters in the style follow suit, as shown in the examples above. The crossbar of *A* should be positioned to balance the upper and lower counters. Otherwise, these characteristics are abominations in a roman alphabet.

AMW

AMWN

Abominable

AMWN

Agreeable

MY FUNNY LETTERFORMS. The order of thick-thin strokes in roman-style lettering results naturally from the use of the flat-edged pen held at a certain angle. When such letters are mimicked by being drawn in outline form, it's easy to confuse thicks for thins. This, of course, looks horrible. Don't guess when drawing roman letters (I always forget which stem of *Y* is the thick one). Pick up a magazine, or anything with type in it, and use that for reference.

AHMNWY

The letters in BadTyp were designed to showcase many flaws, such as incorrect order of thick/thin strokes and inconsistent stem weights. I still shudder to look at these masterpieces!

ZMNVWY

Below, Franklin Gothic Bold and Times Roman from Adobe both display proper order of thick/thin strokes, although the effect is more subtle in heavyweight Franklin Gothic.

ABCDEFGHIJKLMNOPQRSTUVWXYZ

ABCDEFGHIJKLMNOPQRSTUVWXYZ

6. OMIT NEEDLESS SERIFS

As with language usage, errors in letterforms may become standard in time through repetition. A recent phenomenon has been the introduction of the serifed *I* in otherwise sans-serif fonts. I accept blame. BadTyp was one of the first sans-serif fonts to include this anomaly—but I was kidding! The serif *I* in Matthew Carter's Verdana, example below, was a brazen act by a talented designer, though many amateurs have simply failed to comprehend that those horizontal strokes on top and bottom of *I* are indeed serifs, not a part of the letter itself.

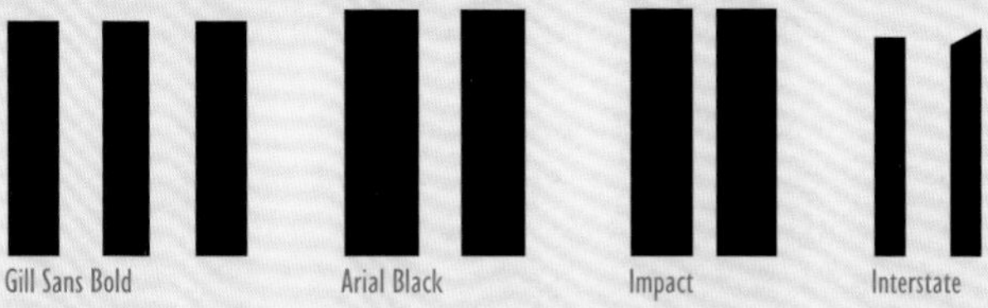

Gill Sans Bold | Arial Black | Impact | Interstate

But... Legibility may be the reason that the serif *I* has become legitimized. Can you identify the above characters? In Gill Sans they are: cap I, lowercase 1 and the number 1. Other examples compare cap I and 1.

INAPPROPRIATE SERIFS R COOL!

Verdana: Microsoft

7. TAKE STEPS TO AVOID CLOG

Achieving a relatively even "color" throughout all letters in a line or in a font is always the goal. Therefore, maintaining equal stroke widths is important to the lettering designer. But of equal concern is how the joining of one stroke to another causes an optical doubling of the stroke weight, unless specific steps are taken to lessen the bulk.

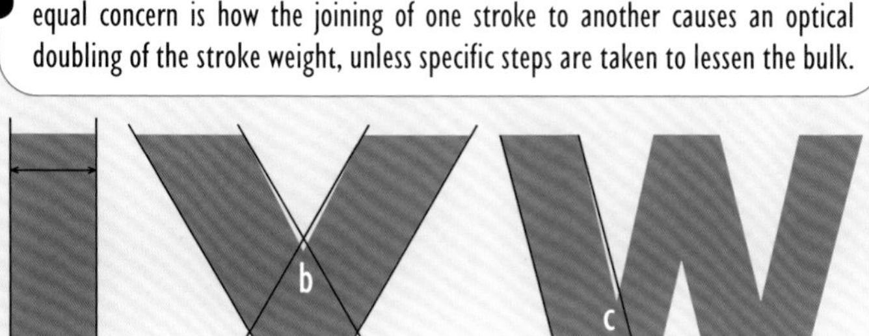
a
b
c

Normally, the opposing sides of a monoweight stem stroke remain parallel for its entire length, a. Both sides of diagonal stems such as *V-W* should also be parallel, yet they may be drawn to taper in width as they conjoin, b and c, in order to minimize their combined girth. This is usually done so slightly as to be hardly discernible to the average man on the street.

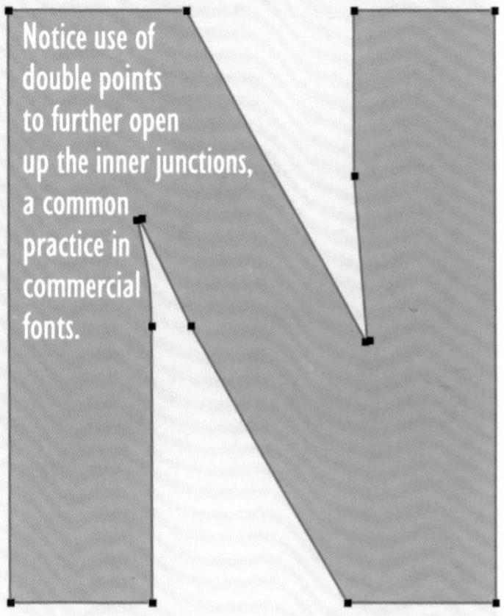
Notice use of double points to further open up the inner junctions, a common practice in commercial fonts.

NA
BM

Matthew Carter's font Bell Centennial Bold, intended for poorly printed telephone books, made clog reduction into a wild, decorative feature.

The *N* above shows an extreme solution to the problems of intersecting strokes and ink clogging up in corners of small characters in print. I would be reluctant to shave letters designed for larger point sizes to this degree, but it is appropriate for small type sizes in print or on the web where such shape distortions would be virtually unnoticeable.

8. BE REGULARLY *Consistent* OR *Consistently* IRREGULAR

NIP INCONSISTENCY AT THE BUD LEVEL

Consistency, rhythm, regularity, evenness of color and (most often) legibility are the qualities necessary for type and lettering to be considered professional. One of my axioms is: *If absolutely every aspect of any piece of lettering were consistent, it still might not be good lettering, but it would be technically beyond reproach.*

But... Inconsistency done with consistency can also be acceptable. The trick is to go just enough off the mark that the result appears intentional, not accidental. A chaotic approach then must be designed so that the appearance of randomness is actually calculatedly harmonious and thus still meets the criteria of what are arguably the most important rules of lettering: Consistency, Regularity and Rhythm.

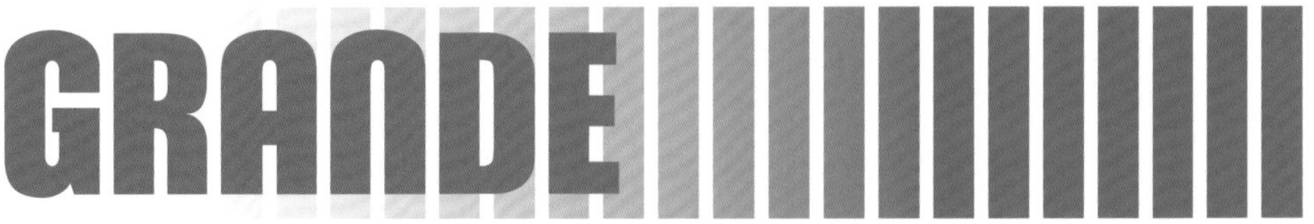
GRANDE

The strokes, interior counters and spaces above are consistent. Regularity is pleasing to the eye, but not all styles allow this level of regimentation. The rest must be made to *appear* this even, through our careful design and spacing of characters.

GRANDE

Above, the erratic inconsistency shown here is disturbing and inexcusable. This is usually the result of simple laziness.

GRANDE

Strokes above are regularly irregular and cannot be mistaken for mistakes. Unifying element: consistent thick/thin strokes.

BERLINS

Type and lettering don't have to be cookie-cutter perfect to be good. David Berlow's Berlin Sans shows some minor inconsistencies (see overlaid letters, above right) yet maintains an even color and rhythm throughout. Also, the flaring strokes are believable: They look as though they really were cut in wood or painted with a brush. This is the "art" of lettering!

Salubra
WALL-COVERING

a
b
c

The 1920s logo above, despite its crude pen inking, has a thrilling rhythm due to almost perfectly consistent stem weights, letter spacing and slant. But something looked funny about it, so I decided to test the veracity of the strokes by quickly reproducing them with a broad-nibbed pen. Normally, if we were designing such a logo, we'd start with the pen, then make our tight drawing of final letterforms based on the information gained by the pen exercise. Aha! I knew that initial *S* didn't quite look right. It doesn't really matter, but my copies of cap *S* prove that the stroke should have narrowed, a and b, as it met the long, straight top stroke. The curious notch at the bottom right corner of the *S* did turn out to be a plausible artifact of the pen, as my sketch at c shows. Hope you don't mind my drawing all over your book.

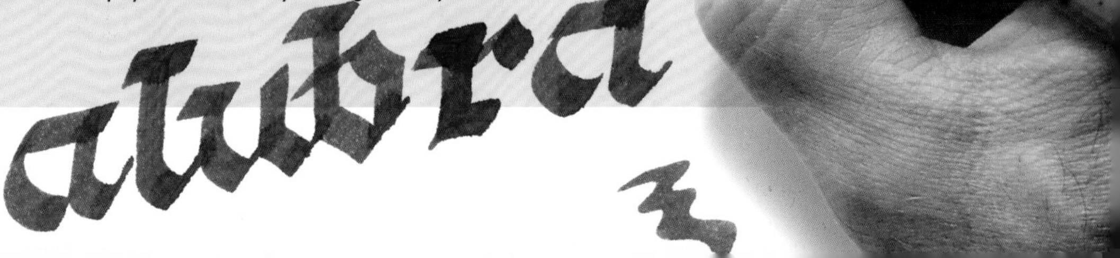
alubra

REPETITION: KEY TO CONSISTENCY

Any idiosyncracy or error in type design, like any lie repeated often enough (as a famous evil person once said), will become regarded as truth—or as acceptable, by virtue of its apparently having been done consciously on purpose. In example a, top right, the one weird *O* is completely out of context in this type style, however, the statement itself makes a statement. In b, a tenuous consistency has been achieved through repetition. In c, the *O* has become established as a legitimate trend through repetitive use. In d, the letter *A* repeats —thereby giving validation to—the style of *O*, and now we may even become convinced that the designer knew what he was doing!

a CONSISTENCY IS SO BORING!

b CONSISTENCY IS SO BORING!

c MOST ANYONE WOULD REGARD THIS ODD "O" AS BEING OUT OF PLACE IN THIS FONT.

d MOST ANYONE WOULD REGARD THIS ODD "O" AS BEING OUT OF PLACE IN THIS FONT.

What is meant by the term "type color?"

The "color of type" has nothing to with CMYK or Pantone. It refers to how approximately dark or light on an imaginary grayscale a column of type, a particular typeface or even an individual letter may appear. The reason we even consider type color usually has to do with an attempt at harmonizing the overall color sense of an entire page layout. Right, type set in Eurostile Medium has a lighter color than the all-caps Eurostile Bold, far right, which looks kind of like the 60% gray halftone in the box below it. In the lower far right example, the gray halftones at bottom show the tonal distribution of the type with unfortunate, though inevitable, "holes" ruining the even type color. Options for helping to eliminate holes are discussed below.

You are now reading body copy, also called text type, set justified in a thin column. Squint at the words so they appear blurry and resemble the tone below.

BOLDER FONT STYLE SQUINTS OUT AT 60%

UNLUCKY COMBINATION

9. THE WORST KERNING PAIR DETERMINES LETTER SPACING

Not all words that we letter or set in type set as compactly as "GRANDE" on the previous page or "MINION" at right. Certain combinations of letters resist a nice, tight set. Solutions include overlapping certain letter pairs where feasible, narrowing troublesome letters, creating ligatures or nipping and tucking letter pairs. In a logo or headline, we can increase the rest of the letter spacing to match the worst gaps.

UNLUCKY
SAVVY MINION

UNLUCKY
SAVVY MINION

At left, words typed with original "factory" kerning that provides general solutions for the average user. Most designers find they have to tweak kerning of headline or display type most of the time.

Here, kerning has been adjusted by increasing all spaces, the foot of *L* has been shortened (first Create Outlines or break apart type—cannot be done in Quark), *K* and *Y* have been overlapped. It's not perfect—the two *V*s look like a *W*—but it's improved.

Below, Caslon is known for having a wide *T* and *L*, two of the very letters that cause big gaps in a setting. Below right, I fixed Caslon's wagon by narrowing the *T* and *L* (also *N* and *E*) and connecting *W-Y-E*, which makes a more cohesive setting.

BOUNTY LAWYER • BOUNTY LAWYER

10. KEEP LETTER SPACING EVEN

Everyone's first instinct when letter spacing is to measure an equal distance between every letter, as in a. No good. Since each letter has a different shape, the amount of space between letters must also be gauged differently. To test the improved spacing in b, we've applied Squint-O-Vision®, c, and found it OK. Many have devised formulas for letter spacing: For instance, the space between *N* and *A* must be one-half or one-third the distance between *N* and *E*. I say, because of the vast variety in lettering styles, that the eye is the best arbiter. Still, once spacing parameters have been established—such as between straight-sided letter *H* and round-sided letter *O*—the same must be consistently applied to *H-C, H-G,* and so on.

a NAVARONE
b NAVARONE
c NAVARONE

A co-worker in a magazine art department once asked me, "How come you guys are always squinting?" Computers for layout weren't in use back then, so it wasn't eyestrain. I explained that by squinting to make our vision blurry, we are able to visualize the gaps and globs in our spacing more clearly.

SECRETS OF LETTER SPACING
Revealed in Startling
SQUINT-O-VISION
INCORRECT
CORRECT

A Argenta
B Argenta
a
b
c
d
e
f
C Argenta
D Argenta

Left, this logo, A, was already trashed on page 11 of the introduction, but now, we have applied the amazing Squint-O-Vision® to help identify spacing and massing issues. In example B, the black masses at a and e stick out as way too heavy; at b and f, incorrectly thin strokes are dropping out altogether; a huge gap at c threatens to separate the one word into two; letters *e-n* are in danger of merging into one ugly mass at d. Example C shows my excellent font Casey Ultrabold, which passes the squint test, in example D, with flying letters. Perhaps there could have been a tad more space between *e* and *n*, but had I lengthened the connecting stroke of *e*, the base curve would have ceased to match the others. Quite often, the design of letterforms in a font involves trade-offs.

HOHIHOH
a OIHVAHIO b
HOHIHOH

Above, an issue related to letterspacing involves the flush alignment of letters in columns. At a, the left edge of *O* has been placed flush with the letters *H* above and below, making it appear to be indented. This ruins the nice, continuous edge we wanted. At b, the *O* has been positioned slightly beyond the two *H*s, so it appears to be optically aligned—as Squint-O-Vision® proves. It is for this same reason that designers often "hang punctuation" like quotes just beyond the vertical boundaries of a column measure.

Think of the spaces between letters as solid areas that should all be roughly equal in size. As a test, I tried filling each space between the letters, right, with 160 circles. I used the space between two vertical letters, a, as the "control," although only 152 circles fit there. At b, we are reminded that sometimes there's no avoiding large spacing gaps. At c, the resulting spacing looks decent.

a b

II LAVATORY
II LAVATORY

c

Not all the spacing we do is on basic fonts like Helvetica or Caslon. At d, a sample of my font Saber to which few rules of spacing, except the rule of the eye, can be applied.

d

Rivendell Valley

But... When spacing lettering that is rigidly mechanical, do we maintain the same, uniform space between all letters to match the counters within the letters, as in **a**, or should we space visually, as in **b**, to compensate for visual gaps or inlets that occur in certain letters like *C, S, E, L* and *T* that don't have nice straight sides like *H* and *I*? Just play it by ear. Note how *S* connects with *E* and *L* yet retains legibility (I think).

a

b

CHISEL TOOLS
CHISEL TOOLS

What is meant by the term "Flush left?"

The examples below should clear up any lingering confusion regarding this difficult subject. *Flush left, ragged right* simply means that all the type in a column will line up straight against an imaginary boundary on the left side, a, and as many words as fit will be set within the given column width. Then the process begins anew on the next line down. The result is an uneven—or *ragged*—right boundary. Example b demonstrates flush right, ragged left, in which the alignment is at the right edge of the column, leaving a ragged or bumpy left boundary line. A ragged edge should undulate, rather than some lines sticking way out beyond others. That's why we refer to a "good rag" or a "bad rag." Hyphenating words can give us smoother rags, but try to avoid it. One of the reasons we may choose to flush type is to not have to hyphenate words, which is considered an obstacle to easy reading.

a

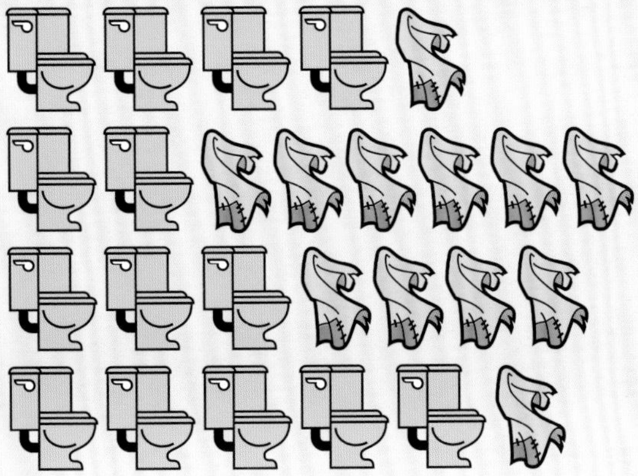

b

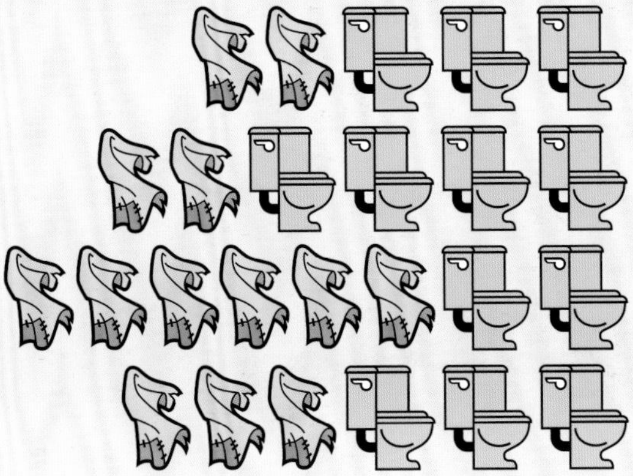

This is flush-left, ragged-right type set in a column. It is all right to let a few words be hyphen- ated if you must.

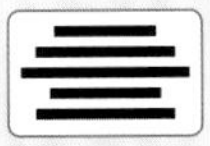

This type is centered within the column width. It's sometimes a good way to present long lists of items.

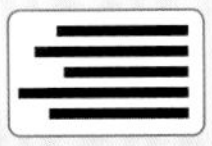

This is flush-right, ragged-left type that some say is hard for the eye to follow as it jumps down to the next line.

This is "justified full lines," which stinks in a thin column like this because big gaps—yes, I said gaps—can develop.

Example of "justified all lines," which has the same problem as the previous style, so it must be carefully written to fit just so.

11. BREAK LINES OF TYPE AT PROPITIOUS PLACES

This is not only a visual issue, but also one that affects readability. It can sometimes be extremely difficult to create good "rags," and we are forced to accept whatever is the best we can achieve, given the copy. Throughout this book, the copy has been changed to effect better rags, breaks, and to avoid gaps and rivers in text (for example, in the fourth line down, I replaced the word *very* with the word *extremely* because it filled up the gaps in the line). The trick, as when writing poetry, is to avoid compromising meaning or intent for the sake of the break—or the rhyme. Of course, much of this book is a "do as I say, not as I do" situation, as often it's been the case that exigency (deadline) has forced me to let my caption type fall where it may for better or worse.

We lose
our freedoms
at the altar
of fear

‡ Kahlil Gibran

Above, the line breaks work out fortunately ideal, making a nice silhouette. Dwiggins cautioned us to not try to make type wrap exactly in a vase like shape—too corny—but I think he'd agree that the shape shouldn't be awkward like above right.

We
lose our freedoms
at the
altar of fear

‡ Kahlil Gibran

Yes, this is certainly ugly. However, in our efforts to create pleasing shapes, we must avoid breaking phrases in unnatural ways thereby sacrificing legibility. By the way, I couldn't source the Gibran quote, but it's a timely statement, in any event.

We hold
these truths to
be self-evident

Above, the decisions as to line breaks in this centered type have resulted in awkward phrasing and a funny, hat-shaped silhouette.

We hold these
truths to
be self-evident

The silhouette here is slightly hokey, but better than the first example. However, the line break separating *to* and *be* is awkward.

We hold
these truths to be
self-evident

This silhouette is not only the best of the three, but the line breaks, fortunately, have fallen into a more natural phrasing pattern.

12. DON'T USE EXPANDED LETTER SPACING INDISCRIMINATELY

Because it's easily done, we are tempted to space letters absurdly wide. If used carefully, this can add a decorative touch, or it can make our work look amateurish and become harder to read. Words set in lowercase, above right, a, are best not widely spaced. Scripts, as in b and c, should not be letter-spaced, because it breaks apart the connecting ligatures. During the Art Deco period, it was popular to design type and lettering with expanded spacing, as shown in example d.

a S i l v e r   S h a d o w

b *S i l v e r   S h a d o w*

c ***S i l v e r   S h a d o w***

d S I L V E R   S H A D O W

S i l v e r   S h a d o w

But... Above is a treatment that I kinda like. The spaced-out script with an offset drop shadow seems more interesting and less haphazard than in its plain incarnation above at c. Perhaps that's because it appears as if thought went into it and that it was done on purpose, rather than ignorantly. When it comes to immutable laws, context is everything. Right, alternating tight and widely spaced lettering within a column was a 1930s shtick, used in posters and sheet music covers.

D E C O
TECHNIQUE
T Y P E
TREATMENT
W I D E

Above, what do the words say? Who knows! But with initial caps followed by lowercase, you'd know.

13. DON'T USE ALL CAPS WITH CERTAIN FACES

Setting words all in capital letters is frowned upon when done with certain fonts and lettering styles. Sometimes it's because the swashes or flourishing strokes bump or overlap, but usually it's because legibility suffers. Remember that context often provides legibility when the design of a face has certain confusing letters that are either too alike or poorly designed. Script fonts, especially, may have capital letters that are hard to read and whose legibility depends very much on context.

But... If Will Dwiggins does it, it's OK, see? At least we have this example of all script caps, right, from his Electra type prospectus to go by. I don't even like it—for the very same reason I said not to do it—but if he did it, it *must* be all right!

ELECTRA

14. STRIVE FOR COLOR HARMONY BETWEEN WORDS AND TEXT

The rule of achieving an even color of letters within a single logo or font should extend further to the entire printed page and the design of a web site. There should be harmony between the color and the feeling of the art and type. At least, that's the ideal. Illustrator Elliot Banfield once told me he believed that the thinnest strokes of the smallest point type on a page should match the thinnest strokes in any accompanying artwork. That would seem to apply to the 1950s business card a, top left, where colors—all in a related key—contribute to this well-integrated design. When both the lettering and illustration are made with the same tool, as in card b, it becomes easier to achieve harmony. The small letterpress type in this card has clogged up, causing it, inadvertently, to match the rest. In card c, the strokes of the sketchy illustration seem consistent with the stroke weights of the chosen font, helped along by a warm gray printing ink that marries all elements of the card by the noted designer George Samerjan.

a

GRELLER · SIEGEL · D'AVANZO ASSOCIATES
G&S&D
150 E. 56, NEW YORK 22, N.Y. · PLAZA 3-6220

b

greta plattry
SPORTS WEAR

c

80 west fortieth street, new york 18, n. y., longacre 4-7257
designer
art director
consultant
GEORGE SAMERJAN

S
⌘

THOU SHALT SAVE OFTEN 15.

This is not exactly a rule of lettering, but it is most important for those of us doing computer lettering. Take it from one who has too often had to redo lost work. Hit Save (⌘-S) frequently, especially after completing any distinct portion of a task. Save your work before you: use Create Outlines (corrupted fonts can crash Illustrator); open any other program; go to print; go to lunch, etc. Above, this is the universal symbol for saving work, which I just invented.

16.

BOLD MONOWEIGHT LETTERS REQUIRE ADJUSTMENTS

When drawing black, bold, heavy or fat letters, we must minimize the optical weight gain, and assure ample "clearance," when two strokes conjoin, such as the bowls of *a-b-d-g* with their vertical stems.

6 Cool Ways to Join Bowls to Stems:

The NOTCH In Franklin Gothic Heavy, the stem bottom has been carved away to create a relief, and the top of the bowl tapers severely as it meets the vertical stem.

The PLUNGE Vertical stem bottoms of *b* and *d* from Kobalt Bold were lowered to provide clearance from the bowls. Counters encroach upon the stems to mitigate telltale weight gain.

The NICK **The SWOOP** **The MEET**

These approaches are but some of the possible solutions to this problem. The methods by which such issues are handled may become significant defining characteristics of a style.

The BOUNCE

The round part, or "bowl" of this medium-weight letter *a* above connects neatly to the vertical stem with ample and clearly defined approaches or reliefs (arrow).

The bowl of this bold-weight letter leaves such piddling reliefs as it grows away from the stem that in small point sizes, these areas will probably "read" as eye dirt.

To maintain adequate reliefs, you might try to move the bowl away from the stem, but that leaves a fat mass on the right side of *a* that will disrupt the even color of our alphabet.

a
b

A solution: Move the center axis of the bowl, a, a bit to the left and taper the strokes as they connect to the stem. Also, move the counter slightly into the vertical stem, b, to reduce optical weight gain there.

Lowercase *a* from Futura Bold, above, demonstrates the principles just described. Futura started out as a monoweight concept, but employed these inevitable, putzy compromises as style weights increased.

Neato solutions like this have often resulted from a desire to maintain a consistent, monoweight stroke width while avoiding the bowl-connecting problems discussed here.

1. 2. 3.

Handling the overweight *e*: (1.) Medium-weight *e*, with ample counters, poses no problems. (2.) Heavy stroke *e*, before tweaking, looks clunky and "nosey." The tiny counters that may close up at small point sizes, are exacerbated by the optical illusion that makes horizontal strokes, like this crossbar, appear even thicker than the stroke overall. (3.) Appropriate tweaking done. All horizontal parts of strokes have been thinned down to open up counters. Also, the terminus of the bottom stroke has been altered to better balance the top. The only problem is that we no longer have a true monoweight form.

Here's the bottom line on drawing heavy, monoweight lettering styles: Check, before determining your stroke width, that you can stack three horizontal strokes atop one another, as in *E*, without the strokes touching...unless you're willing to slim down the center crossbar or apply any of the fancy fixes, right. Remember, if you do choose a diamond center, be consistent and do the same to other applicable letters.

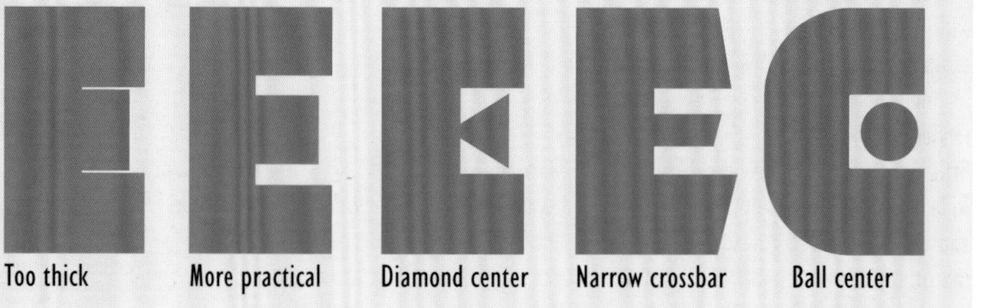

Too thick | More practical | Diamond center | Narrow crossbar | Ball center

THIN | SOMEWHERE IN BETWEEN | FAT

IJ ABCDERSZ MW

IJ ABCDERSZ MW

Above, letter widths are like society in general. You've got your poor and narrow characters on one end of the scale, your rich and wide characters on the other end, but the middle class is always most numerous.

abceghou

abceghou

Left, working outward from counter widths is a good way to gauge overall letter widths. As this example shows, all the counters are relatively equal and since the stroke widths are consistent, too, the result is a nicely balanced effect. Well-shaped counters also indicate well-drawn letters.

HBE

Which of the three letters, *H, B,* or *E* is the widest? To my eye, *E* is the winner, or perhaps *B*, but the equal-size gray boxes in the background prove that E is actually the narrowest of the lot. Bear in mind that the horizontal thrust of letters like *E-B-F* creates an illusion of width that we must cut back to match other letter widths.

17. KEEP LETTER WIDTHS BALANCED AND CONSISTENT

It is not only the widths of spaces between letters that we must consider, but the widths of each individual letter and its relationship to the others within a given style. Once a set of width parameters is established, they should be applied to every alike-shaped letter with as much consistency as we apply aspects such as stroke width or style of serif.

All styles of lettering and type will have their own rules, but generally, there are three basic letter widths in any style: narrow like *i-j-l-t,* wide like *m-w,* and in-between like all the rest. Determining widths of letters is just like spacing, kerning and everything else we do in lettering: Stand back, squint to check for open gaps and closed-up spots, or anything else that sticks out like a sore *T*. Then fix it!

But... Letter widths can also become playthings. Alternating narrow and wide letter widths was a feature of some 1930s lettering styles that I evoked in my font Ojaio Light, right. The font contains alternate narrow characters for *A-E-N-O-U-Y* to break up any places where too many wide characters might occur concurrently in a word.

HOLISTIC THERAPIES
FOR NATURAL HEALTH

What is a "monospaced" font?

Monospaced letter styles are those in which each letter is of uniform width within a generous, uniform space because kerning is undesirable or not possible, such as on the web. The classic example is the font Courier, or the old-fashioned typewriter styles where kerning couldn't even have been considered.

omei

No one would purposely assign equal widths to letters, as in the Courier example above, unless the font needed to be monospaced. Obviously, *o-e* look extended, while *m* looks condensed with silly little serifs and *i* looks absurd with its wide bottom serif. Apply the squint test, and the color difference between *m* and the other letters becomes glaringly clear.

THIS FONT IS COURIER, WHICH MY MAC WON'T LET ME REMOVE. Notice how the apostrophe, comma and period occupy the same width as the *O, M & W*.

IMAGEDOG

License-plate lettering is always monospaced—and condensed (shudder!). I just went outside to copy license plates and then drew the above. They put serifs on the *I* to fill the width; the center point of *M* doesn't reach bottom to give air to what would otherwise be impossibly crowded; the *A* looks pinched; the full-width *E* looks way too wide; and the *D* got serifs so it wouldn't look like an *O*. What machinations we go through when we go monospaced!

18. PLAN THE PLACEMENT OF ALL ELEMENTS WITHIN A DESIGN

Poorly juxtaposed letters and shapes in a logo, lettering design—or any kind of illustration, for that matter—can hurt legibility, contribute to a cluttered feeling and sometimes produce unintentionally ludicrous results. Right, the red rule heading into the nose in the MEP logo is an example of poor placement. The other circled areas are those in which elements have been carelessly placed, resulting in what I call eye dirt: tiny slivers of shapes sticking out where they shouldn't, being neither here nor there. Below right, the logo has been rearranged to eliminate poor juxtapositions and eye dirt.

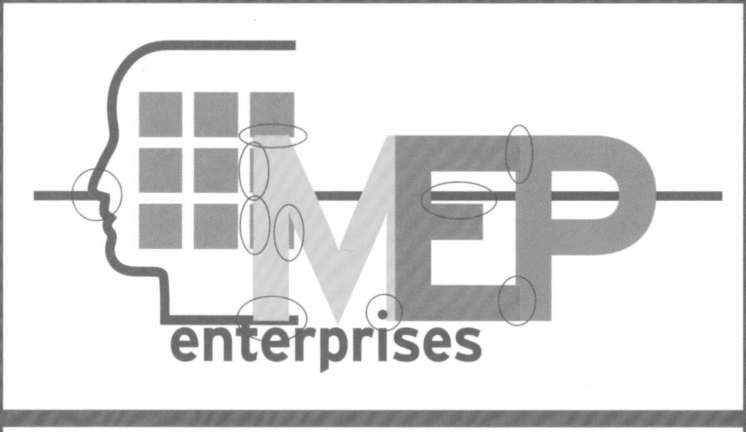
MEP
enterprises

MEP
enterprises

Opposite page, an elaboration of an Emily Brontë quote in highly unruly calligraphy by Rick Cusick. I have featured it here to point out that in 95 percent of instances, Cusick's flourishing strokes that cross over other parts of letters do so at the most astonishingly optimal junctures making it a textbook example of the purposeful arrangement and composition of these abstract forms we call letters. The ideal point, it seems, at which one shape should intersect another is right through the center, or at least far enough from the edges that the two strokes don't visually run together.

a

Stars

b

Stars

In this restaurant logo design, above at a, stars are thoughtlessly placed. Some of the stars badly intersect with the type, causing eye dirt. There are clumped areas of stars and neglected, open areas. The resulting odd silhouette is an important clue that something here is rotten. Any true designer seeing this logo on a menu would lose his appetite. In example b, spacing is random yet even. Several groupings have been created, but they're not clumped. No star lines up with any other. Here we're not reminded of measles, we just think, "Oh, stars," and go right on eating our burgers.

19. COMMIT RANDOM ACTS OF DESIGNEDNESS

In real life, stars clump in the sky and telephone poles may appear to stick out of a person's head as she walks down a street, but our eyes accept all this without question. In pictures, however, we must carefully create the effect of randomness so it does not appear cacaphonous. We do this by placing elements evenly apart yet not obviously so. We create patterns of light and dark areas that seem random, yet none are more light or dark than any others (unless we wish to call attention to a certain area of the picture). In other words, we should create even patterns of groupings.

20. KEEP PARTS OF A DESIGN AT SIMILAR FOCAL RANGE

It's so easy to reduce and enlarge our work to any degree. But bear in mind that all the elements in a logo or design should be comprehensible at one glance without forcing us to move in closer to see a part of it. This is important from a legibility standpoint, but also because combining elements that vary too greatly in line density wrecks the consistent color of a piece. Right, I've drawn this logo to show how badly mismatched are the bold lettering with the fine-line stock illustration.

MOONBEAM
Memories

And this
shall be
my dream
to-night…
I'll think the heaven of glorious spheres,
Is rolling on its course of light,
In endless bliss through endless years.
EMILY BRONTË

The PROBLEM with HORIZONTAL Scale

21. NEVER HORIZONTALLY SCALE TYPE. . .VERY MUCH Having the ability to horizontally scale type is like owning a handgun. Sooner or later you're going to use it—usually with disastrous results. For one thing, there's the oft-mentioned concern that horizontal scaling of a font destroys its creator's intent—which is not so important, because, after all, we got the font free off the Internet and that means it's ours to tweak as we wish. But the main thing is that condensing type by horizontal scaling looks really bad. Forgetting about what it does to letter shapes for a moment, letter spacing decreases proportionately when type is condensed and becomes too large when type is expanded. Instead of using horizontal scale to force a font to fit within a certain measure, it's better to choose an appropriate-width font to start.

STOP

The reason we are always being told to avoid condensing type by horizontally scaling it is that the thick/thin relationship of stroke weights common to a majority of fonts becomes deranged or even reversed and, if excessively done, serifs become thick compared to vertical stems and our type starts looking like the old circus poster typeface, P. T. Barnum.

BARNUM FEAR

One of the problems with expanded letters is a corruption of the curves and angles comprising the letterforms. Above left, the original *a* with its perfect circle corners, and right, the expanded letter with really bad-looking curved corners. Below, the original *S* and expanded version from Kuenstler Script shows

how curves can become crummy when widened.

ERAS

Arial Italic, left, is a monoweight font, so all strokes and stems are about the same width.

ERAS

When Arial Italic is expanded, above, the vertical stems now mimic roman thick/thin letter styles, yet *A* with both of its side strokes wide, instead of just the right stem, and *S*, with its narrow—instead of wide—center stroke, make the resulting font into a bastard. Note also that expansion makes the slant of the letters more acute. When this font is condensed, right, it starts taking on that Barnum problem mentioned above.

ERAS

VIRTUALLY USELESS

USEFUL VIRTUES

I like the font Mekanik Plain OK, but I prefer it after it's been horizontally scaled to as much as 180%. If the scaling is done while in the Adobe Illustrator Character pallet (before we Create Outlines), we should set tracking to way minus to close up the large letter spacing that results from such expansion. To close up tracking manually, after we've Created Outlines, select all the letters except the first. Hit Left Arrow key, say, three times, then deselect the second letter, hit the Arrow key again thrice to move remaining letters over. Continue until done.

But... I always seem to like a bit of horizontal scaling when it is used to expand the width of lettering. To me, it has a unifying effect. Now, all the letters thus expanded, no matter their inconsistencies, at least share this one consistent aspect: They are all too wide. In *Creative Illustration*, 1947, Andrew Loomis explained that mixing a bit of one color into all the others used in a painting "produces an influence on all the colors, drawing them into relationship and harmony." I believe that horizontal scaling wide does the same thing for type.

22. FIND COMMON ALIGNMENTS FOR DESIGN ELEMENTS

Whenever possible, align design elements such as photos, illustrations, columns of text type and headline type to tighten up your work and avoid chaos and clutter. That was the general idea behind the recently popular "grid" craze, but it's always been a guiding principle of design. Left, my very busy layout on the opposite page is shown reduced and with dashed lines to show all the various elements that were lined up.

But... Not everything in a design needs to line up with everything else—that would be really rigid. So do two things: Make elements *enough* unaligned so that the arrangement looks intentional, not just sloppy, and next, compose a dynamic, asymmetrical balance.

Too sloppy Too neat Just right

23. GROUP, DON'T SCATTER TYPE

Right, a is the kind of typographic layout one sees far too often, where the designer has attempted to fill all available space on the page. There's a certain logic to this, after all, and many amateur designers assume that's the goal, but the result is chaos, not good design. In example b, groupings have been created that organize the layout and focus the eye. The number of fonts was reduced from five to three. Also, a concept has been added, with the terrible and ironically named Patriot missile used here, in keeping with the sponsor's motto, for the peaceful purpose of drawing letters.

TYPOGRAPHERS FOR PEACE
invites you to a
PEACE &
LETTERING
R A L L Y
Tonight at
Bodoni Hall 6:00 PM
OUR MOTTO: MAKE TYPE, NOT WAR

a

TYPOGRAPHERS for PEACE
invites you to a
PEACE &
LETTERING
Rally
abc
Tonight at
Bodoni Hall
6:00 PM
Our Motto: Make Type Not War

b

TYPE
KING
SPOT
KING

a b

RACIAL
PROFILE

c

24. ASK WHY

When I was just a fledgling assistant designer under Roger Black, he looked at a page layout I'd done one day and asked me the question, "Why?" He wanted to know why I'd prettified a design beyond the point of function, which in this case meant communication. I responded, "'Cause it looks good." He wasn't buying. There are designers out there who can write a dissertation on the purpose of every dot they place in a layout. I don't go that far, but the lesson Roger taught me was to have a pretty good reason for everything I do (in case I have to defend it). Often, we will use some abstract or decorative elements in our designs that don't require justification—we do it just *because*—but it's always preferable to consider the rationale behind our work and ask ourselves "Why?"

Recently, I saw an ad that looked something like a, above left, with a cool reverse effect in the center of the type. But why did the designer place a meaningless shape there? If the copy had read "Spot King," b, we could say, "Oh, that's a *spot*." Now, if the copy happened to read as it does in c, then there'd be a good reason for using a reversed-out spot effect as the concept.

25. DON'T GO VANISHINGLY SMALL

Increasingly, designers are going real diminutive with type. This is because we lose our sense of scale when designing on computers that give us the ability to view our work at 1200% enlargement so 6-point type looks to us like 72-point. Legibility has as much to do with the point size as with the design of type. Make printouts of your work to find out if it can be read without using a magnifying glass.

ADOBE ILLUSTRATOR BASICS

Most of us never learn more than 40 percent of the functionality of our most-used computer applications. The other 60 percent tends to be techy stuff, silly filters and gimmicks, anyway. The instructions in this book are designed for the reader already 40 percent familiar with Adobe Illustrator. But just in case, the following is a brief refresher course with emphasis on some of the finer points frequently glossed over in manuals. This section does not comprise a complete course. It assumes that you are using Illustrator mainly to set type, tweak type and draw letters, toward the goal of designing logos and fonts. Other essential skills, such as use of the Pen tool, are covered elsewhere in this book. These lessons are written for Mac users, but, except for a few details like key combinations, they apply equally to Windows users.

FIRST, LET'S MEET The GANG

CLICKO

The Selection Tool is his Latin name, but we mostly call him the Black Arrow (or "Clicko" the moniker that he himself prefers). With but one click, Clicko will solid-select all an object's points or many objects that have been grouped.

POINTY

She answers to the Direct Selection Tool, or just the White Arrow, but we call her "Pointy" (AKA "Beziella"). She's the most versatile of the arrow tools. Choose Pointy to select one, some, or all the points in an object or a path.

SHIFT
OPTION

SHIFTY & OP

Formerly part of an a cappella group called the Off Keys, Shifty and Op help Clicko and Pointy add selections and make copies. While depressed, Op gives Pointy the same function as Clicko, so my feeling is, arrivederci, Clicko!

MARKY MARQUEE

He is a prime mover in the Selective Services department. Pointy drags him out of hiding so Marky can select one or more individual points on a path or object, or many paths and objects at once, not necessarily selecting them all.

The COMMANDER

The Commander, chairman of the keyboard, is essential for temporarily toggling back to Clicko or Pointy while using such pals as "Pennis" the Pen tool, "Brushé" the Brush tool, "Abeycee" the Type tool, or "Biggo" the Scale tool.

TYPE and CREATE OUTLINES

Ri

Choose the Type tool and click anywhere on the page to set some type. The blue point to the left of the underline tells us that this type is flush left, which is the default paragraph alignment. You can now choose to Align Center, Align Right, or Justify, if you wish.

Ri

Assuming you'll want to work with the type to edit the letterforms or add an effect, such as a drop shadow, it is advisable to save a copy. Hold down the Option key as you drag a copy away from your working area. Later, you may need this copy if changes or additions to the text are required.

Ri

Unless we're doing a very simple logo, we almost always make type into editable objects. Select type and go to TYPE>Create Outlines (⇧-⌘-0). The paths and points you now see are exactly those drawn by the designer of the font. FYI, the placement of all anchor and bezier points in the example above happens to be ideal.

Ri

So far, we've been working in the Outline View mode, so the fill color of the type is not visible. Above, the type has been deselected (by clicking on any blank area of the page) so the points no longer show. Note, when type is made into outlines, the letters become "objects," no different from any other closed paths or shapes.

MAKING SELECTIONS

With the White Arrow tool, we can select all points by dragging a marquee completely around all letters. Begin the marquee at any corner, provided the start of our drag is well beyond all the objects' points. Look, I messed up. I didn't start my marquee high enough and missed a point.

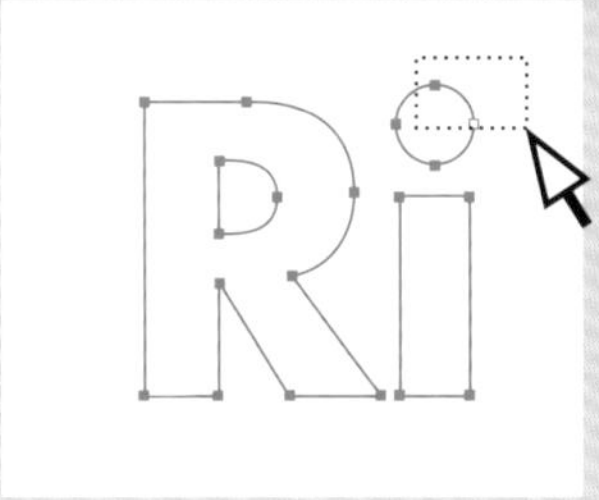

Hold down the Shift key and marquee the neglected point, or just click on it, also with the Shift key depressed. Darn it, I marqueed too deep and accidentally included the 3 o'clock point. See, the Shift key lets us select an unselected point (or points) or deselect ones that are already selected.

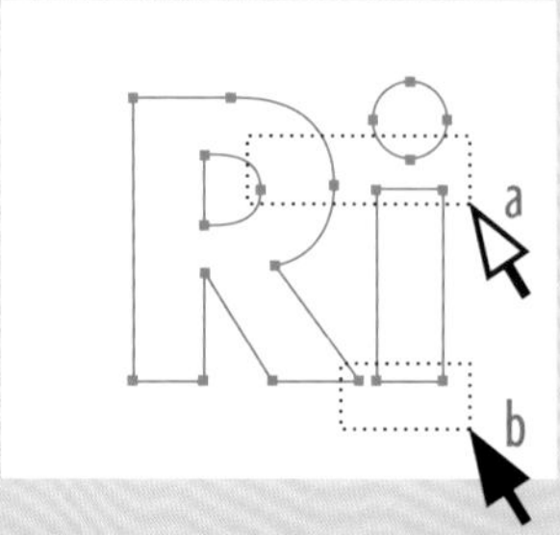
a
b

Another way to solid-select all points in a bunch of objects: Press the Option key while dragging a marquee so it touches some part of every path or object we want to select (a). If we use the Black Arrow tool to select all, don't press Option and marquee only one portion of each letter (b).

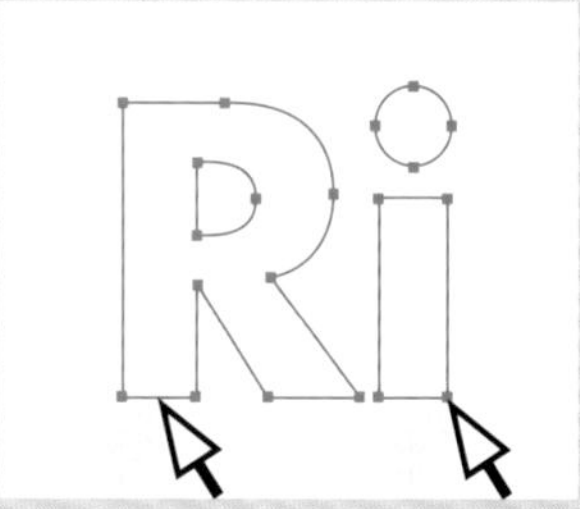

The marquee is, of course, only one way to select points. With the White Arrow tool, hold down Option and click either a path segment or a point to select all, like the *i* and its dot or the *R* and its hole. Two, three or more clicks will select entire groups and the subgroups within them.

When we switch our view to Preview mode (⌘-Y), as imitated above, we can see our objects filled and/or stroked with the colors we've assigned. In Preview mode, we can fully select objects or groups by clicking anywhere within the fill with either the Black or White Arrow tools.

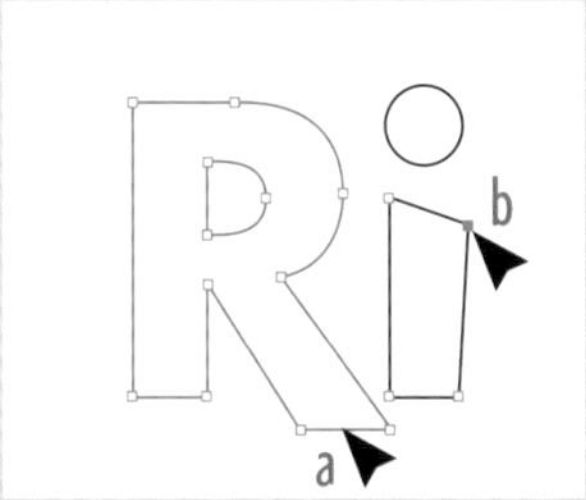
b
a

With the White Arrow, click a line segment between two points (a). Though all points remain hollow-selected, we can still drag the line segment as we like (White Arrow turns to black pointer when it drags). Or click a specific point (b) to drag it alone.

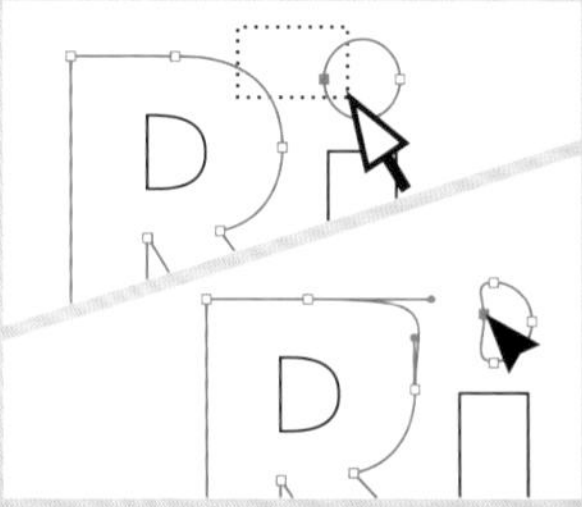

Here's something to watch out for: If we make a marquee around a single point, or even a bunch of them, but the marquee unintentionally crosses over a line segment, when we drag the points, the segment will move also. After a while, we learn to become very precise in drawing marquees.

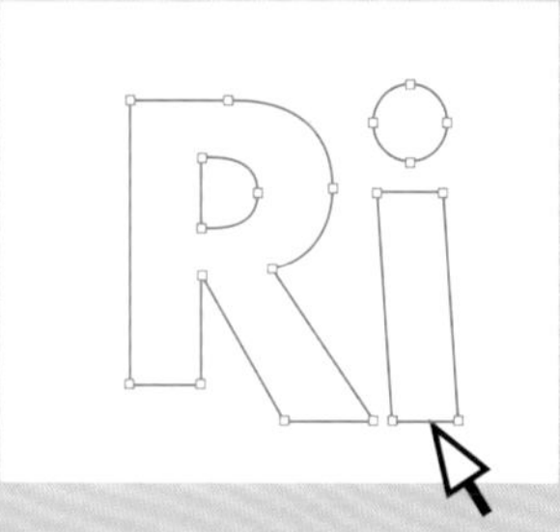

When we want to select several line segments to move them all at the same time, just click on each of the segments—not the points—one after another. Dragging any one of them will move all the line segments.

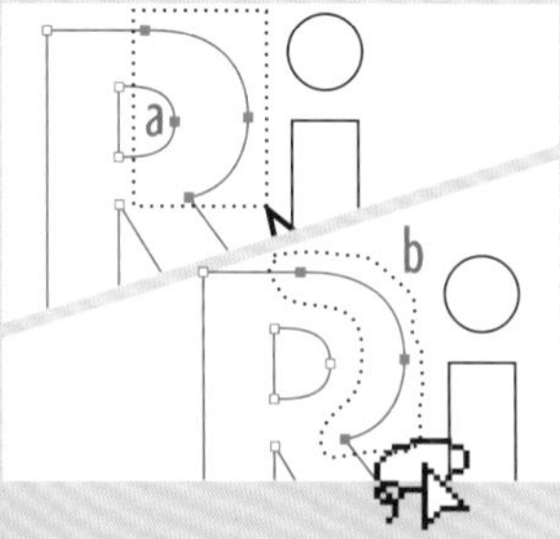
a
b

Often, we want to select the points in a certain area, but the rectangular-shaped marquee can't avoid touching on points we don't want selected. So marquee the desired points, then hold down Shift and click to deselect points, like a, that were unscheduled for selection. Or use the white Lasso tool to draw a more precise selection, b.

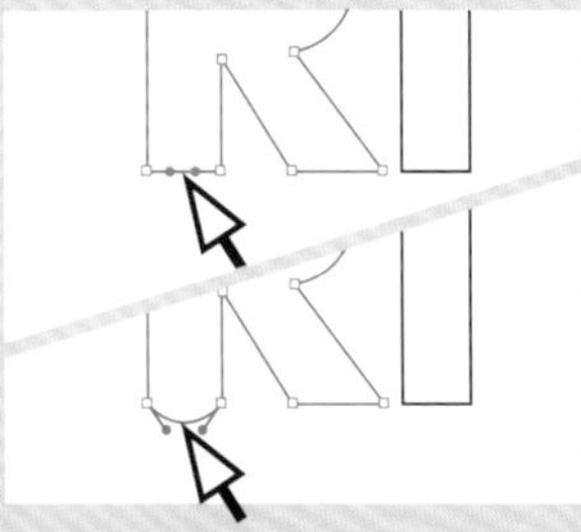

If we click on a path segment between two points whose bezier handles are extended, the path will not drag, it'll bulge. A straight path, as above, shouldn't have bezier handles, but it happens! So drag the handles back into the point (I'm never sure if they're completely in) or just click them with the Convert Anchor Point tool.

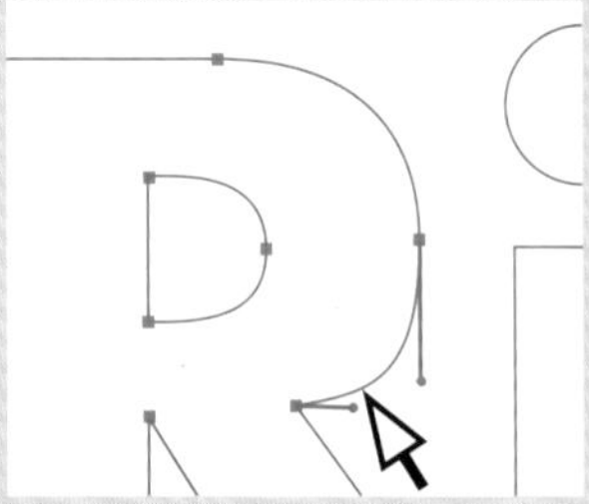

We can purposely drag a path segment between two bezier points to alter the curve. The drag doesn't have to start from the exact center. The spot you drag from—say, nearer to one point than the other—will affect the outcome of the curve. Editing curves this way has never worked for me. Try it, you may find otherwise.

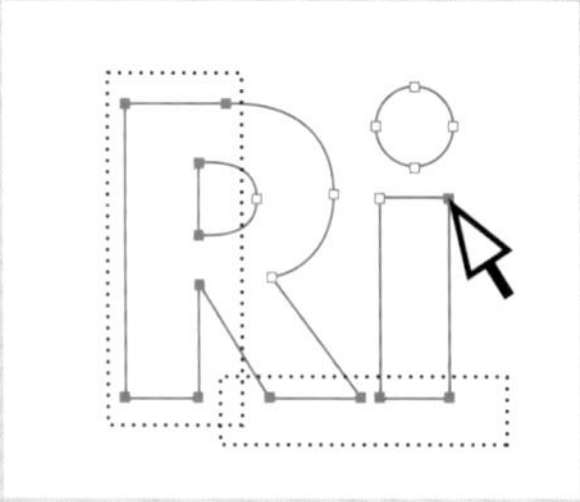

To close this selection lesson, the simplest, though not the fastest, way to make selections is to just click on each point we want and not on the others. The more efficient way is to marquee all marqeeable points, then continue with direct point selection, one at a time, using the Shift key to add and subtract points as necessary.

GROUPING and UNGROUPING

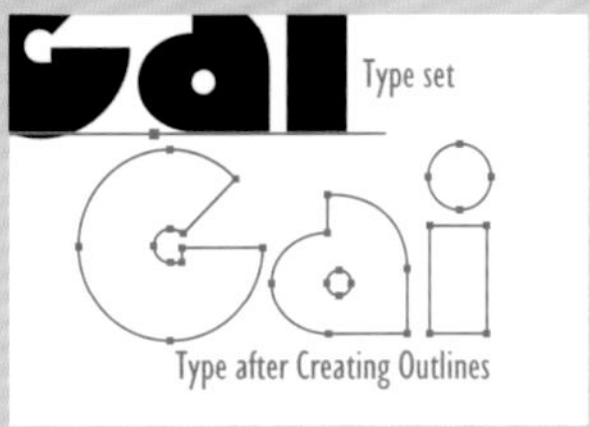
Type set
Type after Creating Outlines

When we set type with the Type tool and then Create Outlines (⇧-⌘-0), all the letters we typed automatically emerge as a unit called a "Group." This makes it easy to select them all with one click of the Black Arrow or an Option-double-click with the White Arrow.

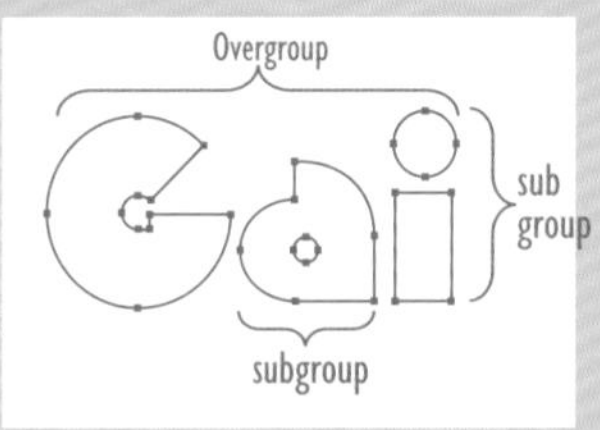
Overgroup
sub
group
subgroup

Within the larger Group, comprising all the letters thus liberated, are the individual letters whose parts, such as the closed paths of the dot over *i* and the holes or "counters" in such letters as *a*, are also Grouped. If we click with the Black Arrow just one point or one line segment of this overgroup, the whole deal will become solid-selected. With the White Arrow, we'd have to hold the Option key and double-click to select it all.

We have said that type and its component parts come automatically grouped. But we can also create Groups of our own, or Ungroup any groupings we don't want grouped. Say we want to make the logo above, with the nifty just-added top and bottom rails, into a Group. We'd marquee the works and go to OBJECT>Group (or ⌘-G). Now we've created an even larger overgroup containing the original type plus the rails.

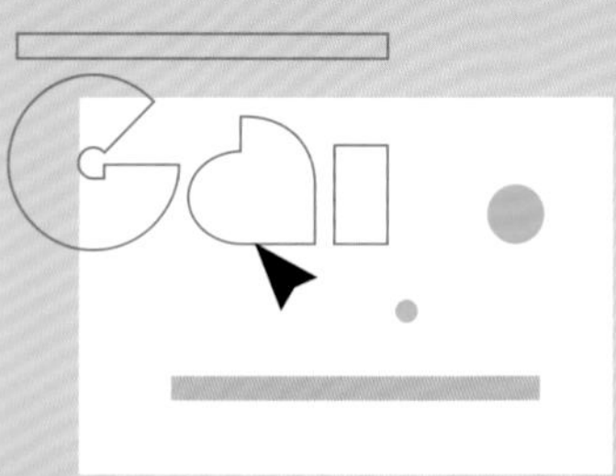

This grouped logo can now be easily selected to be moved or tweaked as one piece. Otherwise, what typically happens to ungrouped logos is that we neglect to select all the "pieces," then try to drag them as one. We end up, as shown above, leaving behind parts, like the dot over letter *i*, and the counter in letter *a*. Did somebody ask why the counter of *a* looks solid orange, instead of clear white? See "Compound Paths," below.

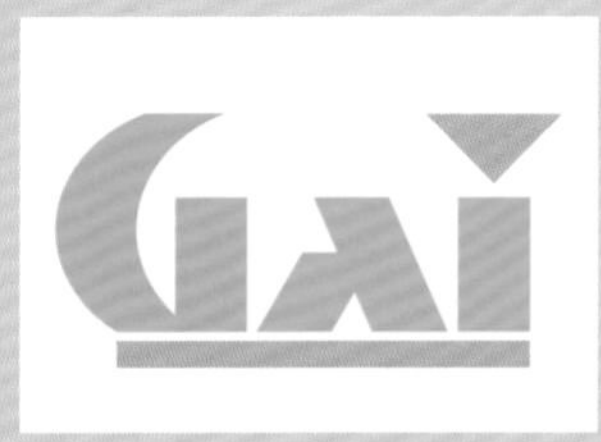

When we draw letters from scratch, we must group them ourselves. In the logo variation above, select letter *i* plus its dot and Group (⌘-G) them (it doesn't matter that the dot has a different fill color). Then select all the letters plus the bottom rail and Group again. Another way to Group: Select all the elements and hit Merge in the Pathfinder pallet. Now I'm wondering if that lowercase *a* reads as an *a*? We have to ask such questions of ourselves.

Groups can be friends...or foes. Say we draw a new dot over *i*. We dutifully try to Group this new combo, but an error message pops up: "*Can't make a group of objects that are within different groups*." When I read that, I just want to strangle Illustrator. Instead, we have to break for tea, come back and Cut (⌘-X) and Paste in Front (⌘-F) until the *i* stem forgets its former associations and agrees to be grouped with its fancy new dot.

Whereas the Group's propensity to stay together is helpful, an annoying aspect of Groups is, as we've just seen, their reluctance to become ungrouped. For example, we place a copy of that *i*-dot off to the side for later use (see it, way over to the right, near the page gutter?). But when we select the *i* above, we may also unintentionally select that copy of the dot because, having been born of *i*, it thinks it still belongs to the *i* Group!

(Can't think of any graphic to illustrate this point.)

To solve this problem, select the copied *i* dot by clicking it once with the White Arrow, then Cut (⌘-X) and Paste it in Front(⌘-F). Doing this, rather than just Paste (⌘-V), replaces the object in the same spot it was Cut from. Also, we can select the *i*-dot and go to OBJECT>Ungroup (⇧-⌘-G). However, I find that when an object's life has included several groupings and regroupings, it sometimes refuses to Ungroup and may take several tries.

COMPOUND PATHS

The first time we computer letterers draw an *O*, we make a large circle and fill it black, then a smaller circle for the counter and fill it white. Then we wonder how to get the background fill color to show through the hole in the center which isn't really a hole, it's just another fill on an upper level. The proper way to punch a hole out of a letter like *O* is to select both circles, then go to OBJECT>Compound Path>Make (or ⌘-8). This will work perfectly provided we apply it to fresh-drawn virgin objects. However, when we've subjected the outer shape to various regroupings, or introduced a new counter shape to an object that had previously been part of a compound path with another hole or two, our attempts to Group may not take. Again, the solution is to repeatedly Cut (⌘-X) and Paste in Front (⌘-F) several times until the object forgets its former identity and through sheer exhaustion at being Cut and Pasted, over and over, agrees to be newly compounded. Another way to compound reluctant parts is to select both objects and use the Pathfinder tools Divide or Subtract From Shape to punch out the holes.

Holes, or "counters," in compound letters appear see-through or white, yet they are actually filled objects. When counters are moved out of their positions within letters, they show their original fills (**a**), or they split the difference (**b**, **c**).

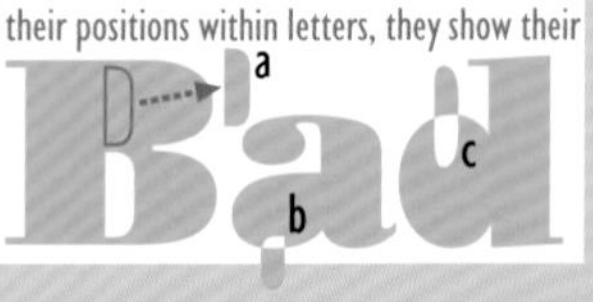
a
b
c

LAYERS, LOCKING, HIDING & GUIDES

We almost never draw a logo from start to finish without major amounts of editing, tweaking, changing our minds, moving and reworking. With really complex logos containing many elements and overlapping layers, it will be necessary throughout the creative process to Lock, Hide or move certain objects and areas of the work in order to "get to" other parts we want to tweak. Adobe Illustrator, like most programs, provides multiple ways of doing the same tasks. Features such as Layers, Lock, Hide and sometimes Cut, Move and Make Guides can all be used to help us clear the way to certain areas for point surgery.

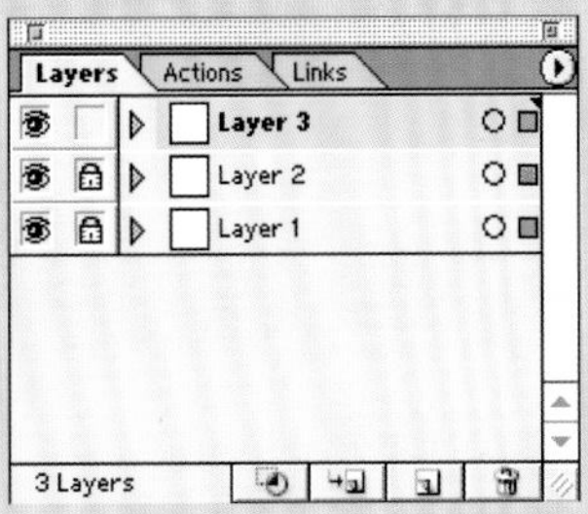
Layers
Actions
Links
Layer 3
Layer 2
Layer 1
3 Layers

If we use the Layers pallet, different parts of our logo can be placed on different layers so we can select one part without accidentally selecting another part. Lock all layers except the one(s) you're working on. Click to highlight a layer to work in it (make sure it's not locked). Above, the lower two layers are shown locked.

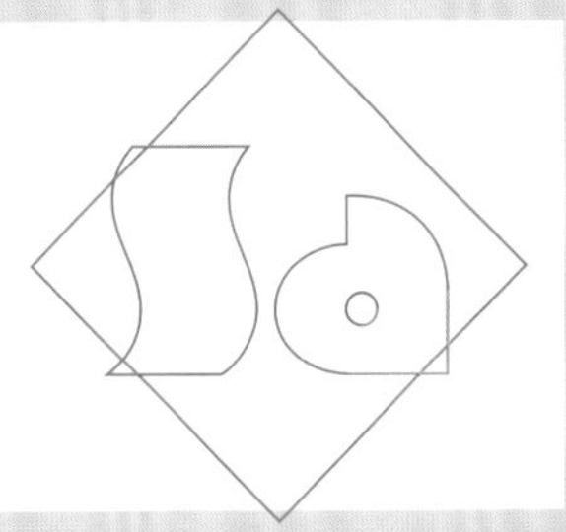

You'll know your logo is built in layers because the selection outlines will be different colors (colors that you can choose and change at will). Above, the diamond backdrop, stroked letter and fill-only letter are on three different layers. (The blue outline of the fill-only letter has been cut away to show the stroked green layer below.)

Switching to VIEW>Preview mode, the logo above demonstrates an instance where layers are useful. By locking the black-fill top layer, it's easy to select the orange-stroked middle layer to change the stroke weight or color. Otherwise, we'd need some way of getting the top layer out of our way in order to access any underlying layers.

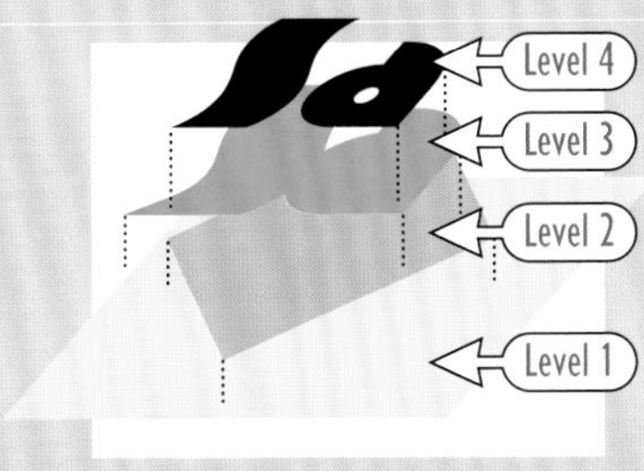
Level 4
Level 3
Level 2
Level 1

Since using the Layers pallet can add extra steps, another way to access objects that are stacked in several levels is to Lock (⌘-2) certain levels while tweaking the art on other levels. Locking (which can easily be undone with Option-Command-2 or ⌥-⌘-2) makes the locked object unselectable.

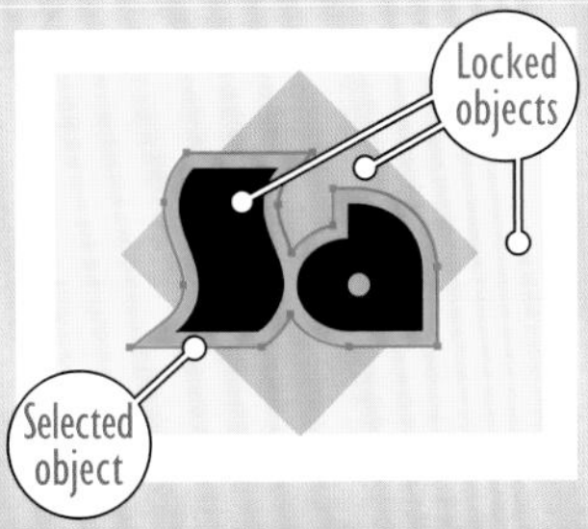
Locked objects
Selected object

By clicking to select, then locking the the yellow background, tan diamond, and both black letters above, we can marquee the orange-stroked letters on level 3 without selecting the art drawn on the other levels. Obviously, we couldn't select level 3 if level 4 above wasn't locked, because we'd end up selecting it, too.

Don't forget, we're Hiding up here!

Other ways to "get at" middle-level objects besides using layers or locking: Hide (⌘-3) will temporarily send objects to purgatory while we work on others free and clear of visual or actual encumbrances. Hide doesn't involve the Mac Clipboard, so objects can stay hidden while still using Copy and Paste. Hit ⌥-⌘-3 to Show all.

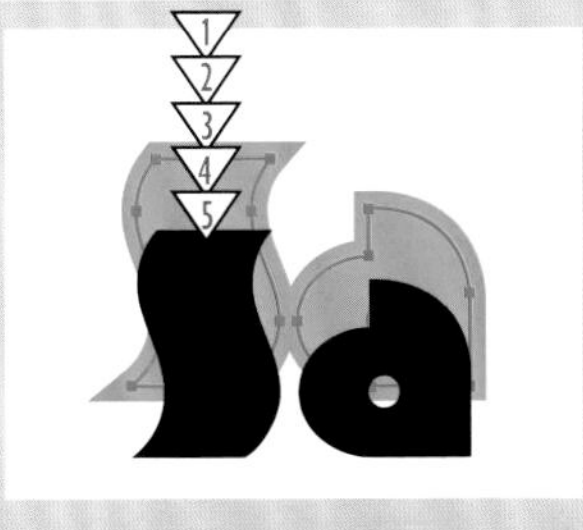
1
2
3
4
5

Another way to access objects or points covered by upper-level objects: Use any arrow key on your keyboard to move the covering object. Above, I selected the black letters and hit the Down Arrow key five times. After editing the orange-stroked letters, I'll hit the Up Arrow key five times to move the black letters back into position.

Objects covering other objects can also be temporarily removed by using the Cut command (⌘-X). This places the removed object on the Mac Clipboard. Later, we can Paste in Front (⌘-F) to put it back. But this is a dangerous approach. We may forget we had Cut objects waiting in limbo and Copy or Cut something else, thereby losing the previous Cut object forever—unless we Undo (⌘-Z), Undo, Undo, etc. to return to before we Cut the second time. However, then we've lost the work we did prior to the Undos. I always make this mistake. So do not use Cut to hide. Use Hide to hide.

Object
Object as Guide
Object & Guide

Another way to get certain objects out of our way is to select them and turn them into Guides (⌘-5). Later, hit the keys ⌥-⌘-5 to Release them from guidehood. But objects made into guides retain their level order, so if an object's point is under a guide, it can't be selected by clicking. It must be marqueed, then first moved a bit out from under the guide with any arrow key before it can be grabbed and dragged with the White Arrow tool.

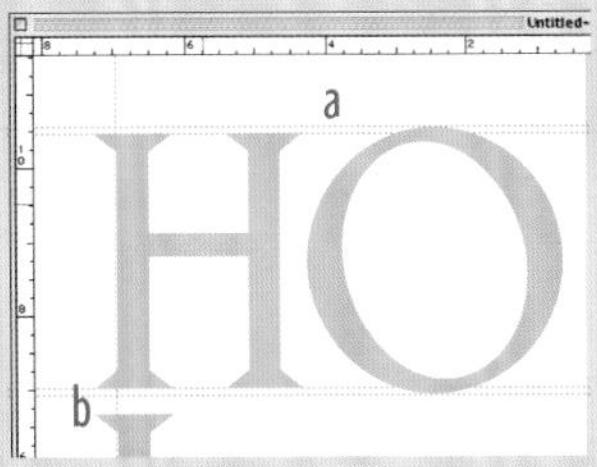
a
b

Guides are used in several ways. If we add Rulers (⌘-R) to our document window, we can drag horizontal or vertical guidelines from them onto our pages. Use these for making baseline, cap-height and overshoot guides for letters we draw from scratch, a, or to vertically align objects, b.

We may also make rough mouse drawings (or slightly better digital pen drawings), then turn them into Guides for more accurate Pen tool tracing. Ruler Guides have also been placed, above, to help keep all letters equal in height. On page 156 see how such letters may be drawn by assembing parts.

ROTATE and SCALE TOOLS vs. FREE TRANSFORM TOOL

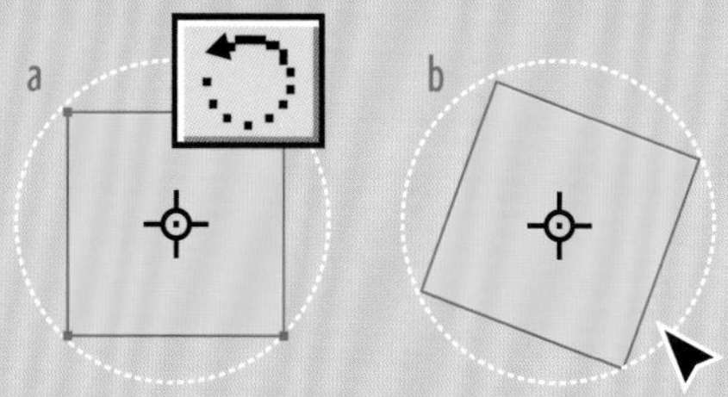
a
b

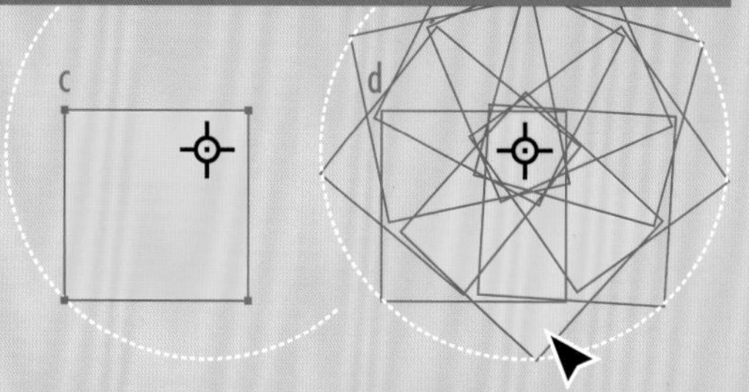
c
d

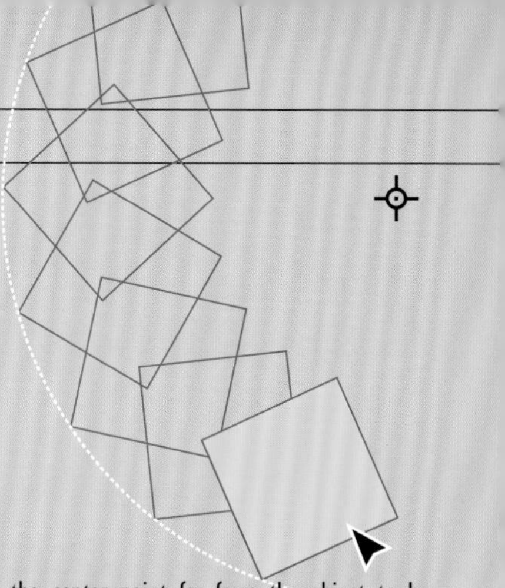

To turn objects, select the Rotate tool in the tool bar, click in the center of a solid-selected object like the square, a, then drag it. The square will spin in place, pivoting on its center, b, which is where we clicked to place the axis of rotation.

If the axis of rotation is instead placed off center, as in c, the overall radius of the spin increases as the object swings around its axis point. Oh, look what a cunning, if asymmetrical, star shape appears, d.

Click the center point far from the object to be turned, as above, and the radius of rotation increases even more. When we are drawing letters, it can often be helpful to place our axis elsewhere than centered.

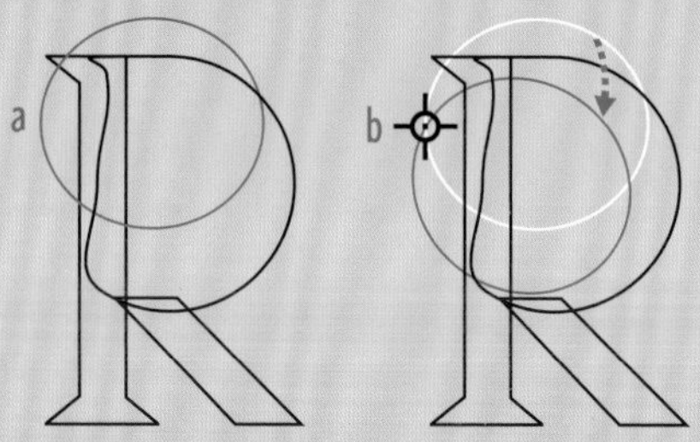
a
b

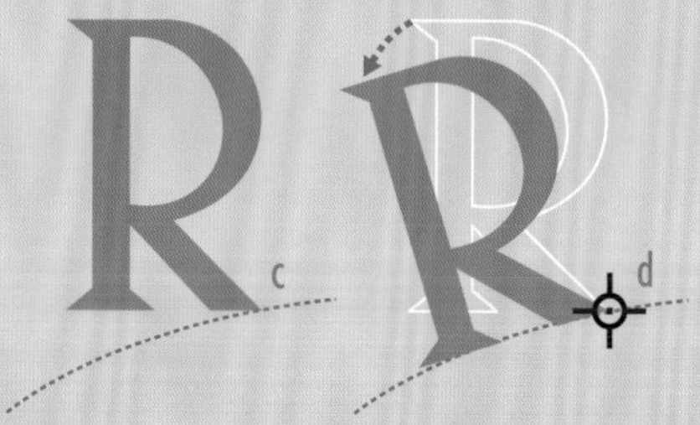
c
d

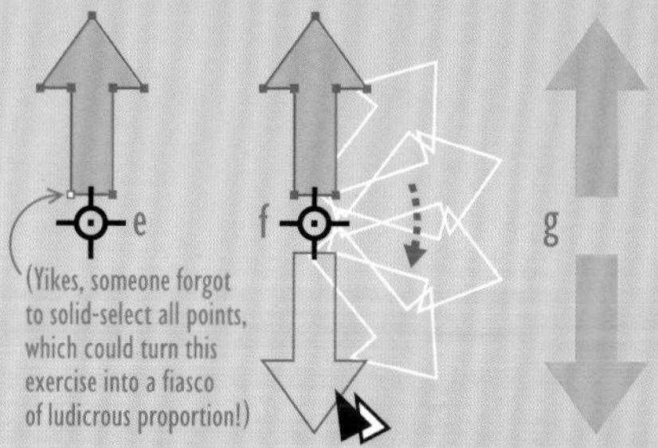
e
f
g

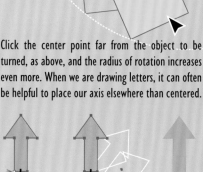

(Yikes, someone forgot to solid-select all points, which could turn this exercise into a fiasco of ludicrous proportion!)

When would we need an off-center axis of rotation? Above, an *R* is being assembled in parts. At a, an ellipse for the counter has been drawn. At b, the ellipse has been rotated from the axis point shown to fall right into place, in one step.

Another use for an off-center axis: If we wanted to rotate the *R* to follow a curving baseline, c, the axis of rotation would best be placed off center as shown, d. (Of course, we'll still need to tweak the stem bases of *R* to better conform to the curving baseline.)

Yet another example utilizing an off-center axis. Axis was clicked below the selected object, e, then rotated while pressing Option and Shift keys, f. Option makes a copy, and Shift snaps the copy to perfect 90° alignment to provide my desired result at g.

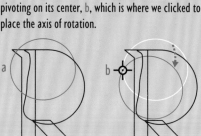

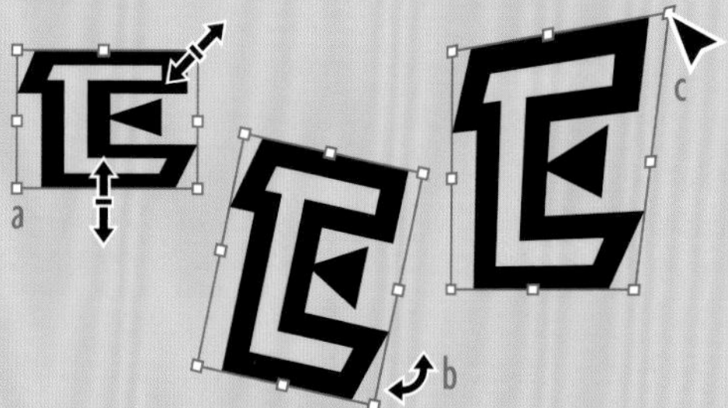
a
b
c

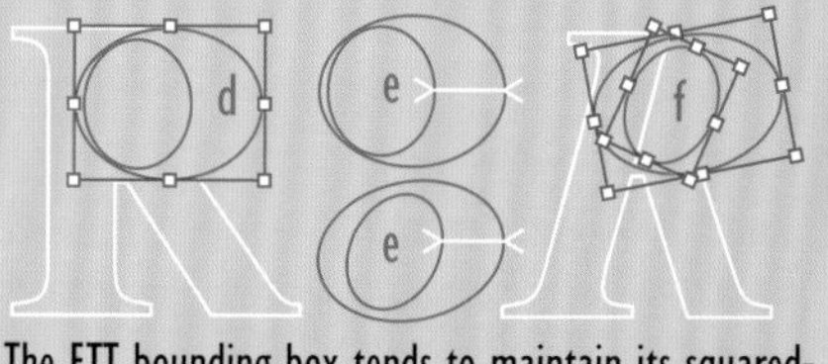
d
e
e
f

The versatile Free Transform Tool (FTT) scales, rotates, shears, reflects, distorts and creates perspective. But it allows rotation from only a central axis within the eight-handled box, above, that bounds selected objects. When using this tool, press ⌘ to toggle to the White Arrow or you can't select anything.

Drag a side or corner handle to Scale an object, a. Rotate from wherever the curly arrow pops up, b. Drag a corner handle to Distort, c, but hold down ⌘ a split second *after* beginning to drag. The FTT does not allow us to make a copy while transforming, as we can by pressing Option (⌥) with other Transform tools.

The FTT bounding box tends to maintain its squared-off relationship with objects (d and f) even if they've previously been transformed with other tools. This is good! Less apparent in the tangent-handled bezier curve system is the concept of center axis orientation that in pencil and compass days helped us to keep inner and outer curves "registered" in some degree of pleasant relationship, e. The FTT's bounding box shows this. It also helps us restraighten spun objects.

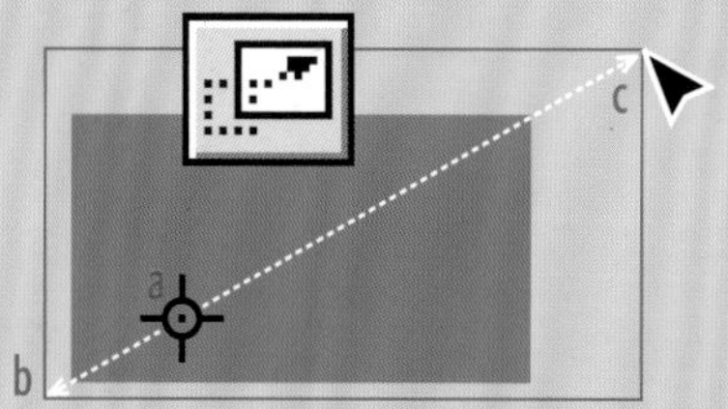
c
a
b

Like the Rotate tool, the Scale tool transforms an object starting from where we click our center axis point. Notice how dragging the rectangle, above, from its axis, a, produced much less enlargment at b, which was nearer to the axis, than at c, farther away.

In addition to dragging objects, the Rotate and Scale tools may both be employed by numerically specifying exact amounts of transformation. Click a spot just as when placing an axis point, but hold down the Option key. Up pops a pop-up window with fields to type desired percentages of rotation, enlargement or reduction. But unless we want to transform a series of objects not all at once, or we need to know the exact percentage to restore an object we'd earlier transformed, the instances when we'd use numerical pop-up windows are limited.

Above left, an object with a 3-point stroke was scaled to 150%, right, so the stroke has also scaled, becoming 4.5 points.

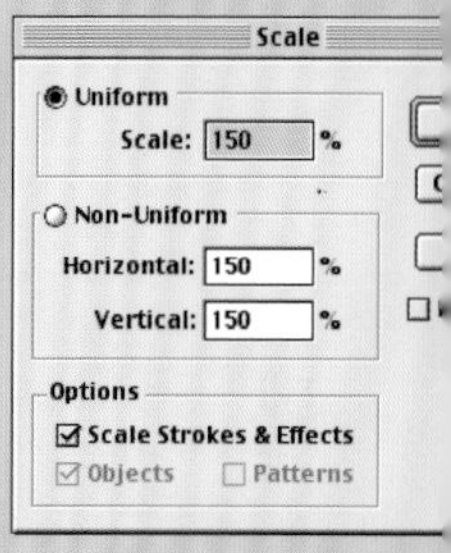
Scale
Uniform
Scale: 150 %
Non-Uniform
Horizontal: 150 %
Vertical: 150 %
Options
Scale Strokes & Effects
Objects
Patterns

The Scale window contains an important option: the Scale Strokes and Effects check box. When scaling a stroked object, should the stroke scale, too—or not? The status of this check box will also affect scaling done with the FTT.

The PATHFINDER PALLETS

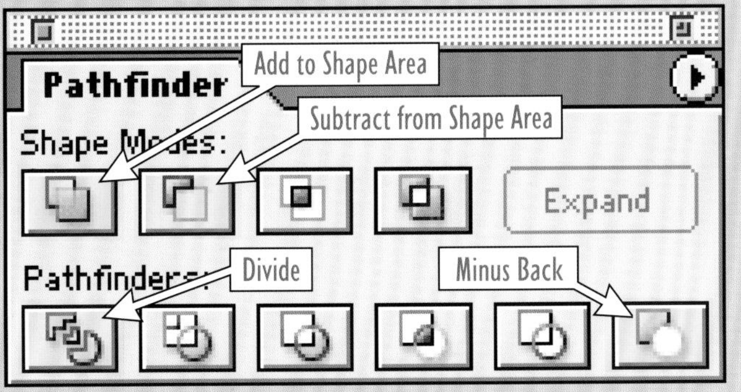
Pathfinder
Add to Shape Area
Subtract from Shape Area
Shape Modes:
Expand
Pathfinders:
Divide
Minus Back

Illustrator's Pathfinder pallet is the main reason I begin drawing fonts in Illustrator, not Fontographer, which can merge shapes, but nothing more. In version 10, Adobe changed the Pathfinder tools to confuse what, in Illustrator 9, had been simple and intuitive. So I will explain the four Pathfinder tools in Illustrator 10 (noted above in red) that are the only ones I've found useful. Perhaps you will disagree with my conclusion that the remaining Pathfinder tools are either too obscure or redundant.

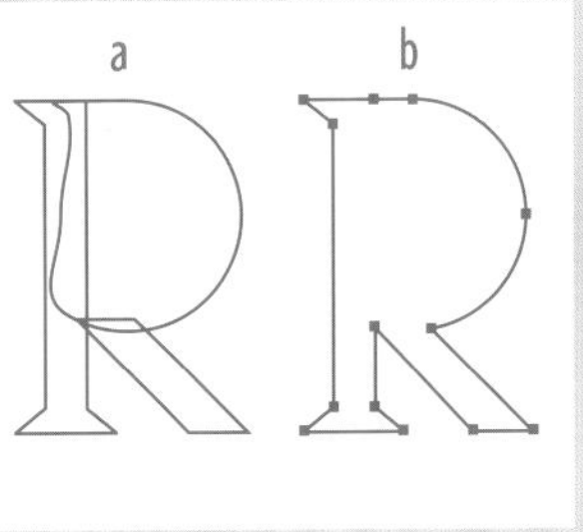
a
b

Use Add to Shape (AtS) to unite parts of an *R*, a. Select the parts, hold the Option key and hit the AtS button. The result is one solid mass, b. Without the Option key, AtS makes fills and strokes of selected objects identical, but each remains an individual. Hit the Expand button to actually unite them.

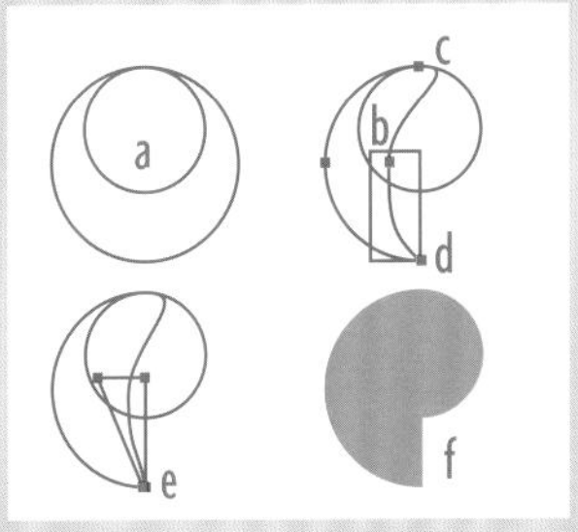
a
b
c
d
e
f

AtS helps us create a shape like f. Draw two circles, a. Drag point b till it's clearly back of c. Draw a rectangle and drag by its southeast point to snap to the large circle's south point, d. Drag the rectangle's southwest point, e, to the circle's south point, also. Hit Option-AtS to unite the pieces into f.

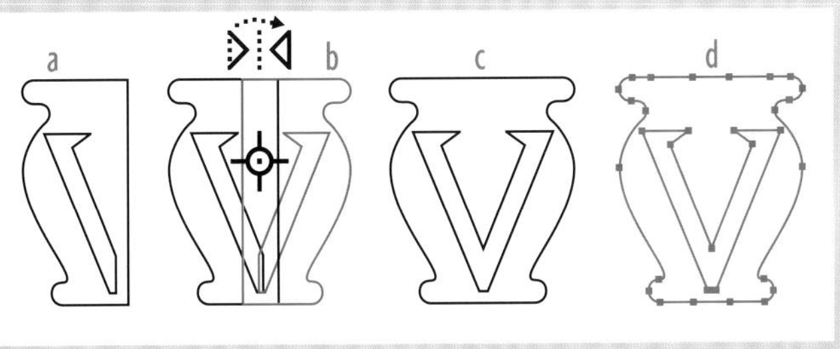
a
b
c
d

Never draw both sides of a vase, a letter *V* or any other symmetrical shape. Draw one side, a, use the Reflect tool plus Option key to reflect a copy, b. Notice that the center axis for both objects is placed so that an overlap shall occur. Objects that don't overlap cannot be united with AtS.

Then, use AtS to unite the two sides into one piece, c (do *V* and vase separately). Notice that superfluous points end up at the perimeters of overlap, d. Excess points complicate shape editing; in drawing letters for fonts, extra points must be removed. For the vase drawing, it's your choice.

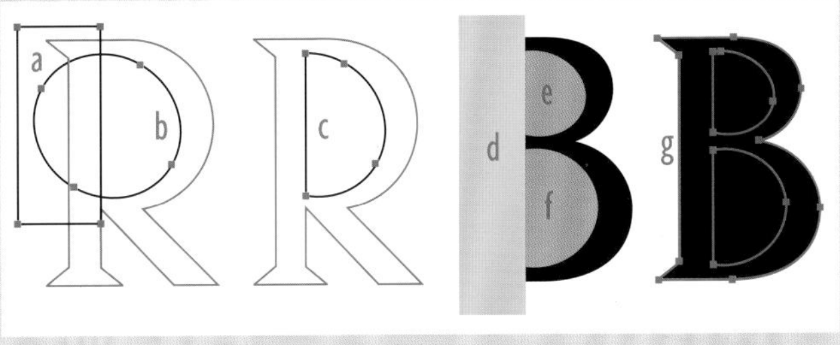
a
b
c
d
e
f
g

Subtract from Shape Area (SfS), previously called Minus Front, cuts an upper object's shape out of one beneath it. Above, rectangle a, aligned with the right side of *R*'s vertical stem, has been drawn over the ellipse, b, that will be the counter. Trim c using SfS plus the Option key.

At d, a rectangle partly covers ellipses e and f that will become the counters for letter *B* (g). Since SfS crops only one object at a time (aggravating!), Copy d, select it plus e, hit SfS then Paste in Front (⌘-F) the rectangle, and this time trim f with SfS. Minus Back just does the opposite of SfS.

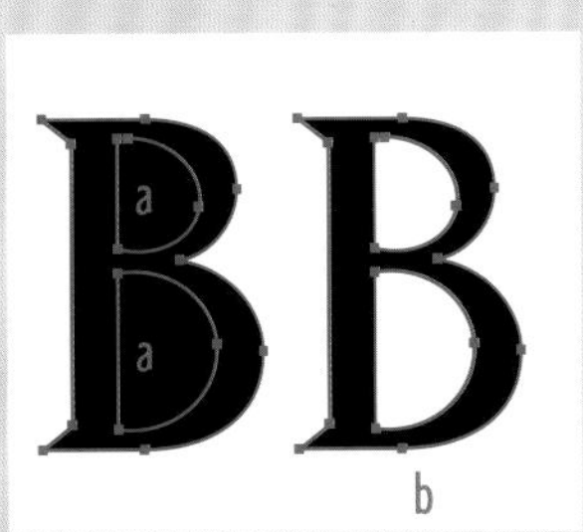
a
a
b

The two counters in *B*, a, must now be knocked out as Compound Paths. Either: (1) Hit ⌘-8 to Make Compound Paths. (2) Select *B* plus one counter. Hit SfS, then select *B* and the second counter and use SfS again. Or (3) select *B* plus both counters and hit Divide, then select and delete the counters. Result shown at b.

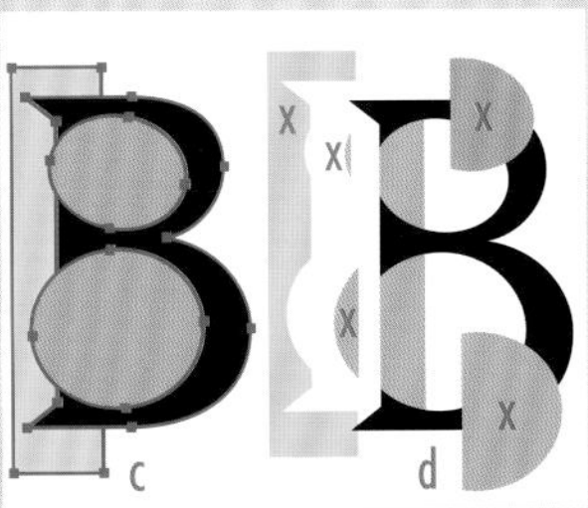
x
x
x
x
x
c
d

Divide could also have been used to make *B*. Divide slices objects along the lines of their intersecting strokes so several objects can be cut apart at once. Then we just delete any excess pieces. Above, select all the parts (c). Use Divide to separate them (d). Select and delete the xs. Use AtS to unite the segmented parts of *B* as one.

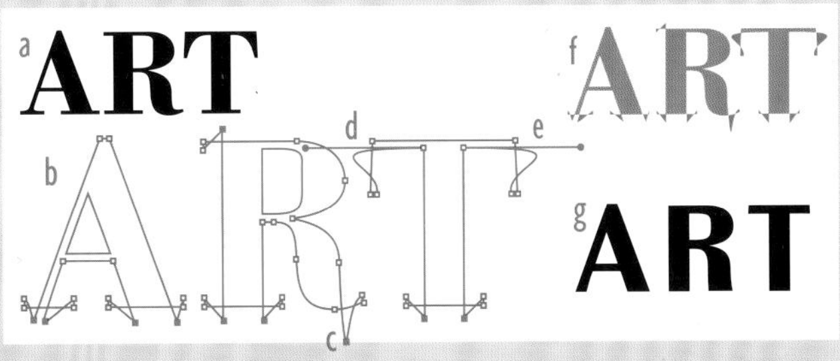
a
ART
b
c
d
e
f
ART
g
ART

Divide can be used on a single object if it has strokes intersecting itself. Above, here's how to turn serif letters, a, into sans-serif ones, b. At c, select then drag all points in red out past the serifs. The c point of *R* must be pulled way down till the stroke gets fairly straight. Pull out the bezier handles, not the points, at d and e until strokes become almost straight horizontal. Now select the letters and press the Divide button. Finally, select and delete excess pieces (at f, shown in red). Final result shown at g (note: I weighted up the thin strokes and squared the leg of *R*). This technique with Divide can also be used to turn rounded corners into square ones.

RANDOM DRAWING TIPS

Many years ago, as a fledgling illustrator, I approached legendary psychedelic-era poster designer Stanley Mouse at a comic-book convention and innocently asked, "Hi, Stanley, would you give me some airbrush tips?" "Oh," he replied, "you can get airbrush *tips* at the art supply store!" and then proceeded to laugh uproariously at his tip quip. I won't repeat this cycle of abuse, dear reader, by advising you not to play in traffic. Here are some actual handy tips you might need to know (that didn't fit anywhere else in the book).

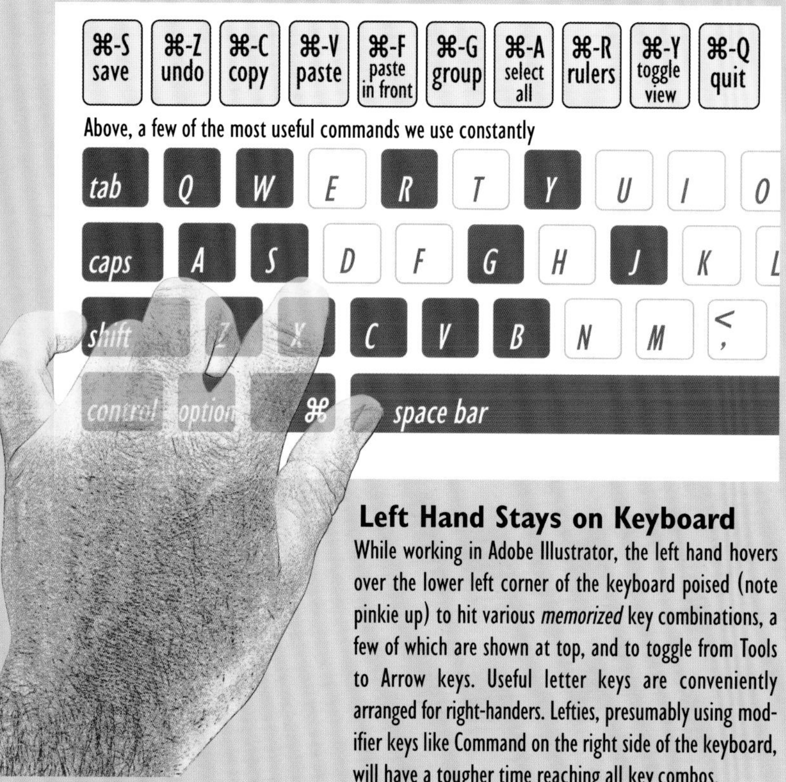
⌘-S save
⌘-Z undo
⌘-C copy
⌘-V paste
⌘-F paste in front
⌘-G group
⌘-A select all
⌘-R rulers
⌘-Y toggle view
⌘-Q quit
Above, a few of the most useful commands we use constantly
tab Q W E R T Y U I O
caps A S D F G H J K L
shift Z X C V B N M < ,
control option ⌘ space bar

Left Hand Stays on Keyboard

While working in Adobe Illustrator, the left hand hovers over the lower left corner of the keyboard poised (note pinkie up) to hit various *memorized* key combinations, a few of which are shown at top, and to toggle from Tools to Arrow keys. Useful letter keys are conveniently arranged for right-handers. Lefties, presumably using modifier keys like Command on the right side of the keyboard, will have a tougher time reaching all key combos.

Key Concepts

When you see "⌘-S," don't press the hyphen key between ⌘ and S.

When pressing key commands, like ⌘-Z (undo) or ⌘-Shift-Z (redo), don't press all keys then release all fingers off the keyboard simultaneously. The Command key (⌘) must be depressed a millisecond before the others. *Then* letter and other modifier keys can be pressed. After all keys have been pressed, the fingers lift off the other keys first, letting the Command key come up last. Otherwise, the Command key may come up sooner than the others and the operation will abort.

Following are a few additional important key commands that should be memorized to avoid always having to go to the toolbars or menu bars.

HAND TOOL Drag page around.* — space bar

ZOOM UP Get magnifying glass to view page larger.* — ⌘ + space bar

ZOOM DOWN Get magnifying glass view page smaller.* — option + ⌘ + space bar

SEND BACKWARD Lower an object to next level down. — ⌘ + { [

SEND FORWARD Lift an object to next upper level. — ⌘ + }]

*Changing screen views and positions can't be undone with ⌘-Z, because they're not actually actions.

SNAP, CRACKLE and SCALE

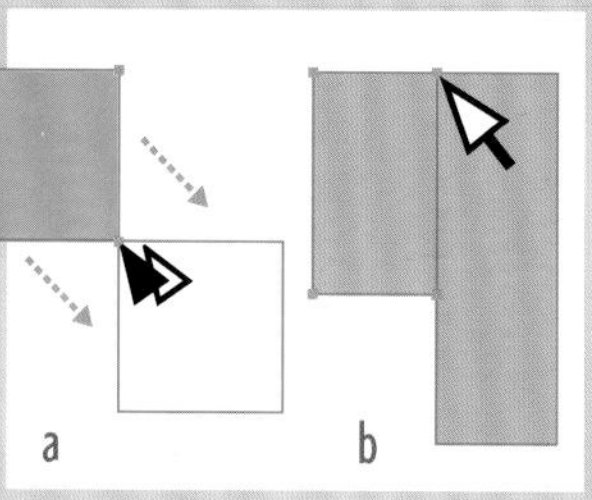
a
b

Snap to it. An object can be selected by clicking on its fill or on one of its paths, but to drag it, it's usually better to drag by one of its points. At a, make a check pattern by Shift-Option-dragging the top square from its NW (northwest) point, snapping the copy to its SE point. At b, the two rectangles were perfectly top-aligned by dragging the smaller's NE point to the larger's NW point. Be sure Snap to Point is checked in the VIEW menu.

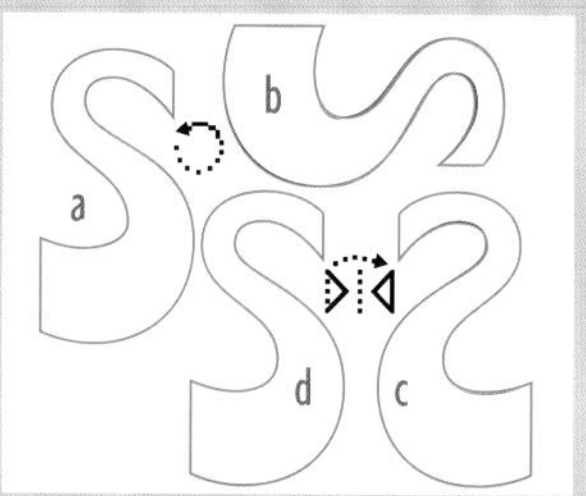
a
b
c
d

New perspective. To fine-tune your art and letters, view them sideways, upside down, 45° and backwards. Save a copy, then use the Rotate and Reflect tools to transform your work. With objective eyes, you'll become aware that curves and shapes you thought were good now seem "off." Tweak points in these new positions, then aright the work and see how it looks. Above, the *S* at a was tweaked in b and c to be finalized at d.

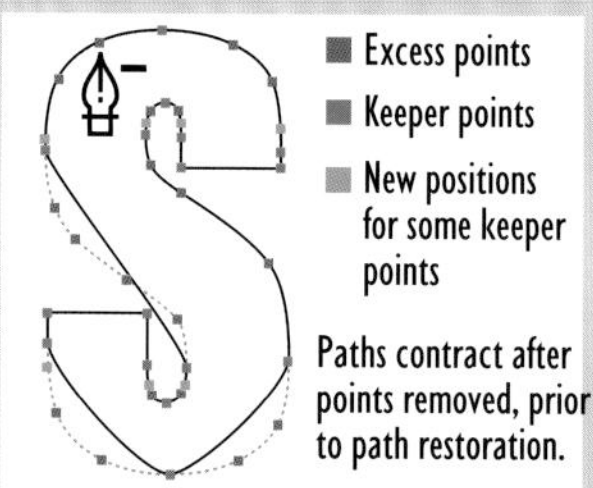
Excess points
Keeper points
New positions for some keeper points
Paths contract after points removed, prior to path restoration.

Fix points. To correct out-of-extrema points, solid-select the object to be corrected. Hit Copy (⌘-C), then make it into Guides (⌘-5). Now Paste in Front (⌘-F). Move, add or subtract errant points knowing that you have the underlying copy to help guide your restoration of the shape. If the original points are hopeless, it's better to trace off the guide from scratch with the pen tool. Make Guides also of quickie mouse sketches to trace for final inks.

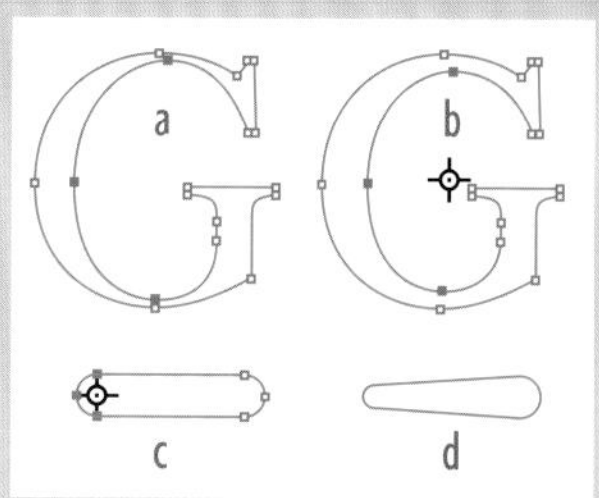
a
b
c
d

Scale don't drag. To decrease the size of *G*'s counter, a, the three solid-selected points could be dragged one by one toward the center. Instead, b, the Scale tool was used to shrink the three points in one move, which avoided any loss of the original harmony between them. Similarly, at c, a Round-Cap stroke was drawn, and Outline Strokes made it into an object. Clicking the Scale tool's center point shown, one end was neatly reduced, d.

SHORTCUTS TO ALIGNING, SPACING

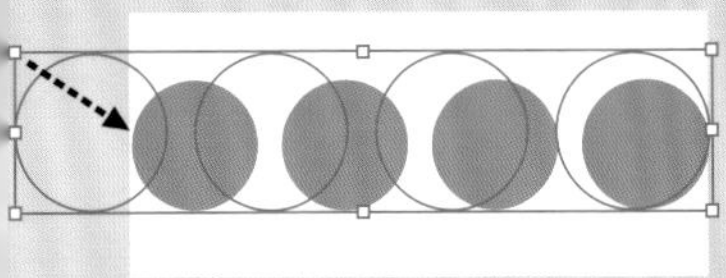

Never measure. Want to fit four objects within a given width? Draw them any size, select them and use the Free Transform tool (hold Shift) to resize them to fit the width.

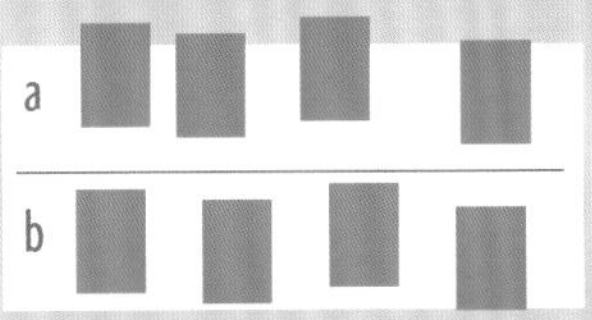
a
b

Never space. Use the Align Pallet tools to Distribute spacing equally or to a specified distance. At a, spacing is random, crummy. At b, it's been equalized with Distribute tool.

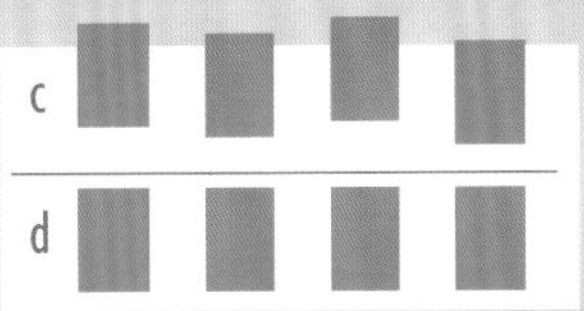
c
d

Never align. Don't line things up by dragging objects to a guide line when one of the Align Pallet's tools can do it. At c, objects spaced well, but crooked. At, d, Vertically Aligned.

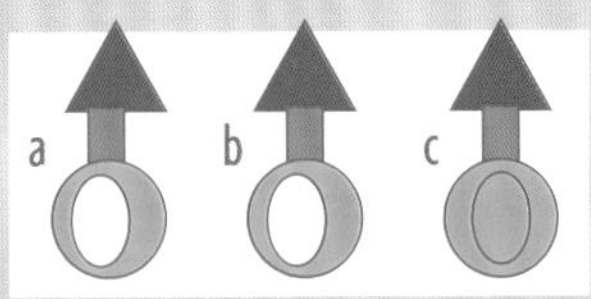
a
b
c

Never center by eye, or by dragging objects. Use the Align Pallet's Vertical or Horizontal Align Center tool. Unaligned objects, a. Aligned, b, except center of *O*, a compound path. Release Compound Path, then recenter, c, then re-Compound.

3 WAYS to DRAW STUFF in ILLUSTRATOR

1. Drawn in Units

Parts of the picture are drawn in groups of pieces—comprised of strokes and fills—built from the bottom up. Each piece is like a unit, with the next level unit and its pieces arranged above. Figures a–d show the lowest unit with a 12-point stroked outline a, filled shapes made from sheared rectangles, b–c, and 3-point-stroke box corners, d. At e, a circle becomes the tag string.

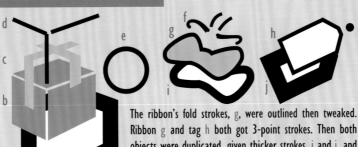

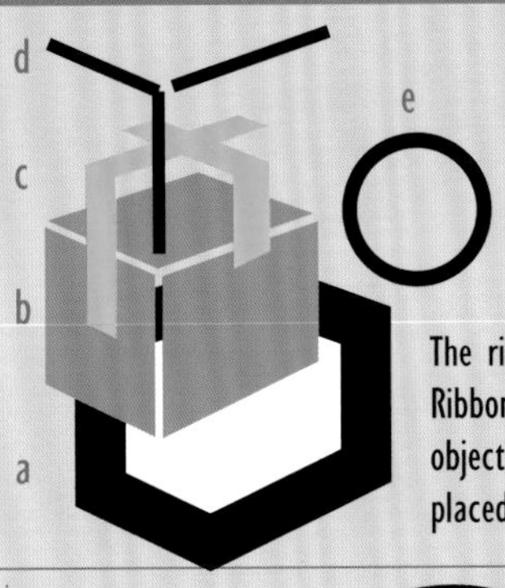
d
c
b
a
e

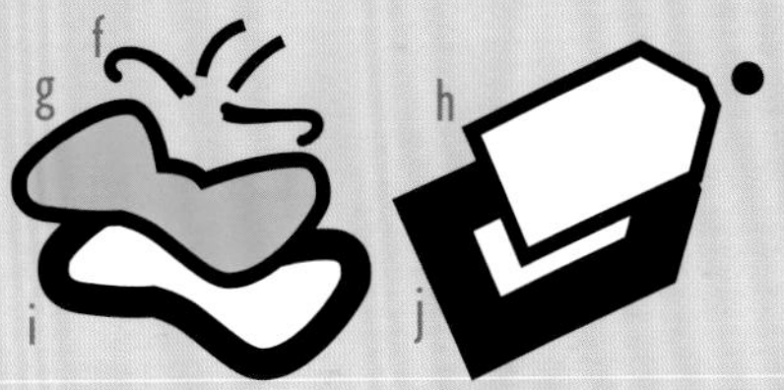
f
g
h
i
j

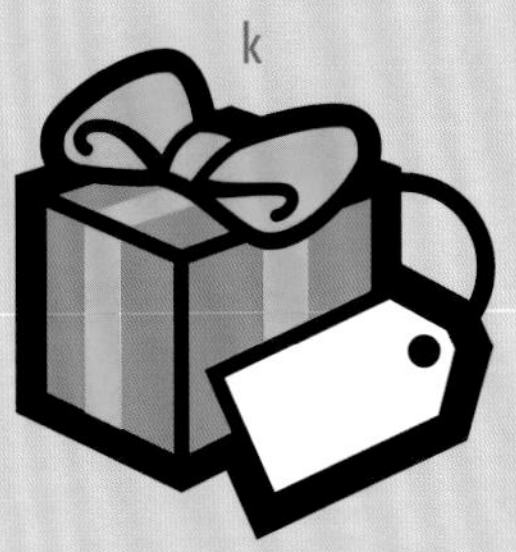
k

The ribbon's fold strokes, g, were outlined then tweaked. Ribbon g and tag h both got 3-point strokes. Then both objects were duplicated, given thicker strokes, i and j, and placed at the lowest levels. Final result was composited at k.

2. Strokes Outlined

As in the first method above, drawing begins with shapes like circles, a, lines (that are parts of circles), b, and rectangles, c. This rectangle was made into a wedge by selecting its SW corner point and moving it with eight Right Arrow key hits, then eight Left Arrows to the SE point. Rectangle d will be subtracted from the bottom of the circle to yield a foot. 10-point Round Cap strokes for arm and leg, e and f, are shown in Preview mode.

a
b
c
d
e
f
g
h
i
k
j
l
m
n

The vertical center guideline, g, is important. That's where we'll click to place our axis point to Reflect-Copy the leg and foot from left side to right. And later we'll use it for making the longitude lines in the background.

At h, all strokes have been selected, outlined and united as three shapes. The diaper wasn't united since it'll be on an upper level. All objects were stroked 1.3 points. Globe grid, i, was made of ellipses, stroked white.

With all red-stroked baby parts selected, hit Release Compound Paths (⌥-⌘-8). Now the inner fills, no longer grouped with the outer, are on a level above the outer. Select leg, j, and diaper, k, and change their fill colors.

A copy of the 4-point black outer circle, l, has been sent to back and filled blue/no-stroke, m. Above, n, the baby's torso and head have now been filled, and the drawing is done (unless you wanted to add a face).

3. From the Bottom Up

This is the most straight forward approach. Working over a scanned sketch, use the Pen tool to draw an overall silhouette of the object, which will become the base-level art, a. The object need not be completely outlined. Inlets, b–c, were left in the contour around the face and hair. Once the drawing is a finished, closed path, begin drawing second-level closed paths, e–f (outlined in blue), which will be given different fills. The face and hair shapes, g, must be drawn through the middle of the black outlined areas, then sent to the very lowest level below the black.* At h (the third level up), Round-Cap strokes, which will remain stroked, add a highlight effect on pants. At i, the final drawing.

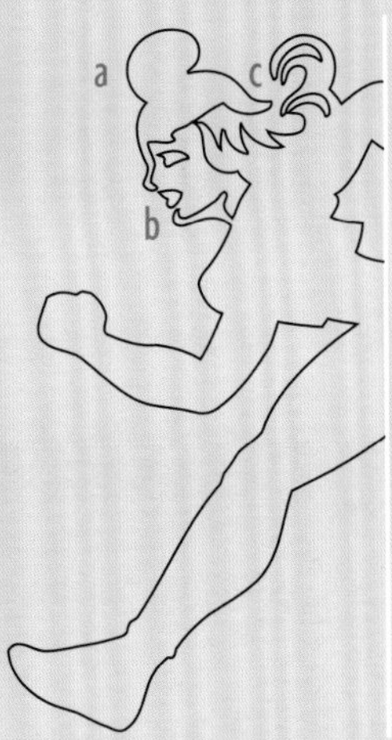
a
b
c

g
d
f
e
h

i

*Add 40% cyan and 30% magenta to 100% black for a "rich black" so hair and face fills won't "show through."

NOT WORKING to SCALE

The way we designed layouts in the past was to block out sections of a piece of paper, as below from *Artistic Signs* (1924), to incorporate all the various sizes of needed text and graphic material. The next step was to sketch the letters themselves, starting as pencil skeletons, and pray they all fit within their designated sections before we ran out of room. Nowadays, some of us still approach computer design in the same way. We block out a design within a page size, create borders and then try to design the type to fit. I maintain that in the computer design age, all space is relative and that it wastes time to work to a size—at least at first. After our designs are finished, we can then adjust stroke weights, for instance, according to the actual size our work will be used.

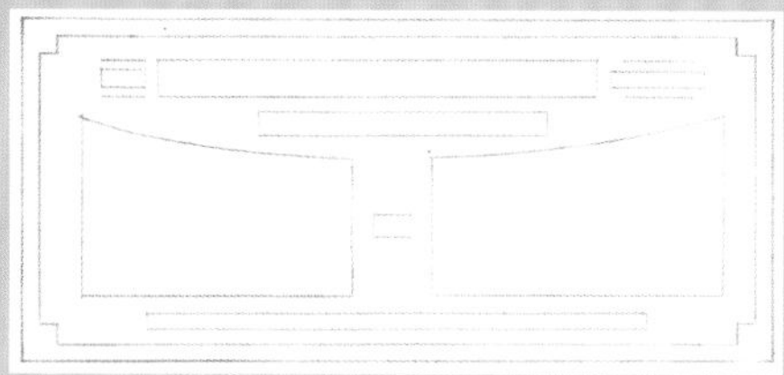

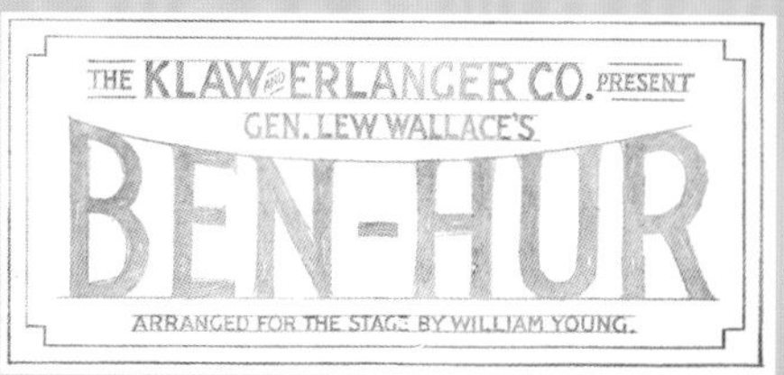
THE KLAW & ERLANGER CO. PRESENT
GEN. LEW WALLACE'S
BEN-HUR
ARRANGED FOR THE STAGE BY WILLIAM YOUNG.

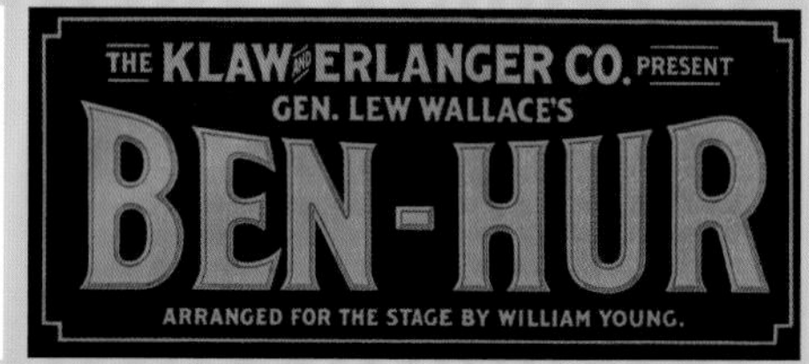
THE KLAW & ERLANGER CO. PRESENT
GEN. LEW WALLACE'S
BEN-HUR
ARRANGED FOR THE STAGE BY WILLIAM YOUNG.

Get art together and set type, any size, any proportion, at first. Then scale, stretch, squash everything to size. Curve type with OBJECT>Envelope Distort>Make With Warp. Finally, scale all the parts as a group to about the size the work will be used.

IRVING KLAW &
SOL WALLBANGER
BEN HER
IRVING KLAW & SOL WALLBANGER
BEN HER
BEN HER

IRVING KLAW &
SOL WALLBANGER
BEN HER

PREPARING ART for CLIENTS

Avoid disaster. Clients sometimes feel they have the right to make changes to our work since they paid for it. Unforeseen computer errors also can result in altering our work in ways that may later embarrass or infuriate us. By learning to properly prepare art, we can reduce later frustration.

a

ALL THE NEWS THAT'S GOOD TO THINK
GOODTHINK
FEELGOOD OPTIMISM H

b

ALL THE NEWS THAT'S GOOD TO THINK
GOODTHINK
Feelgood Optimism Happiness Glee

c

ALL THE NEWS THAT'S GOOD TO THINK
GOODTHINK
FEELGOOD OPTIMISM HAPPINESS GLEE

d

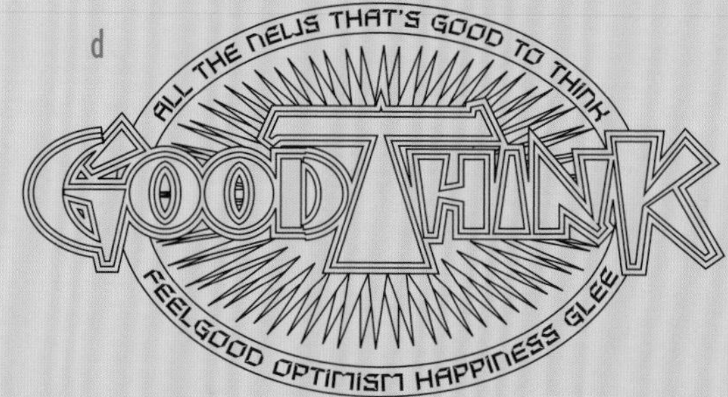
ALL THE NEWS THAT'S GOOD TO THINK
GOODTHINK
FEELGOOD OPTIMISM HAPPINESS GLEE

The fact is, any client with Illustrator or Photoshop skills can change our work, but we can make it a bit harder for them to do so, and at the same time try to prevent accidental mishaps. For example, the logo above at a, got scaled way down, b, but the Scale Strokes & Effects box wasn't checked, so strokes didn't scale. Plus, we forgot to Create Outlines of all fonts. The bottom type was substituted with Helvetica. Yikes! If flawed files are *our* mistake, we may actually be held liable by the client for reprinting or prepress correction costs. Yes, it's happened to me, and to others! A few ways to avoid such situations in Illustrator files are: Create Outlines of any fonts used, Outline Strokes, and unite all objects with the same fill/stroke attributes that also share the same level or layer. These processes simplify our files, sometimes bringing our own "construction" errors to light. Above right at c, single outline type looks simple, but is actually four levels of different stroke weights. At d, all strokes have been outlined and united by level. It looks complicated, eh? That's the point! Clients will find it harder to change art like this. And when we Outline Strokes, we can fine-tune funny stroke problems that often show up. When possible, Paste Illustrator art into harder-to-change Photoshop files to send to the client. Photoshop files are more WYSIWYG than Illustrator, so you may discover errors and protect yourself, as well.

PREPARING WORK for PRINT

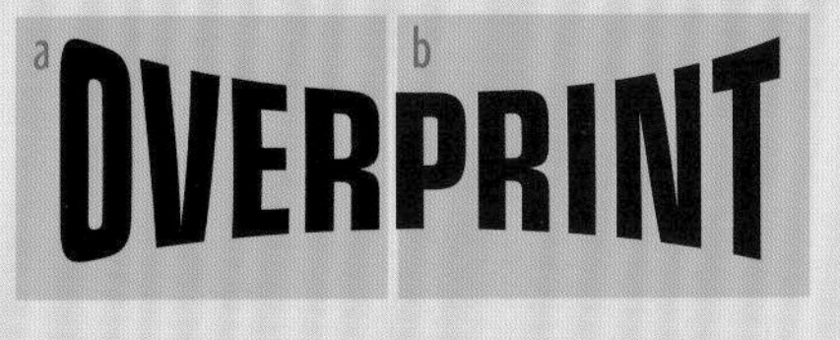
a
b
OVERPRINT

100% black (also called "solid" black) type or art that will print on top of another color is best designated to Overprint. (In Illustrator's menu bar, go to WINDOW>Show Attributes). Now, instead of just black ink on white paper, the black becomes enriched by the underlying halftone color tints. Above at a, black type set to Overprint should look richer than at b, kept at the default setting to "K.O." (knock out) all colors on lower levels beneath it.

OVERPRINT

Blacker blacks! In addition to making the black ink seem richer or "blacker," overprinting ensures that misregistration (when all press plates containing different colors of ink are not printed in precise alignment with one another) won't ruin the appearance of our job. Above, a simulated example of bad registration in which the black printing plate has slipped downwards, leaving slivers of white paper showing between colors.

OVERPRINT
38% C
10% M
77% Y
100% K
77% Y
10% M
38% C

Instead of overprinting, we can enrich the black type itself by including in its fill the same tints as contained in the underlying art. Some designers, however, go for the kill, assuming the boldest black will result from mixing 100% of cyan, magenta and yellow with 100% black. Some printers say this is too much ink coverage and that it muddies the black and delays drying. Though it is not necessary to do this, I think it's OK to do in small areas.

a
b ENRICH SMALL BLACK TYPE?

Enriching solid black is usually done by adding 40% cyan. Sometimes, 30% magenta is also added. This is thought to be sufficient to avoid most overprinting problems such as "show-through," which will be discussed next. Since printing registration is rarely absolutely perfect, it is not advisable to enrich smaller point-size black text type. Slightly off-the-mark registration, which might go unnoticed in larger type, a, can cause smaller type, b, to appear unnecessarily muddy and blurry.

Showthru
a
b

Show-through is when unenriched solid black overprints other colors, therefore becoming undesirably and unevenly "enriched," as seen above at a. Any color that overprints others, such as the magenta ring, also at a, may suffer from show-through. At b, none of the colors were set to overprint. The black type has a fill of 40C/30M/0Y/100K. Our monitors and ink-jet printers don't reveal overprinting and show-through issues to us. We must try to anticipate printing problems and plan our work accordingly.

Without trapping
With overprinted trap stroke

Trapping involves making a color slightly overlap its neighbor to provide leeway if print registration is poor. Adobe Illustrator can trap objects using Pathfinder pallet options. Or trap manually by adding to a filled object a 0.25-point stroke of the same color and setting the stroke to Overprint in the Attributes pallet. Trapping is more important when using PMS spot colors, which usually are not mixed together as tints, than with CMYK, where well-planned fills may obviate traps.

Spread the lighter color, rather than the dark, by adding an overprinting stroke. The impact of misregistration will be less noticeable if the lighter color encroaches upon the darker. When assigning a stroke for trapping and setting it to overprint, remember that only half the stroke counts. The other half falls within the object area. So if a 0.25-point trap stroke is suggested by your printshop, assign 0.5-point strokes. Many printshops will automatically add trapping "in-line," so we don't have to.

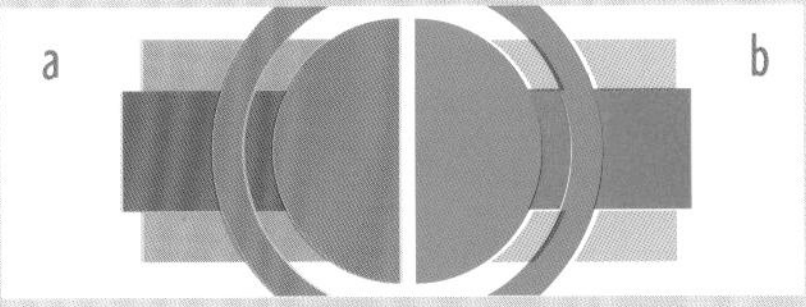
a
b

Avoid traps by mixing each four-color halftone tint with a little bit of the adjacent neighbor's colors, a. For example, when both background and foreground objects contain some percentage of magenta halftone, if registration goes awry, a sliver of less obtrusive magenta, rather than white paper, b, will show. Approach a is felt to be preferable to b, but the best approach may be to choose a better printshop. I usually make traps only for PMS-color jobs or any job where I, not my client, deal with the printer.

RGB

RGB for web, CMYK for print. Be sure your Illustrator files designed for print do not contain any RGB colors, or that the Document Color mode is not RGB. When negs are made by a service bureau or printshop, art in RGB—unless it's discovered and fixed—can come out as gray scale. Don't use PMS colors and spot colors in four-color CMYK jobs. They indicate to a service bureau output device that we want to use additional ink plates. PMS colors in a four-color job may just drop out altogether.

This is only a test. At a, how dense must a halftone screen tint be for the press to hold the image? At b, what is the finest point size of line that can be printed without dropping out? At c, for your edification and mine, a comparison of blacks with and without enrichment. Results of this test will vary according to size of screen, paper stock and press used. This book uses a 200-line screen. Screens of 100—150 lines are most common.

a 5% 4% 3% 2% 1%
b .02 .05 .1 .2 .3 .4 .5 .6
c
100% (S) black
40C-SK
40C-30M-SK
SC-SM-SY-SK

Lettering DON'TS & DOS

The law of being consistent in all aspects of our lettering has already been mentioned many times and should be enough to make the following examples of inconsistency unnecessary. Still, it may be helpful to point out some of the more common, yet insidious manifestations of inconsistency. Many cases of faulty lettering are the result of resistance to reference. If we were willing to refer to a font similar to the one we intend to draw, we might avoid committing some basic errors in letter shapes. I call this the authorship dilemma. We are afraid to copy or use reference because the result will be "copying," and the final job won't be "ours." Perhaps so, but at first, we will need to copy until the correct forms of letters are more or less permanently etched into our minds. Copying is the best teacher. Finally, there is the problem of lack of overview and reluctance to self-criticize. I read that the illustrator Maxfield Parrish would hang his works in progress on a wall and sit and stare at them for long periods. I can almost guarantee you that Parrish was thinking, "OK, what sucks about this?" Just to sit back and take the time to stare at our work—or put it away for a while and come back to it—gains us an invaluable perspective that can make problem areas suddenly become obvious. Lack of ego helps in this. We are all so fragile and deathly afraid of criticism, but I feel that the ability to listen to criticism, whether from our own intuition or the constructive criticism of another, is the only way to become better at what we do. For example, my font Magneto originally had a rather buxom dot over *i-j* that was quite a bit larger than it now is. David Berlow of Font Bureau, which publishes Magneto, told me the dot should be smaller. We argued over this for days until one day I woke up and realized he was right: The oversize dot was inconsistent with the color of the rest of the alphabet. So I changed it . . . and the rest is typographic history. :)

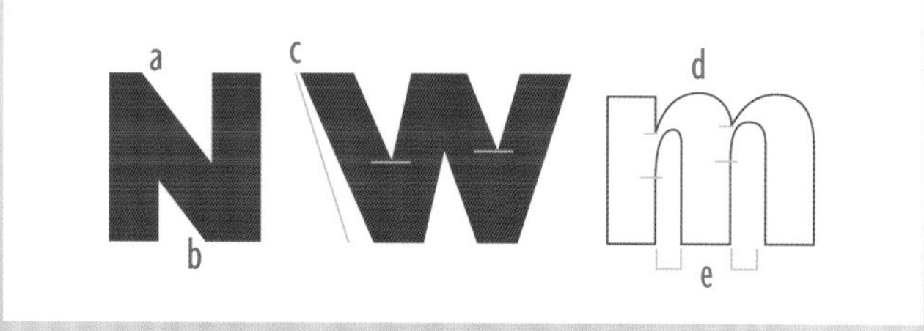
a
c
d
NWm
b
e

DON'T let unenclosed counters, sometimes called "admitted spaces," within letters become unbalanced. At a, the diagonal stem meets the vertical stem too narrowly at the top. At b, the base juncture is too wide, leaving unbalanced upper/lower counters. At c, left and right slopes of *W* don't match, and the height of the diagonal stem junctures are different. At d and e, nothing is right. See what I mean?

a
c
b
mba

DON'T mix too many neat ideas into one style. There are too many shapes happening in the logo above, like perfect circles next to quarter circles of varying radii, so the letters don't match as a style. And just what is going on, a, with the top of *m*? Rounded corners are so easy to make on a computer, it never ceases to amaze me how often I see bumpy transitions from curve into stem as at b, c.

baks

DON'T let your lettering become a mishmash of too many cool angles, shapes and weird, small spaces that contribute to eye dirt. In this logo above, there is much too much going on. Pick one or two angles, curves and shapes and leave it at that. This is an example of lettering that's too hip for its own good.

basey

DON'T confuse top and bottom weights. Well, what'll it be—a top-weighted letter style or a bottom-weighted one? Choose one and stick with it. Note also that a thin vertical stem has been well established until the last stem of *y*, which suddenly becomes wide. Also, the spine of *s* is too low, making counters unbalanced.

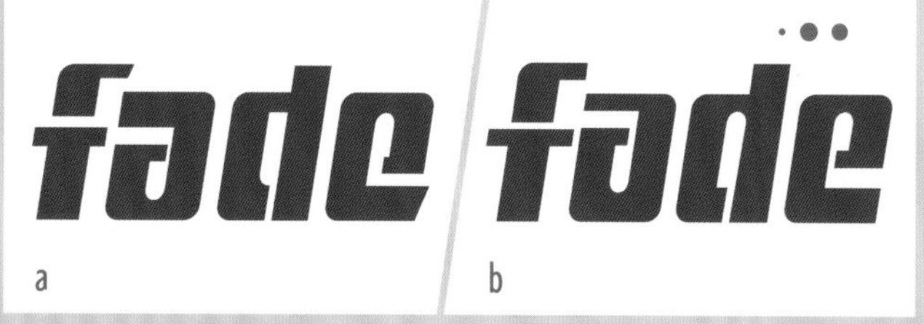
fade
fade
a
b

DON'T let all the spaces between shapes, which for lack of a better term I'm calling *slots*, be of different widths. They should follow the same law of consistency that demands that stem widths, counter widths, letter angle and letter spacing all remain the same. Nothing disturbs the eye more than slots of different widths, as at a. The logo is improved at b.Gauge balls were used to keep widths consistent.

a
b
c

DO "draw through" when drawing letter outlines, a, so that stems passing through other stems within the same letter will follow through accurately. Don't unite shapes too soon. If you tweak stem widths later, you may mess up the follow through, b. If you do need to realign stems, draw several *s*-curve strokes, c, from extrema point to extrema point as guides to help you regain correct follow-through.

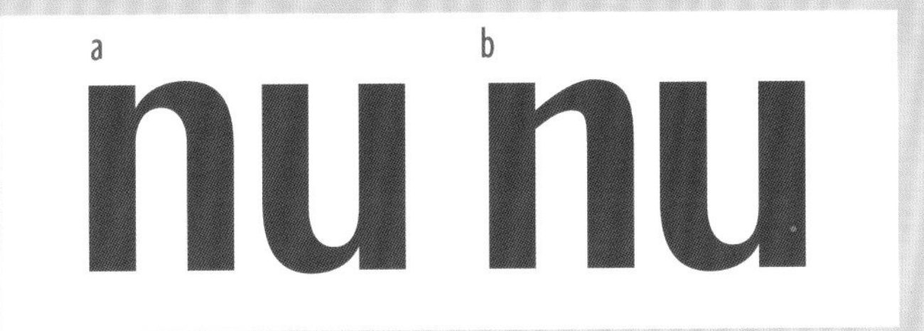
a
b
nu nu

DON'T be inconsistent with letter shapes. At a, the letters *n-u* are a matched set. They should be: *u* is just *n* rotated (although for there to be subtle differences between them is not unusual). At b, each letter was drawn independently, without using standard parts, so naturally they are mismatched.

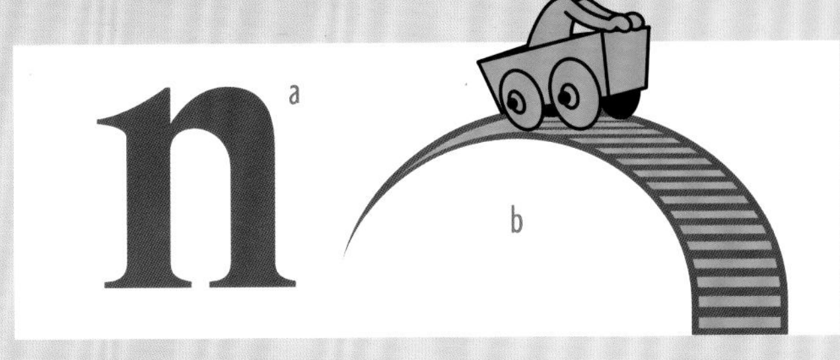
n
a
b

DON'T let the top part of the curve, a, come around too fat. This is obviously a contour-drawn *n*, rather than a pen- or brush-drawn *n*. Think of these curves as roller-coaster tracks seen in perspective, b. Common sense tells us the tracks are parallel, and as they diminish or come forward, both sides remain in parallel relationship.

a
b
c
d
C S E p

DON'T be guilty of any of the following errors: At a, the ball of the *C* is too small compared with the weight of the letter. At b, the spine of letter *S* narrows in the center instead of coming to its fullest width at this point, as it should. At c, none of the serifs on this letter *E* are the same size. At d, the bowl of *p* tilts forward though the rest of the letter is very upright. A posthumous tip of the hat to Mortimer Leach, who discussed these bad examples, which I've redrawn above, in his excellent book *Lettering for Advertising*, 1956. (It actually upsets me to look at these letters.)

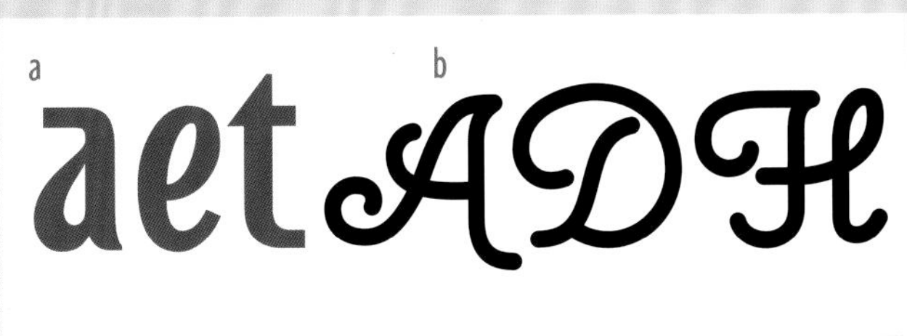
a
b
aet
ADH

DON'T accidentally italicize. At a, the thrust of letters *a-t* are clearly vertical, yet the *e* seems to be slightly slanting. This can happen because *e-c-o* have no upright stems to anchor them in verticality and we start to lose the objectivity to notice. It helps to check our letters backwards by holding a printout to a mirror or just flopping/ Reflecting letters on screen. At b, an example of a semi-script style that is clearly upright—except for *D* that slants forward. I've recently observed this in several fonts: designers don't realize that stem angles are mismatched.

a
OBJECT
b
OBJECT

DO create "accommodations" whenever possible so letters may fit better together and the incidence of spacing gaps will be lessened. At a, the original type, Kobalt Black. At b, the sizes of all counters were increased, which decreased overall weight; letter *B* was turned upside down so *J* could tuck; letter *C* was rotated backwards so its lower right stem could tuck under *T*, resulting in closing up the usual gap there.

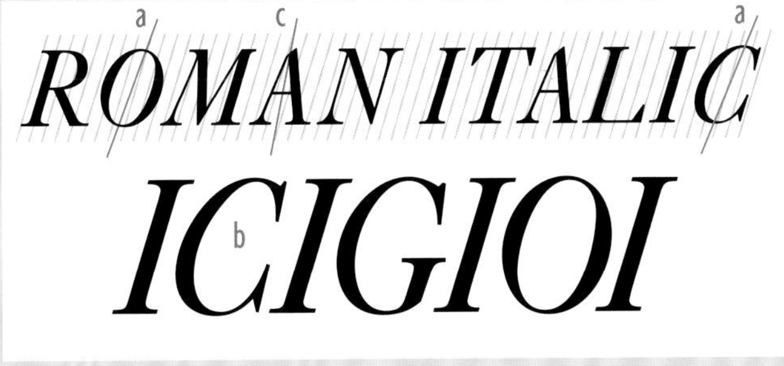
a
c
a
ROMAN ITALIC
b
ICIGIOI

DO increase the angle of slant for italicized round letters like *C-G-O-Q*, and also for applicable lowercase letters which may even include the bowls of *b-d-p*, and so on. I have found that the axes of rounded characters must be more acute, a, than those with straight sides or they may appear to be falling backwards, b. Apply this rule also to diagonally-stroked letters, like *A* at c, whose degree of slant is insufficient here.

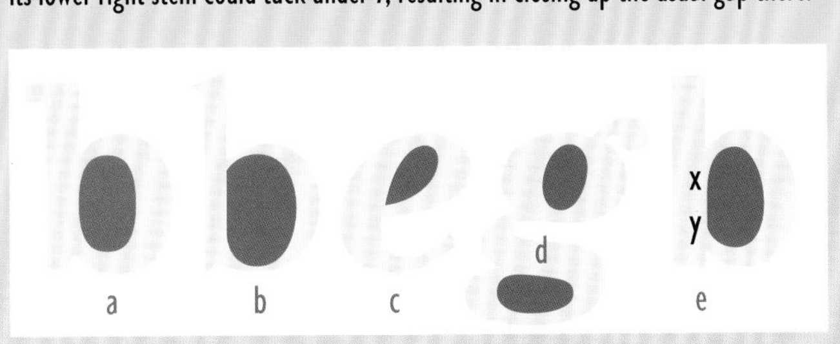
x
y
d
a
b
c
e

DO keep the interior shapes of counters pleasing. Counters can be absolutely symmetrical as in a, or asymmetrical as in b, c, d, yet still be nicely shaped. The lumpy counter at e branches slowly away from the stem in a clockwise direction at x, but on its return at y, the attachment is more abrupt. True, the counter at b is drawn similarly, but there it's forcefully, consciously and more gracefully done.

DON'T be afraid to draw logos, fonts or lettering. Fear of trying may be the biggest mistake of all. Sure, your first efforts may stink, but, hey, Rome wasn't burnt in a day! Give it time, keep trying. Careful, intelligent and diligent application of all the principles put forth in this book can absolutely compensate for any lack of native talent. Did you know that s/he who perseveres furthers? And that confidence and persistence will take you much farther than mere talent alone?

Bezier Curves for Cowards

POINTS IN EXTREMA

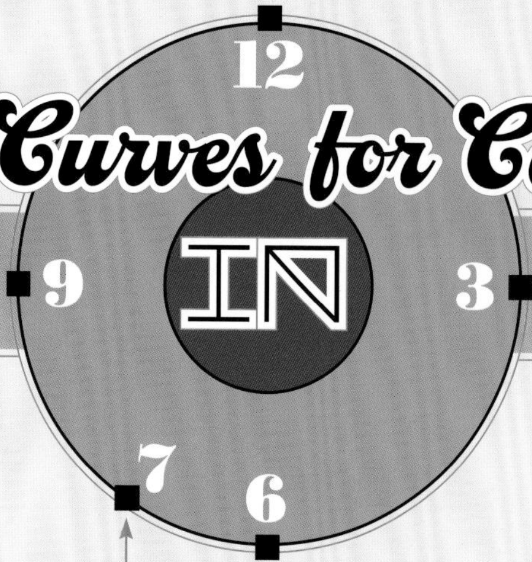
12
9
3
7
6

The best placement of Bezier points is at the most extreme edges of the curve: the 12, 3, 6 and 9 o'clock positions. A study of the point placement in any well-drawn font will demonstrate this truth. Points in "extrema" (Latin, I guess) enable easier tweaking or point editing to ensure the smoothest and most agreeable curves. Equally important, points in extrema improve autohinting and PostScript interpretation of our fonts.

(But sometimes, darn it, you just gotta place an extra point or two along the path to achieve the shape you're wanting.)

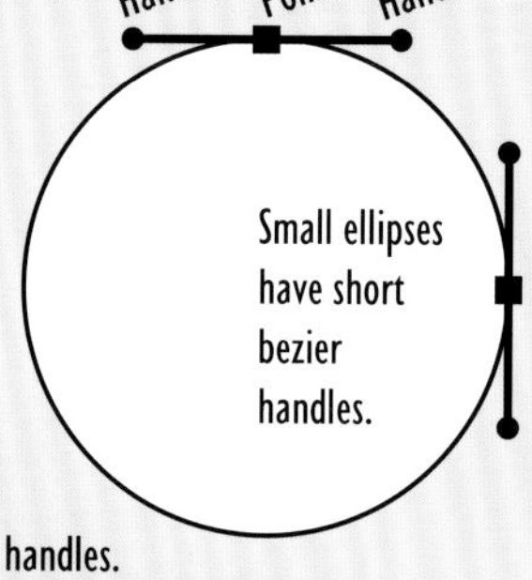
Handle
Point
Handle
Small ellipses have short bezier handles.

Big ellipses have long bezier handles.

Whenever we are drawing in Illustrator or Fontographer, whether pictures or letters, we should ever attempt to place all points in extrema and keep all handles orthogonal (straight, vertically or horizontally) by holding down the Shift key as we drag them away from each new point we draw.

The straight side of a curve should not have a bezier handle.

A point that transitions from a large curve to a smaller one will have one handle longer than the other.

How do I find the extreme position?

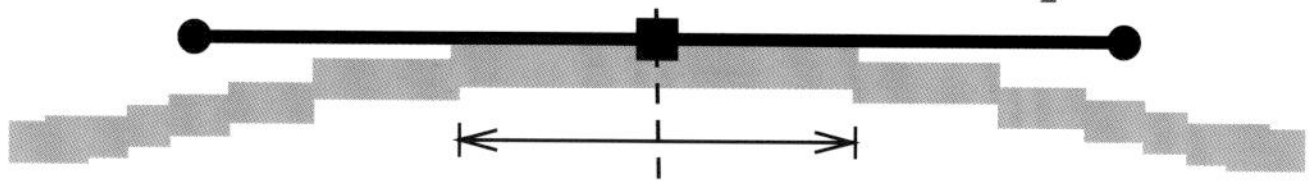

Enlarge your view of a stroke, or a scan you are tracing, to see the bitmap rendering. The extreme point is where the "stairsteps" level out. The very center of the straight part is where the point goes.

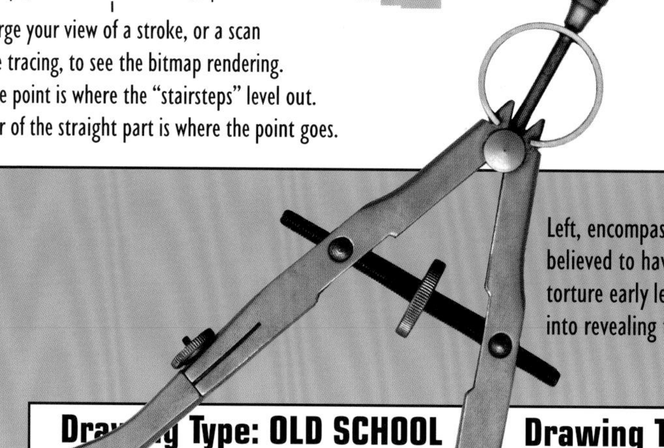

Left, encompassing device believed to have been used to torture early lettering scribes into revealing trade secrets.

If we are not drawing a font, the extrema rule is not absolutely essential, except, as mentioned, it makes curve editing easier.

Some designers may assume, incorrectly, that using more points guarantees better rendering of letter shapes in printers and on-screen. Actually, the fewer points the better, so long as the extrema rule is observed. Fewer points usually also means smoother curves.

I've seen many commercial fonts designed on now-outmoded font creation software, containing tons of extraneous points. Sometimes the process of converting a font to TrueType causes extra points to be added. Autotracing from scans also places too many points and puts them in the wrong positions, i.e. not in extrema. Such fonts can give the wrong impression about point placement.

(continued on opposite page)

Drawing Type: OLD SCHOOL

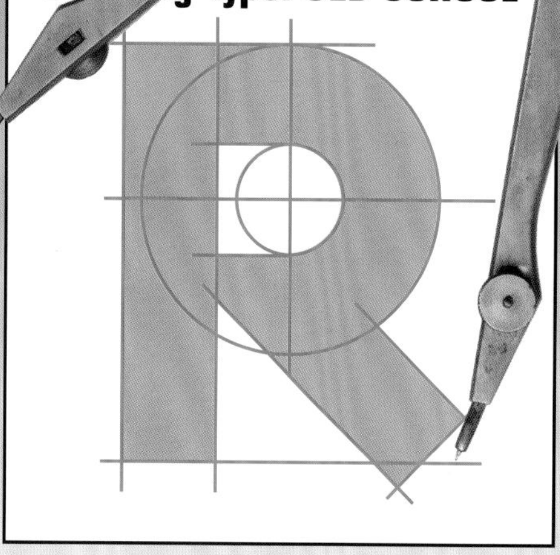

Drawing Type: NEW SCHOOL

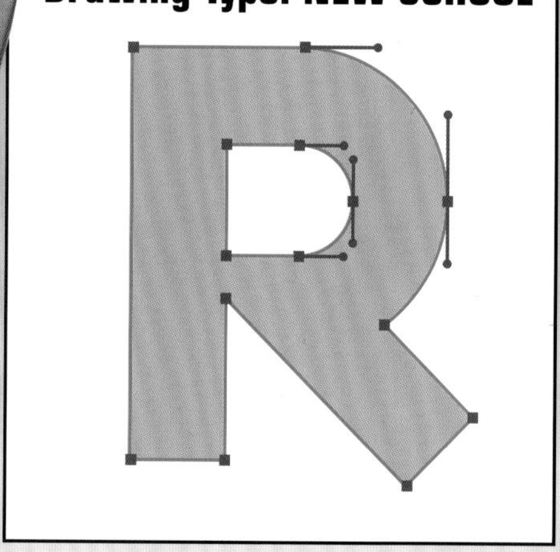

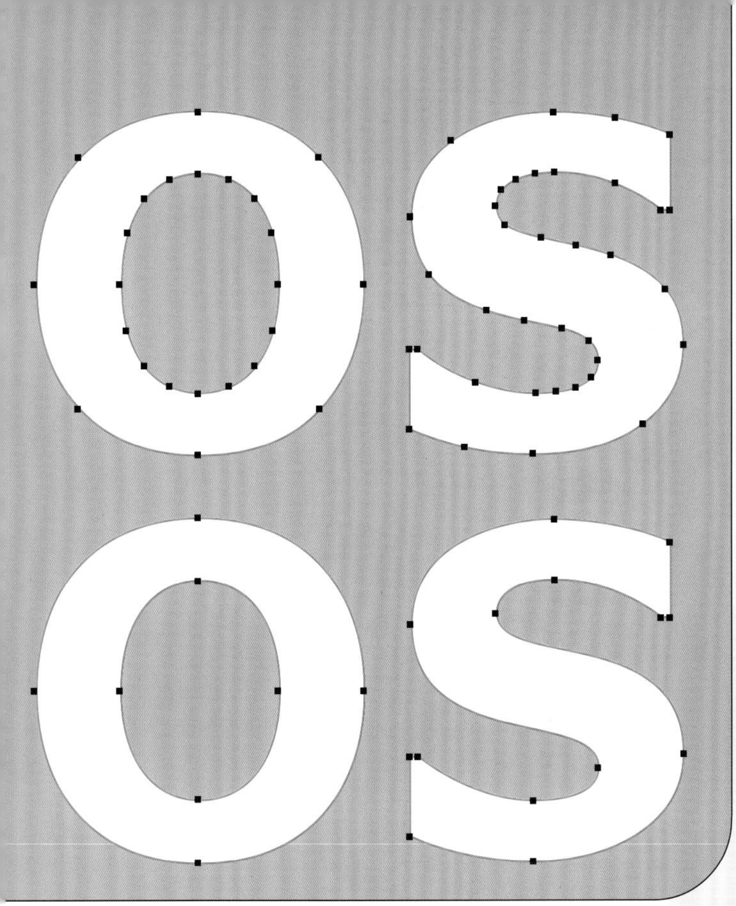

In 1990, when we had 80MB hard drives and 16MB of RAM, too many bezier points may have contributed to a general slowing up of font loading or printing, but now, if you use too many points, it really doesn't matter.

Except as previously mentioned: Points in extrema may produce better "hinting" for viewing fonts on computer monitors and the web. Hinting is the manner in which a letter arranges itself into stairstep pixels on-screen. Some conscientious designers edit hinting to ensure their fonts look good in all sizes and situations. But I'm told that other reputable designers never bother with hinting. Personally, I couldn't care less about hinting because I don't consider the appearance of a font at 12-point size on-screen, on the web or coming from a 300 dpi laser printer a true "end use." You may very well disagree. In print, a font will look only as good or bad as the designer designed it.

Which of these sets of letters, left, would be easier to tweak?

Compare results of point editing using both methods...

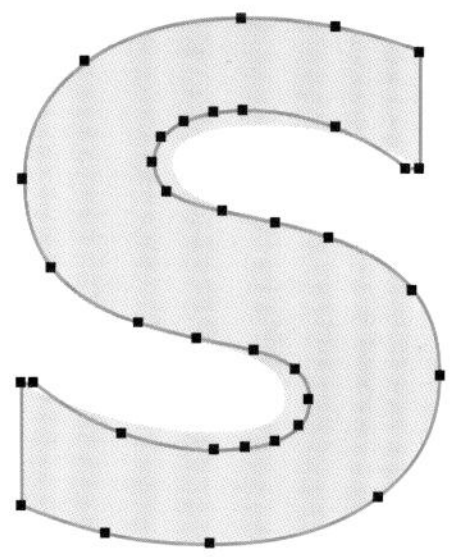

1. Pretend we want to tweak this *S*, left, so the shapes of the inner curves match the blue-shaded letter in the background. Just look at how many points we'll have to move while still attempting to retain smooth curves.

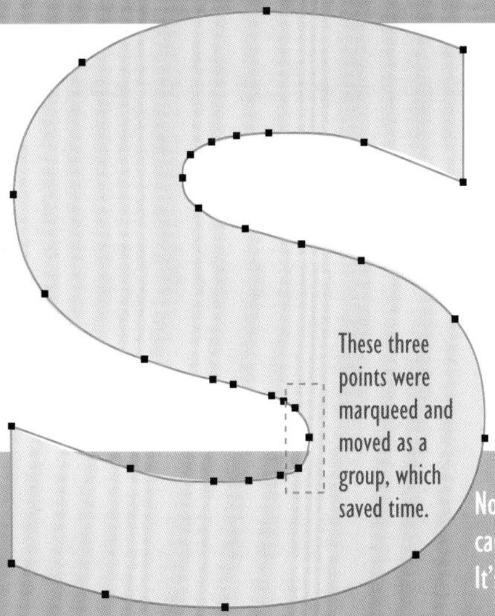
These three points were marqueed and moved as a group, which saved time.

2. Left, first steps have been taken by dragging points to the edges of the background *S*. Next, the bezier handles will all have to be adjusted to make the curves smooth again. That's work! But could we get away without bothering to fix the points? (Hey, most users of our font will never notice the rough edges.)

Here's that shaky *S* from step 2 at 12 and 24 points. Looks OK, huh?

Well, if you're like me, ever striving for perfection in letterforms, you'll want to design your lettering for the *most* discriminating eye, not the least.

Note: Too many points defining a shape won't necessarily cause bumpy curves, not if one adjusts them all carefully. It's just—who would want to?

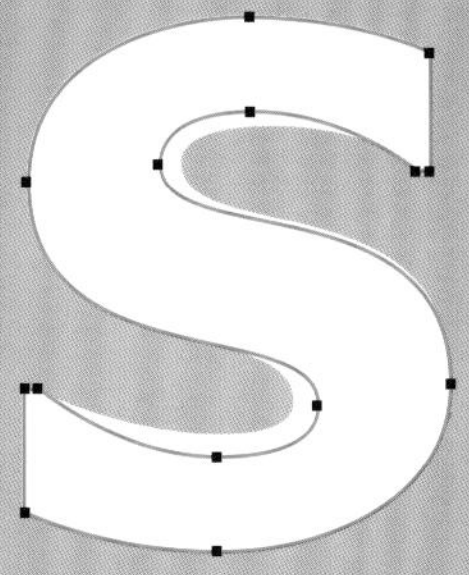

3. Here's that *S* again—This time, with points in extrema. As we drag each bezier point to its new position, the resulting curves will remain beautiful, requiring only minor adjustment of handles.

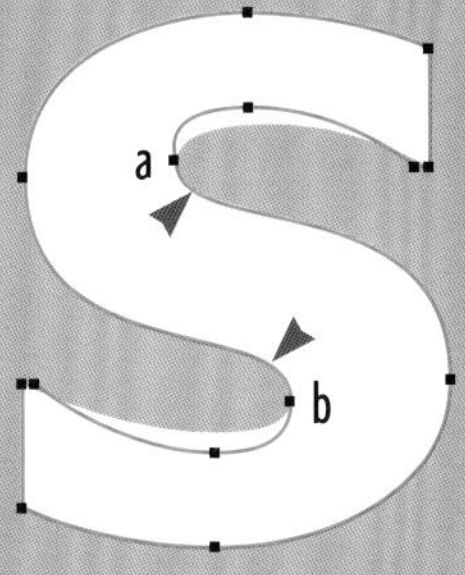
a
b

4. Left, the points at a and b have been dragged to their new positions. Arrows show that resulting curves have remained nice. Right, points c and d have been repositioned. Only the point at d will have to be slightly tweaked by raising the lower bezier handle a bit.

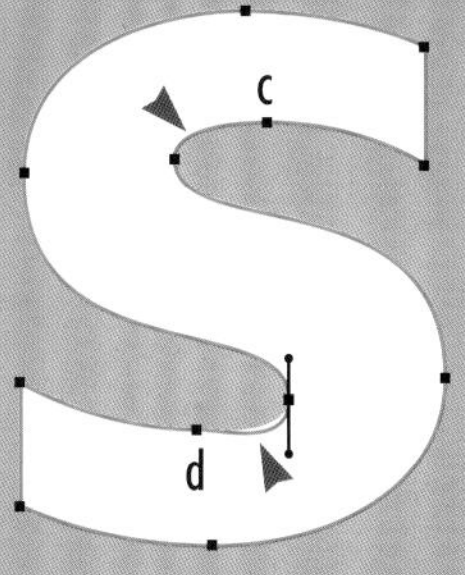
c
d

Handling Points

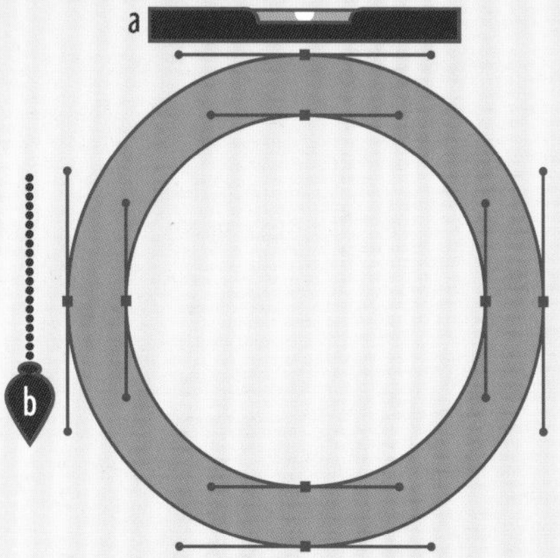
a
b

The handles of points in extrema should be positioned perfectly straight either vertically or horizontally. When making an ellipse, any Ellipse tool will place points correctly, but when we draw curves with a Pen tool, we must hold the Shift key so handles stay level, a, or plumb, b.

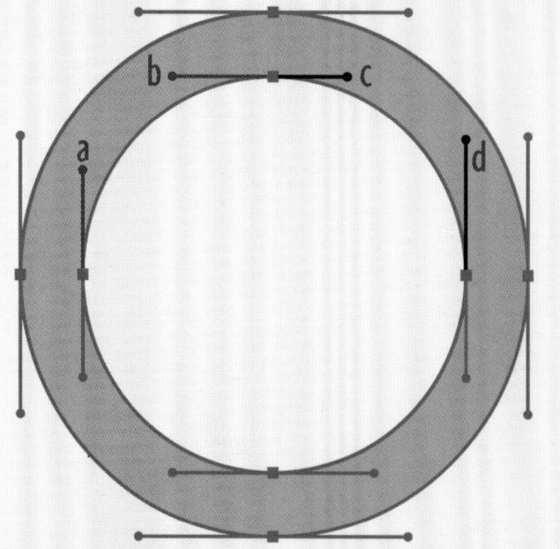
b
c
a
d

When properly drawn, the two point handles bordering a constant curved path, such as a, b, should always be the same length to equally bear the burden of the curve. Sure, we can still, more or less, achieve the same curved shape with an arrangement like c, d, but it is not ideal.

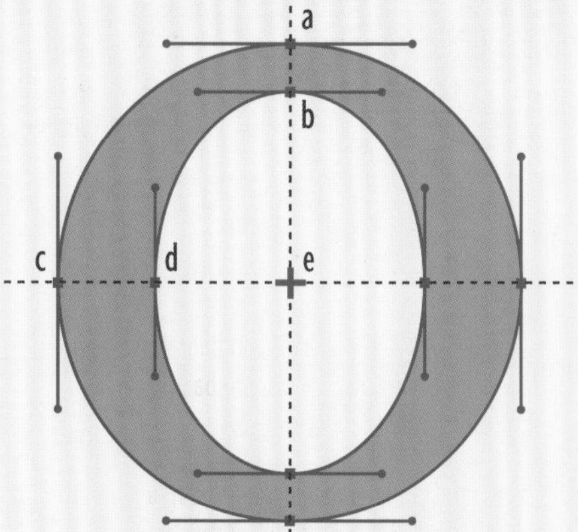
a
b
c
d
e

In most lettering styles, the two adjacent points on inner and outer curves, such as a, b, or c, d should always be in alignment with each other. In a symmetrical letter like *O* above, all four sets of extrema points should be lined up horizontally or vertically with the center axis e.

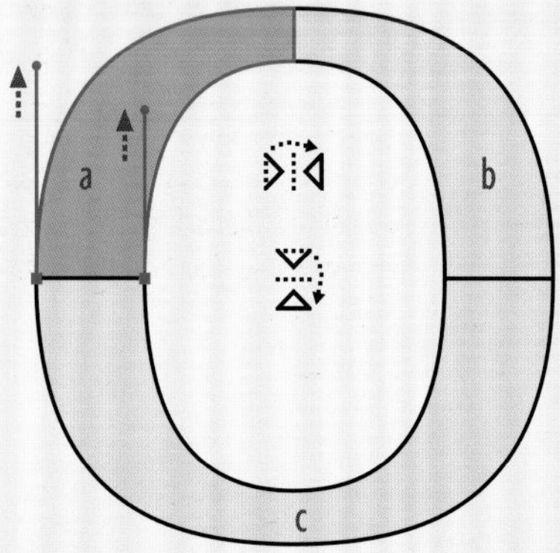
a
b
c

Handles can be dragged up for a squarish ellipse. Illustrator's and Fontographer's Info pallets show numeric point coordinates so bezier handles on all sides of a symmetrical curve can be made exactly the same. Or, Reflect-Copy quadrant a to create b, then Reflect-Copy a and b to make c.

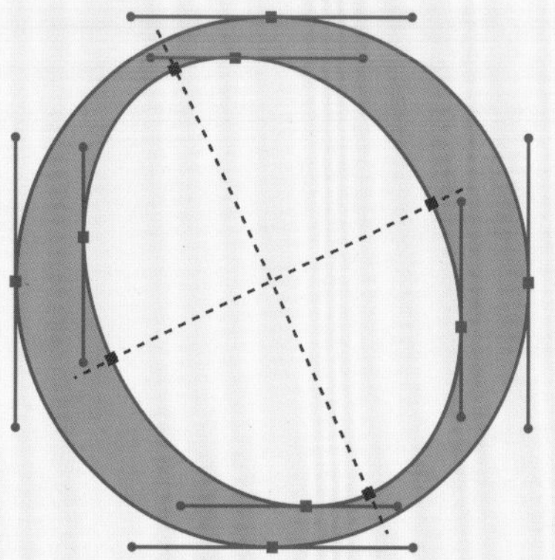

Rotating the counter, or center hole, of the *O* gives a keen, old-fashioned look. But it requires moving the positions of the points back to extrema. In Illustrator, this may be done manually, or if making a font, Fontographer's Clean Up Paths filter will do it automatically.

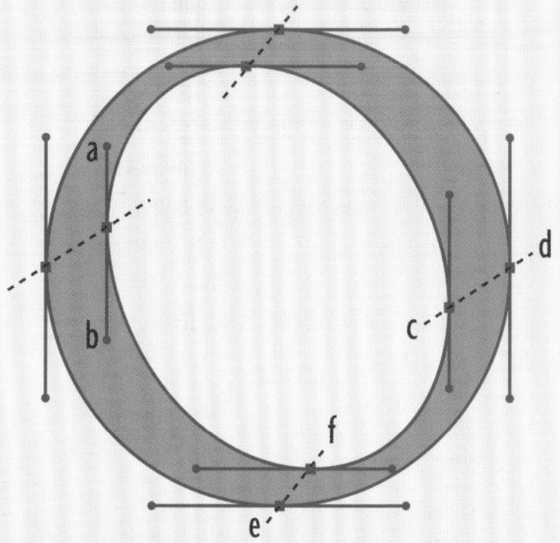
a
b
c
d
f
e

Notice, above, that the handles of the inner ellipse points, such as a, b, are no longer the same length, and that the angles of inner and outer points like c, d and e, f are in alignment with each other and in oppositional symmetry with the points on their adjacent sides.

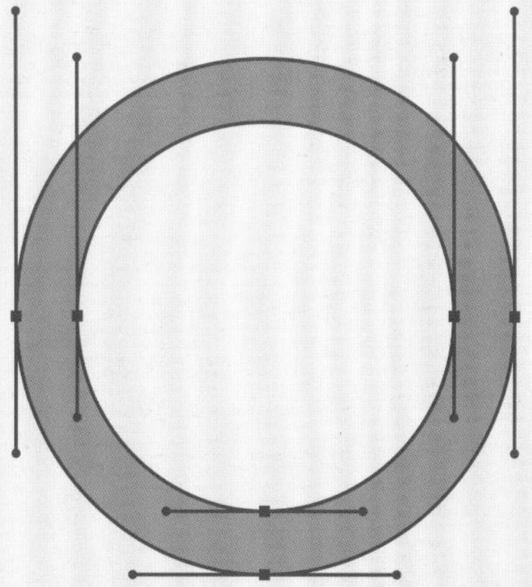

By extending bezier handles ridiculously, one can eliminate points such as would properly appear in the 12 o'clock positions on the inner and outer circles above. But not only will most curved shapes suffer from the omission, the rendering of our fonts on-screen and in print may worsen.

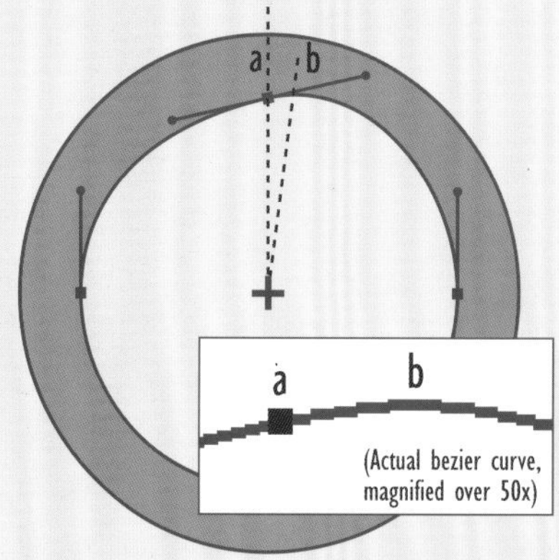
a
b
a
b
(Actual bezier curve, magnified over 50x)

The world won't explode if points aren't in extrema and handles are crooked. If we're not drawing a font, points need be in extrema only for ease of curve tweaking. Notice that when we angled the handle, above, the extrema position shifted from a to b, where the point ought to go.

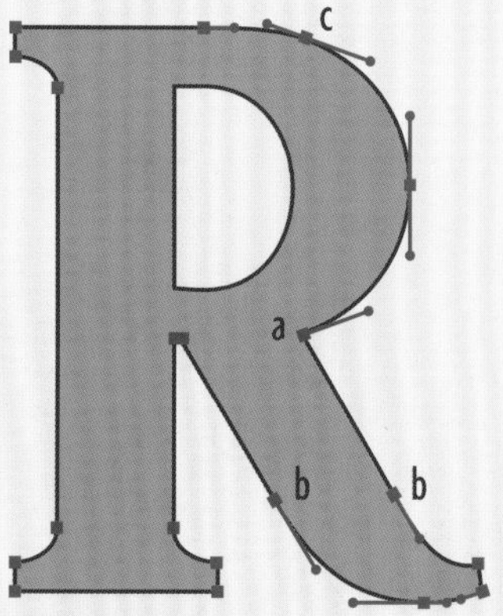
c
a
b
b

So, do try to place all points in extrema and make all handles straight up or down. But these rules don't apply to corners (a), straight lines that are diagonal that transition into curves (b), and the occasional extra point (c) that may be the only way to achieve just the elusive curve we want.

DRAWING *with* BEZIERS, Point by Point

7–8. Shift-click points to constrain them straight.

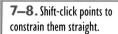

9. Shift-click point, drag out a long handle. Drag left side handle back into point.

10. Click point at 3 o'clock, now hold Shift, drag out (and keep) two handles to make a *smooth point.*

11. Click point (not with Shift key), drag handle toward left, angling it to match curve of bowl. Click point again to delete the prodigal left handle. Option-click this same point and drag a new handle out, but in the direction of the leg of *R.* This point is now a *corner point with beziers.*

6. Click point. Drag out handle toward left—always in the direction we're heading. Click prodigal handle to kill it.

5. Shift-click the point. Pull handle upward. Drag prodigal lower handle back into point and proceed to next point.

12. Click point, drag short handle to the right. Let up mouse. Hold Shift and drag the left handle wide until the ogee curve between points 12 and 11 matches the scan.

4. Click the point, hold down and drag a handle upward. Let up mouse, again click the point. The prodigal handle disappears. This is a way to kill off an outgoing handle. Straight path segments don't need handles.

PS: Note the extra-long handles between points 24 and 25. This arrangement creates a gently rounded, pointless, virtual corner.

13. Click point, drag handle up. Click again to kill it, adjust lower handle to achieve desired curve.

3. Again, Shift-click the point to constrain (force) it into perfect horizontal alignment with point 2. Keep Shift down and don't let up on click until you've dragged a short bezier handle toward the right, away from point. A prodigal (unnecessary) handle emerges also on left. Press ⌘ to toggle to the White Arrow tool. Drag left handle back home to point. This is a *transition point* (from straight to curve).

14., etc. Problem: caption space is no more. Reader must leave nest, fly on own wings. Remaining steps will follow same four point models as already explained: corner, transition, smooth with beziers, and corner with beziers. Got it, then? OK, proceed.

2. Hold Shift key as you click (Shift-click) so this next point is forced into perfect vertical alignment with point 1.

1. Draw points in clockwise direction. Read captions from bottom up. Click first point.

Usually, we draw letters by following the shapes of scans of rough sketches placed on a template layer locked beneath the working layer. See page 158 on tracing scans.

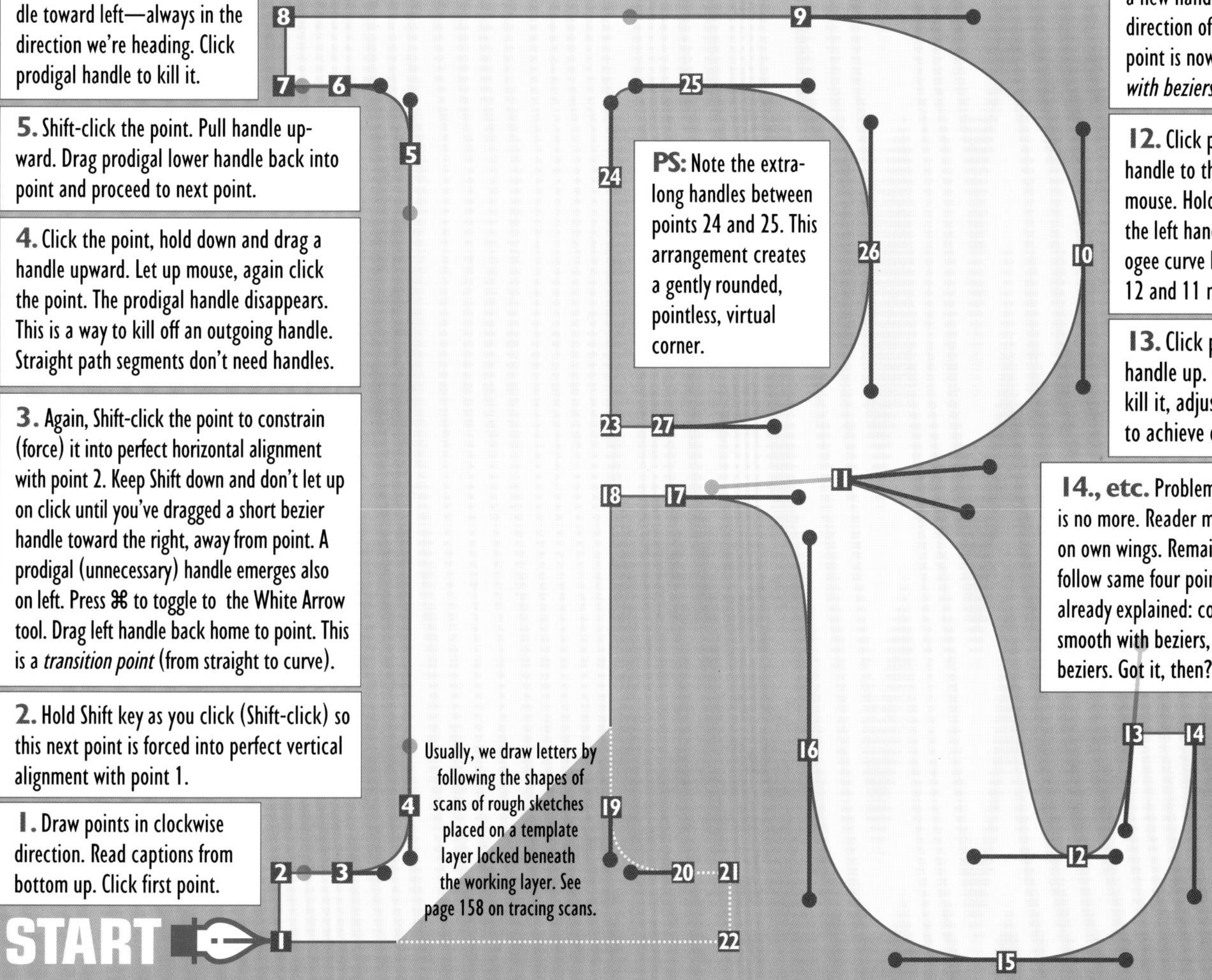
START
1
2
3
4
5
6
7
8
9
10
11
12
13
14
15
16
17
18
19
20
21
22
23
24
25
26
27

FAQ: Bezier Pointers........................

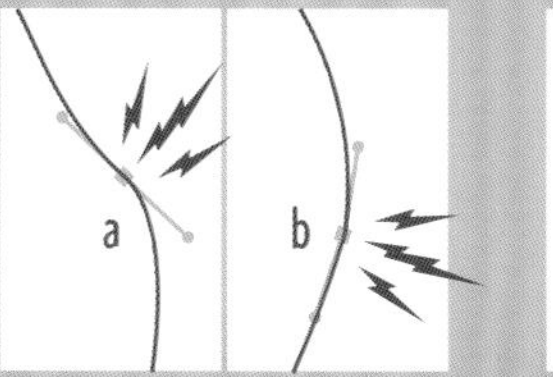
a
b

Why do I get weird bumps in my curves? Always drag the handle in the general direction your curved path is heading, or at least tangent to the curve. Beginners always start wildly spinning handles, a. Or you may have a corner point where a smooth one should go, b.

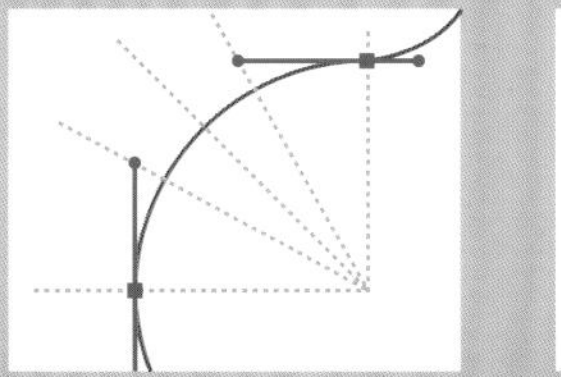

How long should a bezier handle be dragged out? A handle should extend about one-third the way to the next point. Don't make one handle do all the work; both must share the curve. After you finish drawing a path, you'll go back to adjust all handles.

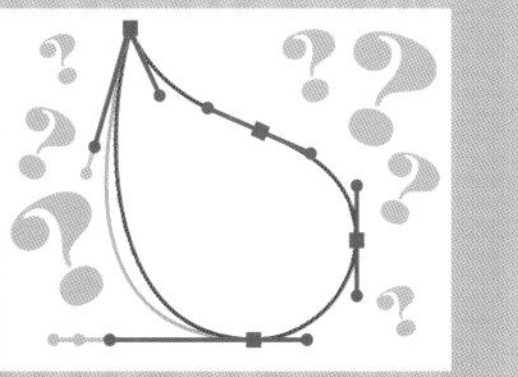

Which of the two handles bordering a curve do I adjust in order to get the curve the way I want it? After a while you'll get the feel for it. Usually, adjusting both handles—perhaps one more than the other—is required to perfect the curve.

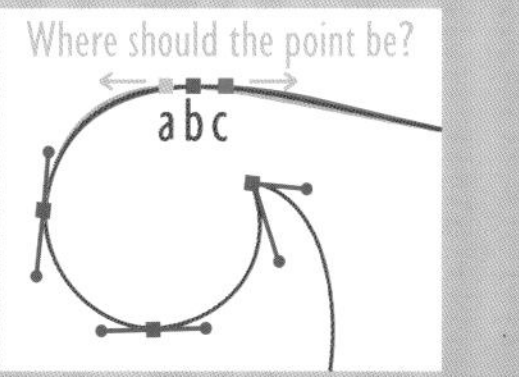
Where should the point be?
a b c

Points are in extrema, but the !#@$! curve won't do what I want. Just because a point is in extrema doesn't mean it's ideally placed in space. Above, which point, a, b or c, will give the desired curve? Also, try adding a point between the stubborn two, or tilting point handles out of square (just this once).

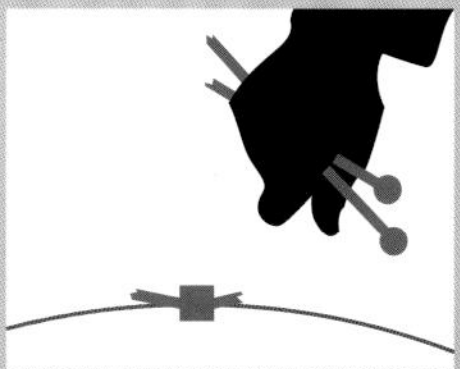

What should I do if the point don't work 'cause the vandals took the handles? I get the feeling that some of you just aren't taking this subject seriously enough.

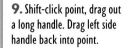

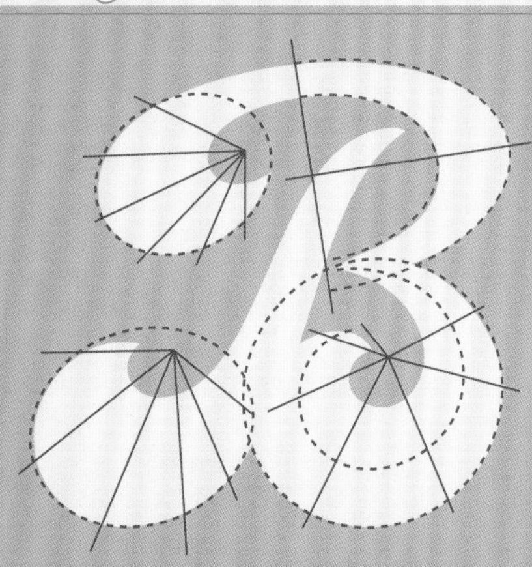

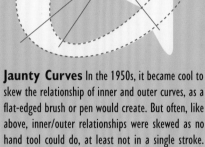

Round Curves These flaring cat-tail curves emulate the strokes of a fat, pointed brush. Most of the curves' axis points are off-center, yet a brush would need to be held perpendicular to the work, not at an angle, to make such strokes. Swells grow organically from wrist pivot position as brush is borne down upon.

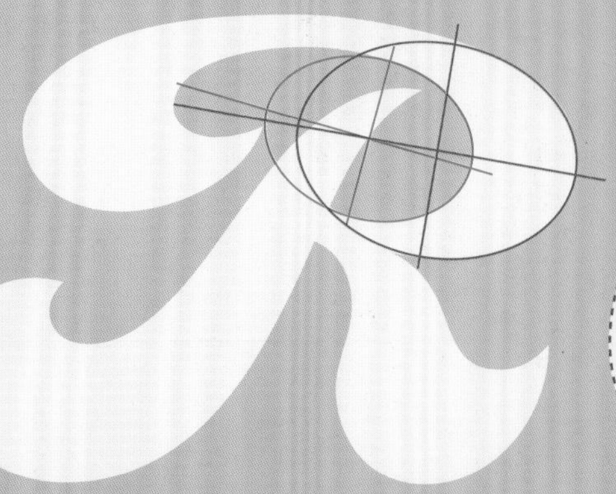

Off-Round Curves In drawing Casey Ultrawide, I noticed the discrepancy above, between the inner and outer angles of the bowl of *R* that—though suitable for another font—was contrary to the round curve concept, torturously described in the previous caption, that I tried to achieve. Later, I corrected it.

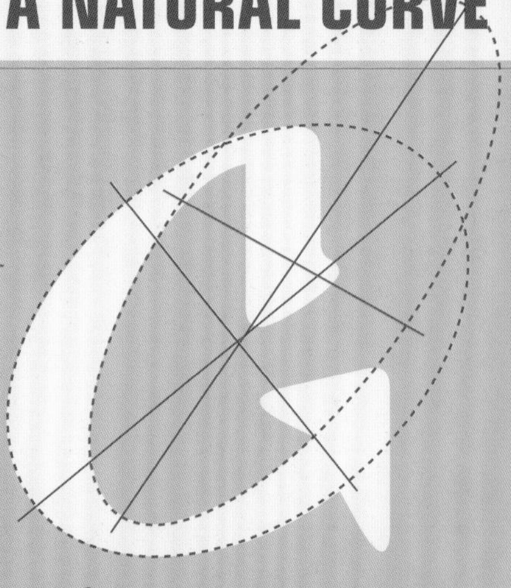

Jaunty Curves In the 1950s, it became cool to skew the relationship of inner and outer curves, as a flat-edged brush or pen would create. But often, like above, inner/outer relationships were skewed as no hand tool could do, at least not in a single stroke. Nonaligned center axis points characterize this style.

Comparing Inking Styles to Letterforms

The best lettering, like cartoon inking, has calligraphic qualities that come from a pen or brush drawn at a consistent angle, any given curved segment of which can be a masterpiece of graceful nuance, or an awkward and inharmonious rat's nest of unrelated contours. Following is a comparison of cartoon inking styles and their lettering equivalents to show that a consistent and well-reasoned plan ought to precede any curves we build with beziers.

Side Swell Swelling occurs along the lengths of strokes, tapering at the turns. This style, produced virtually automatically with any flexible pen point, can be found in early 1920s and 1930s animation inking on both coasts.

Heavy Mono Outline, Thin Inline Originated with Winsor McCay, was perfected by Max Fleischer animators Dick Huemer and Willard Bowsky. The slightly flaring outer stroke gives a sense of volume. A bold, decorative approach.

Bottom Swell Were this example inked with a brush (all examples were done with beziers—*and it was no picnic!*), the inker's wrist would have had to freely pivot to create such curves. Typical of mid-1930s Hollywood cartoon inking.

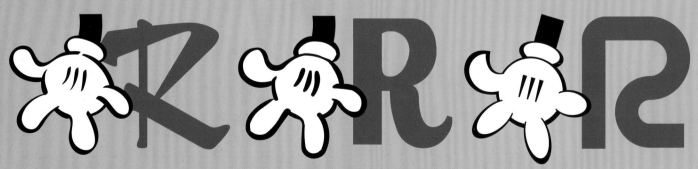

Energetic Swell The above, imitating chisel-point-brush inking, was done with Illustrator's Brush tool. Will Dwiggins called this style of curve "energetic" (as his own tended to be). The wrist is held static and strokes are sort of sideswiped in.

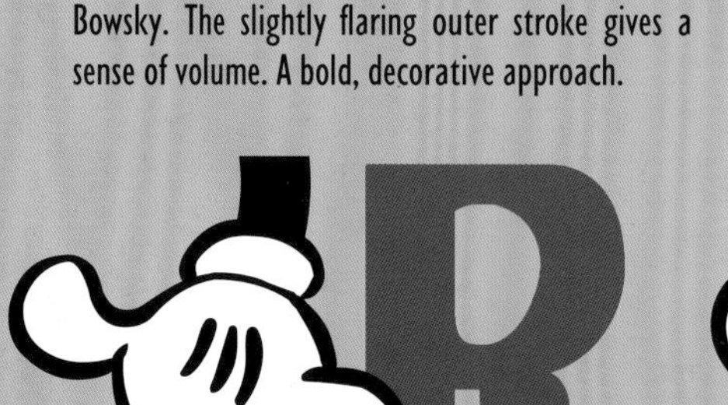

Internet Low-budget animation's exigencies preclude careful inking. Drawn with Macromedia Flash's lousy Brush tool on a digital tablet, the above is typical of much Internet cartoon inking. The choppy hand and Internet *R* adhere to no style; strokes are bastards.

Computer Geometric Created entirely of ellipses, rectangles and segments of ellipses, such drawings can lack the warmth and realism of drawings made by hand. Instead, there's a clean precision that, when well done, is very appealing.

ARTS & LETTERS: *Perfect Curves*

What do good art and good lettering share? Good lines and curves. This is something some designers do naturally, and others have to work at. It's easier with a pencil or brush to draw a gorgeous curve, which a speedy wrist can facilitate, but beziers present major technical impediments that detach us from the tactile immediacy of the hand on paper. This page features hand-done works whose every curvaceous stroke—virtually any curved line segment we may inspect—serves as a goal for those of us attempting to wrangle such results out of recalcitrant mice.

GENE DEITCH ASSOCIATES, INC.
43 WEST 61 NEW YORK 23 NEW YORK CIRCLE 7-1970
COPYRIGHT 1959 BY
GENE DEITCH AND ALLEN SWIFT

Right, there is deliberateness in every stroke of animation artist Shane Glines's pencil sketch. Such beautiful curves are not merely the result of his expertly stylized depiction of nubile female anatomy. You can't be stupid and be able to draw this well. Glines's obvious intellect, his ability to store visual information and reproduce what he observes, his restless enthusiasm for inquiry and fearless self-correction are indicated by every line he draws—It seems to me, anyway.

Above, brush drawing by Gene Deitch, legendary cartoon director. Deitch's is the classic cartoon inking, and each of his curving forms is picture perfect. Even the copyright legend—obviously just dashed off—is beautiful. The letterhead sports a really hip logo, too.

HA!
IF ONLY SHE KNEW, IF ONLY SHE KNEW!
Sigh..

Left, his curves and energetic, chisel-stroke inking do more than ape classic, comic-book styles, they epitomize it. Choose virtually any one of Mitch O'Connell's strokes, blow it up and isolate it from the rest, and see if it doesn't embody every characteristic of grace, rhythm, and balance that we strive for in letter design.

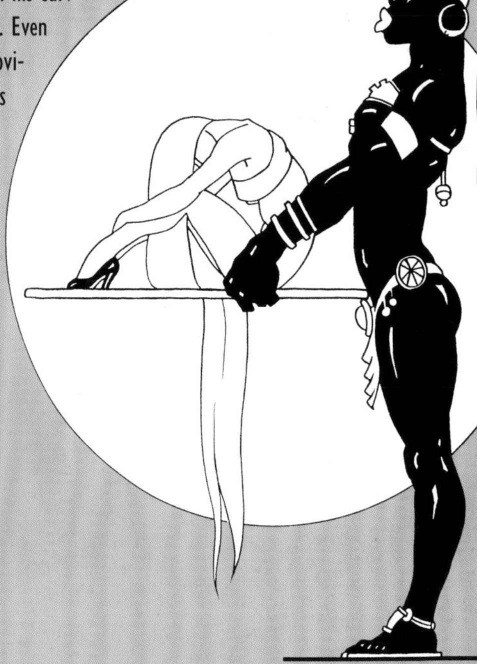

Above, Ernesto García Cabral ("Chango") was the premiere caricaturist and movie poster artist of Mexico, 1930s–1950s. Every line he drew was delicious, and according to *Mad* cartoonist Sergio Aragonés, who sought out and met his idol, Chango was a wonderful and humble man. As Sergio once observed to me, "The better artists [in a technical sense] are also usually nicer people."

CURVE CLINIC

Bezier Curves for Cowards

Can a segment of a curve be scrutinized out of context and still be deemed good or bad? Yes. And when every curved segment of every letter possesses a rhythmic beauty unto itself—as well as in context with the whole—we can be sure that our lettering is gonna look right. It takes a good eye and practice, and with beziers, it also takes lots of patience.

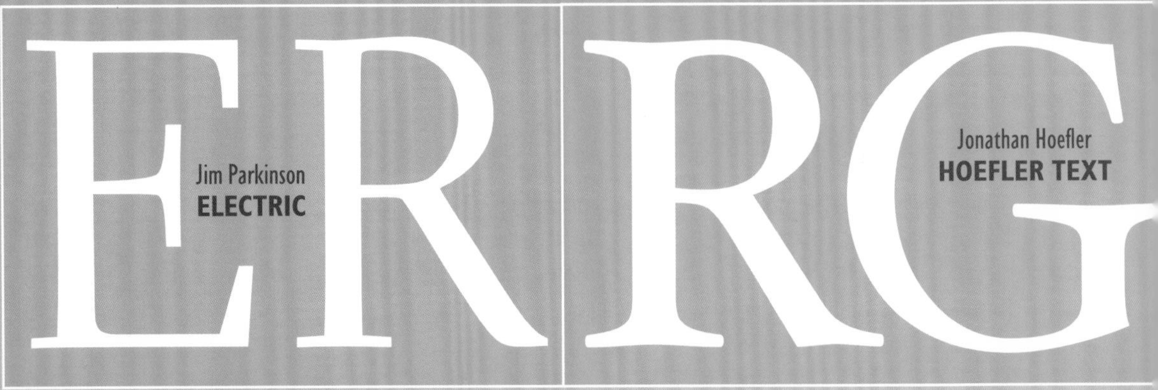
ER
Jim Parkinson
ELECTRIC
RG
Jonathan Hoefler
HOEFLER TEXT

Jim Parkinson and Jonathan Hoefler are two type designers who do a better job than most at finessing curves. The examples above are entirely without rudeness or lapses in artistic judgment. This, I believe, is the goal.

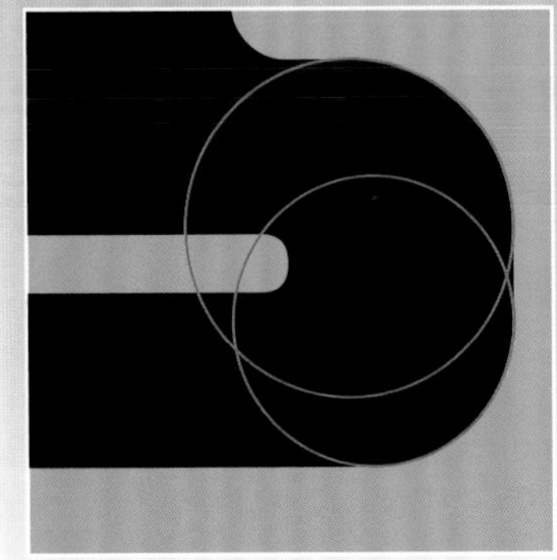

I read somewhere that, whereas we can use tools to mechanically construct a letter, there are sure to be places where we've no choice but to draw a certain portion by eye. I'm always amused to notice those places where the logic of a designer's geometric structure breaks down, as in the letter fragment above, with nonmatching perfect circles on what should be identical corners, and the blunted circle in the counter that totally breaks style.

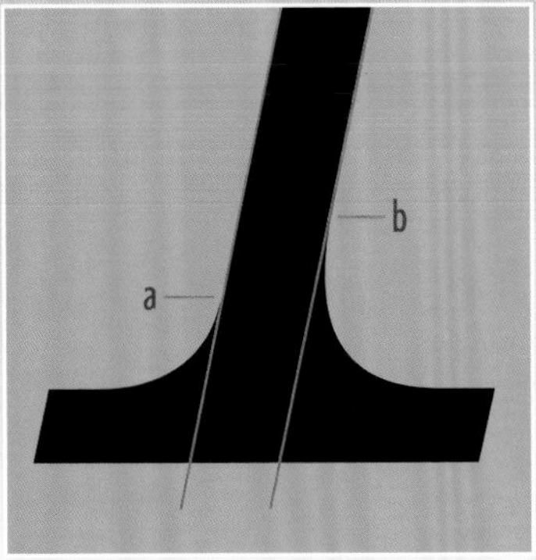
a
b

Above, although the two sides of this serif cannot, of course, be identical, they ought to appear to have once been a matched set prior to italicization. Instead, these serifs are of different parentage, and they're just ugly curves, besides. For starters, it would be an improvement if both bezier points, at a—b, which transition from the straight stem into the curving serif, had been placed at the same height.

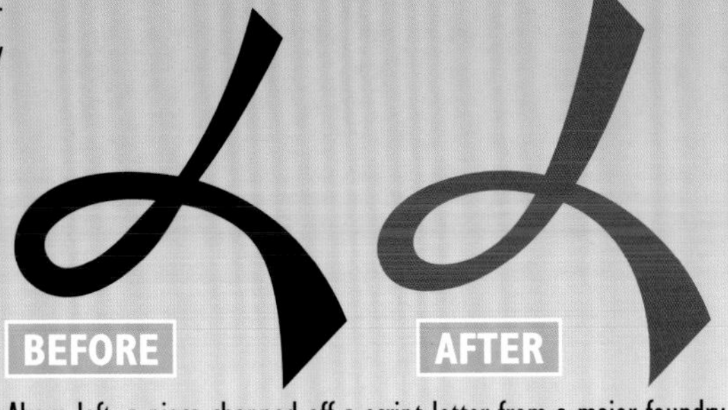
BEFORE
AFTER

Above left, a piece chopped off a script letter from a major foundry. Aside from ugly, lumpy curves, the lines of the stroke don't follow through as they loop around. In the designer's defense, I will admit there's nothing more difficult than rendering delicate scripts. And I certainly was reminded of this as I tried to improve these curves, above right, which are now reasonably beyond reproach.

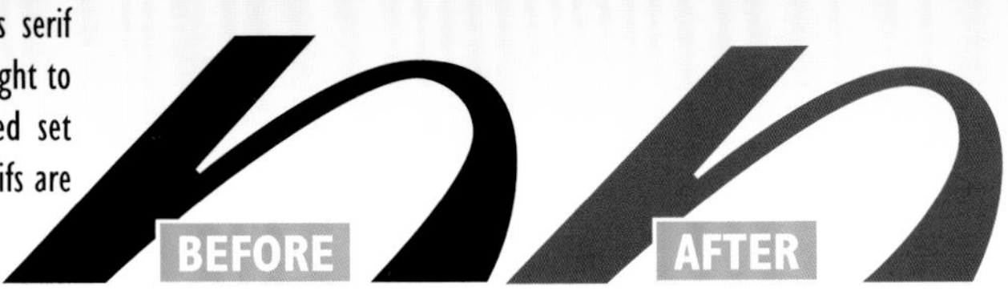
BEFORE
AFTER

Above left, the outer curve of the hump is awkward but acceptable. The inner curve, however, is obviously flawed. My corrections in the version, upper right, consisted mainly of making the inner curve echo the arc of the outer as if made by a single brushstroke.

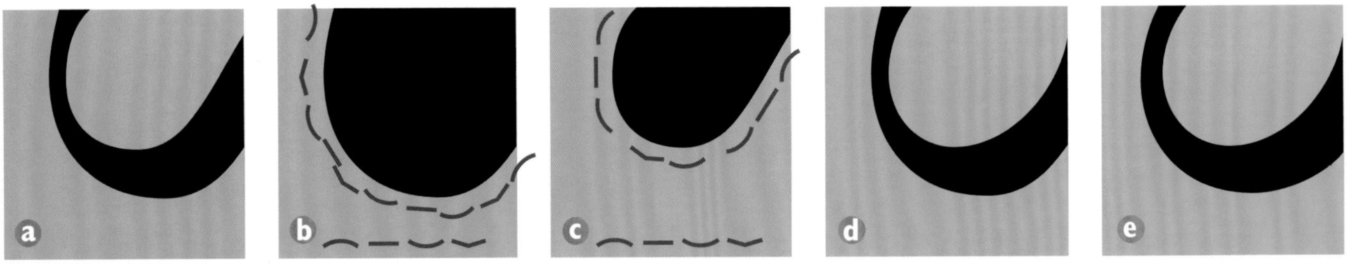
a
b
c
d
e

Often a curve is good or bad relative only to its opposite side. Either inner or outer could be good, but paired as opposite edges of one stroke, they don't properly relate. We must choose, then, which curve to fix so the two flow as one. At a, we see the original portion of a letter whose curves I don't like. At b, the outer curve is isolated to better scrutinize its very subtle bumps, flat spots, dips and corners.

At c, the counter is isolated, and my shorthand notational system indicates flaws in the counter's curves. Basically, wherever we find a bump, flat spot, dip or corner, we are sure to find bezier points placed out of extrema, with handles poorly adjusted. At d, the inner curve has been fixed, the outer left alone. True, if you saw these curves in a whole-letter context, they might make more sense. Or not.

At e, both sides of the curve have been designed to flow smoothly and work together. This was fairly difficult for me to correct and that's the point: It takes time to make good curves!

In Conclusion...

All that we draw, whether logos, fonts, icons or illustrations, will benefit from having points placed in extrema.

Our Master's Voice:

"During the early sixties at the Renault corporation, where I was an engineer at the time, I went to see my supervisor to tell him that I had found a new mathematical method for drawing curves that would replace all previous rough calculations and other lathed shapes and models. He saw my project, looked at me, and said, 'Monsieur Bézier, if your thing worked, the Americans would already be using it.'"

—Pierre Bézier

(by permission of Christian Lavigne, from *La Sculpture Numérique*.)

9 BEZIERRORS: (When Good Beziers Go Bad)

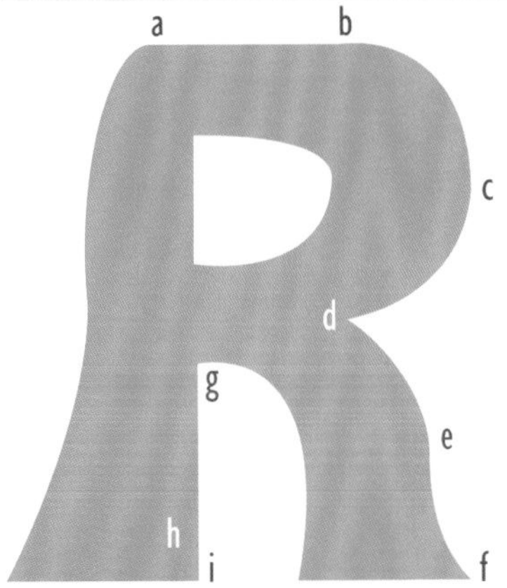
a
b
c
d
g
e
h
i
f

I created this pathetic *R* to demonstrate "Bezierrors." These are common errors that the major font foundries consider unacceptable. Some of them are rendering mistakes that we all commit, and others are problems inherent in Adobe Illustrator or result from the way in which our computers render our work on-screen.

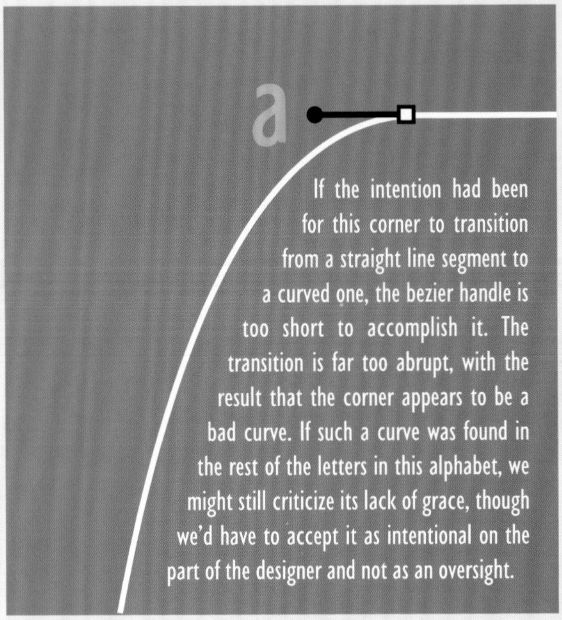
a

If the intention had been for this corner to transition from a straight line segment to a curved one, the bezier handle is too short to accomplish it. The transition is far too abrupt, with the result that the corner appears to be a bad curve. If such a curve was found in the rest of the letters in this alphabet, we might still criticize its lack of grace, though we'd have to accept it as intentional on the part of the designer and not as an oversight.

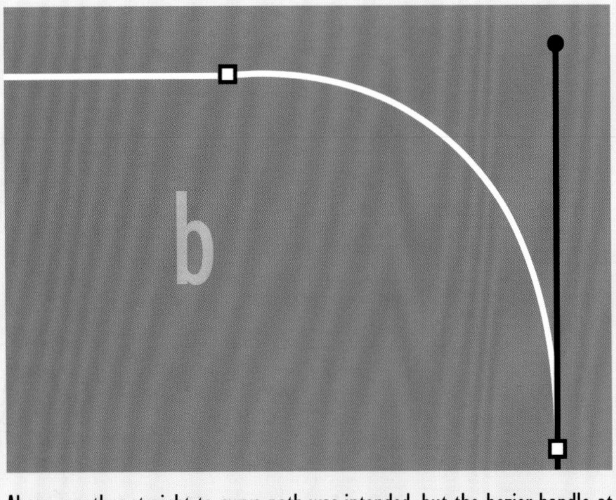
b

Above, another straight-to-curve path was intended, but the bezier handle at the 3 o'clock position overshot the top line of the letter, creating a hump before the curved segment hitches up to the straight one. Ideally, the 12 o'clock point (the top one) should carry half the bezier burden by having a handle of its own. This handle would push the line in the direction it faced thereby—most likely—avoiding the hump, though another hump could occur a little farther down path, if the 3 o'clock handle still jutted too far up.

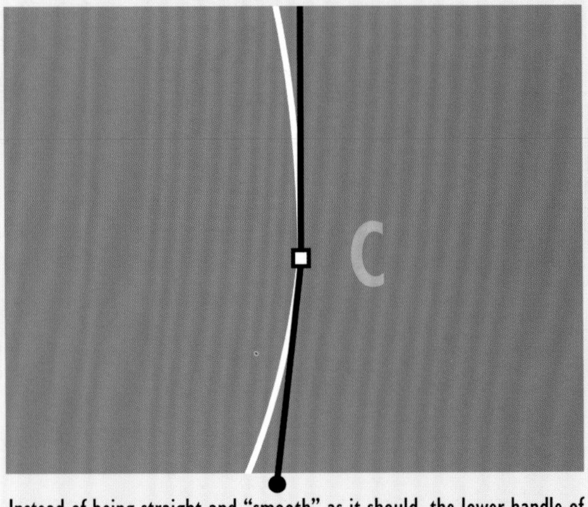
c

Instead of being straight and "smooth" as it should, the lower handle of this point changes direction from the top handle, proving that it is a corner point which has no business in the 3 o'clock position on the bowl of this *R*. Bezierrors such as this one often result from letting a draw program autotrace from a scan. Autotracing, as we explain on page 159, always requires an enormous amount of reworking before the paths can be considered acceptable.

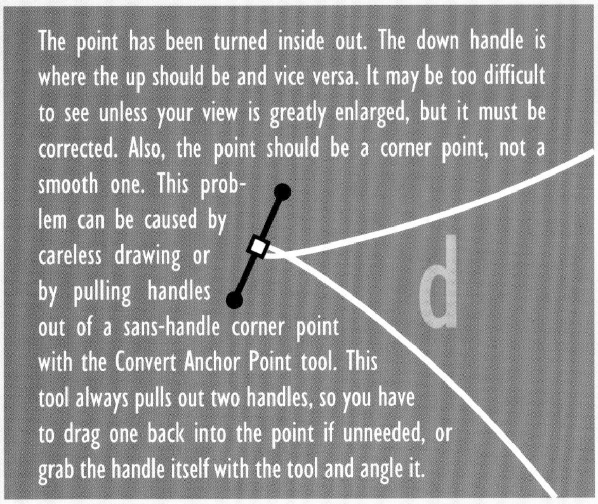
d

The point has been turned inside out. The down handle is where the up should be and vice versa. It may be too difficult to see unless your view is greatly enlarged, but it must be corrected. Also, the point should be a corner point, not a smooth one. This problem can be caused by careless drawing or by pulling handles out of a sans-handle corner point with the Convert Anchor Point tool. This tool always pulls out two handles, so you have to drag one back into the point if unneeded, or grab the handle itself with the tool and angle it.

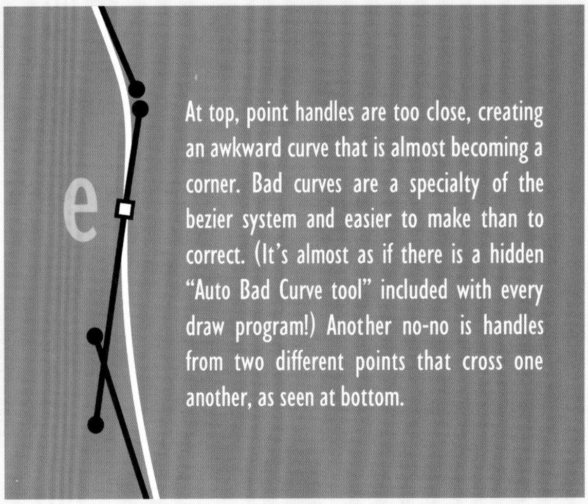
e

At top, point handles are too close, creating an awkward curve that is almost becoming a corner. Bad curves are a specialty of the bezier system and easier to make than to correct. (It's almost as if there is a hidden "Auto Bad Curve tool" included with every draw program!) Another no-no is handles from two different points that cross one another, as seen at bottom.

f

When is a line not a line? When it's ajar. There's nothing more annoying than seeing slightly off-straight straight lines. Most of the time, you cannot successfully correct this by manually moving a point to level the line. It may be because the line isn't a line, it's a bunch of pixels and our monitor screens have to decide whether to display them at level 24354647362562545 or at level 24354647362562546, so they split the difference and you see one or two bumps in the line, indicating it isn't straight. Even when we drag down a guideline, the guide will snap some points right to it, and others above or below it. And you thought it was just that you were stupid? No, it happens to all of us. To alleviate the problem, always hold the Shift key down while drawing a straight vertical or horizontal line. But if you notice a path is crooked, you can select the points at both ends and go to OBJECT>Path>Average, then choose the Horizontal (or Vertical) Axis radio button. Another path-straightening technique I use often is to draw a rectangle on top of a crooked line segment and use Subtract From Shape Area to chop off the crooked part. I demonstrate variations on this technique in the Type Trix section (pages 166–193). But there is a larger issue with regard to straight lines that keeps me up nights worrying. The question is whether or not infinitesimally crooked lines matter. For example, what if the builder didn't perfectly square up the walls of your house? Chances are, you'll never notice it. Likewise, with 9-point or even 96-point type, will a slightly crooked line or two be perceptible? In any event, we must endeavor to make all vertical and horizontal lines truly on the level.

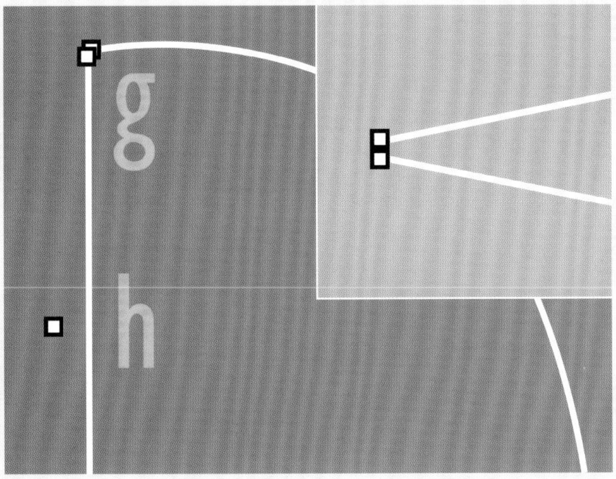
g
h

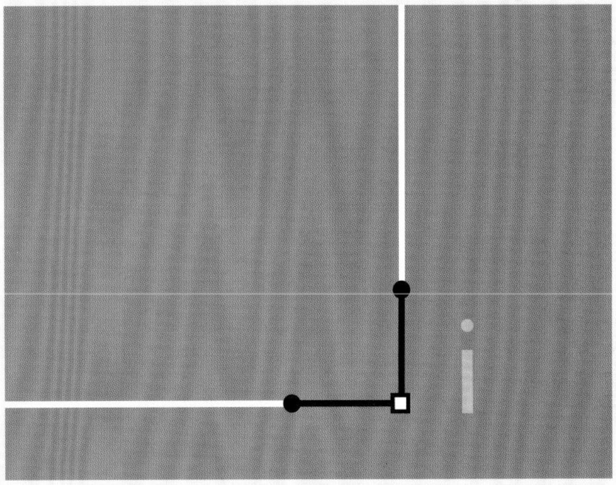
i

The top Bezierror at g is use of two points where only one is needed. This usually results from Uniting two or more parts, especially if the parts are not precisely aligned to one another before going to Unite. It is sometimes advisable to use double points (though not atop one another) to terminate a long, sharp pointed shape (inset) so that it doesn't either dot-gain or disappear on press at small point sizes. The bottom Bezierror at h is stray points: vestigal points that serve no purpose and must be deleted. Go to EDIT>Select>Stray Points, then delete, or select manually and delete.

Here is a perfect 90° corner point...with bezier handles. Why? This point should have no handles. It seems that with the two most recent versions of Adobe Illustrator, the program has begun to add these unnecessary handles to the corner points of straight paths when Outline Strokes is used to turn strokes into filled, closed-path objects. Handles make it impossible to drag from the middle of a straight line segment, as can be done when no handles are present on either end of the line. Click once with the Convert Anchor Point tool to remove handles from a point.

Drawing Letters
The Leslie Cabarga Way!
"Do as I sa
not as I do!

METHOD ONE: Skeleton Strokes

Letters that start out as "stick figures" are the easiest letters to draw. That's because we need draw only one line, not two, to define a letter's inner and outer contours. The paths can then be stroked to any desired width. This method is best suited to drawing monoweight letters, not thick/thin roman letters. But roman *can* be done, too, as demonstrated.

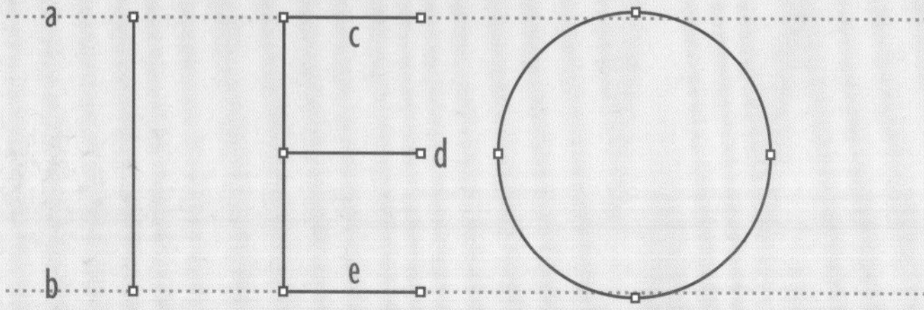

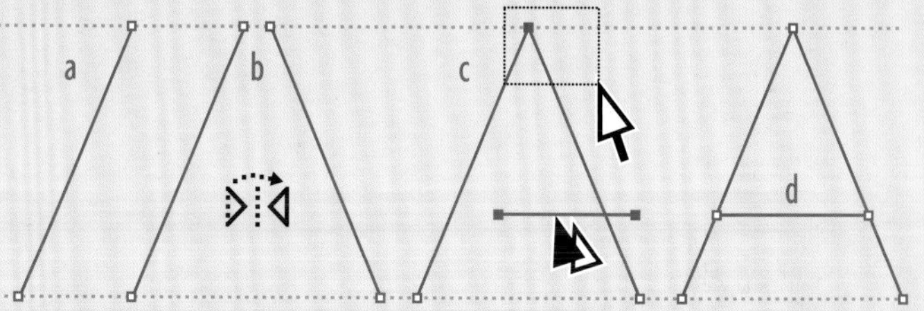

1. Create top and bottom guidelines, a, b, to establish letter height. Height can be arbitrary now, as the beauty of skeleton letters is their flexibility. Draw letter *I* by holding down Shift as you draw the second point to ensure an absolute vertical line. Drag-Copy this *I* stem over to start the *E*. Draw top horizontal arm, c. Drag-Copy it down to make the crossbar, d. Drag-Copy it again to make the bottom arm, e. For *O*, make an ellipse, drawing it slightly beyond the guidelines. Why? See page 112.

2. For now, make all letter shapes and widths normal, like the "block letter" alphabets we copied in kindergarten. Draw the left stem of *A* as in a. Use the Reflect tool and hold down Shift-Option to flop a copy of the stem for the right side, b. Drag the right stem by its top point until it snaps to the left stem's top point. Marquee both top points so they're selected, c, and Average-Join them in one step with Shift-Option-Command-J (⇧-⌥-⌘-J). Drag-Copy the crossbar from *E* for *A*, d.

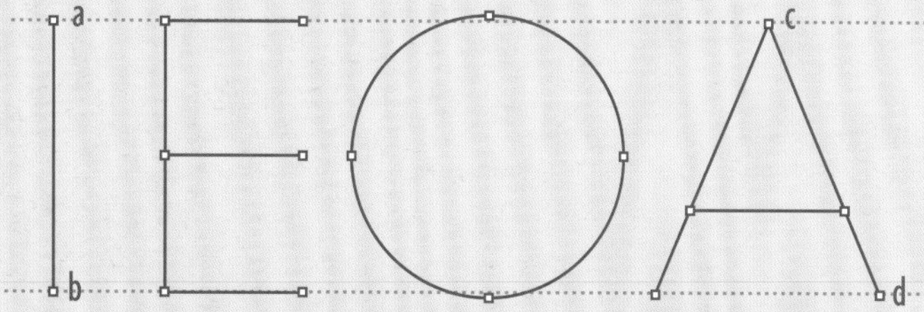

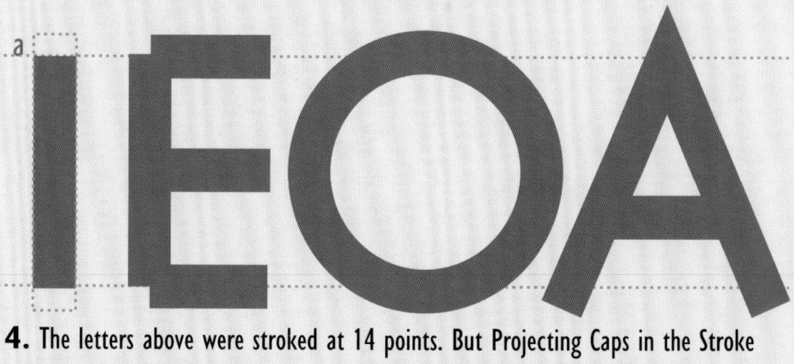

3. All the rest of the letters will be created from the stroke-parts collection above, plus a few more lines we'll draw as needed. Take care to place points such as a–d exactly on the guidelines. Next, assign stroke weights to thicken up letter stems.

4. The letters above were stroked at 14 points. But Projecting Caps in the Stroke pallet needs to be assigned so the vertical stems of *I*, *E* and *A* will extend to the same height as *E*. The dotted line at a shows how Projecting Caps changes letter *I*.

5. Above, Projecting Caps have been assigned to all strokes. (The thin blue lines are our original paths. Notice that I neglected to place my points exactly. The bottom arm of *E* is not exactly on the baseline, a, and the crossbar of *A* extends too far right, b. Also, the left stem of *A*, c, will have to be dragged down past the baseline, like the right stem, d, so that the strokes can later be trimmed off square to the baseline.

6. More letters have been built from skeleton strokes. A circle was made for the bowl of *R*, then the 9 o'clock point, a, was deleted. From the 12 o'clock point, b, a line was drawn to c. The same thing was done to the bottom of the bowl. At d, a leg for *R* was drawn past the baseline so it could be trimmed. Points e and f were also extended so they, too, can be squared off. A point was added to *O* at g, then the line segment between it and h was deleted and a crossbar added. Later, *G* will become *C*. *R* will become *P*. *N* may become *M*, and so on.

Outline Strokes makes unneeded points that should be deleted.
a
b
c
ARN

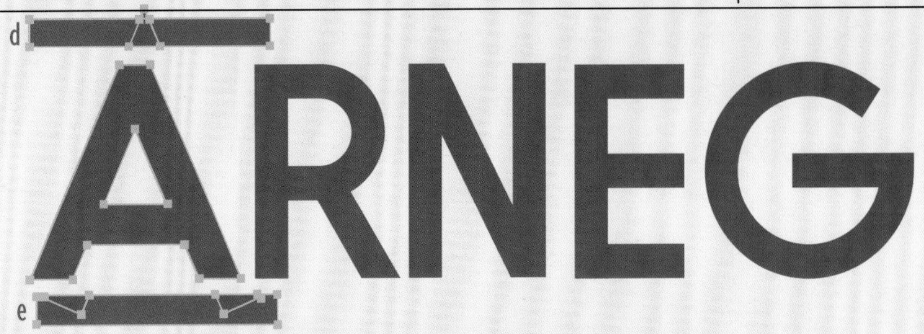
d
e
ARNEG

7. Here is one way to trim letters. Select all strokes (Save a Copy of the skeleton strokes off to the side of your page!) and go to OBJECT>Path>Outline Strokes, so paths become filled objects, a, not 14-point strokes anymore. Then hit Add to Shape in the Pathfinder pallet. This will unite the stems of *A* and the crossbar into one piece. Now create two rectangles, like b and c, positioned exactly against the top and bottom guidelines. Select the rectangles plus all letters to be trimmed. In the Pathfinder pallet, hit Divide. Select and Delete all extraneous pieces, like d and e. Above right, some of the finished letters. Gasp! We've reinvented Futura!

The Versatility of Letters Drawn From Skeleton Strokes

Right at a, letters have 3-point strokes and at b, the very same paths were given 11-point strokes. Naturally, each weight will need tweaking, like respacing and repositioning the crossbars of *E*, *A* and *G*. Letters *A*, *R* and *N* will need to be trimmed to the guides. It would, in fact, be highly useful to a letterer who wished to rely mostly upon custom lettering to prepare in advance entire skeleton alphabets then tweak and stroke as need demanded.

a
IEOARNG
b
IEOARNG

a
RAINBOW
RAINBOW
b
RAINBOW
RAINBOW

c
RAINBOW
RAINBOW

Ability to Stretch and Squash

We can Scale skeleton-stroke letters endlessly and still retain the monoweight effect. At a, the word *RAINBOW* has been set in Futura Bold (in black). Beneath it, letters stroked at 7 points spell the same word. (Since this process requires untrimmed stroke letters, I've lightened the parts that will later be chopped off) In b, both sets of words were condensed with the Free Transform tool. The Futura now looks dumb with its too-wide horizontal strokes, but the skeleton letters have survived the change with mono stem weights intact. At c, both *RAINBOWs* were squashed, or horizontal scaled, wide. The Futura's widened vertical stems make the style look haphazardly roman, but the stroke letters maintain their monoweight characteristics (although lots of tweaking must now be done to open up those clogged counters).

a
b
b
b
RAINBOW

How to Make Stroke Letters Into Roman Thick/Thin letters

Start by excessively condensing the skeleton letters, a. Assign narrow 4-point strokes, then Outline Strokes. Similar to the K.O. (knock-out) mask technique shown in step 7, I drew some red rectangles, b, then selected them, along with all the letters, and used Divide on the bunch to crop off tops and bottoms of letters. Above right, at c, I selected all the letters from a and scaled them wide with the Free Transform tool, which caused the vertical stems to become thick and the horizontal stems to stay thin. But all is hardly hunky-dory.

c
RAINBOW
d
RAINBOW

Above, example c reveals that the counters in *R*, *B* and *O* have lost their smoothness. And *A*, *N* and *W* do not observe proper thick/thin order as per the roman style. All these corrections were made in d, manually done. My god, we've reinvented Optima! Note the red circles overlain on letters *N* and *I*. I use these "gauge balls"—the larger corresponding to the width of thick strokes and the smaller to measure thin strokes—to guide me in assuring consistency of all stem widths. I don't use squares for this purpose, because circles apply to diagonal and rounded stems as well as straight ones. Yes, it's a lot of work drawing letters, but then you wanted to know how the professionals do it, didn't you? Turn the page, the fun's only beginning!

METHOD ONE: Skeleton Strokes

Further Adaptability of Stroke Letters

Amazingly, all the examples of medium-weight lettering you see at right were created from the skeleton stroke paths shown below them. In example a, a single circle, broken into quarters and connected up to horizontal and vertical strokes, formed the basis for the consistency of this style.

The b version of the word *WIRELESS* was created by stretching the strokes tall and adding some hooks on *L* and *S*. Note, however, that stretching curves kind of ruins what should be smooth transitions into the straight paths.

The word *CURRENTS* in c was largely made out of circle paths variously joined together. Stroke ends were assigned Round Caps.

NEW WORLD MUSIC, example d, was created with two copies of the same stroke letters on two levels: The bottom level has a 10-point yellow stroke, and the top level was given a 5-point terra-cotta red stroke.

There would seem to be endless variations on the monoweight stroke letter, and indeed, this being an easy style to draw, there are already hundreds of stroke fonts. In fact, experts reckon that the last conceivable variation on the monoweight stroke font will show up on a free font web site sometime in the year 2009, and that all horizontal stroke terminals will be sheared at 30° angles.

a
WIRELESS
WIRELESS
b
WIRELESS
WIRELESS
c
CURRENTS
CURRENTS
d
NEW WORLD MUSIC
NEW WORLD MUSIC

Capturing the Elusive S-Curve

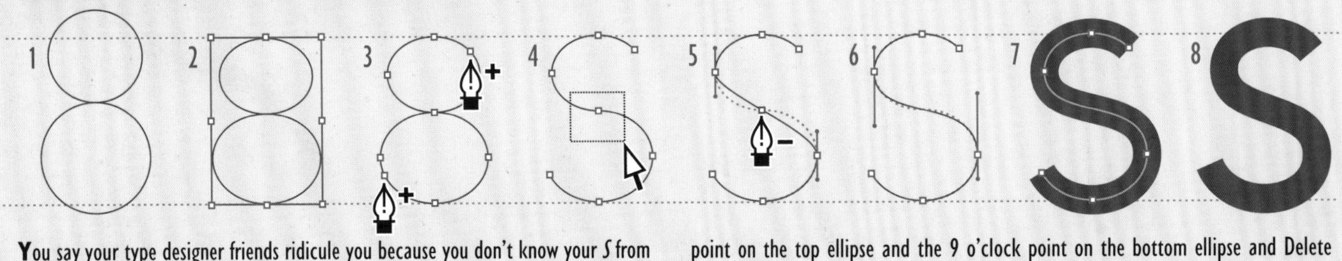
1
2
3
4
5
6
7
8

You say your type designer friends ridicule you because you don't know your *S* from your elbow? Take heart, you're not alone. We who breeze through our *E*s with ease and laugh at our *P*s and *Q*s, still cringe at the thought of drawing an *S*. Above is one technique: 1. Make two circles, the bottom can be slightly larger than the top. Select both and use Horizontal Align Center in the Align pallet so they…align. 2. Use Free Transform tool to squish them to size within your guidelines. It doesn't ever matter what size we initially draw things, because we can change them. 3. Add Points approximately where shown, then, with the White Arrow tool, click on the 3 o'clock point on the top ellipse and the 9 o'clock point on the bottom ellipse and Delete them. 4. Marquee the two center points and Average-Join them (⇧-⌥-⌘-J). 5. Copy the *S*, then make the original into Guides (⌘-5). Paste in Front the copy. Now delete the center point. Notice how the curve retracts. 6. With the underlying guide-*S* you just made, pull the bezier handles to restore the curve (it'll be smoother now without the center point). 7. Here's our *S*, stroked at 11 points. Damn, it looks crooked! 8. Select the *S* and Create Outlines. Rotate the final *S* till it looks straight. Your *S* may not come out crooked. The placement of those added points in step 3 will affect this.

The Swelling Skeleton

To draw a letter style with flourishy strokes such as a script, or the uncial-style lettering below, it is best to start with skeleton strokes and then add swells where needed by expanding parts of the strokes. This way, the thinnest strokes are assured of maintaining uniform weight. Copying from an old book of alphabets, I drew these skeletons of uncial-style letterforms.

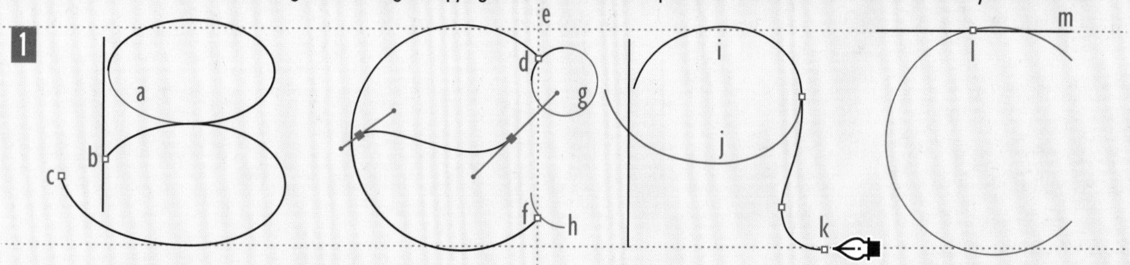
1
a
b
c
d
e
f
g
h
i
j
k
l
m

1. Draw two ellipses for the bowls of *B* and delete the segment at a. Add a point at 10 o'clock on bottom bowl, b, delete the segment between it and 9 o'clock, then drag the point at c. For letter *E*, make a circle, add a point at 1 o'clock, d, then drag over a guideline e, which helps locate our second added point at f. Delete the 3 o'clock point between d and f. Draw a small circle touching the d point. Delete points to remove the g segment shown in red. Reflect-Copy the resulting quarter circle down to make h. To make *N*'s upper ellipse, i, drag-Copy the lower ellipse of *B* and delete its bottom half, j. Whenever possible, reuse previously drawn parts as a way of maintaining consistency. Continue *N*'s bowl stroke, using the Pen tool, to k. For letter *T*, drag-Copy over the circle from *E*, add point at l, then Delete the remainder of the circle shown in red. Draw a straight top stroke, m.

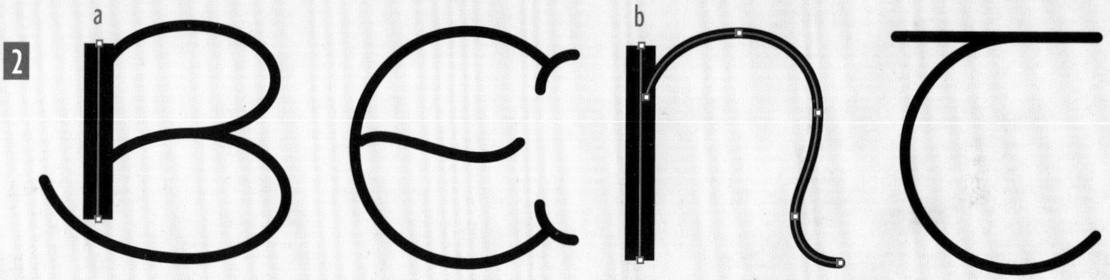
2
a
b

2. Stroke a and b at 11 points. Assign 4-point strokes to the rest of the lines and give them Round Caps in the Stroke pallet window.

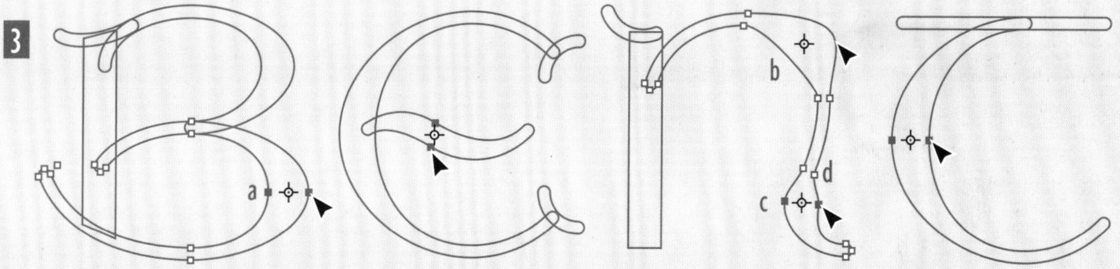
3
a
b
c
d

3. Select all paths. Go to OBJECT>Paths>Outline Strokes. Use the Scale tool to create swelling strokes as shown. Here's how: With two adjacent extrema points selected, a, click once between them with the Scale tool, then drag one of the points outward to expand the stroke. At b, this was attempted by locating the center of the Scale tool where there were no points. At c, the two selected points were too close to another set, d, so in both cases, the attempt to swell the stroke was unsuccessful. Notice that "serifs," also created with strokes, were added to the tops of *B* and *N*.

4
a
b
c
d

4. After the swelling is done, unite all parts with Add to Shape in the Pathfinder pallet. At a, add the two points shown and remove the existing corner point (in red) to round the corner. Do this in similar corners, as shown. At b, add two points to the stem leading up to the serif, then remove the existing points in red to soften the corners. Stroke ends were fattened up by selecting the three points in these former Round Cap strokes and Scaling them slightly larger. At d, the center point of the Scale Tool was placed off center and the bottom point dragged to expand the stroke. It usually works better to use the Scale tool to create swelling strokes than to move points by hand, but we'll still have to tweak tons to get pleasingly round results. Above is the finished lettering. What do you think: Should the square bottom on the thick *N* stem have been rounded?

METHOD TWO: Parts Department

With this method, we draw an archive of "parts" and combine them to build all the letters in an alphabet. Usually, these parts will apply to only 90 percent of our letterforms, after which we must create additional parts as we go along. Since consistency in lettering is our goal, the best way to achieve it is to use an archive of parts.

Magneto

My font Magneto Bold is a perfect example of the use of spare parts in constructing an alphabet. Of course, it is a font designed to be predictably repetitive and so lends itself well to the parts treatment. At right are the nine basic parts used to construct all the lowercase letters. One-of-a-kind parts are shown in black. The uppercase required its own slightly more extensive set of parts.

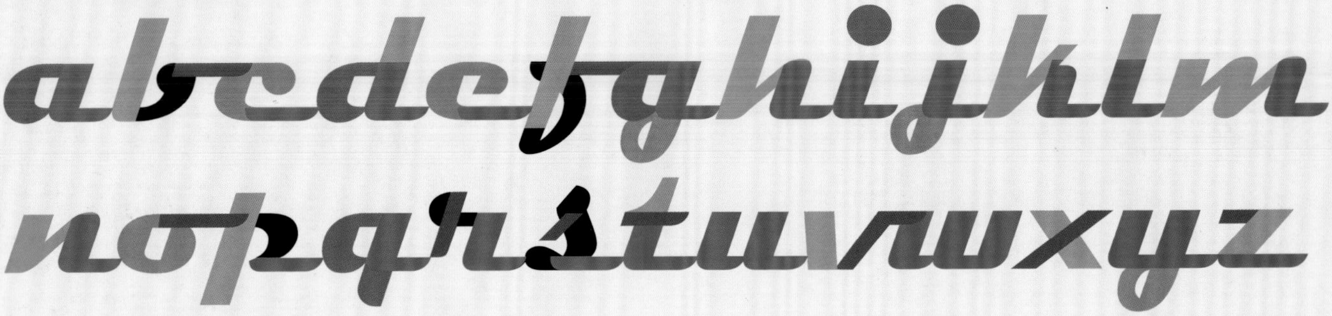
abcdefghijklm
nopqrstuvwxyz

Konstruct It Like Koch

Rudolf Koch was hip to the parts idea. These *aufbauzeichnungen,* or construction drawings, for his font Kabel show the seven "systems" he devised, based on the four divisions of the square, to create this uppercase alphabet. We take sans-serif fonts so for granted, it's hard to believe that when such fonts as Kabel began to come to America from Germany in the 1920s, many printers considered them a type heresy.

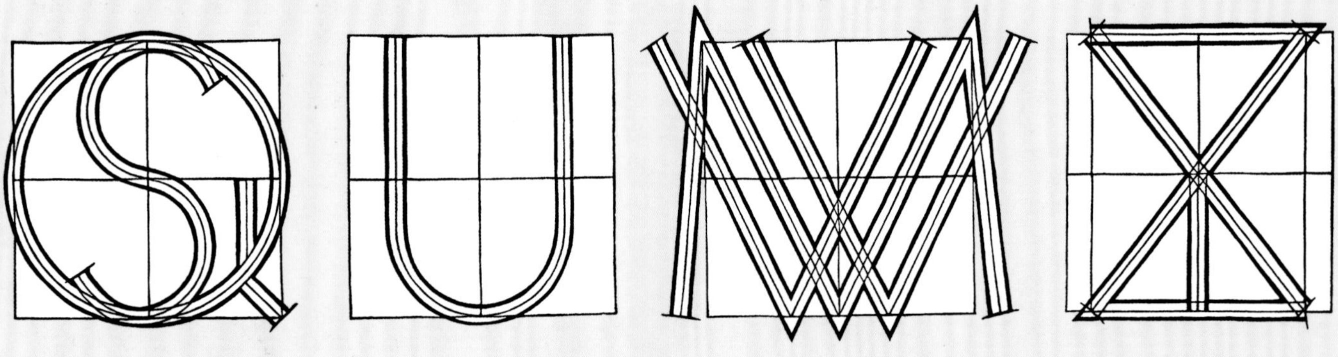

From an idle musing that produced this sketch of an *r*, left, I was inspired to design the alphabet below. It is a complicated style that, due to the angled bottoms of the letters and rounded corners, is especially difficult to draw. Because I like to go right to computer instead of working from tight, measured sketches, I must first choose the best portions of the best letters in my sketch to determine basic shapes and sizes for my parts archive. Next, I create as few parts as possible and hope they'll work with as many letters as possible. Then I compose the parts into letters, nipping and tucking as I go along. The final letterforms, some of which are seen at the bottom of the page, are always affected by how the parts come out. We discover that certain shapes that seemed viable in the sketch don't work in reality. This alphabet won't be completed here, but you can see it beginning to evolve. Plenty of tweaking comes next. Practically speaking, this style is too unusual so if it were a font, sales would be limited.

1. Determine Basic Shapes and Sizes

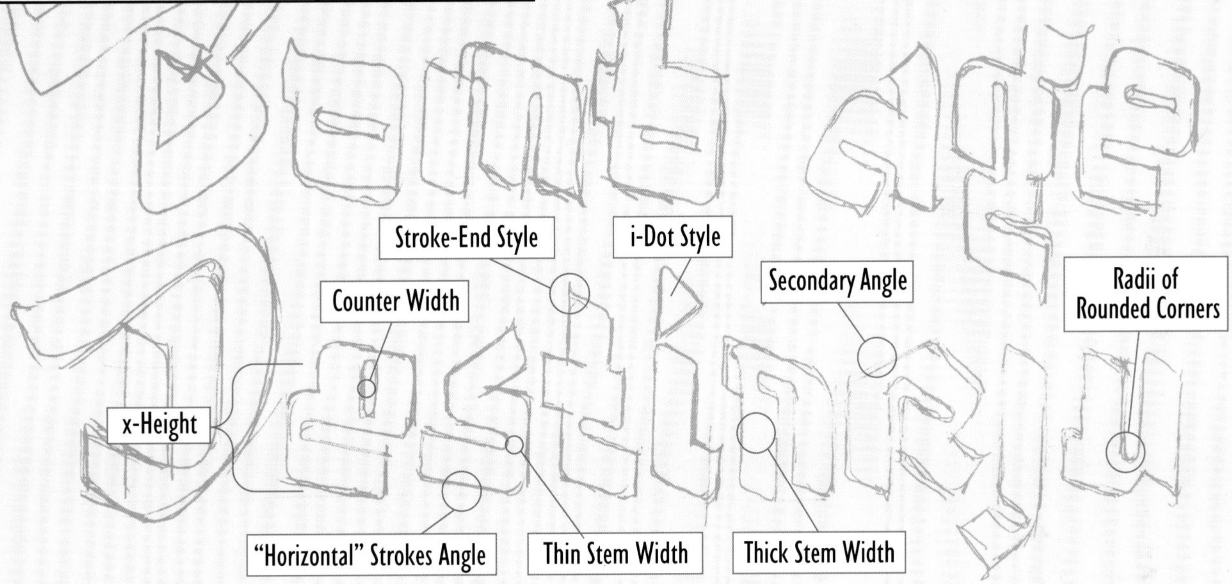
Stroke-End Style
i-Dot Style
Counter Width
Secondary Angle
Radii of Rounded Corners
x-Height
"Horizontal" Strokes Angle
Thin Stem Width
Thick Stem Width

2. Create Parts

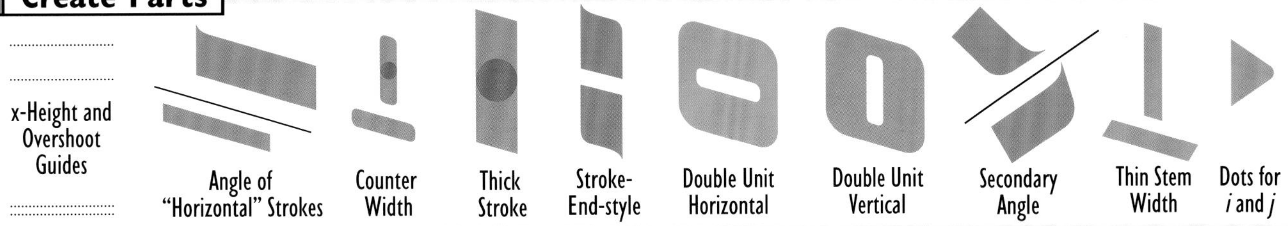
x-Height and Overshoot Guides
Angle of "Horizontal" Strokes
Counter Width
Thick Stroke
Stroke-End-style
Double Unit Horizontal
Double Unit Vertical
Secondary Angle
Thin Stem Width
Dots for *i* and *j*

3. Make Letters

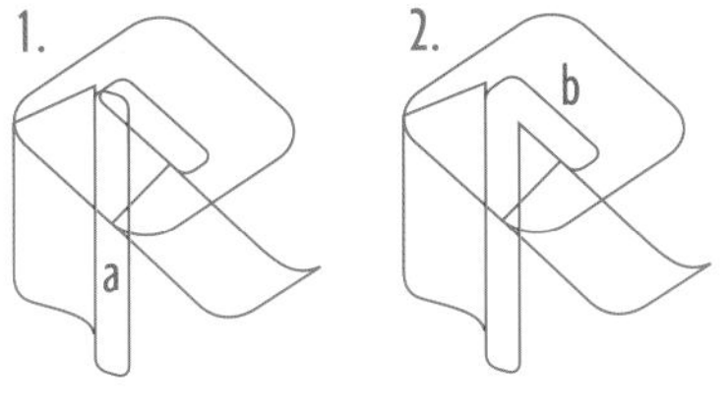
1.
a
2.
b

Now that the parts (at least the basic ones) are done, it's time to make letters. **1.** Three parts of *r* have been assembled. The tall counter part, a, will be used as a knockout. **2.** Two parts united, b, with the Pathfinder tool Add to Shape. **3.** Three parts comprising the letter shape have also been selected and united. **4.** The two composited parts were selected, then Subtract From Shape knocked out the counter to make the final *r*. Below, more letters composed of parts. Weird shapes, especially within letters *b*, *i* and *e*, result from dragging points out of the way when we're using only pieces of parts. The process is complex, but I know no other way.

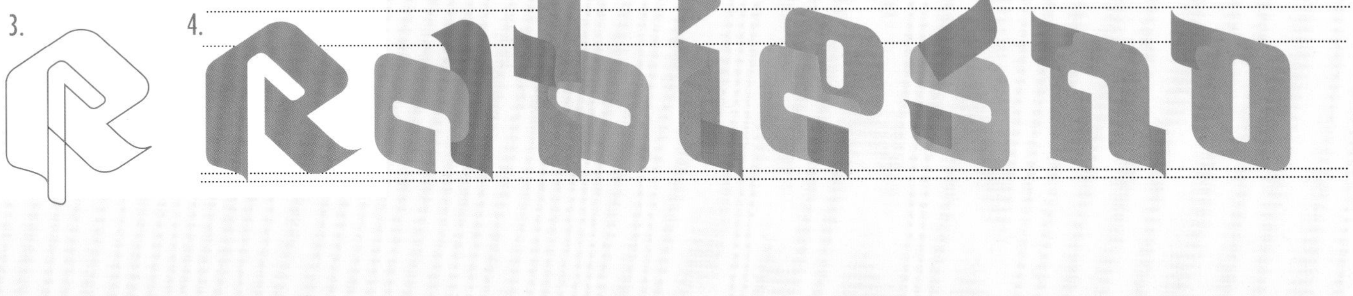
3.
4.

METHOD TWO: Parts Department

Make a Serif Part

There are almost as many ways to draw a serif as there are styles of serifs that can be drawn. Here's an approach to creating one basic style. We'll add this serif to the skeleton letters we drew and made into filled objects on previous pages. So this means we'll be combining the Spare Parts method with the Skeleton Strokes method to accomplish this task. Actually, combining methods is common practice. We'll do whatever works!

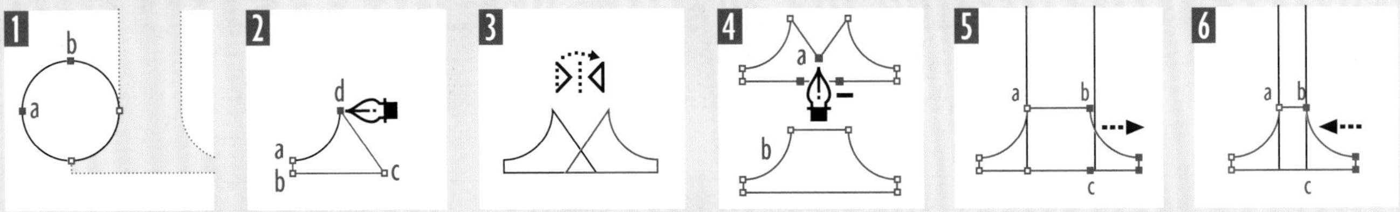
1
b
a
2
d
a
b
c
3
4
a
b
5
a
b
c
6
a
b
c

We will create classic "bracket" serifs. **1.** The gray area represents our goal shape. Draw a circle. Delete points a and b. **2.** Starting at point a on the remaining quarter circle, draw with the Pen tool to b, then to c (hold Shift key to constrain points straight). Close the path at d. **3.** Reflect-Copy the half serif we created so it becomes a full serif. **4.** Use Add to Shape to unite the two halves into one shape. With the Delete Anchor Point tool, remove the points caused by uniting, shown in red at a. The result is shown at b. **5.** Drag this serif that we've just created and align it with the left side of a thick vertical letter stem. Select all the points on one side of the serif and drag them in or out until they align with the right edge of the stem. Use an enlarged view to do this accurately. **6.** Apply the serif to a thin vertical stem. Drag half of the serif in or out until it aligns with the right edge of the stem. Continue to apply copies of the serif to the rest of our letters.

Add Serifs to Letters

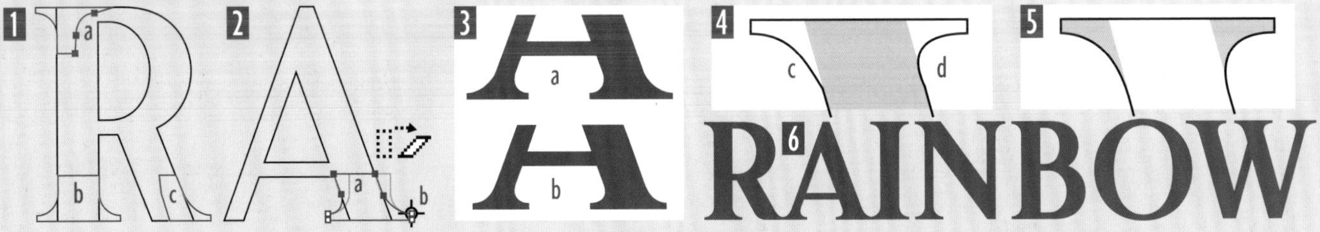
1
a
b
c
2
a
b
3
a
b
4
c
d
5
6
RAINBOW

We will attach serifs to the expanded stroke letters created on page 151. When all serifs are in place, serifs and letters will be united using Add to Shape in the Pathfinder pallet. **1.** At a, a full serif was put in place, and the three selected points were dragged away to avoid overlapping *R*'s counter. At b, a full serif was used. At c, half a serif has been sheared to the angle of *R*'s leg. **2.** We'll demonstrate the shearing on letter *A*. Select only the serif's four upper points (we don't want the lower part of the bracket to shear), a. With the Shear tool selected in the toolbar, click the axis point shown at b and drag any one of the serif's selected points leftward until its angle matches that of the *A* stem. **3.** At a, we see the final result of the previous step. Shearing has caused the outer serifs to grow wider than the inner serifs. This looks bad and will also cause letter spacing problems later. At b, the outer serifs have been pushed in closer to the letter to make them appear equal in width to the inner serifs. Also, various tweaking has been done to the bracket's bezier curves to make them transition more smoothly from stems into the curves. **4.** Look out for crummy transitions like c and d, both of which are the result of bezier handles not in line with the angles of the stems the serifs spring from. **5.** Transitions smoothed out. Think of serifs as having bulk. Though the two sides of a diagonal serif have different shapes, they both should appear to be twin brothers and be of equal length and girth. **6.** Here is the lettering with serifs added (inevitable tweaks were made to letters *and* serifs).

METHOD THREE: Straight Ahead

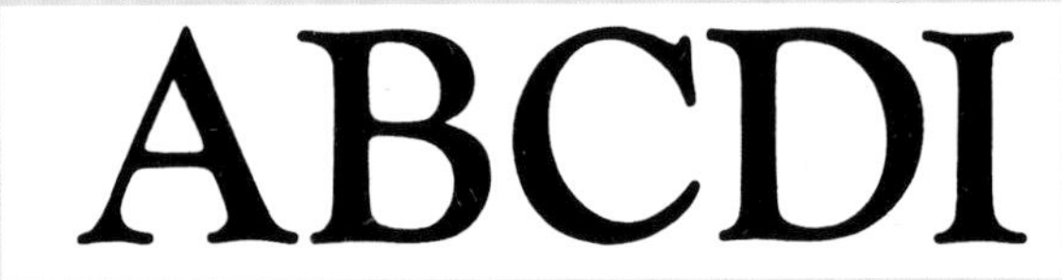
ABCDI

All the rules change when we consider creating a letter style with all the (intentional) hand-drawn idiosyncrasies of a face like Goudy Bold, left. For this style, which has a minimum of cookie-cutter repetition and geometric predictability, we can employ skeleton strokes, spare parts and straight-ahead drawing to get the job done. To make a font like Frederic Goudy's, we'd have to start out with really tight drawings, just as he did. (That part is up to you.) Following is an outline of just a few aspects of digitizing complicated letters.

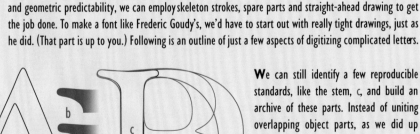

The first thing we notice is that Goudy Bold has almost no straight lines and no symmetrical ellipses. Serifs on the tops and bottoms of letters are unalike, a, and not even the same from letter to letter, b. This is definitely old school—and cool! To draw such artistic letters requires an eye that is mightier than the Pen tool.

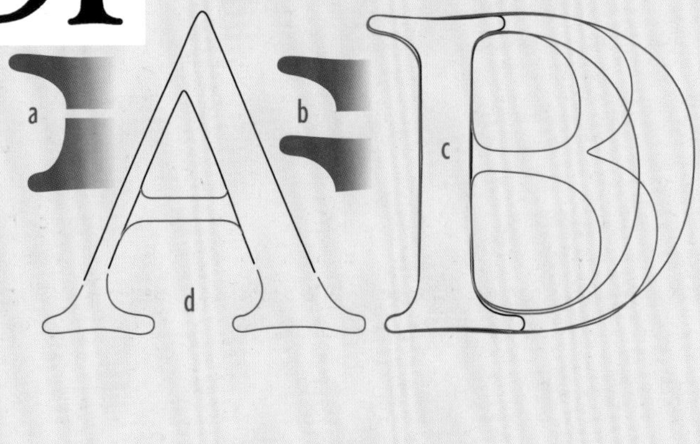
a
b
c
d

We can still identify a few reproducible standards, like the stem, c, and build an archive of these parts. Instead of uniting overlapping object parts, as we did up above, we can leave serifs and stems as open paths, d, then Join all the paths together. Or if we are tracing a scan of a very tight sketch, we can always draw straight ahead, point to point, without using parts.

METHOD FOUR: Modifying Type

a
MURDERERS
MURDERERS
MURDERERS

Right, the word *MURDERERS* was set in ITC Machine, a font whose regularity makes for ease of adaptability. In the second version, the same type has been horizontal scaled wide. The third version shows the type after modification. The circle, a, was the only extra part used to make this amazing transformation from Machine to Murder.

Modifying type to suit our specific needs is a practice that existed long before computer fonts and drawing programs. Thankfully, it's a lot simpler to do now than when we were using white-out and inking over photostats. Usually, it is easier to work from existing letters than to create our own from scratch. In most cases, we can retain much of the existing work. For instance, most of the basic strokes, letter widths, spacing and kerning have already been taken care of for us.

Often, however, it is best just to start from scratch—depending upon the style of letter you are designing—than to have to mess with another designer's decisions. This is especially true if we are trying to manipulate a poorly drawn font. A surprising number of fonts, even some from major foundries, are drawn with stems of slightly different widths, points drawn on top of one another, extra points and slightly crooked vertical and horizontal lines that are a pain to correct. So why bother adapting from such a font?

It is bad form to take somebody's font, make changes to it in Fontographer and call the work your own. But, in this writer's opinion, it is acceptable to tweak a few words of type—especially if you do it beyond recognition.

REMINDER: Drag copies, off to the side of your artboard, of all parts and pieces you make at all stages in the process of drawing letters. Never burn your bridges behind you by destroying parts that could later be recycled.

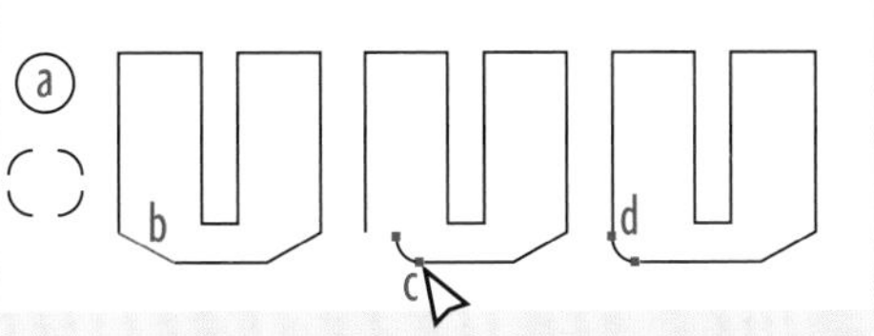
a
b
c
d

1. Start with letter *U* because two *U*s rotated 180° make *M*. Parts of the circle a will replace diagonal corners. Delete line segment b. Join a lower left circle corner to *U* at c and drag over to *U's* left stem, d. Marquee the overlapping points at d and Average-Join. Then, round the opposite corner of *U*, too.

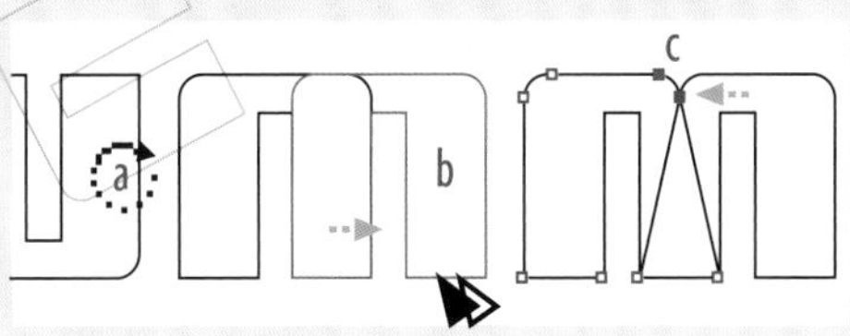
a
b
c

2. Rotate the *U*, a. Hold Shift-Option to straighten and make a copy. Hold Shift-Option to Copy again as you drag the upside-down copy, b, to the right. Select the two points at c. Hit the Left Arrow key eight (or so) times to move them left, then do the same to the other side. Now *M* and *U* are done.

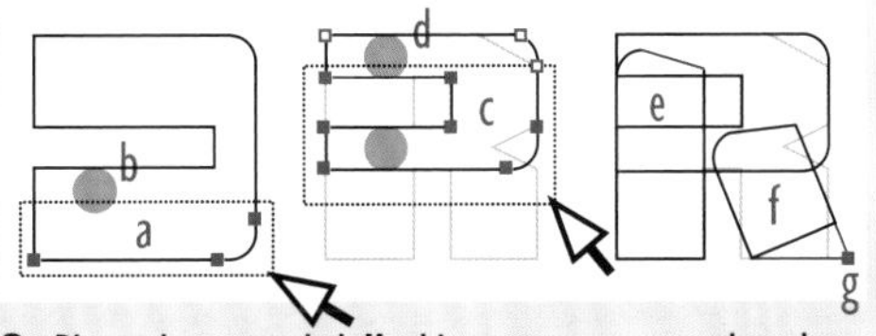
a
b
c
d
e
f
g

3. Place the expanded Machine type on a template layer beneath our working layer so we can refer to its proportions. To make letter *R*, Rotate-Copy letter *U* so it's on its side. Make a gauge ball to our thin stem width. Marquee the selected points at a. Drag them up to the bottom of the gauge ball, b. Marquee the points shown at c. Drag them to the gauge ball, d. Chop off half of an *M*. Close the path again, e, to use as a left vertical stem. Copy then Rotate this same stem again to make the leg of *R*, f. Drag the g point to the baseline to make the bottom of the leg sit flat.

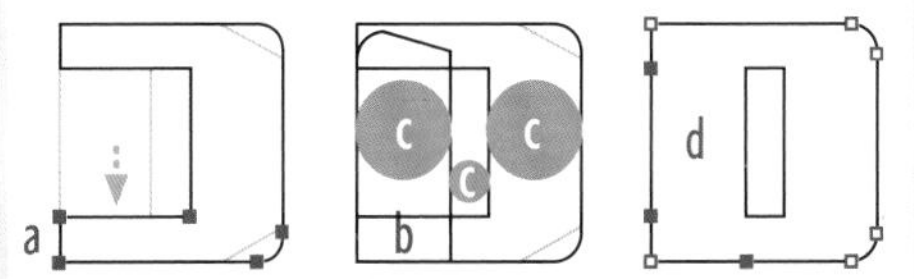
a
b
c
c
c
d

4. To make *D*, drag over a copy of the top half of *R* that we made in step 3. Select the points shown at a, drag them down to the baseline (always hold Shift when dragging points that should remain straight in line). Drag a copy of the left stem, b, that we used for *R*, and make it the left vertical stem of *D*. Horizontal Align Left in the Align pallet can be used to perfectly line this stem up with the body of *D*. At various points in the process, gauge balls like c can be used to ensure that stem and counter widths are staying consistent. If you choose to unite letter parts, d, delete excess points (in red).

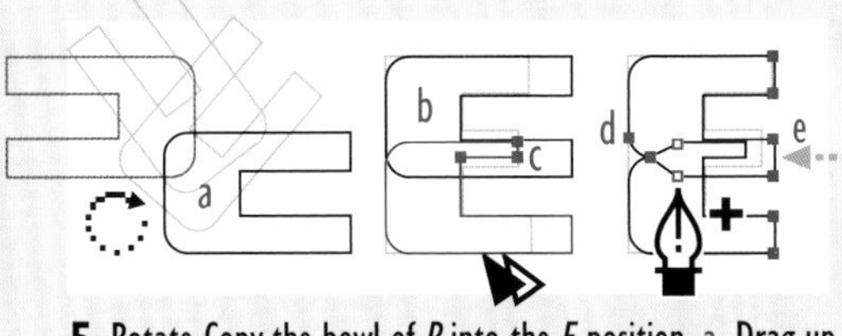
a
b
c
d
e

5. Rotate-Copy the bowl of *R* into the *E* position, a. Drag up another copy, b. Move points shown at c to reduce the lower crossbar, so it won't add excess points when both parts are finally united. Add two new points (in green), then select the two points at d and hit the Up Arrow key maybe three times. Select the adjacent two points on the bottom lobe, moving them down three Arrow keys. Marquee the letter's right side and drag the selected points leftward to reduce *E*'s width.

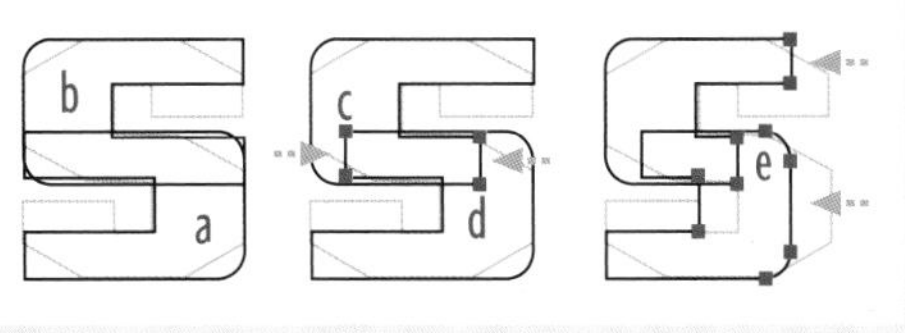
a
b
c
d
e

6. Drag over yet another copy of *R*'s bowl, a. Select and Reflect-Copy it to make b. Drag the two selected points, c, to the right so they don't stick out. Drag the points at d to the left. Select all the points shown at e to drag the right half of the letter to the left to reduce its width. We now have all the letters assembled. It occurs to me, this hasn't really been a lesson in modifying type. It's been more about using parts. But perhaps this is, in the computer age, how to modify type.

METHOD FIVE: TRACING SCANS

Most of what we draw on computer starts with the tracing of scans. For some of us, the process automatically precludes use of parts because we just trace scanned images straight ahead from one corner, around and back to the starting point. This is fine if the image scanned was perfected in the sketch form. Auto tracing has always seemed to be the great grey hope, but in actuality, it usually takes more time to fix poorly placed points than if we had drawn the object from scratch. Following is a closer look at some of these issues.

1. Right, a scan out of *Strong's Book of Designs*, 1905. When preparing to scan, try to line up the edge of the book page, or paper sheet, along the raised lip or glass edge of the scanner as straight as possible. Since our best efforts at this often fail (pages are sometimes bound into books crooked), we usually have to straighten the scanned image once we've opened it in Adobe Photoshop.

2. In Photoshop, hit ⌘-R to show Rulers. Pull a guideline down to a point touching the bottom or topmost edge of the image. Draw a marquee around the area to be straightened. Hit ⌘-T for the Free Transform tool. Handles form at mid and corner points on the Transform marquee, and a center point appears. Drag this center point, which will be the axis of rotation, to the guideline.

3. grab a corner point somewhere opposite to the center point axis and drag the image until it appears straightened. (Tip: Try dragging the corner handle not straight up or down but diagonally upward or downward, which allows more minute, incremental movements.)

4. Finally, in Photoshop, use curves (IMAGE>Adjust>Curves) to remove any gray in the background and to strengthen the blackness of the image for autotracing. The configuration of the Curves palette shown is the one I always use, more or less. Photoshop's Brightness/Contrast filter does not seem, to me, to remove gray middle tones as well as the Curves filter does.

5. Adding a bit of Photoshop's Unsharp Mask (FILTER>Sharpen>Unsharp Mask) can further enhance the clarity of a scanned image. The final result is a straightened scan made crisp and clear, ready for tracing.

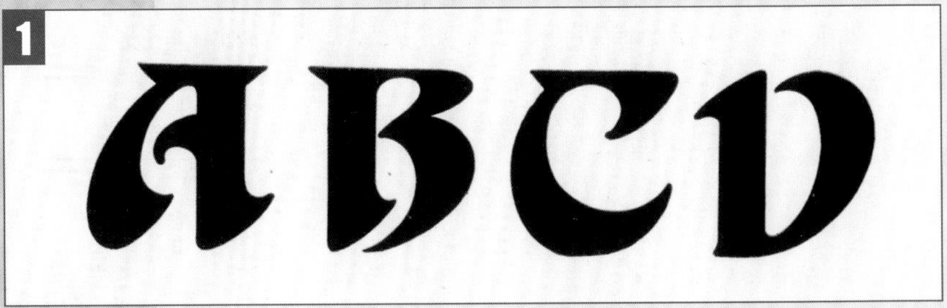
1
ABCD

2
ABCD

3
ABCD

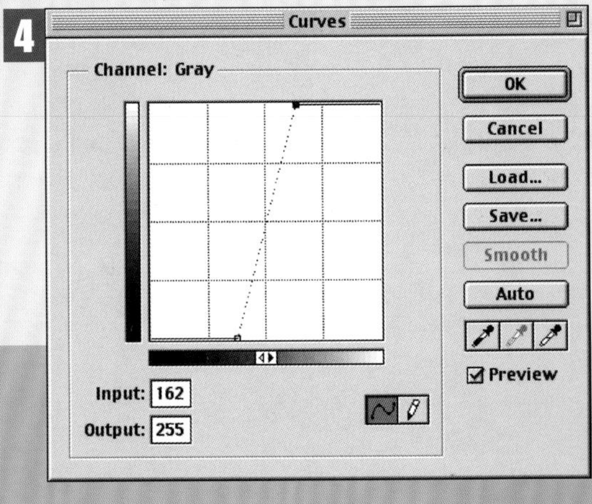
4
Curves
Channel: Gray
OK
Cancel
Load...
Save...
Smooth
Auto
Preview
Input: 162
Output: 255

5
ABCD

Which Image Is True? The Curves filter can alter the density, and thus the shapes, of the letters we scan. The examples below show how each Curves profile alters the scanned image. Take care to determine optimal density when manipulating a scan that should preferably be true to the original.

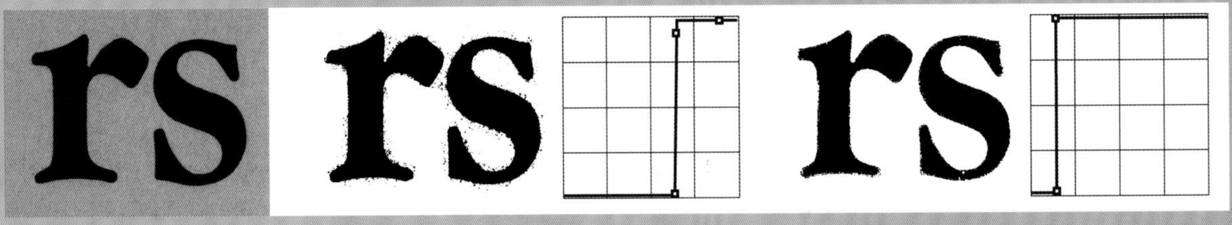
rs
rs
rs

1. Scan before manipulation **2.** Curves profile that fattened up the image **3.** Curves profile that slimmed down the image

OUGHT WE AUTOTRACE?

Autotracing always requires plenty of handwork to move points around, delete unwanted points and add points where they should have been. Autotracing varies in quality from program to program according to the size and resolution of the scan and the various settings that some programs allow in order to fine tune the degree of accuracy. Below left, Strong's *A* as Autotraced in Adobe Illustrator. Fidelity to the scan is poor, points are not in extrema, but there are not too many points, so fixing them will not be difficult. Below right, the *A* scan Autotraced in Fontographer. Fidelity to every nook and cranny of the scan is good and points are in extrema—and lots of other places! This Autotracing would be a nightmare to fix in Illustrator, but Fontographer has features like Clean Up Paths and allows us to delete multiple points in one key command that speeds up this task. Personally, in both cases, I'd start with each program's respective Pen tools and trace the scan by hand, placing points correctly from the start.

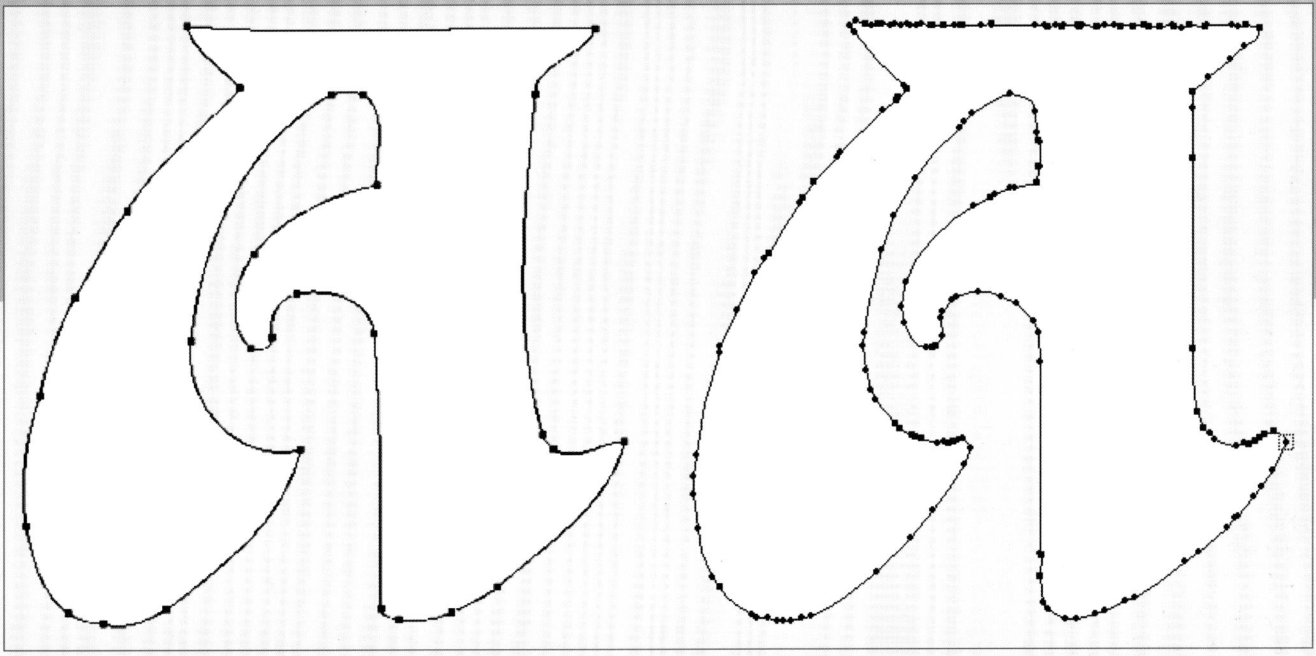

Working From Scans

Images that we scan for the purpose of tracing should be scanned at high resolution, and at a large enough size so the image's edges will appear distinct when we enlarge our page view to work up close. Below, scan a was 300 dpi, but scanned only about one inch wide, making its edge contours difficult to interpret when blown up. Scan b was also 300 dpi, but the image was scanned at 200% so its edges are more clearly defined. Scan c is a bitmap, line-art scan at 1200 dpi and 200%. I usually never scan as bitmap. Gray scale comes out cleaner and allows us to use the Curves filter. But, though it looks dirty, the bitmap scan seems to provide an unambiguous edge to trace.

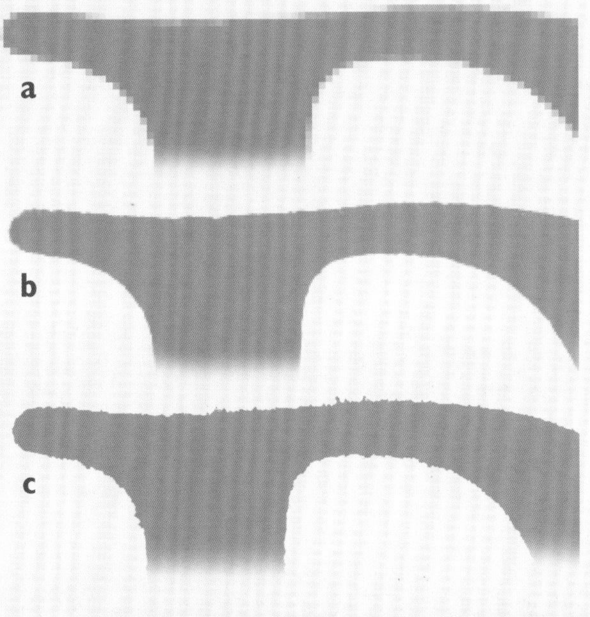
a
b
c

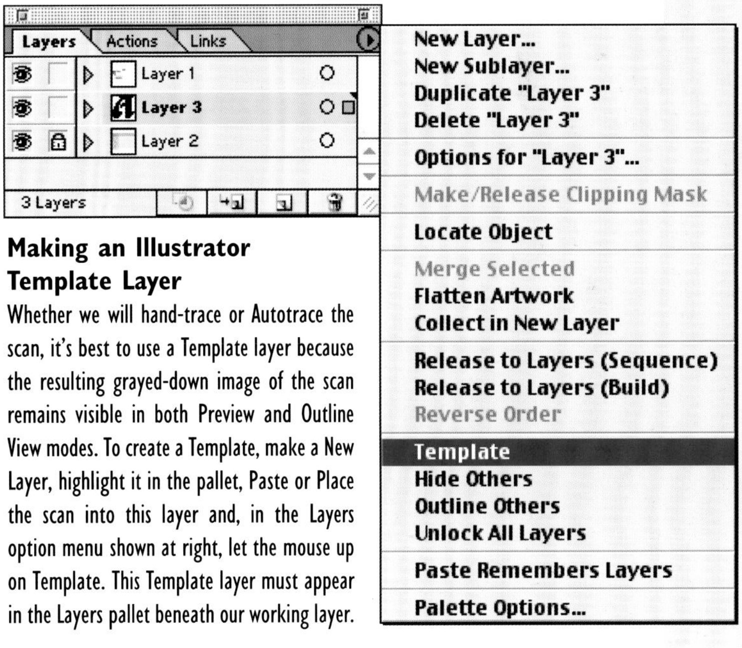
Layers
Actions
Links
Layer 1
Layer 3
Layer 2
3 Layers
New Layer...
New Sublayer...
Duplicate "Layer 3"
Delete "Layer 3"
Options for "Layer 3"...
Make/Release Clipping Mask
Locate Object
Merge Selected
Flatten Artwork
Collect in New Layer
Release to Layers (Sequence)
Release to Layers (Build)
Reverse Order
Template
Hide Others
Outline Others
Unlock All Layers
Paste Remembers Layers
Palette Options...

Making an Illustrator Template Layer

Whether we will hand-trace or Autotrace the scan, it's best to use a Template layer because the resulting grayed-down image of the scan remains visible in both Preview and Outline View modes. To create a Template, make a New Layer, highlight it in the pallet, Paste or Place the scan into this layer and, in the Layers option menu shown at right, let the mouse up on Template. This Template layer must appear in the Layers pallet beneath our working layer.

How to Trace Scans

There is no difference between the way we use the Pen tool to trace a scan and to draw straight ahead or by any other method. All the same rules of bezier curves and points in extrema still apply. Working with a scan does not mean we can't also use skeleton strokes and spare parts. These techniques can insure consistency, which the scanned art may lack.

Yes! You Can DRAW ICONS
Spots and Dingbats...Like the Pros!

A close cousin to the logo is the icon. Often the two are interchangeable. In previous pages we've explored the idea that letters and drawings are both really designs adhering to the same basic ideals of shaping and composition. In the icon, spot (a small illustration) and dingbat (a funny old term for a small, type-high decorative character designed to add a spot of cheer to a dull page of text), we are, in a sense, dealing with a form of logo that emphasizes the graphic over the typographic. These are images that—similar again to the logo—may or may not contain extreme shorthand narrative, clever concepts, humor, or functional and instructive aspects. But in that case, they'd better be darn decorative or visually stunning. "Punch" is something no decent icon should lack. Because we usually associate iconic symbology with being shown at very small sizes, icons must be drawn boldy enough to withstand such reduction. In the following pages we will look at various styles of icons and at some of the artists who specialize in their construction.

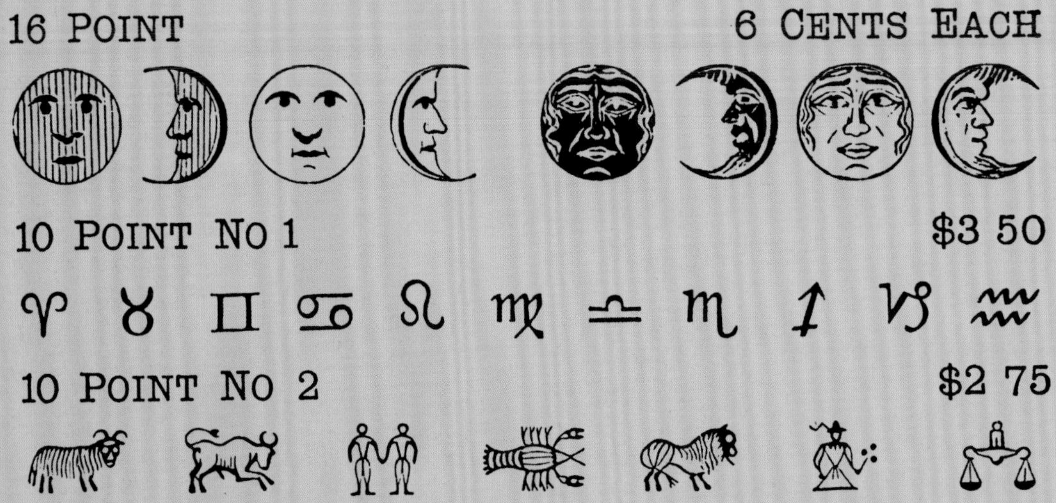
16 POINT
6 CENTS EACH
10 POINT NO 1
$3 50
10 POINT NO 2
$2 75

Sidebar left, comparison of old and new icons, showing the typically bolder style of modern icons. Above, astrological icons (at popular prices) from the 1885 MacKellar, Smiths & Jordan Foundry catalog. Below, an icon for every occasion from the 1936 catalog of Empire Type Foundry.

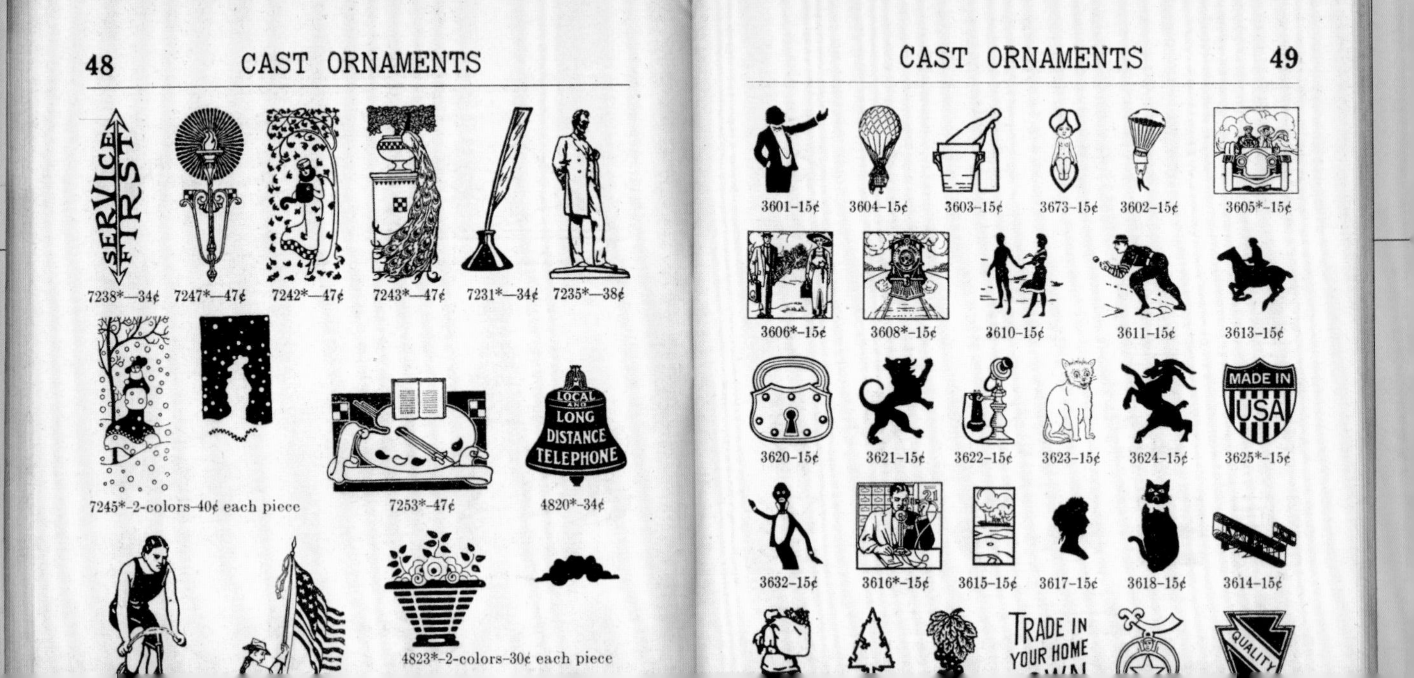
48
CAST ORNAMENTS
SERVICE FIRST
7238*—34¢ 7247*—47¢ 7242*—47¢ 7243*—47¢ 7231*—34¢ 7235*—38¢
7245*-2-colors-40¢ each piece
7253*-47¢
LOCAL AND LONG DISTANCE TELEPHONE
4820*-34¢
4823*-2-colors-30¢ each piece
CAST ORNAMENTS
49
3601–15¢ 3604–15¢ 3603–15¢ 3673–15¢ 3602–15¢ 3605*–15¢
3606*–15¢ 3608*–15¢ 3610–15¢ 3611–15¢ 3613–15¢
3620–15¢ 3621–15¢ 3622–15¢ 3623–15¢ 3624–15¢ 3625*–15¢
MADE IN USA
3632–15¢ 3616*–15¢ 3615–15¢ 3617–15¢ 3618–15¢ 3614–15¢
TRADE IN YOUR HOME

LESLIE CABARGA

Vignetted

Unenclosed within the typical circle or square, this type of icon relies upon dynamic composition to hang together. The designs above were drawn with strokes that were expanded as outlines and then point edited to make them swelling and variweighted.

MILK

Tool-Drawn

Icons created with rectangle and ellipse tools are easy to draw, but no apologies need be made. Such simple symbols evoke powerful primordial memories from an age when square, circle and triangle were the only shapes we knew.

Silhouetted

Powerful and evocative, silhouette icons are still cheaters because much detail may be omitted from the drawing.

Bezier Feathers

Rotate or drag-Copy a single pointy stroke, then hit ⌘-D to keep duplicating and achieve the look of brush "feathering."

Symmetrical

Computers were made for this type of icon. Draw one half of something, flop-copy it and get the other half for free. There is something noble and dramatic in symmetrical design—unless too obvious.

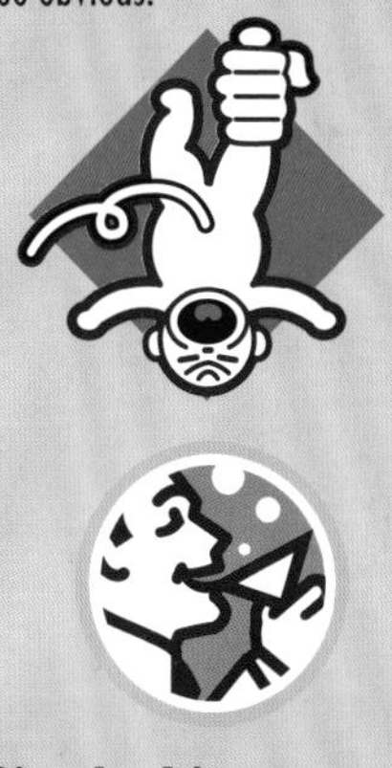

Single Line

Icons can be drawn with the Pen tool in one or two stroke weights to take vast reduction.

Autotraced

When it's just too complicated to draw point by point, and/or if you want an interesting, distressed look that can't be achieved through artifice, then autotracing may be for you. But you'll still have to first draw or scan an image and clean up the points some.

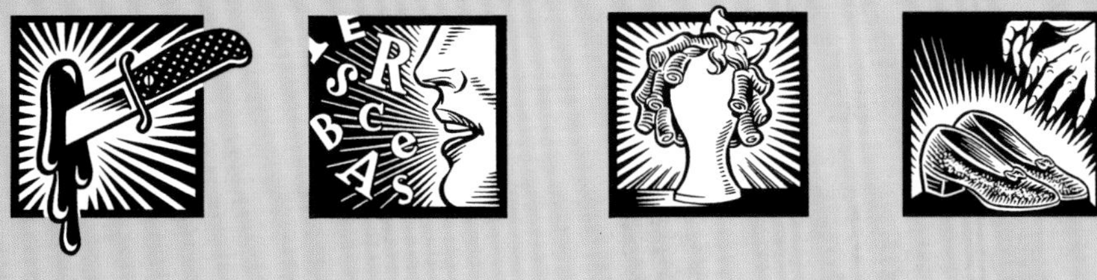

Faux Woodcut

Left, icons done for *Premiere* magazine initiated a vogue in the late 1980s for fake woodcut style (I did them with brush) and radiating lines.

NIGEL HOLMES

Pixelated

This style (drawn with rectangles stuck together) might appear to be easy to draw, but a discerning eye is required to design pixel icons as sharp as these.

Continuous Line

Each icon is drawn with a single (or sometimes several) meandering lines. Holmes maintains consistent "density" of linework throughout the series from icon to icon.

fax
PBX
firewall
person at terminal
factory
office building
terminal
clock
delivery truck
house
store
walking

Signage Icons

Drawn by Holmes for the Smithsonian Institution, these samples (just a few from the larger set) display deceptively simple solutions to creating imagery for global comprehension.

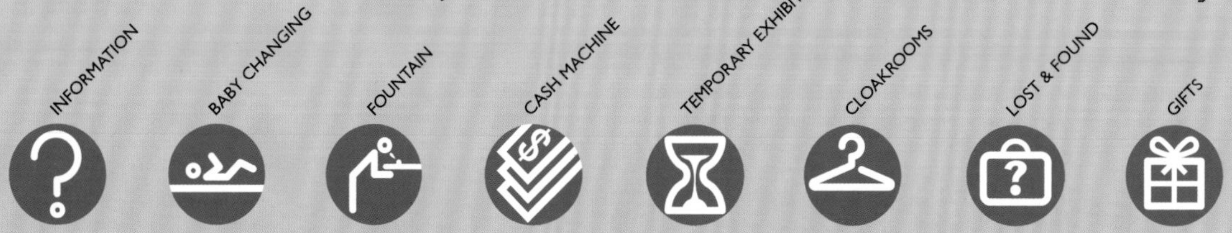
INFORMATION
BABY CHANGING
FOUNTAIN
CASH MACHINE
TEMPORARY EXHIBITS
CLOAKROOMS
LOST & FOUND
GIFTS

Chart Figures

These modern variations on classic chart and graph stylized human figures show greater animation and more vivid color than would have been the case in these fellows'earlier incarnations.

RIAN HUGHES

Round-Cap Chubby Style

A font is the perfect delivery medium for a series of icons as Hughes has done, above. Select his font called Pic Format from Device foundry, type any key and you'll get an icon. Keep typing to discover what's where. Each icon comes in both positive and negative versions.

MARK FISHER

Nouveau Retro

Inked by hand, these clever calendar icons commemorate notable occasions. Fisher does an amazing job of imitating the oversaturated line quality of old printed advertisements.

URP!
Newport Seafood & Wine Festival

Spring Break

Dr. Seuss's Birthday

Mother's Day

DANIEL PELAVIN

Chubby

Search no more for that dancing cow or elusive cotton ball box icon. Pelavin's got it and thousands more, all drawn with his signature friendly fat stroke.

MARK FOX

BMW 325i:
Speed and Sex and Steel

Surfboard:
Plasticity in a World of Flows

Baseball Bat:
Power Plays

Luxor Hotel:
Slow Buildings for Fast Space

@:
Marking the Electrosphere

Freeways:
Iconic Foundations

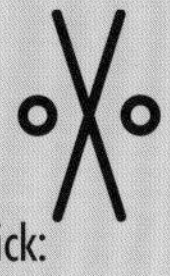
Lipstick:
Masks of Beauty

Blue Jeans:
Uniforms of Modernism

SFMOMA:
Iconic Monumentality

CBS Logo:
Co-opting the Corporate

Minicam:
You are Big Brother

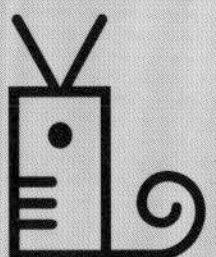
KitchenAid Mixer:
Gadgets Galore

Split Screen

Top, in navy and lemon, a system of icons by Mark Fox of BlackDog for an Oracle Corporation annual report. Note that all the designs maintain consistent light/dark ratio, line width and live area within the enclosure. There's an art to drawing cohesive series of consistent icons like this.

Abstract Conceptual

Above, Mark Fox produced this exercise in free association for the San Francisco Museum of Modern Art exhibition "Icons: Magnets of Meaning." (The larger logo at right spells out the word *ICON*). Just looking at this amazing series starts my mind pondering the limitless creative possibilities of the icon. . . unleashed!

Hobo Signs

These chalk-marked icons were scribed on sidewalks or fences to lead other hoboes to safe places for a handout or to direct them away from dangerous houses and neighborhoods. A complex lexicon developed, and an illiterate hobo was plumb out of luck. A few of the many signs are shown on this page. Too bad hoboes didn't have Adobe Illustrator, because these 7-point round-cap stroke icons that I researched off the Internet were really easy to draw.

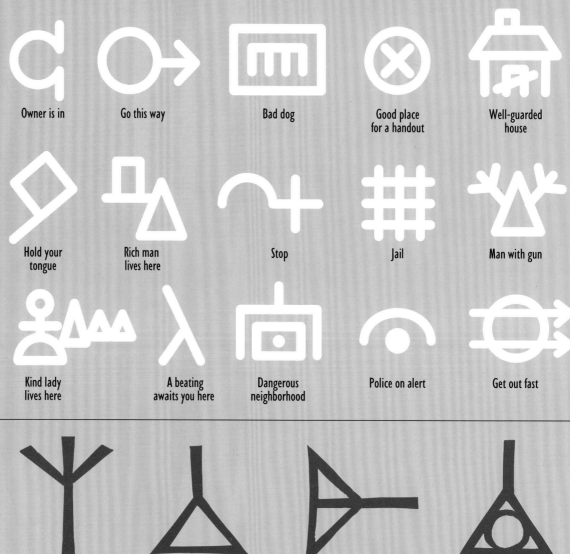

Owner is in

Go this way

Bad dog

Good place for a handout

Well-guarded house

Hold your tongue

Rich man lives here

Stop

Jail

Man with gun

Kind lady lives here

A beating awaits you here

Dangerous neighborhood

Police on alert

Get out fast

Ancient Icons

In his 1926 treatise *The Book of Signs*, Rudolf Koch does not give specifics as to the origin of these ancient icons. But we take him at his word since he is Koch. Originally cut in wood by Koch's assistant Fritz Kredel, these icons were scanned and autotraced by the author, then carefully point edited for accuracy. The flairing strokes lend a monumental quality that could be used for styling modern icons.

Man

Woman

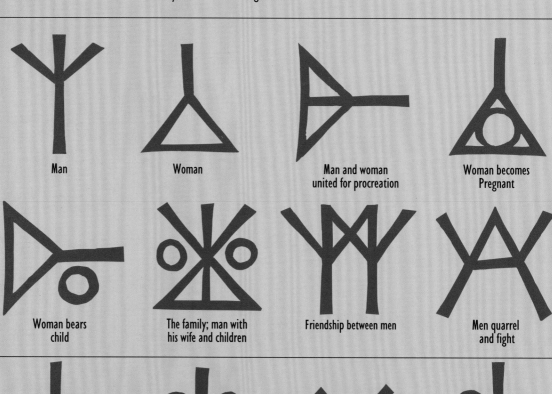

Man and woman united for procreation

Woman becomes Pregnant

Woman bears child

The family; man with his wife and children

Friendship between men

Men quarrel and fight

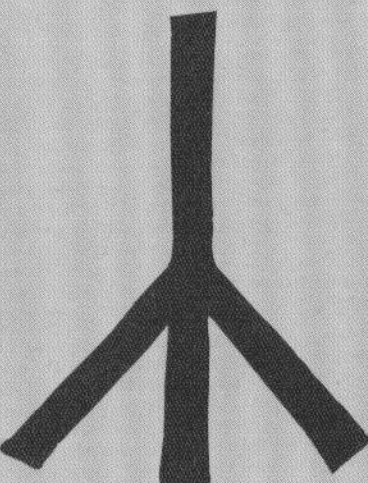
The man dies

The widow and her children

One child dies

Forlorn mother with remaining child

Crop Signs

The speed with which crop signs appear in fields overnight, the miraculous manner in which the stalks are bent and interwoven yet not broken, the uncanny precision of the forms and their unique complexity, along with the amazing interplay of positive and negative space—carved out of corn!—leaves no doubt in my mind as to their otherworldly origins. While interpreters of these signs await their Rosetta stone, researcher Wolfgang Schindler, who created the carefully measured drawings of actual crop circles shown on this page, jokingly suggests that they represent messages meant for *him*. Your intrepid author has, in the meantime, divined the true meaning of these outer space icons and captioned each accordingly.

Morgan's Hill, 1994

Keep moving, devilish big brother watching

Chilcomb Down, 1990

Don't settle here, ozone hole too large, icecaps melting

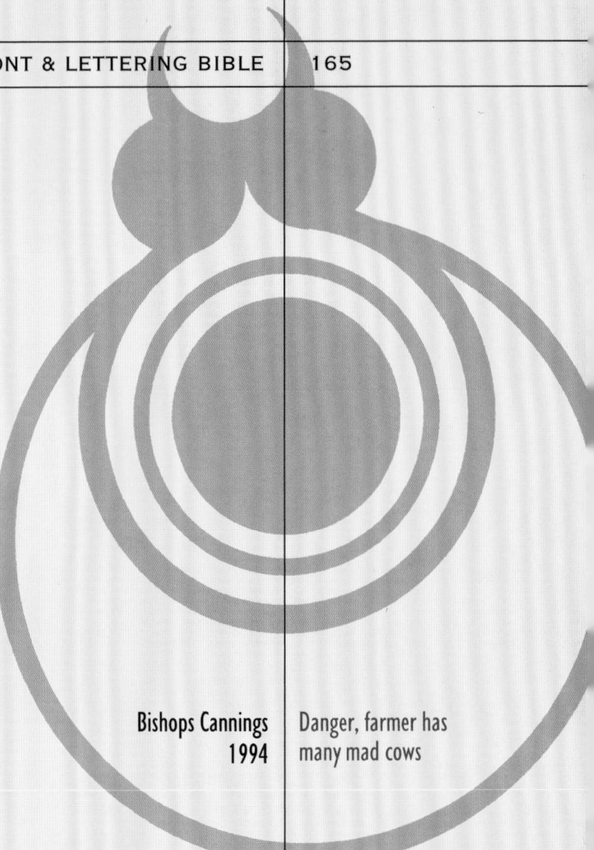

Bishops Cannings 1994

Danger, farmer has many mad cows

Longwood Warren, 1995

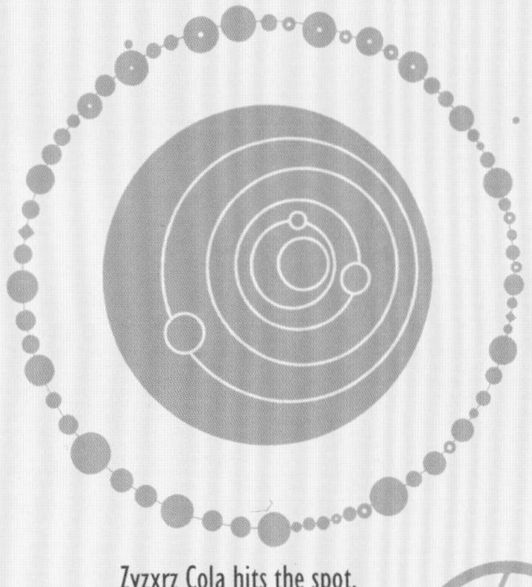

Zyzxrz Cola hits the spot, 12 full dnydrs, that's a lot; twice as much for your pyngl, too; Zyzxrz Cola is the drink for you.

North Lancing, 1990

Bare midriff zone

Neudorf, Annaberg, 2001

Ripe for conquest, natives too busy watching video box

Barbury Castle, 1991

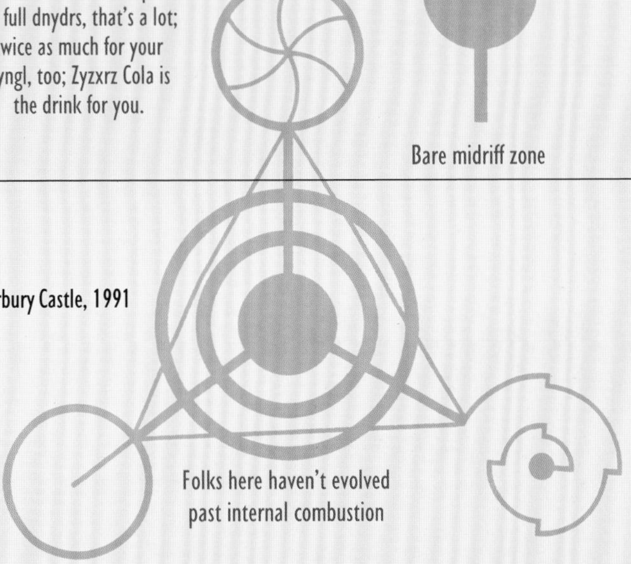

Folks here haven't evolved past internal combustion

FRENCH CASINO
HOTE
NEW
VINCENT
HOTEL ASTOR
ALL STAR CAST
OR BAR
ROSE MARIE
IRVINGTON
ASTOR BAR
DINNER $1

Above is a classic 1930s neon signage montage, of the sort always used in Hollywood movies of the period. And though it was accomplished with multiple exposures in a photo shop, it was not done in Photoshop.

They laughed when I sat down at the computer, until I showed them...

INCREDIBLE TYPE TRIX

Most type effects involve bringing an illusion of dimensionality to flat drawings of letters. There are really only four main categories, and all type special effects are essentially variations on and combinations of these: the outline, the drop shadow, the dimensional block shadow and the dimensional letterface.

Outlines around type—whether glowing in Photoshop, or hard-edged in Illustrator—help unify groups of letters and/or words and are also used to separate lettering from its background for better contrast and legibility. Outlines around letters can also provide a pleasing, decorative effect.

Drop shadows were originally inspired by dimensional sign letters that cast actual shadows against their actual backgrounds. Drop shadows improve contrast between type and background by creating the impression that the letters have been lifted off of the flat art plane.

Dimensional block shadows imitate sign letters that have been cut from blocks of wood or formed with sheet metal sides. The Type Trix lettering above proves that a dimensional-block-shadow effect really makes lettering pop!

Dimensional letterface effects include chisel edging or faceting, as well as embossing, debossing and pillow edging, all of which can be done in Adobe Illustrator. These effects can often be better achieved in Photoshop or Corel Bryce, but such programs are beyond the scope of this book, which aims to teach basic letterforms and the happy combining of same, using vector-based tools. Whatever cool surface-mapping effects you apply to your type afterwards, you can sleep easier knowing the fundamental construction of your letterforms is sound.

A gallery of type trix from the past and present follow, with tutorials on how to apply these effects to your own logos.

EXERCISE Design a logo starting with basic black-filled lettering, then enhance it by creating four variations utilizing each of the categories of special effects listed above. Instructions for achieving these FX begin on page 176.

EXHIBITORS HERALD
THE INDEPENDENT FILM TRADE PAPER

Above, a very nice outlined lettering job, c. 1927, with gracefully flowing letters and interesting ligatures. The piece was undoubtedly done by one artist, which goes to prove that if you can draw a border like this, the lettering part is a piece of cake.

Right, a brochure, c. 1900, for Ashtabula Tool Co. that, typical for the Victorian age, has all the stops pulled out. Again, one artist designed the whole piece, including the small lettering. With lots of patience, one could replicate all these effects in Adobe Illustrator.

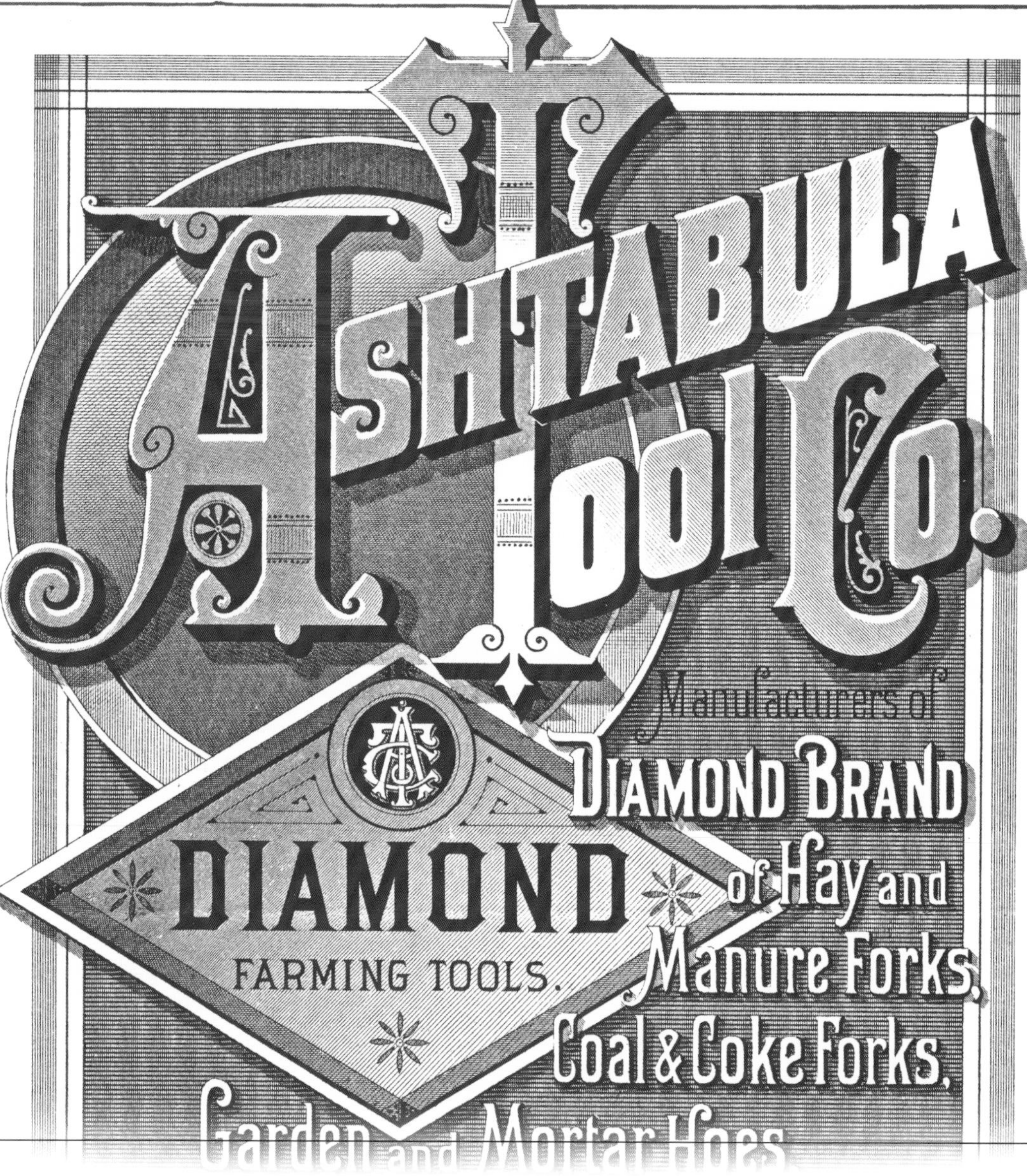
Ashtabula
Tool Co.
Manufacturers of
DIAMOND BRAND
of Hay and
Manure Forks,
Coal & Coke Forks,
DIAMOND
FARMING TOOLS.

Left, Michael Samuel created this logo worthy of M.C. Escher for Design Visionaries. And he added a fuzzy drop shadow to really spiff it up. Above, Samuel plays with flip-flopped 45° block shadow letters, superimposing a field of horizontal lines that further confuse the planes of this logo for the ISM Company.

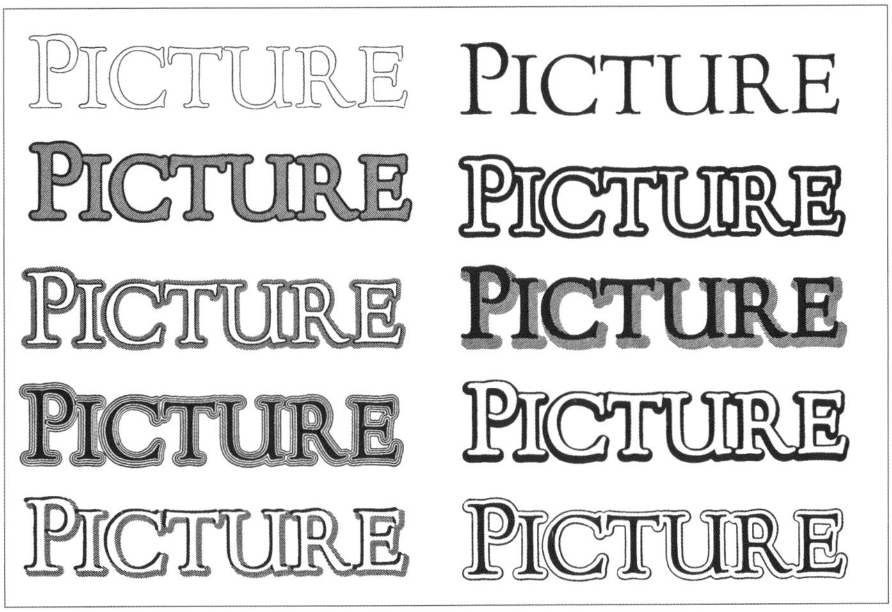
PICTURE
PICTURE
PICTURE
PICTURE
PICTURE
PICTURE
PICTURE
PICTURE
PICTURE
PICTURE

There are virtually no graphic effects that we create today that could not have been achieved in the old days—albeit with much greater difficulty. At left is a 1939 example from the Martin Weber Studios in New York. All the effects shown were created photographically from the single line of black type in the upper right corner.

Clueless at Remyco, a long-defunct company of a bygone era. And is it any wonder! Had their logo sported a correctly made block shadow, they might today be competing with Sony for market share. Granted, the logo designer had to ink this job with a ruling pen and didn't have a computer to help him out. But he still could have slid a tracing of the logo down to the right at 45° and used it to guide him. Instead he made it up and drew it by eye. "Never rely upon memory, for you might be betrayed by it," said Andrew Loomis, illustration luminary.

Fortune

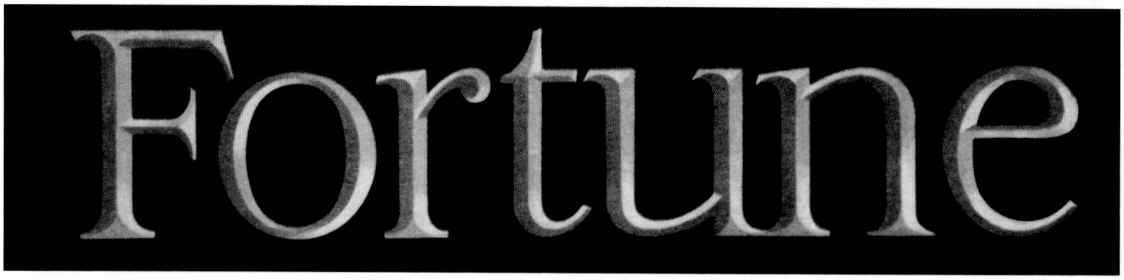
Fortune

Right, from a 1932 edition, the *Fortune* magazine logo was designed by Thomas Cleland. Drawn with pen and ink, the letters appear to have been cut from platinum. By 1942, below right, the logo had become more stylized, though an airbrushed version retained the original dimensional effect.

SIGN LAYOUTS.
CHOICE
GROCERIES
AND FRUITS.
WEST & BRO'S
TAILORS.
GENTS FURNISHERS.

Above, a page from an 1892 sign lettering manual, showing two styles of drop shadows and elegant floating baselines. In those days, the rule was to place a period after every word or phrase. Silly, huh?

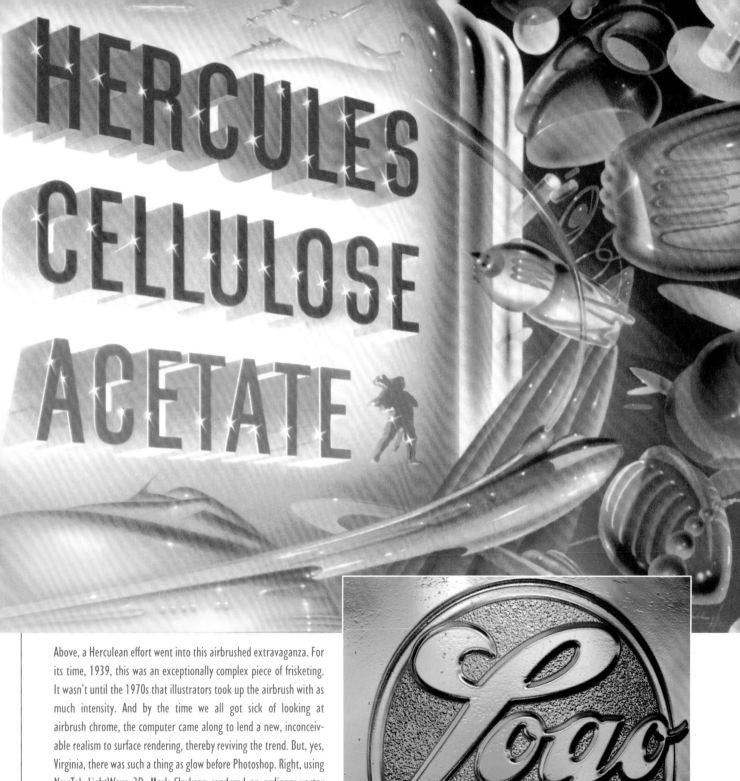

HERCULES
CELLULOSE
ACETATE

Above, a Herculean effort went into this airbrushed extravaganza. For its time, 1939, this was an exceptionally complex piece of frisketing. It wasn't until the 1970s that illustrators took up the airbrush with as much intensity. And by the time we all got sick of looking at airbrush chrome, the computer came along to lend a new, inconceivable realism to surface rendering, thereby reviving the trend. But, yes, Virginia, there was such a thing as glow before Photoshop. Right, using NewTek LightWave 3D, Mark Clarkson rendered an ordinary vector logo design into the spitting image of a molded glass soda bottle.

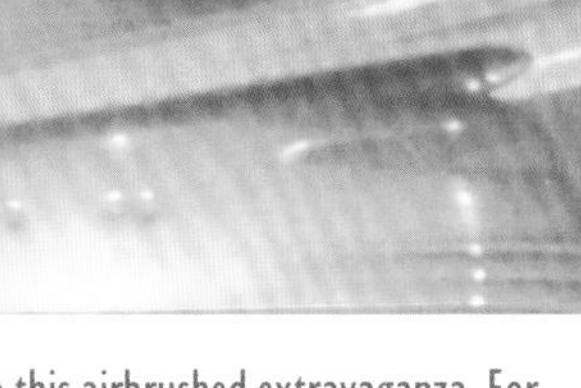
Logo

Logo

R
G
FULLY
ASHOK
LEYLAND

S
INSURED

Above and above left, Sri Lankan food-wagon sign painters have developed an amazing style of decorative lettering, as shown in these photos by Viktor Kaganovich. The sign painters draw inspiration from such sources as engraved bank notes and American "kustom" auto detailing. Left, these real-life carved wooden letters from an 1890s sign company catalog are not designers' concepts of how dimensional letterfaces should look, but the real thing. Below, it's not a rainbow gradient blend—which they didn't have in the 1950s when this pencil packaging design was issued—but a split fount printing effect. Try asking a modern printer to use several PMS colors separated by rags in the ink fount so the colors blend as the press rolls and he'll instantaneously invent a plausible-sounding excuse as to why it cannot possibly be done.

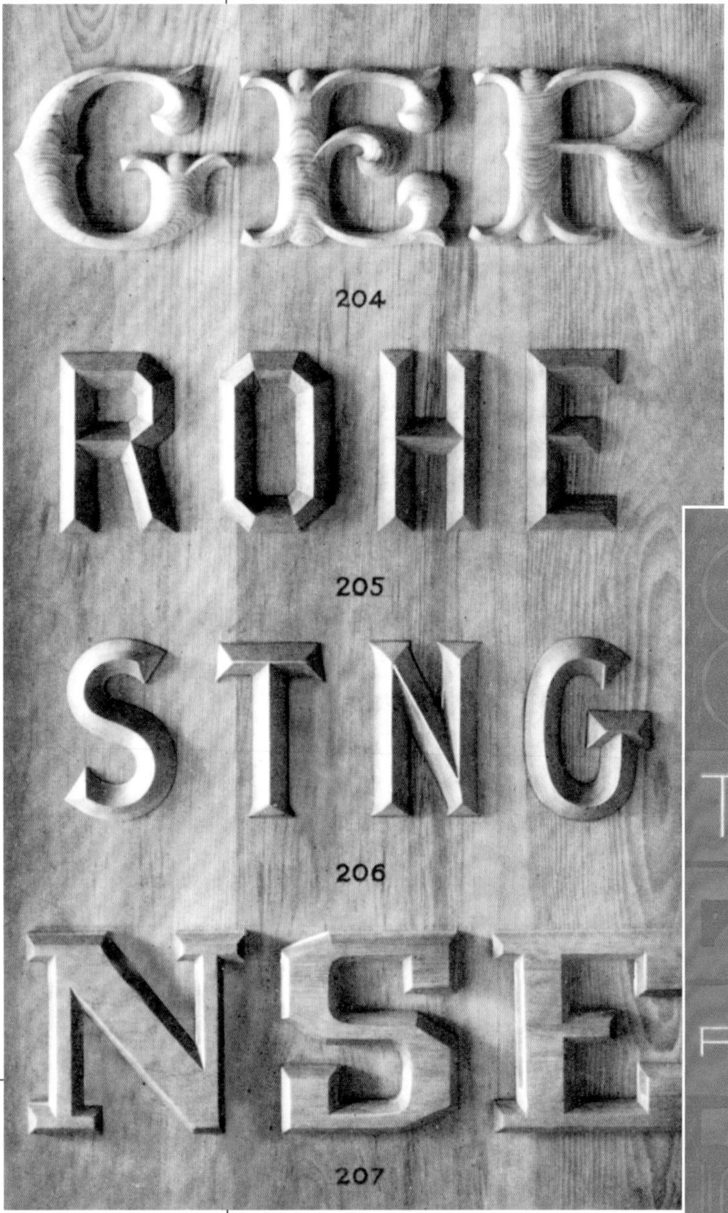
GER
204
ROHE
205
STNG
206
NSE
207

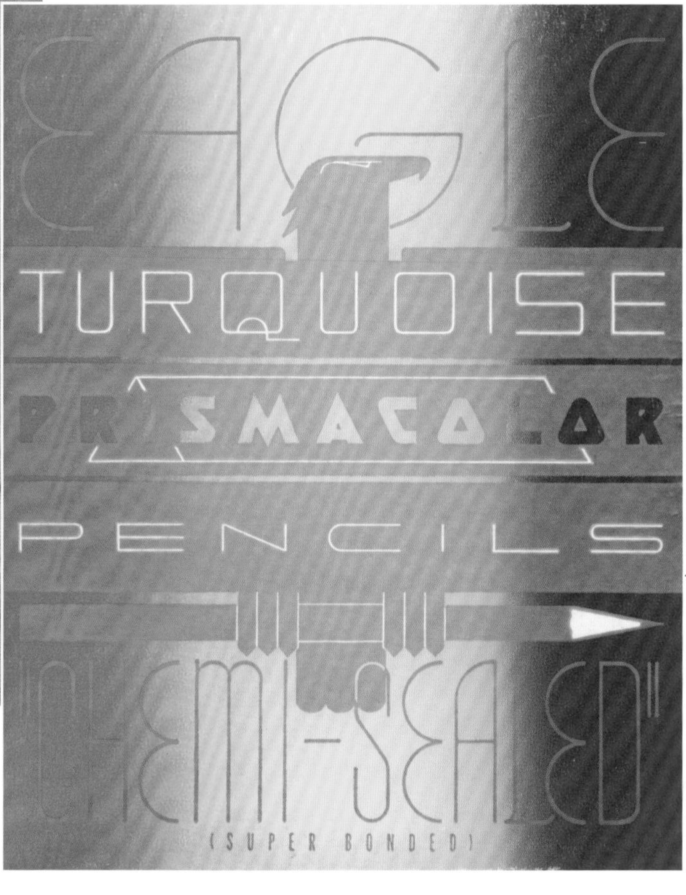
TURQUOISE
PENCILS
CHEMI-SEALED
(SUPER BONDED)

Political cartoonist Lalo Alcaraz always seems to hit the mark with his own incisive perspective on current events. And he's no slouch in the drop-shadow department, either. His cartoon, right, sheds a telling light upon what many believe is the shadowy secret behind the 9-11 story. As novel as we find Alcaraz's approach, this concept—the shadow revealingly differentiated from its source—has shown up from time to time through the years as one bit of shtick in the thinking designers' arsenal.

9 11
LALO ALCARAZ ©2002
DISTRIBUTED BY UNIVERSAL PRESS SYNDICATE

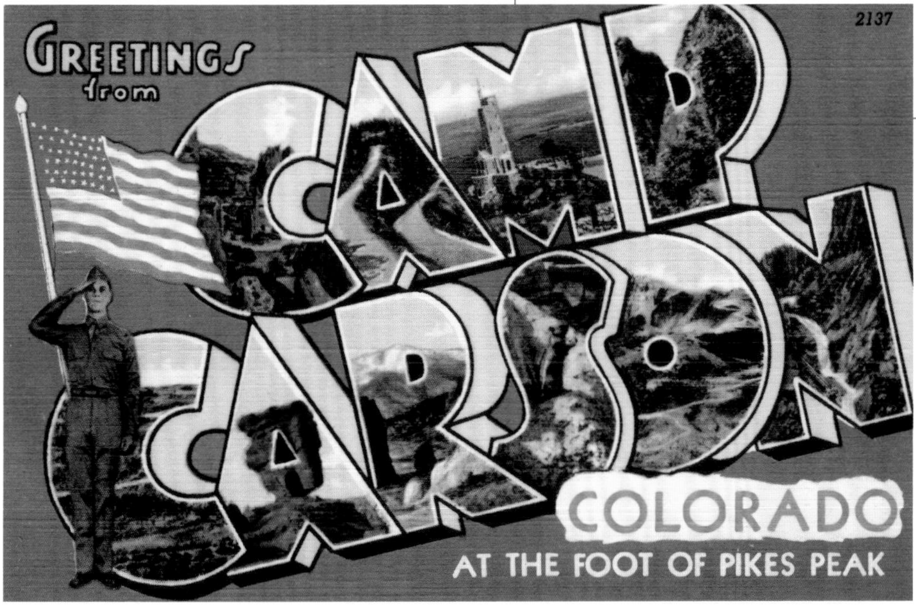
2137
GREETINGS from
CAMP CARSON
COLORADO
AT THE FOOT OF PIKES PEAK

IN THE ARKANSAS VALLEY
2370
LA JUNTA
COLO.
ON THE SANTA FE TRAIL
© CURT TEICH & CO., INC.

No catalog of cool type effects would be complete without examples of classic American postcards with their wonderfully clunky letterforms and awkward block shadows. These two examples are typical. Imagine my surprise in finding the Camp Carson card, above left, since I was born in the camp hospital while my father spent his tour of duty painting signs like "LATRINE."

Tom Nikosey, whose work fills this page, shares credit with other designers such as Michael Doret and Daniel Pelavin, for pioneering the “logo illustration.” This is a type-driven illustration so richly decorative that the letters themselves take center stage and nobody minds the absence of a pictorial element. I was shocked to discover that Nikosey’s extravagant tonal blends were not the product of Photoshop, but were all done with Illustrator’s gradients. And that means they are vector and thus fully scalable.

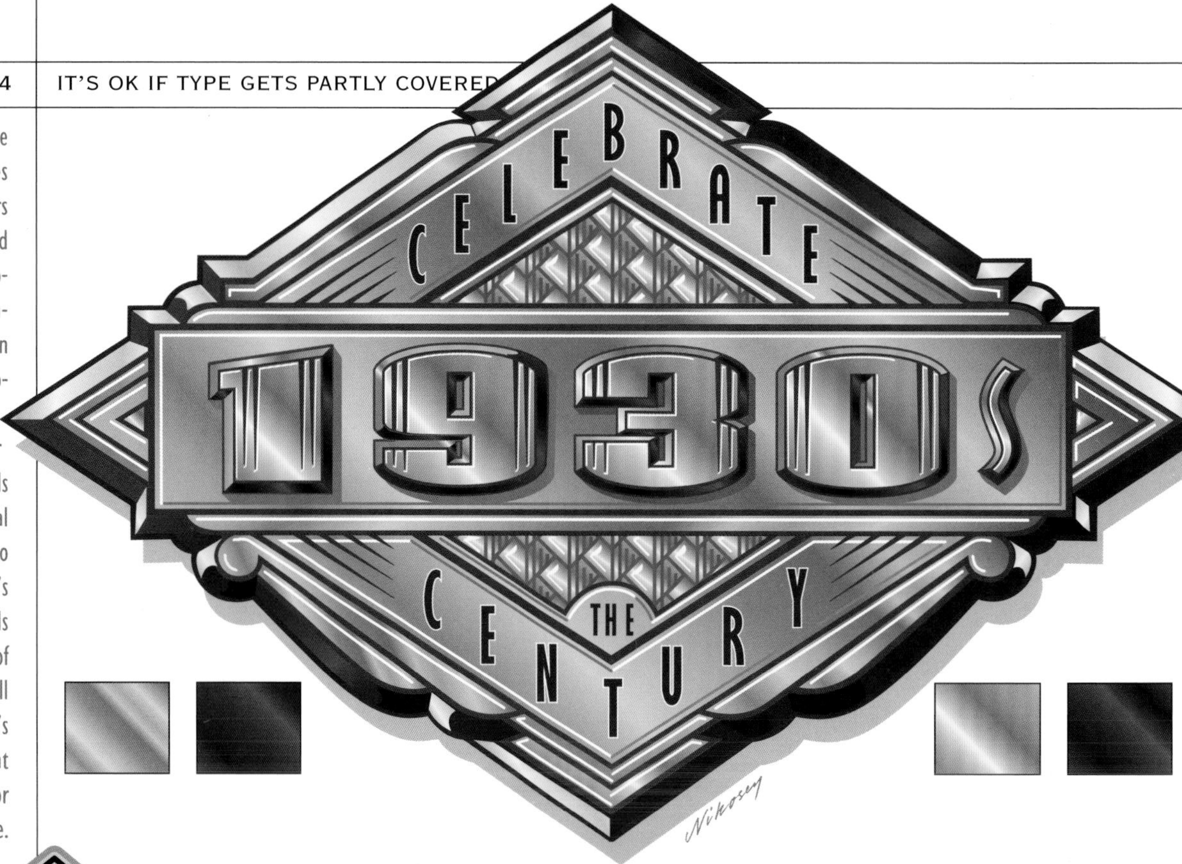
CELEBRATE
1930s
THE
CENTURY
Nikosey

CELEBRATE
1920s
THE
CENTURY

Above, Nikosey created four amazingly complex gradients for this logo for the U.S. Postal Service. To create a metallic surface effect, the Gradient pallet for just the first of these blends (swatches shown above) utilizes eleven different, subtly coordinated colors! Left, another in the postal logo series. Below left, merchandising emblem for Crosby, Stills and Nash. Below, a beautifully drawn and modeled carved surface treatment for an Indiana Tourism logo.

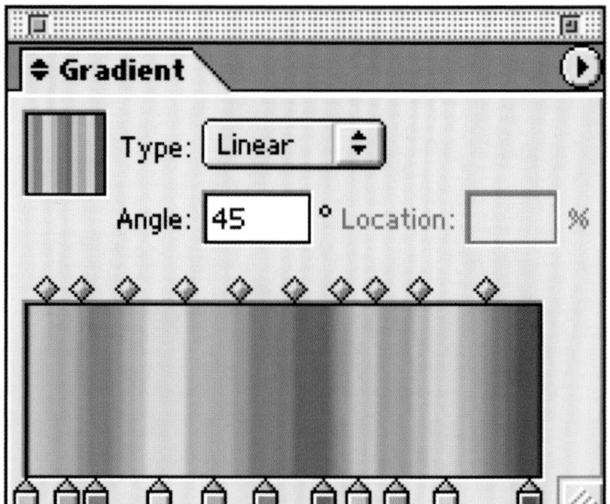
Gradient
Type: Linear
Angle: 45
° Location:
%

CROSBY STILLS
NASH

ENJOY
INDIANA
WHERE THE WELCOME MAT IS ALWAYS OUT!

I once accused Daniel Pelavin of maximally utilizing Illustrator's capabilities such as Rotate-Copy and Duplicate to achieve detailed effects that once were within the purview of only the skilled engraver. One such example is Pelavin's logo for the Type Directors Club, right. The underlying complexity of this many-layered job is revealed in the wireframe portion shown far right. In the logo Red Hot in Latin America, Pelavin's done it again, this time in color. And we got his permission to reverse engineer this piece for you.

THIRTY
EIGHT

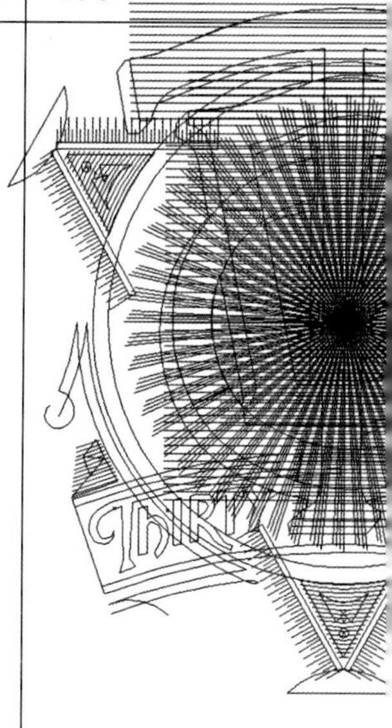

RED HOT
IN LATIN AMERICA

a
b
c
d
e
f
g
h
i
j
k
l
m
Stroke
Weight: 1.08 pt
Cap:
Miter Limit:
Join:
Dashed Line
.02 pt
2.7 pt
dash
gap
dash
gap
dash
gap

The background shape was drawn and filled with gradient a. Gold curlicues were first drawn as stroked lines. Outline Strokes turned the lines into objects, which were point edited to swell and taper as desired, b, and filled with gradient c. Letters like d were drawn and filled with gradient e. Wide strokes, circled, were applied to the letters, and Outline Strokes turned them into objects. The blue line, f, indicates the letter's original outline. The new outline of the letter, g, was drag-Copied and recolored to form the yellow highlight at h and the brown drop shadow at i (shown exaggeratedly pulled out). For the lavender letter highlights, circled, two copies of the inner outline, j, were dragged down at 45°—the second slightly lower than the first—and Subtract From Shape Area left just the highlights remaining. A stepped gradient blend between two round-cap, dash-stroked (specs shown at l) copies of the basic letter outlines, d, became the raised-ball letter border at k. Shown blown up and also exploded at m, the effect required eleven steps. This ball effect was also applied to the curlicues around the background shape. Don't worry, special effects like these are more fully demonstrated in the how-to section that follows.

Before adding effects to type, it's best to select the type, then go to TYPE>Create Outlines so the letters become objects. To place an outline around type, such as A, the obvious approach would be to simply add strokes to the black-filled letters. However, unless the outline will be thin, such as a 1- or 2-point stroke, this is usually not advisable.

When we add wide, 4-point strokes to letters, as in example B, the weight of the letters is reduced and distorted interior shapes result. This is because half the width of our stroke falls within the letter itself. (I know—you're looking at C and thinking, "Hey, this would make a really cool font!" Don't bother, it's already been done, and you can no doubt download it for free off the Internet right now!)

The proper way to get an outline effect, while preserving the original shape and weight of the type, is to stack two (or more) copies of the same type on different levels, as in D. Here's how:

1. Select and then Group (⌘-G) the lettering to be outlined (when we Create Outlines of type, all letters become automatically grouped). It's easier to select all parts of objects in a Group, even when they're enmeshed in multiple levels.

2. Copy (⌘-C), but don't Paste yet.

3. Assign a 6-point stroke to the type.

4. Hit Paste in Front (⌘-F). There are now two copies of the logo—the bottom stroked, the top unstroked—exactly on top of one another, as seen in E.

5. Add a 1-point white stroke to the black-filled letters on level 2, as shown in F. Because it's only 1 point, the stroke does not encroach too much into the shapes of the letterforms.

6. The preferred method would be to give level 2 a white fill and white 2-point stroke, then Paste a third copy—black fill only—on top. The result, G, shows interior junctions, such as x, ending in points, whereas without the third copy, those junctions would be blunted, as in z.

A

HORACE
MELBATOAST

B

C

HORACE
MELBATOAST

D

Level 2
Level 1
HORACE

E

HORACE
MELBATOAST

F

G

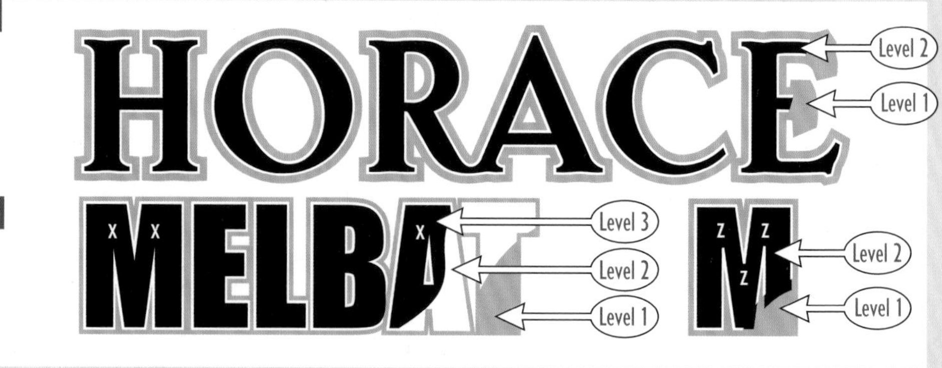
HORACE
Level 2
Level 1
MELBAT
x x x
Level 3
Level 2
Level 1
M
z z z
Level 2
Level 1

A
FUTURISMO
B
FUTURISMO
Level 3
Level 2
Level 1
C
FUTURISMO
Level 3
Level 4
Level 2
Level 1
D
FUTURISMO
6
5
4
3
2
1

Fred Cooper likened the prettying effect of an outline placed around lettering to "sending a plain girl to a competent beautician—glamour results." In 1939, Cooper could get away with that comment, but still, he wasn't exactly wrong. Although they can carry a retro connotation, outlines really jazz up lettering. Left, two copies of A have been Pasted atop one another to form a three-level outline, B. Level 1 has a 6-point red stroke; level 2 has a 5-point white stroke. The top level 3 is filled black with no stroke.

You can go nuts with outlines. There are endless variations. In C, level 1 has a 14-point black stroke; level 2 has a 9.5-point red stroke; level 3 has a 3-point white stroke; and top level 4 is filled black with a 2-point white stroke that reduces the weight of the black letter itself. Note, all strokes have been assigned Round Join corners.

At D, a six-level outline treatment. The letter *O* is shown expanded at bottom. Modifications, like lowering or squaring the points on *M*, would have to be made to avoid its sticking out so alarmingly. Notice that the multistroked counters of *R* and *S* are looking lumpy as shape flaws in the drawing of the font become exaggerated by the series of strokes. Also, as stroke weights increase, their outermost edges naturally look funky. Then we can Outline Strokes and hand-finesse them.

OUTLINE CLINIC

Out-of-the-box letter spacing that looks fine when we first set type sometimes requires fine-tuning later, after outlines and effects are added. The widths of outline strokes should be as carefully planned as the spacing of the letters themselves. Right, some problems have been highlighted.

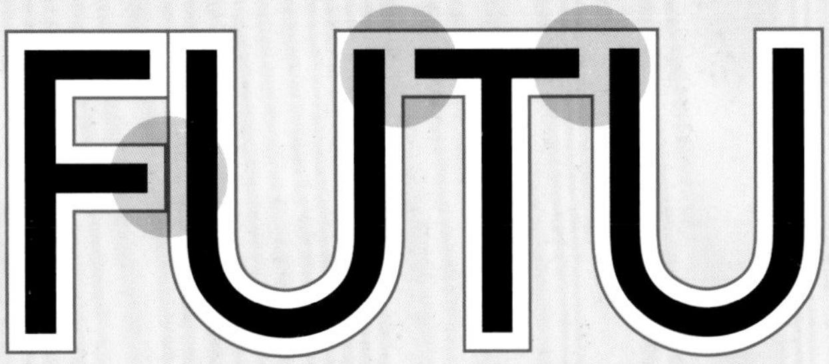
FUTU

Below, two different solutions. Both require adjusting spacing, either to tighten or open up areas where outlines became doubled in width, spoiling the uniformity of the effect. The crossbar of *F* needed to extend the same length as the upper arm—or be cut back—to avoid the awkward proximity to the stem of *U*.

FUTU FUTU

ADJUSTING LETTER SPACING

A. Here are three levels of type. On top is the type itself, Cartier Book Bold, as set with its original "factory kerning." The middle layer has a 6-point green stroke, and the bottom layer has a 7-point black stroke, leaving a 0.5-point stroke "reveal." Problem areas are noted.

B. Improvements have been made by tightening letter spacing to reduce areas where the outline became double-thick as at d, and where the thin black strokes, falling too close together, cause eye dirt as in c, e, f. Also, teensy counters, such as a, b, g have been deleted altogether.

C. Here's another way to avoid the problems noted in B. *Increase* letter spacing. Try to create an even rhythm in the white spaces between letters. To better achieve this, I adjusted a few letters at a, b, c by dragging parts of them out to close or open up space as needed.

A

RadioMan
a
b
c
d
e
f
g

B

RadioMan

C

RadioMan
a
b
c

OUTLINE CLINIC

KEEPING OUTLINES CONSISTENT

A neat trick is to enlarge an initial letter several point sizes over the rest of the letters. For balance, the last letter may also be enlarged. However, if an outline is applied to such a treatment, its width should remain consistent for all letters, including the enlarged ones. Think of it this way: First the sign painter made the black letters, then, he took one flat-edged brush and outlined the perimeter of all the letters.

A. The wrong way to do it: First and last letters have 8.5-point strokes, and the smaller letters in between are stroked only at 5 points.

B. Problem corrected. All strokes on level 1 are now 7 points. Let's start nitpicking the shapes of outlines themselves. Depending upon the angle of convergence, pointy corner strokes will either stick way out like a, d, g, h (to mention a few) or get chopped off as in c, e, f. Also, the outline strokes connecting *R* and *A* at b would look better if they matched up.

C. All corrections have been made. First, all stroked letters on level 1 were changed to objects with Outline Strokes. Then points were added and subtracted, and bezier curves were tweaked as necessary. Notice, the pointy strokes no longer perfectly parallel the letter contours but taper to shorter and narrower endings. Can you identify other subtle changes I made?

A

RABELAIS
Level 2
Level 1

B

RABELAIS
a
b
c
d
e
f
g
h

C

RABELAIS
BEAT COFFEE SHOPPE

CELERY tonic
GEFILTE fish

1 If you want to thin down an existing font, you can take out a pocketknife and start whittling, or try the following method. Be aware that in doing this, it will almost always be necessary to make corrections to the resulting letterforms. Above, sample words typed out in Arial Black and Times Roman Bold.

CELERY t
a
GEFILTE
b

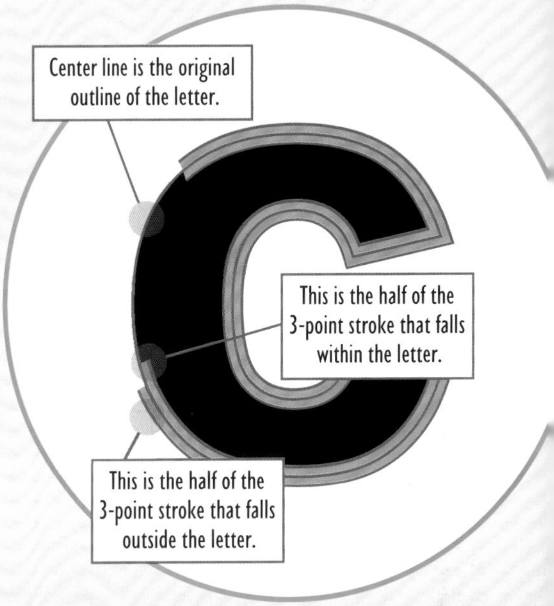
Center line is the original outline of the letter.
This is the half of the 3-point stroke that falls within the letter.
This is the half of the 3-point stroke that falls outside the letter.

2 Create Outlines of these words and add strokes. *Celery* got a 3-point stroke, and *Gefilte* got 2 points to avoid having the thin stems disappear. Next, select all the type and go to OBJECT>Path>Outline Stroke. Above, at a and b, I've triple-stroked some of the letters to imitate the selection outlines you'll see when you Outline Strokes. See explanation in circle, right.

CELERY tonic
d
e
c
b
a
GEFILTE fish

The removed parts of letters look strange because they are compound paths.

3 With the White Arrow tool, Select and Delete the fills, a, and the outermost outlines, c, but leave the innermost outline (which is actually the inner contour of the stroke), b. As parts of the letter are deleted, counters like d and e become filled in. Select the *R* and its counter and go to OBJECT>Compound Paths> Release Compound Paths (⌥-⌘-8). Do the same with letter *o*. If Release Compound Paths doesn't punch out the holes (a never-fixed bug in Illustrator), hit Divide in the Pathfinder pallet, then Delete the counters. Now that the letters have been slimmed down, letter spacing should be tightened up and certain letters, such as the *R* in *Celery*, the *n* in *tonic*, and the *h* in *fish* should be tweaked to restore their shapes. I've done this manually, below.

Rnh

Drop shadows are the most common type effect, partly because they are easy to make. They add a decorative touch to "plain" lettering like A. More importantly, drop shadows are used to add emphasis to type, especially where a busy tonal or colored background would cause a lack of contrast, legibility or coherence.

MAKE A SIMPLE DROP SHADOW

B. Select some letters, then Group (⌘-G) and Copy (⌘-C), but don't Paste yet. Next, give the type you just copied, a different fill color. Now Paste in Front (⌘-F) a second copy of the type, and while it remains selected, hit the Up Arrow key a few times, then hit the Right Arrow key the same number of times. Note: Drop shadows can be made whether or not Create Outlines has turned the type into objects.

C. The tonal values are shown reversed, with the letter being dark and the drop shadow light. Drop shadows can be overdone. In D, the shadow has been dropped down too far, resulting in a confusion of masses and perhaps poor legibility. Also, the drop shadow no longer seems to relate to the type as a shadow.

A similar problem develops in E. The shadow from this thin-stem font, Progressiv, is dropped too low. The slivers of white showing between letters and shadows cause visual clutter (eye dirt) that's best avoided.

There are several ways around this problem: Raise the drop shadow to avoid spaces between letter and shadow; add an outline stroke to the drop shadow to thicken it up (F combines both approaches); make a blurry drop shadow with Photoshop's Layer Styles effects (blurry drop shadows not only look more realistic, but the blur interferes less with legibility of the type itself); or make the drop shadow three-dimensional as explained on the next page.

MAKE A CAST SHADOW

In G, a cast shadow is shown. Select and Copy the type (don't Paste yet). Change its fill color (this will be the shadow). Use the Free Transform tool to shear the type, a, so it leans right or left (hold Command key and drag the FTT's top-center handle). The height of the shadow can also be increased with this tool. Finally, use Paste in Front (⌘-F) to lay the original version of the type, b, over the shadow. A cast shadow is, frankly, a little too hokey for frequent use.

MAKE A RELIEF DROP SHADOW

Example H shows the three levels required for a relief drop shadow in which the shadow appears separated from the letter. Select the type. Give it a 2-point stroke, same color as the fill. Holding down the Shift and Option keys, drag the type upward and to the right (Shift will constrain drag direction to 45°, and Option will create a second copy of the type). Color this second copy of the type the same as the background so it appears invisible. Change the stroke to 1 point and color it the same as the fill. Finally, drag the second level (which should still be selected) diagonally upward, again holding the Shift and Option keys, to make the third and top level. Give this level a different fill color and no stroke.

Note: Avoid assigning drop shadows (or outlines) to type in Quark XPress with its Type Styles submenu or Measurements pallet. Few options are provided, and the effects look ugly and amateurish.

A

DROPSY

B

DROPSY
Level 2
Level 1

C

DROPSY

D

DROPSY

E

SHADOW

F

SHADOW

G

a
b
DROPSY

H

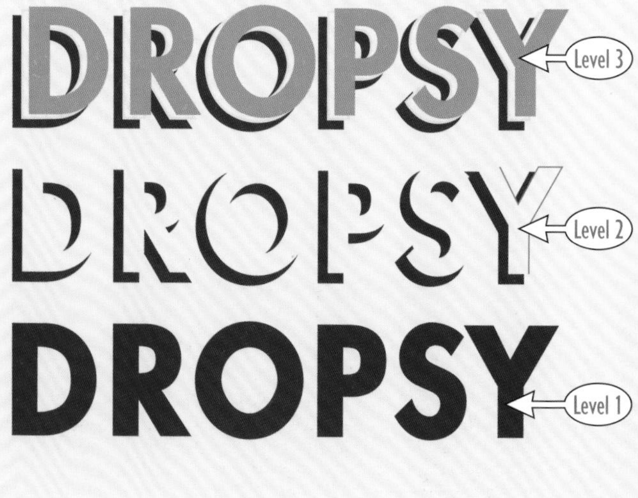
DROPSY
Level 3
DROPSY
Level 2
DROPSY
Level 1

This is a fun effect that always packs a punch and has a retro connotation (think *Superman* and *Amazing Stories*). Unfortunately, there are no simple ways to achieve it. Points will have to be adjusted by hand. Computer graphics are all about strategy. Following are a couple of approaches.

METHOD ONE: 1. Select the lettering or type (make sure to first Create Outlines if type is being used).

2. Hold down Shift and Option keys. Drag the letters 45° northeast so a new copy is made. Select it and hit Copy (⌘-C) to Paste another copy later.

3. Select both layers of type and use Add to Shape Area in the Pathfinder pallet to unite them into one connected mass.

a
c
b

4. With the Delete Anchor Point tool, remove the points shown in red to create diagonal edges. Points a, b, c have already been removed. Also, delete the counters outlined in red.

t
u
v

5. Use the Add Anchor Point tool at t, u, v on curved areas to make a curving transition into the diagonal. After removing the points in red, we should be left with shapes like the above.

x
y
z

6. We may need to adjust certain points, like lowering x, y, z to get consistent 45° angles. (I told you this effect was a pain.) Finally, Paste in Front (⌘-F) a copy of the type and change its fill color.

METHOD TWO: 1. Select the type. (We should already have Created Outlines, or broken it apart.) The blue outline around the type above is to show that it is selected.

2. Hold the Shift and Option keys and drag a copy slightly 45° southeasterly (we'll drop a different direction this time).

3. Press Duplicate (⌘-D) twenty times or so to repeat the action of Copy. Then make a copy of the final duplicated copy so we can Paste it later.

4. Select all the copies of the type and use the Add to Shape Pathfinder to unite them into one mass. With this method, curved corners project smoothly, requiring no more work from us.

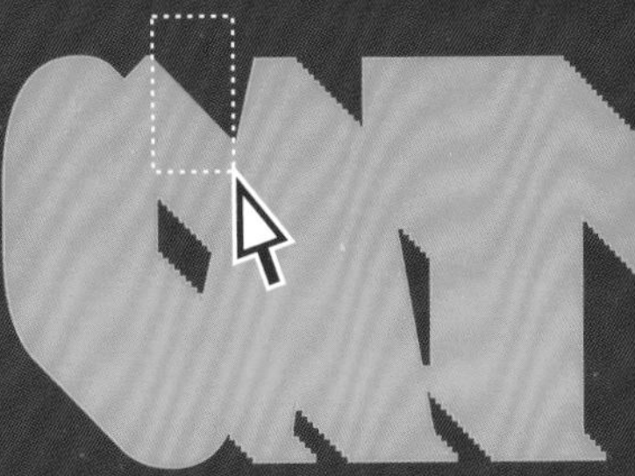

5. With the White Arrow or Direct Selection tool, marquee a stairstepped diagonal area (leave beginning and end points unselected). Delete the selected points and hit Join (⌘-J) to connect beginning and end points with a single line.

6. Repeat previous step, area by area, deleting all the stairsteps and re-Joining to smooth the outline of the shape. Finally, Paste in Front (⌘-F) the original type and assign it a new fill color. The top-level type can also be positioned in the upper left.

A NEW SLANT ON 3-D BLOCK SHADOWS

Designer Stan Endo likes to play with perspective, creating updated Escher-reminiscent optical illusions like the one at right for twentyFive, a Los Angeles clothing company. To create dynamic, dimensional drop shadow and outlining effects like these, all you need are the lessons given on these pages—and tons of talent. Also, patience. There's no magic way, that I've discovered, to create shapes like these automatically. They've gotta be drawn out point by point.

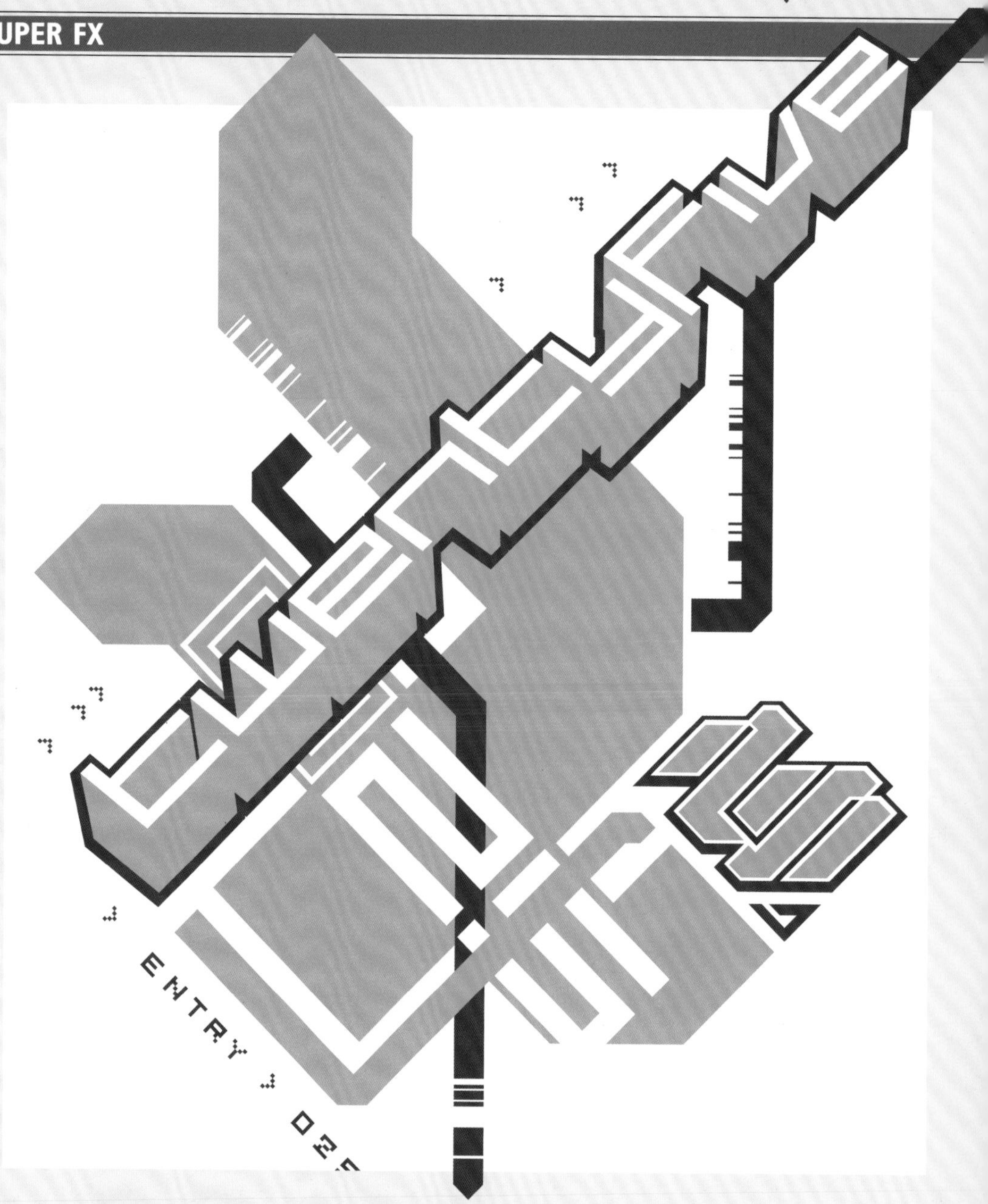
ENTRY 025

CHEATING THE ANGLES

When you're a logo designer, your relatives always come to you for their logos. I used to charge them, but wound up feeling guilty about it, so now I do them for free, like this one, below right, for Ralf, my German brother-in-law. Luckily, this logo reminded me of something I should tell you. When we create a two-level drop-shadow effect, letters such as *A, N, W, Y,* and *Z* always look awkward because the drop shadow sticks out less on diagonal stems than on vertical or horizontal stems. Below, at a, we see this phenomenon in action. At b, I've cheated the angle by dragging the diagonal stem unnaturally wide to please the eye. The problem and the correction principle are the same whether we are using a block shadow, a, or a plain drop shadow, b.

a

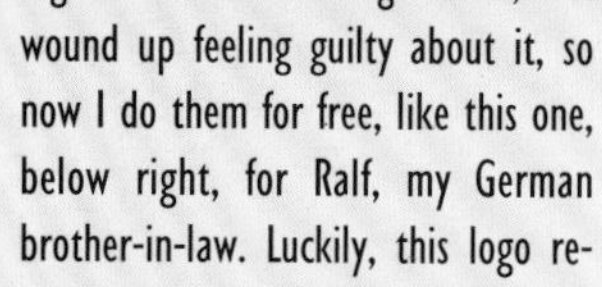
ENH

b

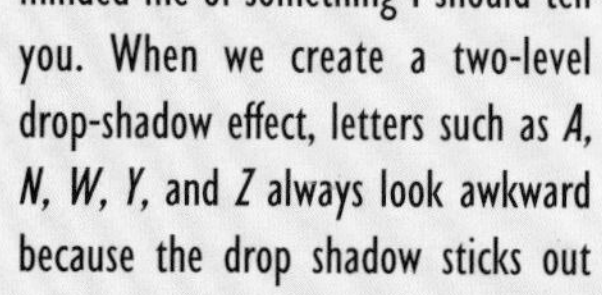
ENH

RalfBeck
Kfz-MEISTERBETRIEB

c

I faced the problem of the uneven diagonal reveal (*reveal* means the part that shows) when I created the highlight effect on Ralf's logo. What happened was that when I drag-Copied down the letter faces to make the orange level, highlights along the diagonal tops of letters like *a* came out wider than along the flat tops of letters like *e*. I opted to go for uniformity over naturalism. I made gauge balls in two widths, c, and used them to measure all white highlights to assure consistency. Note the style of drop shadow in this logo. It's off to the left, not downward. Hopefully, logo designers have small families.

1
MIDNIGHT

A SKELETON-STROKE BLOCK SHADOW

1. Create 3-point skeleton-stroke letters with the Pen tool. Group them (⌘-G). Keep a copy of the letters by dragging a copy somewhere off to the side, or by hitting ⌘-C. Beware: When we keep a copy in memory too long, we often forget and Copy something else, thereby losing the first copy altogether. That's bad!

2
c
e
d
f
a
b

2. Select all letters and drag them diagonally downward, holding down Option to make a copy. With the Pen tool, draw lines connecting the original letters to their copied brothers. Join the strokes where possible, as in a to b. Don't join, just draw lines from corner strokes like c to d. The path from e to f has not yet been connected.

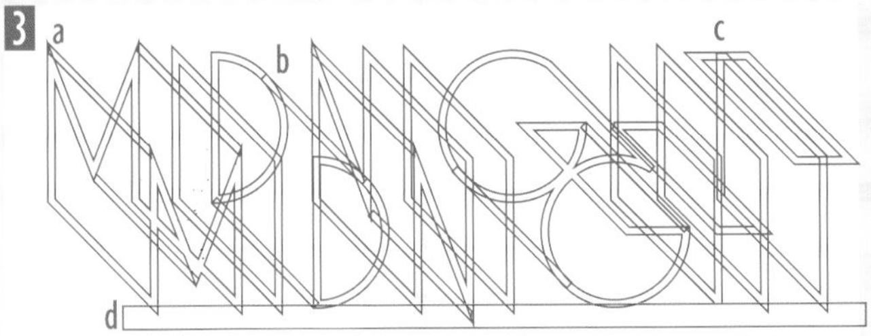
3
a
b
c
d

3. Select All and Outline Strokes. Shown above in Outline View are the strokes, now turned into objects. Make corrections, like dragging points to match them up neatly as in a, moving the stroke down to the *D* curve at b and lowering the pointy top of *T* at c. Create a rectangle, d, along the baseline as a knock-out mask to chop off pointy stroke ends. Make another rectangle to chop off pointy ends at cap height.

4

4. Again Select All. Hit Add to Shape Area in Pathfinder pallet. Hit ⌥-⌘-8 to Release Compound Paths. Hit Add to Shape again so one contiguous mass is created. Because the first operation will have brought the shadow to the foreground, Select it, Cut it, then Paste Behind. Now the shadow sits on the lowest level.

5
MIDNIGHT

5. Paste in Front (or drag over into position) the skeleton lettering we originally drew and made a copy of. Outline Strokes of the skeleton strokes and hit Add to Shape to unite individual strokes that formed *H* and *T*. Of course, depending upon the particular letters in your logo, some of what I just covered may not apply.

6
a
MIDNIGHT

6. Add 5-point strokes to both the lettering and the shadow. Look what we get—a whole 'nother logo! But notice the strange triangles sticking out of *M*, *N*? They're the culminations of strokes from the interior angles as at a. To remove them, Outline Strokes, and before you unite the letters with their former strokes, drag those triangles inward.

BLOCK SHADOW HELL

For this logo utilizing complicated gradient blends, it was necessary to first draw the block shadows for each letter individually and then drag them together into position as a group. Divide was used to knock counter shapes out of foreground letters. Many levels of letters and block shadow planes had to be arranged in proper stacking order, as seen in the exploded view, far right. Various methods were used to get the job done.

LOGO

1
COMMONMAN
2
COMMONMAN
3
COMMONMAN
a
4
COMMONMAN
5
COMMONMAN
6
COMMONMAN
7
COMMONMAN
COMMONMAN
8
COMMONMAN
COMMONMAN
a
b
c
d
e
f
g
h
i

MAKE A CURVED-BASE BLOCK SHADOW

1. *COMMONMAN* was set in Kobalt Bold. Create Outlines turned the letters into objects so their shapes could be edited. You may type any word in any font of your choosing.

2. Pointy tops were flattened on *M, N, A* because points break up the smooth flow of the line at cap height. Always feel free to edit a font's characters in Illustrator, whether or not you designed the font.

3. An ellipse was created, a, for a new baseline and then made into Guides (⌘-5). Use the Free Transform tool to individually enlarge each letter, bringing them down to the baseline. *C-O-M-M-O* have already been done. The Free Transform tool is seen ready to transform *N*. The remaining letters haven't been resized yet. Letter spacing can be readjusted as we proceed.

4. Resize all letters (I tweaked the *A*) and one by one, pull all the vertical stems down below the elliptical baseline. Be sure you're using Illustrator's White Arrow tool (Direct Selection tool) so you can select specific points of a letter and not the entire letter.

5. With the Pen tool, draw a rough shape that overlaps all the lowered stems (but never touches the elliptical baseline). Select all letters whose stems we dragged below the baseline along with the rough shape, and unite them with the Add to Shape Area tool (hold down Option) found in the Pathfinder pallet.

6. Go to VIEW>Guides>Lock Guides. By letting up the cursor on this menu item, we will unlock the elliptical baseline that we previously made into guides. Now go to VIEW>Guides>Release Guides. The elliptical baseline becomes an object again. Select it along with the united letters and choose the tediously named Subtract From Shape Area tool (hold down Option) in the Pathfinder pallet to neatly trim off all the stems so that they now perfectly follow the elliptical baseline as shown.

7. Select all the letters. Drag them northeasterly, while holding the Option key to create a copy. Assign this new top-level copy a different fill color. Now select the base-level letters. With the Free Transform tool, they can be slightly reduced and rotated, and the lower left corner even enlarged slightly (click and hold mouse on the FTT bounding box's southwest handle, *then* hold Command key while pulling downward to distort just that corner). These transformations of the base-level copy are to make it appear to be receding from view in the distance behind the top-level letters.

8. Begin dragging points from the bottom copy so they "Snap To" target points in the top copy. (Go to VIEW>Snap to Points if this feature is unenabled.) It looks bad if points are slightly misaligned, so enlarge the page view as you work. Points a, b, c in letter *C* already have been hooked up. Eliminate points d, e with Delete Anchor Point tool. The last *N* has been started by adding a point (Add Anchor Point tool) to the middle of the stroke, f, and dragging it to position g. Next, point h would be dragged to top position i, and so on.

9. More letters have been completed by moving or adding points and dragging them up to meet their top-level mates. I've outlined the resulting jumble of shapes this method creates. This approach, which I call the Straight Ahead Method, is the third method we can use to create 3-D block shadows (methods 1 and 2 were shown on the previous spread). It requires more thought than the other methods, because we have to logically figure out where to add and delete points, and to which relative point to drag them.

10. All the lines are connected now and united into one black-filled shape. Points were added at a, b to maintain the bottom curves of *O*. At c, I cheated the angle, rather than have no visible black edge (which would have otherwise been the case).

11. Naturally, you'll want to add an indication of underglow. Make a rectangle like a, any size. Drag this rectangle under *N*. Connect corner point to corner point, such as from b to c. Drag-Copy the altered rectangle and place this new copy under the stem of the next *N* and edit the points as required to match up corners.

Curved letters like *O* have no hard line dividing the side plane from the bottom plane. Unless you choose a gradient fill to blend from the bottom blue into black, the hard-edge solution shown here is a classic. Create gradating strokes, as shown at d, using the original rectangle. Place them so they extend beyond the bottom edges of the 3-D shadow, e, and well into the letter *O*. Continue to put the rest of the bottoms in place, matching point-to-point the flat bottoms, and extending the bottom planes of remaining curved letters *C* and *O* past the edges.

12. Select the entire lower-level 3-D shadow and the gradating shading lines under the *C, O* and *O*. In the Pathfinder pallet, click Divide. In a, the bottom pieces of the shading lines have been dragged away to show how Divide has cut through all the intersecting lines. But this operation has brought the divided items to the foreground. Select them and Cut (⌘-X), then Paste Behind (⌘-B) so the top-level type and the rest of the underglow rectangles will again be in the foreground.

13. This is the finished logo.

14. But why stop there? Marquee the entire logo to select it, then Copy it. Unite the selected logo with the Add to Shape Area tool in the Pathfinder pallet. Give the resulting monolithic slab an outline of 6 points. Go to OBJECT>Path>Outline Stroke. Unite the whole mess again. Give this a 2-point stroke, then Paste in Front the logo you copied. Now, I think we're finished.

9
COMMONMAN

10
COMMONMAN
c
b
a

11
COMMONMAN
a
e
d
c
b

12
c
b
a

13
COMMONMAN

14
COMMONMAN

a
a
b
c

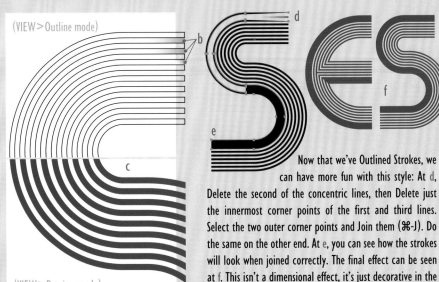

These neat effects begin with skeleton letters, a, stroked at 1 point. Above at b are the five levels of strokes this effect required. To achieve this style, start with a 9-point stroke on bottom. Copy and Paste in Place a second layer on top but make it a 7-point white stroke. Then Paste a 5-point black stroke, and so on, alternating black/white strokes, each 2 points less than the preceding one, until the top level is the 1-point skeleton stroke we first drew. Example c, above, goes a few steps further into our Op Art odyssey by utilizing nine levels of graduated-width strokes. This time the white strokes have been assigned the same color as the page background. The key to this effect is to always add or subtract the same number of points to each successive stroke so an even effect is achieved.

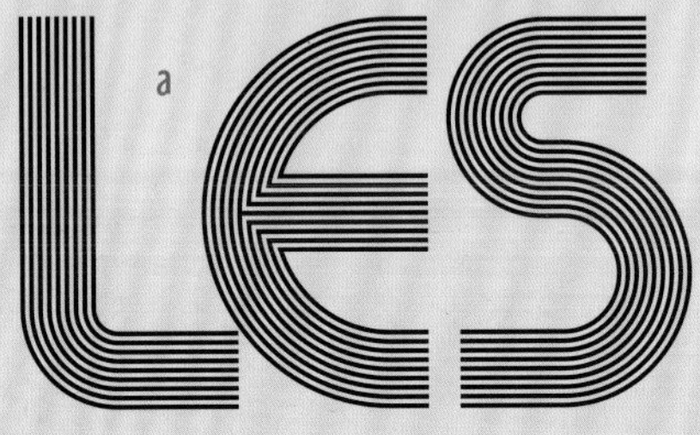
a

Geometric-style letters, a, work well with a concentric lines effect. To try some variations, select all strokes and change them into filled objects with Outline Strokes. Hit Divide in Pathfinder pallet, and then Delete all the unneeded in-between shapes shown at right, b, in the enlarged view of letter *S*. Here the top of the *S* is shown in VIEW>Outline mode to show that these lines are now filled objects. The bottom of *S* shows the fills in VIEW>Preview mode.

(VIEW>Outline mode)
b
c
(VIEW>Preview mode)

d
e
f

Now that we've Outlined Strokes, we can have more fun with this style: At d, Delete the second of the concentric lines, then Delete just the innermost corner points of the first and third lines. Select the two outer corner points and Join them (⌘-J). Do the same on the other end. At e, you can see how the strokes will look when joined correctly. The final effect can be seen at f. This isn't a dimensional effect, it's just decorative in the "Fake-o Deco" style that became popular in the 1970s.

g
h
i
j

There are plenty of variations on this style, all starting with skeleton-stroke letters. Example g was adapted from example f shown in the middle row of this page. Example h contains five layers with 16-, 13-, 10-, 6- and 3-point strokes all with Round Caps. All strokes forming the crossbar of *E* were sent backwardseneath the curving outer stem strokes. The variation shown above at i was also begotten from the previous example f. Three of the center lines were deleted and then the two outer strokes were copied and placed off to the side where they were merged manually into an overall white silhouette, which was then placed on the bottom level. Our last variation, example j, simply consists of five layers of strokes, alternating red and black going in 4-point increments from 20, 16, 12 and 8, to 4 points wide. As in h, the crossbar strokes have been sent backwards, placing them under the C-shaped stem. Notice that Adobe Illustrator does a very good job of maintaining parallelism as stroke widths increase, so all these concentric line effects were kept nice and even without imperfections to cause visual disturbance.

1. STONED DROP SHADOW Set some type. Create Outlines. (Some simple drop shadow effects can be made without Creating Outlines, but for complicated work, it's better to do so.) Fill type red.

2. Add 2.5-point white-stroke outlines. Select the letters and Outline Strokes. Now the strokes have become filled compound paths and the red letters are separate objects underneath the white outlines.

3. Select only the outlines (really, they're now fills) and give them 0.5-point black strokes (use heavier stroke widths than I'm specifying if you're creating your letters very large on the page).

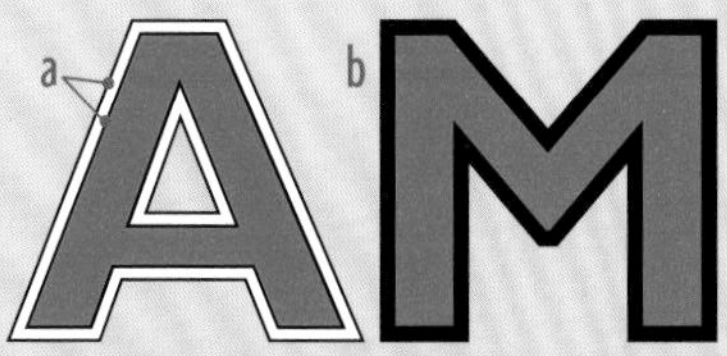
a
b

4. Select the white outlines with the black strokes (be sure to select both the inner and outer lines, a, including surrounding the counter hole in letter *A*). Hit Copy, but don't Paste yet. Before Pasting, fill the white outlines black, as shown in b.

5. Now Paste in Front the white outlines, but before deselecting them, hit the Up Arrow and Left Arrow keys twice each. The black-filled outlines will show underneath the white outlines and the letter faces will have a recessed look.

6. To add block drop shadows, Lock all the levels of the letters just made. Paste the same outlines again, but now Paste Behind (⌘B). Drag them 45° southeasterly. Paste Behind once again. Select and unite these two copies. Proceed as on page 181.

1. FACETED LETTERS Draw some skeleton-stroke letters (see page 150) and stroke them fat. Above are 18-point dark blue strokes (the thin blue inlines are to show the original skeletons).

2. Copy skeleton letters. Apply Outline Strokes to the fat-stroked letters. Draw rectangles and use Subtract From Shape to cut off bottoms and top of *A*. Above, bottom stems done, top ready to be chopped.

3. Above, with the letters trimmed, Paste in Front a copy of the original skeleton strokes. If you dragged the copy off to the side, make sure it is perfectly centered when you drag it back on top.

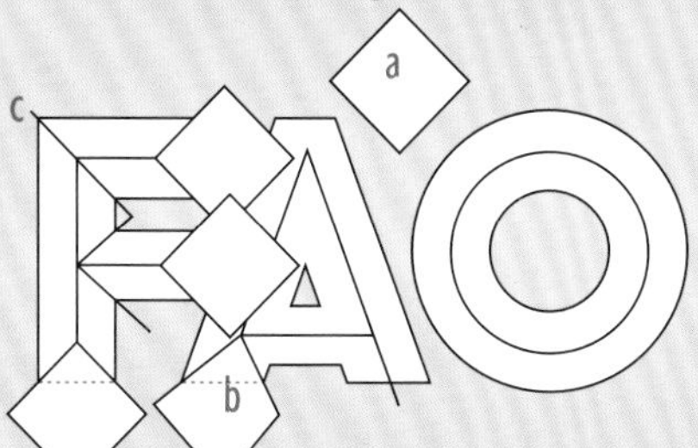
a
c
b

4. (Above shown in VIEW>Outline mode.) Rotate a square shape 45° as at a. Drag copies of this "diamond" over the ends of stems. Distort the diamond at b to make it align. Draw 45° strokes, as in c, that extend beyond the edges of the letters. Diamonds and 45° strokes must intersect corners.

c
d
a b

5. Place all diamonds and draw the rest of the 45° lines as at a, b. Drag strokes c and d up to the top points of the diamonds. Draw a 45° line through *O*. Now select all letters, lines and diamonds and hit Divide. Delete excess shapes that fall outside of the letter boundaries. Letter *F* shows the final result.

a

6. Select different facets of the letters and fill them as you wish. Letter *F* has gradient fills, each facet carefully modeled with the Gradient tool. The *A* has solid fills with white strokes added. For *O*, I created gradating lines, a, rotated them 45° and knocked them out of the *O*, again with the Divide filter.

OTHER FACETED EFFECTS For a flat-faced, chisel-edge effect, Paste a copy of your original skeleton-stroke letters over the facet treatment you completed above. Assign thicker stroke weights to the skeletons, then drag stem ends in toward the centers of the letters as in a, b, c so the 45° lines meet right at the corners of the strokes, as in x. Apply Outline Strokes to the skeletons and then unite them. In y, these new letter faces were given thin white outlines. In example z, four flat fills, from yellow to red, were assigned to the letter face and its facets.

a
b
c
x
y
z

a
b
RF

The ALGONQUIN. Select and Copy skeleton letters, a, that are stroked at 17 points. Don't Paste yet, but now increase the stroke width of these same letters to 25 points and change the stroke color to a darker one. *Now* Paste in Front (⌘-F) and hit Up and Right Arrow keys same number of times to move this top-level type 45° northeasterly until top and bottom edges of letter and drop shadow align, b.

RF

The IDYLWILD. Shear the type or lettering so it leans hastily forward. Add 1- or 2-point white speedlines (strokes), arranging them artistically so they don't clump or bump. Select all these white speedlines, Copy, then Paste in Front. Hit Up Arrow key twice, then change stroke color to orange. A gray drop shadow can be Pasted Behind by adapting the Algonquin technique just described.

RF

The PRINCE of CHICHESTER. Use filled letters, not skeleton stroked. Assign 1-point strokes to outline the filled letters. Drag (hold down Shift and Option) a copy a little to the left. Hit Duplicate (⌘-D) five times. Assign the fifth copy (the one on the top level) a different fill color, like the orange above.

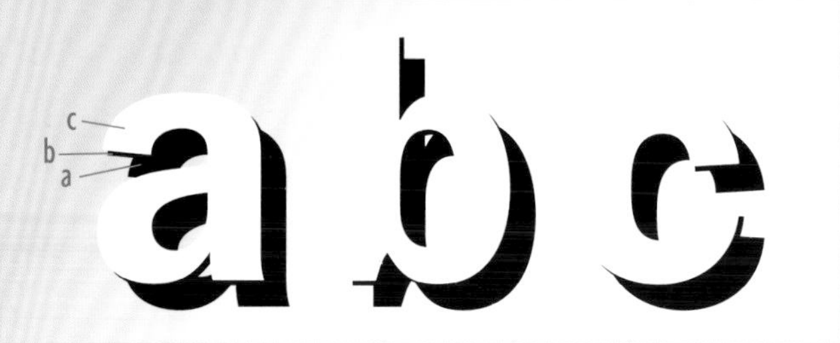
c
b
a
abc

The SHADOWNOSE. Set some type, fill it black, a. Drag a copy 45° north-westerly, b. Drag another nor'wester but not far, only a few points' worth of distance, c. Give this third, top copy a white fill. Now you see it, now you don't.

b
c
REPO
a

The BILDERBERGER. Set type, drag a copy to the side. Make a deep block shadow (see page 181). Select type and block shadow. Copy them and Paste in Front. Unite the two. Draw a white rectangle like a. Select the white rectangle and the united shadow/type. Make them into a Compound Path (⌘-8), b. Place the original type that you first copied on top. Place a pattern like c in the background.

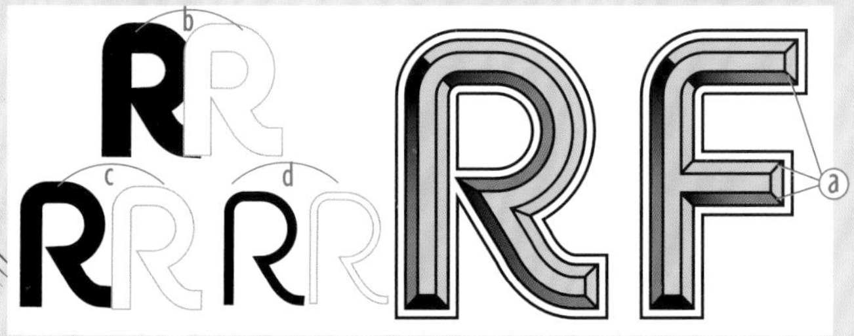
b
RR
c
d
RRRR
RF
a

The METROPOL. Utilizes six stroke layers. Bottom to top they are: 21-point black, 19 white, 15 black, 13 white, 7 black and 5 white. Draw 45° diagonal strokes, such as a, by hand. Outline all strokes and Subtract From Shape, one at a time, each of three pairs, b, c, d, of black/white strokes. Select All and Make Compound Path. Then Release Compound Path and assign different fill colors to each facet.

REPO a
REPO b
d
REPO
c
e

The FLORA-DORA. Set type, a. Shear the letters (hold Shift to keep verticals vertical), b. Pull letters down one by one to a horizontal baseline, c. Create block shadows, then Subtract From Shape each letter from its shadow. As shown in the exploded view, d, draw rough shapes such as e to separate the planes (only the lines shown in green must be drawn accurately). Use Divide to cut these shapes out of the block shadows. Assign different fills to each plane.

b
a
c
RSE

The ELMO AARDVARK. Use filled letters: Copy them, Lock them, then Paste in Front. Assign this level a 5-point stroke, no fill. Outline Strokes and Delete the outermost part of the outline, a. The inner edges of the outlines, b, should now look filled. Select these "inner letters" and drag them southwesterly 45°, holding Option to make a copy. Select the inner letters, b, and the copy, c and use Subtract From Shape on them (do it letter by letter). The result is inline highlights, as above.

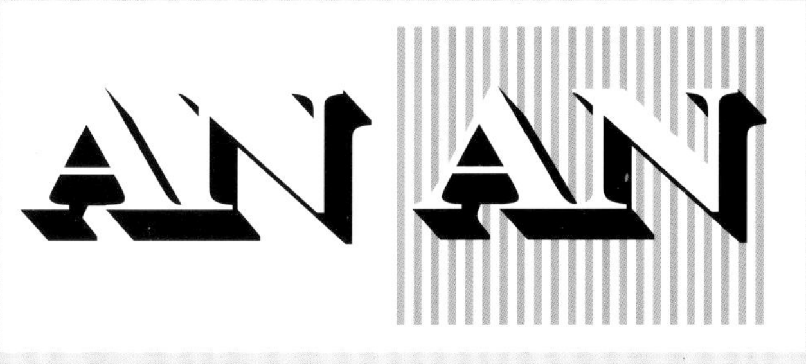
AN AN

The MERRY WIDOW. Make a block drop shadow and color the type white (or the same color as the background). Notice that, from the drop shadow alone, you can still read the type. Adding a pattern behind it gives another dimension.

ES

The TRILATERAL. Make shallow block drop shadows about the depth of the blue level shown above. Drag-Copy the drop shadow 45° upward once, then hit Duplicate to make a copy again. Color the copies red, white and blue just like the French flag. Reposition letters on the top level and assign 1-point white strokes.

a
b
c
d
ES

The MORGENTHAU. Draw a block drop shadow for your letters, a. Copy the orange letters, then refill them white. Paste in Front the orange letters but move them northeasterly upward, b. Make a series of 45° strokes—enough to cover all drop shadows—Outline Strokes, then unite them along bottom edge, c, so you can Subtract From Shape them out of the drop shadows in one step, d.

a
b
c
d
ES

The CHESTERFIELD. Paste filled letters, b, over a black-stroked copy, a. Create horizontal gradating lines and unite them with a shape covering one side, c. Place the gradating lines over the letters. Select the filled letters, b, plus the lines and hit Divide. Delete excess pieces, such as d.

a
b
c
ES

The ILLUMINATI. Assign 4-point strokes to filled letters. Outline Strokes. Lay fancy shapes like a or b into position over the former outlines, c, that we just made into objects. Unite them with Add to Shape. Select the outlines, assign 1-point black strokes, then hold Option key and hit the Up Arrow key once. Release Option, hit Left Arrow once. Finally, add Chesterfield gradating lines to the letters

ES
a
b

The WINKYDINK. Using skeleton letters, put a 23-point stroke on bottom and a 4-point stroke on top. Push the upper stem ends back, so they extend less than lower-level stems. At a, the stroke hasn't been pushed back yet. Outline Strokes and draw masking shapes like b to Subtract From Shape any stroke ends that stick out or whose angles don't parallel those of stroke ends on the bottom-level letters.

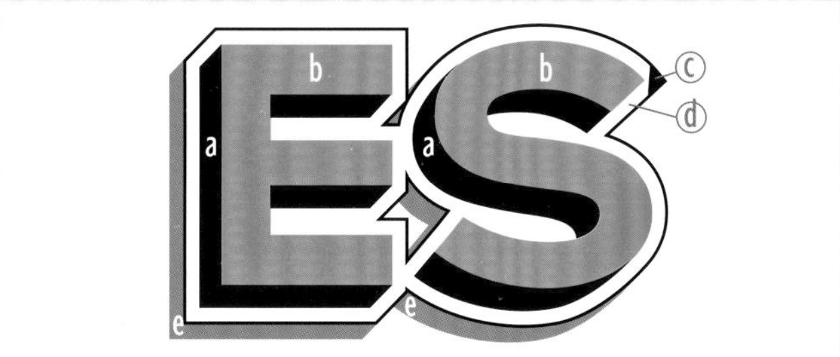
ES
a
b
c
d
e

The CLIQUOT CLUB. Make block drop shadows like a. Select a and b. Copy and Paste Behind. Unite them with Add to Shape and assign an 11-point black stroke, c. Copy again and Paste in Front, assigning a 9-point white stroke, d. (You may have to bring levels a and b to the top levels again.) Now Paste Behind and assign an 11-point purple stroke and fill, e. Drag the e level 45° southwesterly.

ES

The BEAUMONT. Letters were given dimensional block drop shadows. Then both the letter and the shadow layers were selected, Copied, Pasted in Front and united. This combined shape was filled and stroked gray, Pasted Behind and moved southwesterly downward. Gosh, "The Beaumont." What funny names the old sign painters used to give to drop shadows and lettering effects, eh?

There are right and wrong ways—or shall we say, good and better ways—of making type run around a circle. The basic approach, as shown at right, is to create a circle or ellipse, then click on it with the Path Type tool (select Align Center in the Paragraph pallet so the type will be centered) and start typing.

GIAMBASTI

GIAMBASTI

Look closer. Each letter has been placed perfectly tangent to the ellipse baseline, but that does not mean the letters follow it perfectly. Instead we get a bumpy effect, especially with wide-bottomed letters like *A* and *M*. In some cases, if the type is being set small, or if the client is a jerk and we resent him because he wouldn't know a good logo if it jumped up and bit him, we might leave the letters as they are with the program's standard curvature. Notice also that kerning usually gets messed up (look at *S-T*) when we set type on a path. This should be corrected.

GIAMBASTI
a

1. One way to get all the letters to truly follow the curvature of the elliptical baseline is to extend them past it and then trim them: Select the ellipse, a, and make a copy of it. Create Outlines of the type. Drag all the stems down past the baseline. Round-bottomed letters like *G* and *S* won't need to be extended or cut off. Letters like *I, A, M, T* can be easily pulled down. Letter *B* takes some finesse, and the center stroke of *M* requires pulling left and right side points individually to avoid widening it. Above, *I, A, M* and *B* are ready to trim.

GIAMBASTI

2. Continue dragging all the flat-bottomed stems down below the baseline. Draw a circle, of a smaller diameter than the baseline but large enough to overlap all the pulled-down stems. Select this circle plus all the long stem letters and unite them with Add to Shape in the Pathfinder pallet.

GIAMBASTI
a
b

3. This is what it'll look like after you've united the letters with the smaller circle, especially if your smaller circle was a different color than the letters, as mine was. Release the ellipse that was made into guides for our our baseline. Copy and Paste in Front. Marquee-select both the baseline ellipse and the smaller one that's now united with all your letters (I showed only a portion of the ellipse, a, so you could see b behind it.) Hit Subtract From Shape in the Pathfinder pallet to trim the letters to the baseline in one shot.

d
c
GIAMBASTI
a
b

4. Here is the final result, with all bottoms following the curve perfectly. So we're done? Not necessarily. Ideally, we have to trim off the tops of the letters, too, though they're not as important to trim as the letter bases. Draw a large circle from the center point of the original baseline ellipse. Add points at a and b and drag up point c, then d and e to turn the circle inside out while maintaining the portion of the curve we need to form a knock-out mask to trim off the tops of the letters. Follow the procedure already given to trim the bottoms of letters. (Hint: Horizontal center strokes of *A-B-A* should also follow the curve, but that we'll have to do by hand—see next page.)

HERMANN

1.CREATING A CURVED-BASELINE EFFECT Start by setting some type (or use lettering you've created). Make a circle or ellipse and center it under the type. Turn the ellipse into guidelines (⌘-5). This will become the curved baseline for our letters.

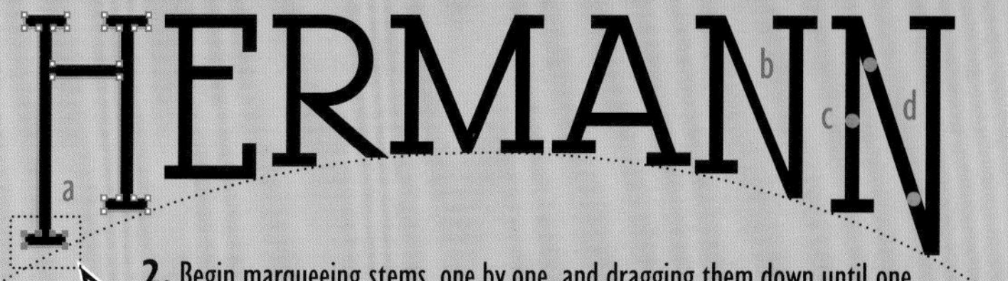
HERMANN
a
b
c
d

2. Begin marqueeing stems, one by one, and dragging them down until one of the base points touches the curved baseline, as shown at a. Notice that only the points of the lower stem and serif are solid-selected for dragging. When the right stem of *N* was lowered, b, the diagonal stroke became too thin. This has been fixed in the last *N*. As I always do, I made a gauge ball—a perfect circle, c, the exact width of the stem—then dragged two copies, d, over to the diagonal stem to use as guides in editing it to match the rest of the stems.

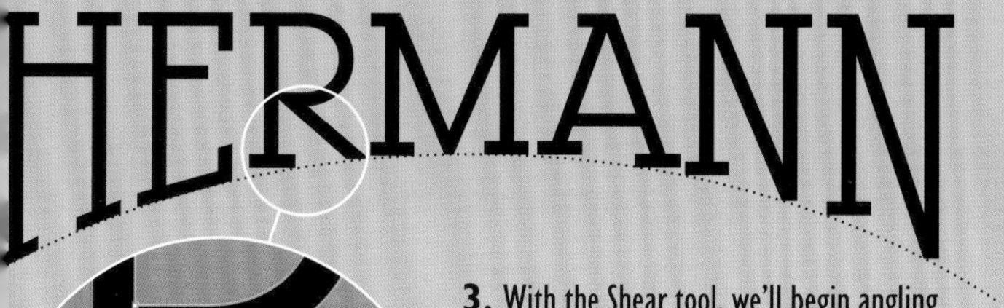
HERMANN

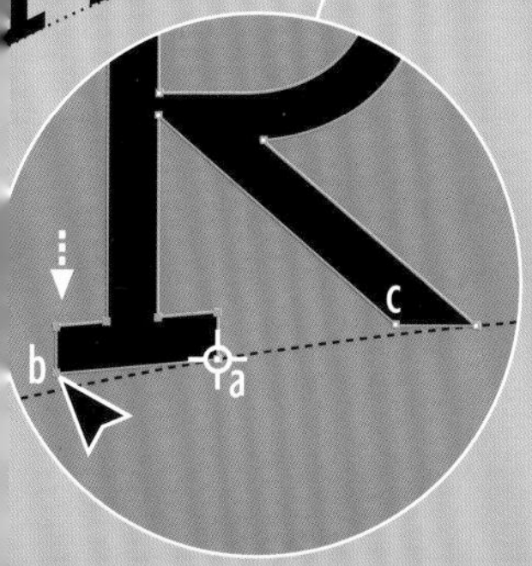
b
a
c

3. With the Shear tool, we'll begin angling the serifed stems to match the curved baseline. Click on point a which touches the baseline. That point becomes the axis of rotation, or shall we say, "Shearation"? While holding the Shift key to maintain verticality, drag point b to the baseline. Point c can simply be dragged down by hand, without using the Shear tool.

HERMANN

4. Above, the letters have all been curved along the baseline and the crossbars of *H* and *E* have been lowered to adapt to the increased cap height. True, each of the serif bottoms are straight against the curved baseline, as we worked so hard to cure on the previous page, but most of these serifed letter bottoms are narrow, so they hug the curve acceptably well.

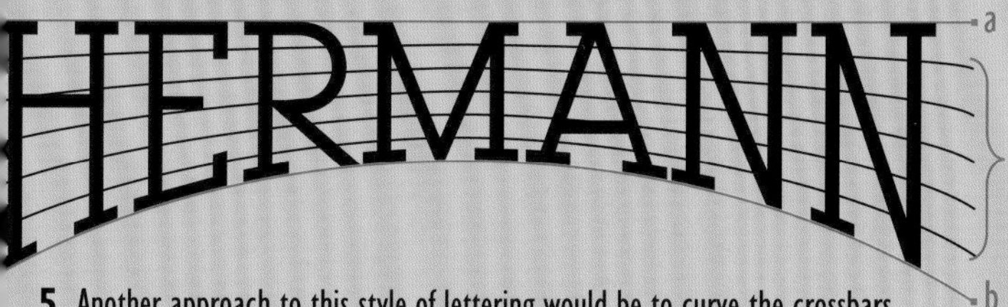
HERMANN
a
c
b

5. Another approach to this style of lettering would be to curve the crossbars like the baseline. Draw a line at the tops of the letters and Release your curved baseline guide back into a line. Choose the Blend tool by double-clicking it so the Blend Options window opens. Choose 5 as the number of Specified Steps. Select the corner points a and b, then click with the Blend tool first on a then on b to create the intermediate lines at c. Go to OBJECT>Expand. The Expand box opens. Click OK. Now these intermediate lines are released from the Blend.

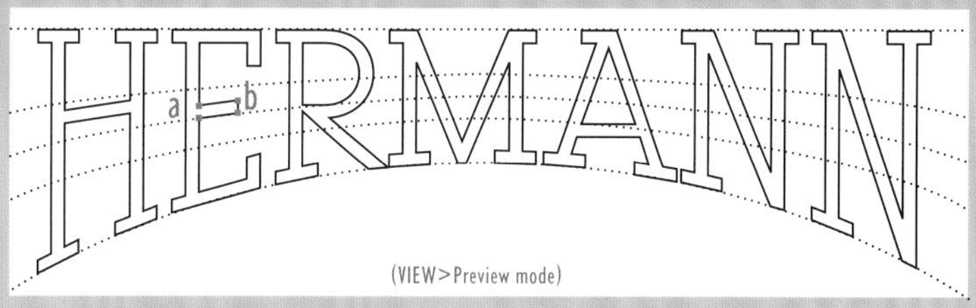
HERMANN
a
b

(VIEW>Preview mode)

6. Delete all the Blend lines that don't fall near the crossbars of *H, E* and *A* and make guides of the ones that do. The *H* crossbar has been tweaked. Notice that since it didn't fall exactly on one guideline, I centered it between two of them. Perhaps the *H* crossbar should have been placed on the same line as the *E* crossbar. What do you think? For the *E*, select the two points at a and drag them to the guideline. Do the same for b. The *A* crossbar remains to be repositioned.

And Furthermore... Ideally, serifs and crossbars should follow the curved baseline and the axis point of the original ellipse. In example X, at a, the serif has been aligned with the curved baseline to begin the process. At b, the Convert Anchor Point tool was used to drag bezier handles out of a corner point. After dragging the unnecessary handle b back into the point, adjust handle c until the serif follows the baseline curve. In example Y, the crossbar has been deleted and a new curved crossbar stroke f has been drawn to stem width. What is stem width? Make a gauge ball like g, exactly the width of the stem, and center a copy on the f line. Increase/decrease stroke width until it matches the diameter of the circle. Rejoin both sides of the *A* at d and e so they are closed, Outline Strokes of the crossbar line, clip off excess crossbar that may stick out, and unite it with rest of letter *A*.

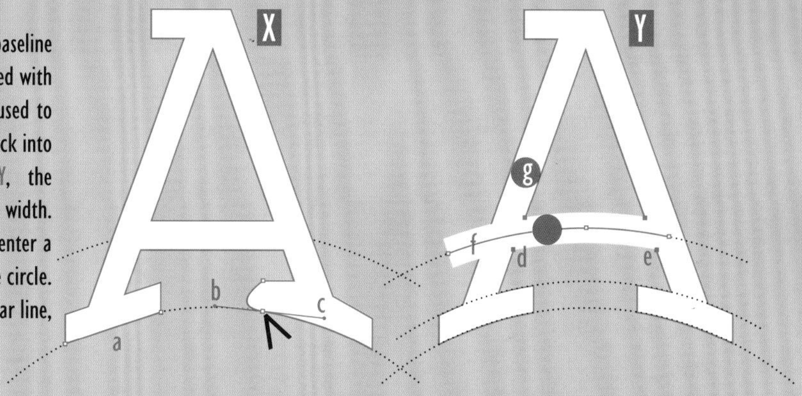
X
Y
a
b
c
d
e
f
g

Heretica

Helvetica
Outmoded

I was going to say never set certain fonts, like this Magneto script, around a circle—and that still goes!—but it turned out I like the above example that I set hoping to discourage you. So I gave it an offset outline and a central image, and made it into a logo. The image has no closed paths. Fills result from end points connecting.

Now above is what I meant: I made this into a logo, too, but it's hard to read, the shapes of the letters do not lend themselves to being spun around a circle, the kerning gets ridiculous, especially around the bottom arc, and perhaps worst of all, the connecting ligatures between letters no longer connect. (Why do I get the feeling that everything I say "Don't do," you're gonna do?)

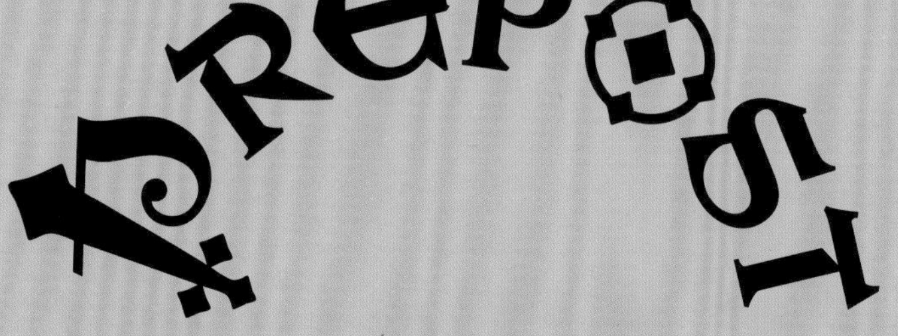
PREPOST

Here is another sort of font, Saber, that is too eccentric to be set around a curve. The larger the point size of the letters in relation to the diameter of the curve, the worse the setting will look—and that goes for almost any font, actually. The goal is for enough of the mass of each letter to be able to hug the path so as to clearly establish that there is a path. Above, we have an impression of a center circle, but we're not really sure what's going on: Something looks awry.

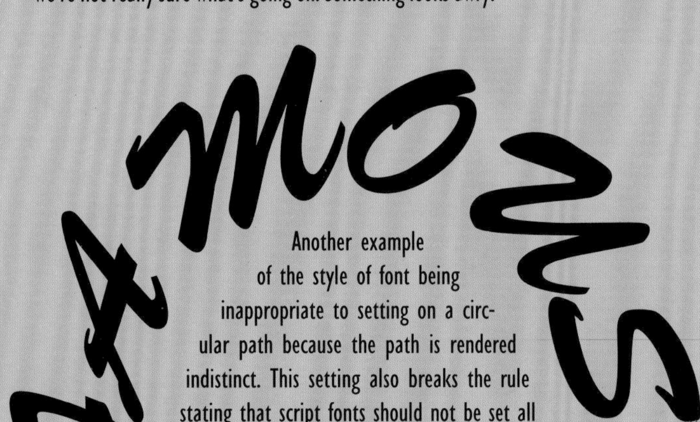
FAMOUS

Another example of the style of font being inappropriate to setting on a circular path because the path is rendered indistinct. This setting also breaks the rule stating that script fonts should not be set all caps. Also, the first letter *F* hangs lower than the last letter *S*. Usually, the two will be in alignment unless there's a good reason for not doing so.

A ROUND ABOUT WAY OF SETTING TYPE

HELVETICA TYPE
IS OBSOLETE
IS OBSOLETE
a
b
c
d

The setting above, with lettering rounding the top and bottom of a circle, is a common arrangement. The secret is to draw two circles, one for each line of type. Make a circle, a, and set type along the top. Choose Align Center in the Paragraph pallet so the type is centered around the circle. Create a second circle, b, using the same center point, c, and extend it to the cap height of the type we first set. With the Path Type tool, click on the 6 o'clock point of this second b circle. Set type, then click on any Arrow tool. Drag the I-bar, d, upward until the upside-down type rights itself. It's sort of hard to position the type straight—it'll jump around—but you can straighten it with the Rotate tool afterwards.

(PS: I don't actually dislike Helvetica, it's just a foundry envy kind of thing.)

Always I'm getting frantic e-mails like this one: "Dear Mr. Cabarga, my boss wants rounded type with an Infinity Peacock Block Shadow on his desk by 9 o'clock and I'm suffering from feelings of inadequacy. What should I do? Signed, Technically Blocked in Bloomington." Well, "TB," here's how it's done:

1. Set type along an elliptical path and crop the bottoms as shown on page 190.

2. Start the peacock fan splay at the center point of the baseline ellipse and draw each of the peacock splays. With the letter *L* as an example, draw the first point, a, at the farthest-out left edge of the letter. Make the next point at the center point, b. Continue drawing up to c and finally close the path by connecting up to the original a point. Go ahead and draw the last letter, *A,* in the same manner.

3. When all the splays are done, select them all, then use Add to Shape in the Pathfinder pallet to unite them into one piece. Why draw the individual splays just to unite them? It was necessary to draw them in order to get the proper angles as each line met at the center point. Notice that I cheated the angle to close up the narrow sliver that would have come between *D* and *A.* Actually, the font I used for this (Angle, one of mine, of course) is too unusual for this treatment. A regular sans-serif type would have worked better because the spaces between letters would have been less variable.

4. Lock the united splays and draw a new single splay, a, for the underplanes. Place point b at the center point and Rotate-Copy it repeatedly until each copy lines up with the left edge of each letter or stem. Drag the right side of each splay in or out so it matches the width of the letter or stem. You'll have to drag up the tops of the splays to underlap curve-bottomed letters so slivers of color don't show as at c. Finally, I outlined the letters and the united splays with a 1-point stroke.

1

RONDALA

2

RONDALA
a
c
b

3

RONDALA

4

RONDALA
c
a
b

The type warp effects, right, were created with Strider TypeStyler 3. This is a handy program, but it is not advised for professionals who want high-quality output. Of course, we can draw any nutty shape with pen tools in Illustrator or Macromedia FreeHand, though it's nice to have a program do it for us. Some of TypeStyler's simpler shape maps are useful, but most, like Fish, right, are really silly and no decent designer should ever use them.

HAMBONE
HAMBONE
HAMBONE
HAMBONE
HAMBONE
HAMBONE

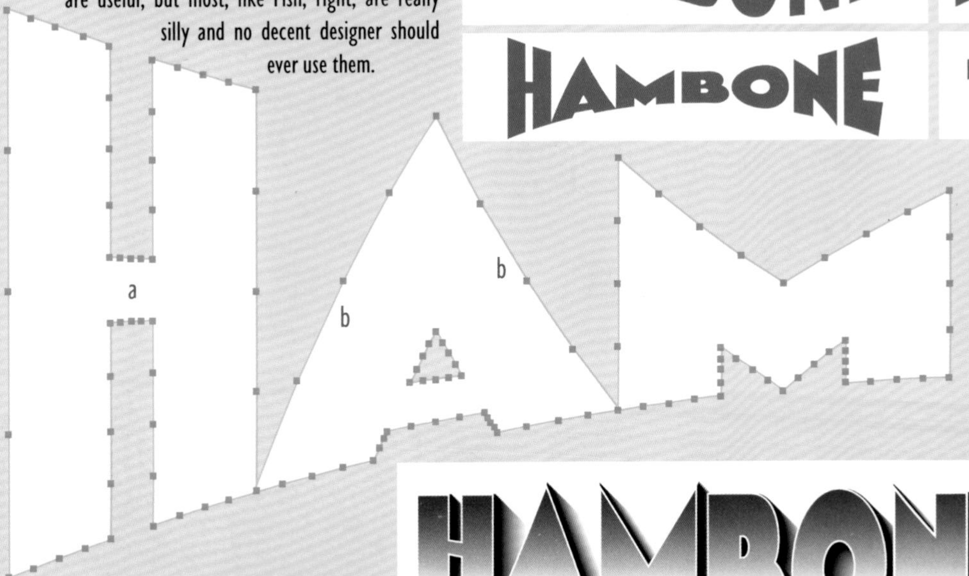
a
b
b

HAMBONE

Even when TypeStyler makes shape maps we like, there are rendering problems that limit their use. In order to warp type, TypeStyler adds too many points, often distorting letter shapes in undesirable ways. Above, for starters, notice at a, the wiggly crossbar of *H,* and at b, the bowed sides of *A.* Errant points can be manually removed, though that is arduous. TypeStyler can also be used to create an amazing array of tacky gradient and tonal effects. Use of them will mark your work as amateurish. The enlarged *E,* above right, reveals that the blending method used is suitable only for low-res projects. Out-of-the-box gradient fills, like the blend used on the face of this letter, always look cheap and superficial. Lastly, I really dislike very thin outlines, like the white stroke around this type. I think the reason they disturb me is because a dimensional block shadow and gradient blend letter face imply that the letter has a certain weight and volume. A thin white outline seems to negate that weight, and also is just tacky-looking.

ILLUSTRATOR GETS WARPED

HAMBONE

New in Illustrator are Warp effects (OBJECT>Envelope Distort>Make With Warp) that produce astonishingly good results. Above was created with Arc/Horizontal: 30%. To then release paths into point-editability requires going to OBJECT>Expand (hit OK). Unlike TypeStyler, which adds excess points to shapes in order to curve them, Illustrator uses only existing points, adding and tweaking bezier handles as needed. This is great! Illustrator also now offers 3D extrusion for block shadows that work quite well.

HAMBONE

Above, this is one of those creepy effects that is too hokey to ever be used—but it's nice to know we could if we needed to. In the Make With Warp dialogue window, use these settings: Flag/Horizontal: 60%, Distortion/Horizontal: -15%, Vertical: 20%. The perspective, and the flag-waving effect are very realistic, but notice that the *H* and *E,* especially, are badly distorted. Unless we purposely *want* this perspective effect, warped letters like these should *never* be used in a logo (unless we ourselves are also warped).

Another kind of warp can be achieved with OBJECT> Envelope Distort>Make With Mesh. After selecting desired number of rows and columns, a grid forms over the selected type or object. Any of the corner points can be dragged any which way to make fairly useless distortions, as in the example, right.

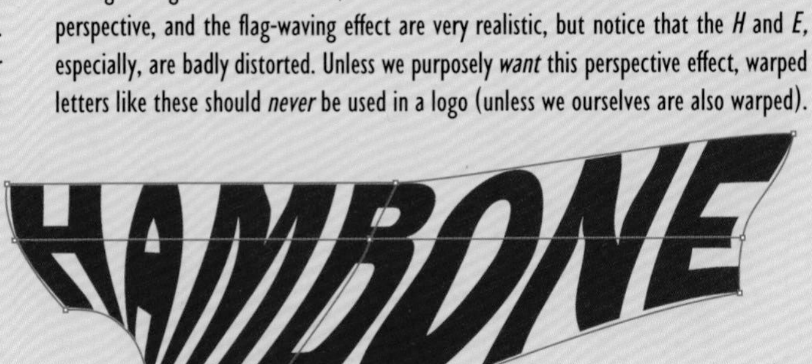
HAMBONE

HAMBONE

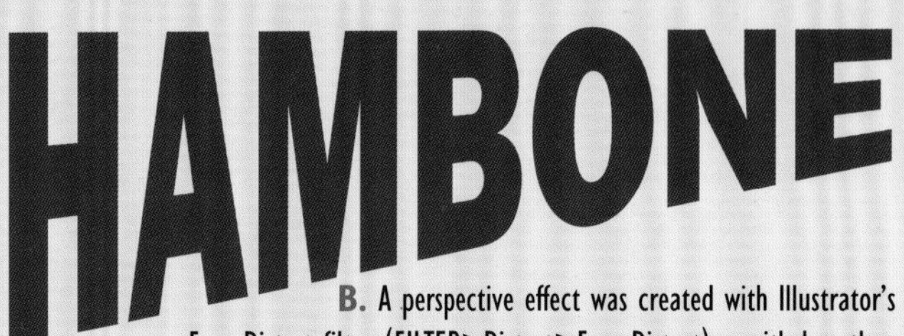
HAMBONE

Semicool type FX can even be created in Illustrator with the program's older shape distorting features. We can Shear, Scale, Rotate, do various warping and get perspective effects. Combining some or all of these adds extra thrills. Other filters, like Illustrator's Punk and Bloat, produce weird and interesting effects, but they are rarely useful.

A. Above is a word set in Franklin Gothic Heavy. Now we'll play.

B. A perspective effect was created with Illustrator's Free Distort filter (FILTER>Distort>Free Distort)...with less than great results. The first few letters, *H-A-M*, became horizontally scaled narrower and out of proportion with the remaining letters.

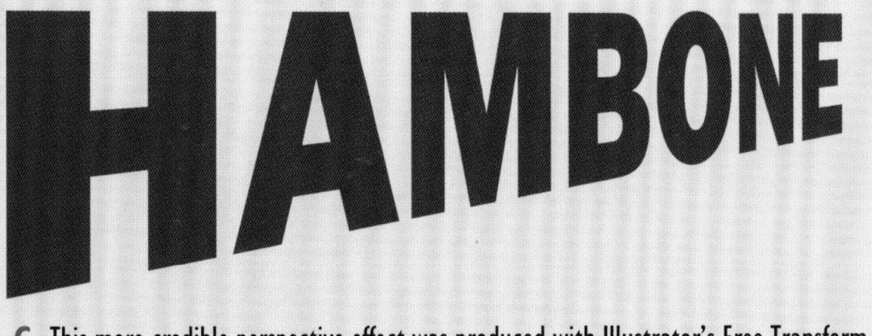
HAMBONE

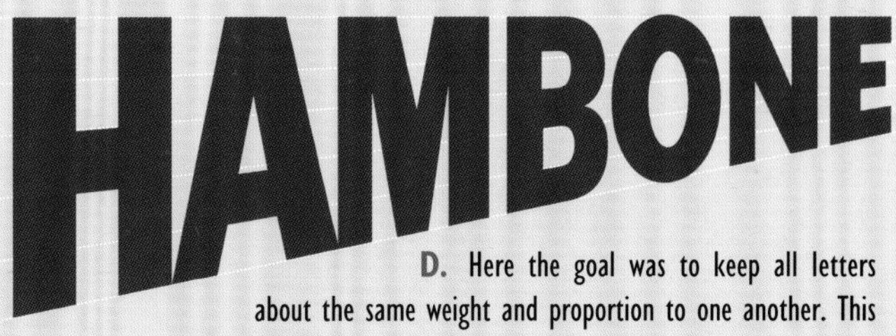
HAMBONE

C. This more credible perspective effect was produced with Illustrator's Free Transform Tool. With the tool highlighted, select the letters, and a box with eight handles surrounds the type. Begin to drag the lower left (or southwest) handle straight down, *then* hold down the Command key and continue to drag for the distortion to work.

D. Here the goal was to keep all letters about the same weight and proportion to one another. This version had to be hand tweaked. A vanishing point was chosen and—just as we did in the old pencil days—perspective lines were drawn, but with the Pen tool, and made into guides (⌘-5). This isn't a perspective effect. The letters just become smaller at the right side.

HAMBONE

HAMBONE

E. With the Free Transform tool, I've sheared the type by first grabbing the lower middle handle, holding down the Command key and dragging toward the right. Then a perspective effect was created by dragging the lower right corner handle, again while holding the Command key. The effect looks exciting, like there's this band Hambone, and all your friends are going, and you really want to go see them, too.

F. This effect, like the previous one, was done with the Free Transform tool, but the results are unsatisfactory because the letters, while in perspective, seem to be turning in space so the last letter is way out of whack with the first one. I conclude from this demonstration that we may have to draw such dimensional effects ourselves, rather than relying upon the programs to create them for us.

FONTLAB'S FUN FX

FontLab, a program designed for font creation, also offers some effects filters. Hit Shift-Command-T to open the Transform window. In a folder called Effects are such wonders as the College outline (applied three times, below at a) and 3D Extrude, at b. Fontlab's renderings of these effects is pretty good, but will yet require tweaking for professional use. Problems like out-of-parallel stroke widths and nonconverging corners have been circled. Still, FontLab was the first to automate true block shadows.

a b

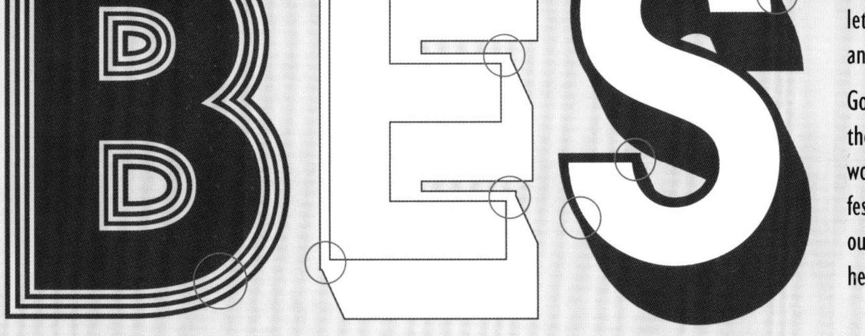
BES

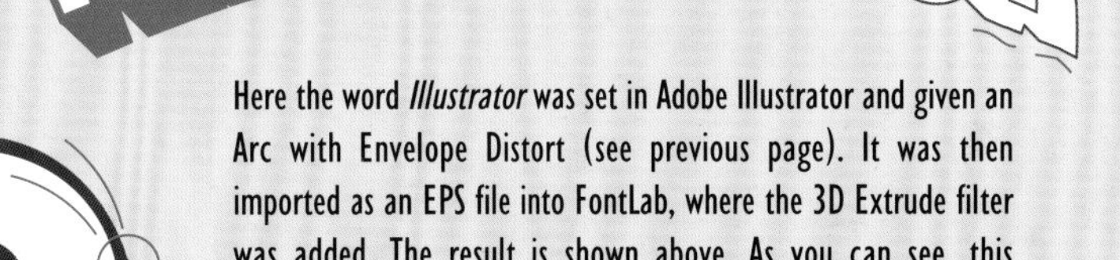
ILLUSTRATOR

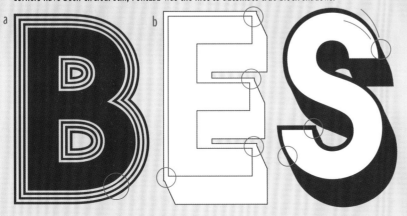

Here the word *Illustrator* was set in Adobe Illustrator and given an Arc with Envelope Distort (see previous page). It was then imported as an EPS file into FontLab, where the 3D Extrude filter was added. The result is shown above. As you can see, this lettering will require a lot of tweaking. Red lines on the right show an exaggeration of just some of the distortions.

Gosh readers, you must think me awful for nitpicking every flaw in these otherwise wonderful programs, but here's the point: Sloppy work like this just doesn't fly in the high-stakes world of professional design. If you were to show a portfolio full of untweaked, out-of-the-box type effects like these to a New York art director, he'd escort you out of his office in a New York minute.

Is Good Taste in Letter Design Subjective?

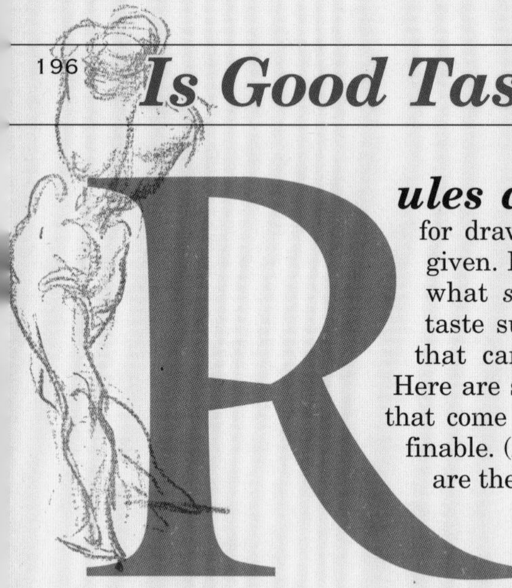

Matthew Carter's Mantinia

***R**ules and procedures* for drawing letterforms are easily given. But is it possible to outline what *should* be drawn? Is good taste subjective, or is it a quality that can be universally defined? Here are some opinions on this topic that come close to defining the indefinable. (All unattributed comments are the author's.)

Restraint

"The definition of good taste in all art is restraint, and having the talent to implement it. This can be learned by objectively studying the masters." ***— John Homs***

Context

"First we must define what we mean by 'good taste.' Jan van Krimpen said that he didn't want to draw 'beautiful letters, but only good letters.' It's a question of semantics. Good letters come from an understanding of what two thousand years of letter usage has produced and what has been perceived as good, I think mainly by persistent usage. Beautiful letters depend on artistry. The classic roman letters are beautiful, and good, but they can be used incorrectly. A social critic once defined good taste as the right thing at the right time and place." ***— Doyald Young***

Suitability

"Good design is always practical design. Good type is like a good chair that has a suitability to the nth degree to be sat in, or stamped on paper and read...one that is neither clumsy and thick, nor skinny and weak." ***—W.A. Dwiggins***

Honesty

Whenever inferior materials are used in imitation of natural materials—linoleum resembling an inlaid parquet floor, a "cultured-marble" sinktop, polyester instead of silk, "antiqued" modern furniture built of particleboard, or a pencil-drawn "brush script" whose strokes don't ring true—a crime against taste has been committed.

Rhythm

"Without rhythm there could be no poetry or music. In drawing and painting there is rhythm in outline, color, light and shade....to express rhythm in drawing a figure, we have in the balance of masses a subordination of the passive or inactive side to the more forceful and angular side in action, keeping cons–antly in mind the hidden, subtle flow of symmetry throughout." ***—George Bridgman***

Spontaneity

"The best letterers have a quality in their work that is almost musical. This is evident in the way a curve is drawn and resolved. The most difficult thing is to draw beautiful letters with the feeling that the result is completely spontaneous. Tom Carnase has it, Tony DiSpigna has it, as does calligrapher Michael Clark. These are the virtuosos." ***—Gerard Huerta***

Sincerity

"That thirteenth-century urn is the legacy of thousands of years of people making urns, contributing, adding and subtracting ideas until it became the culmination of the efforts of a lot of sincere craftsmen." ***—Ted Cabarga***

Composition

The greatest of the old master painters, in addition to being good at drawing and painting, were usually also better designers than their contemporaries.

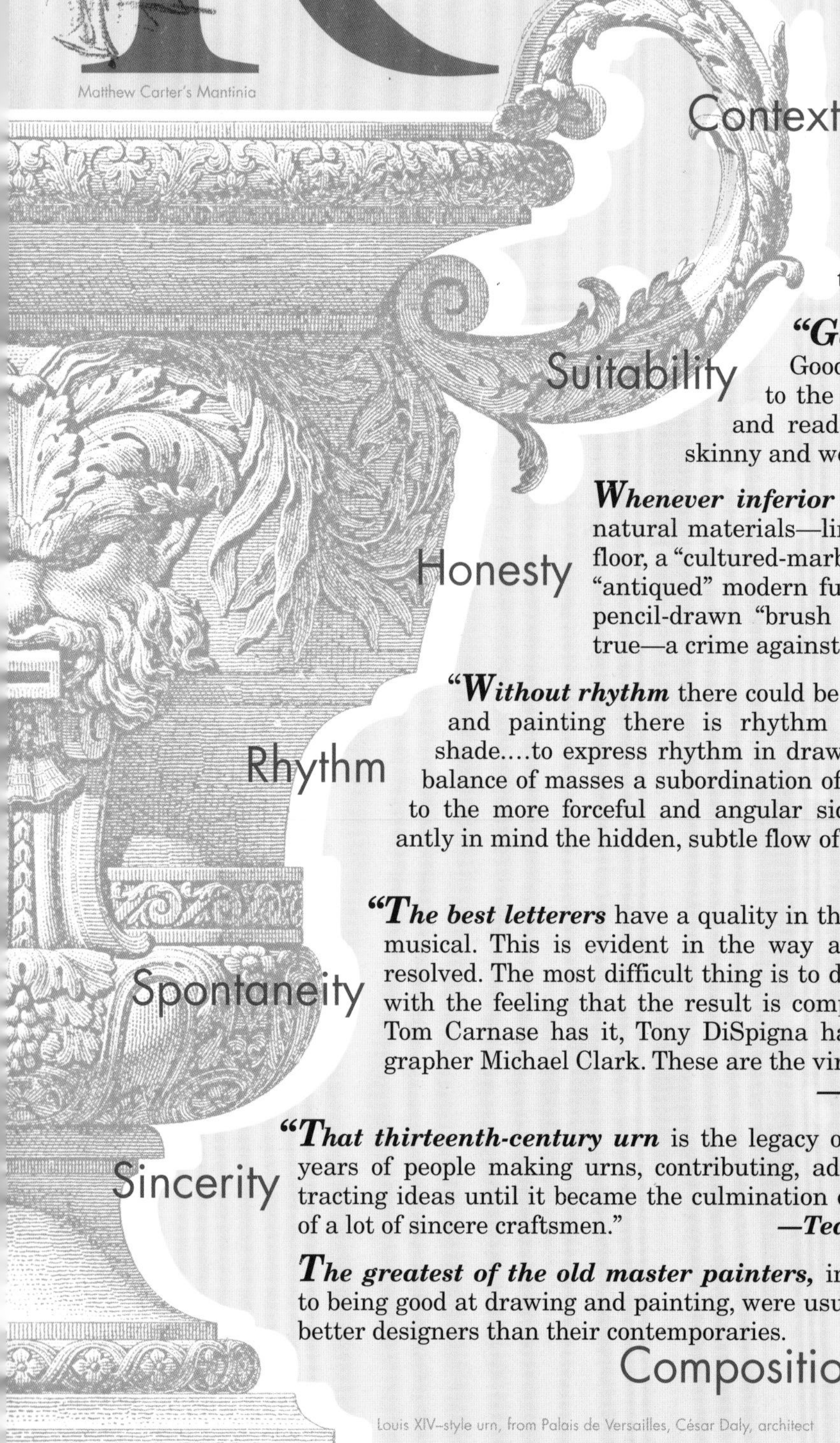

Louis XIV–style urn, from Palais de Versailles, César Daly, architect

Hermann Zapf's Palatino

&HEART

Giovanbattista Palatino, 1540

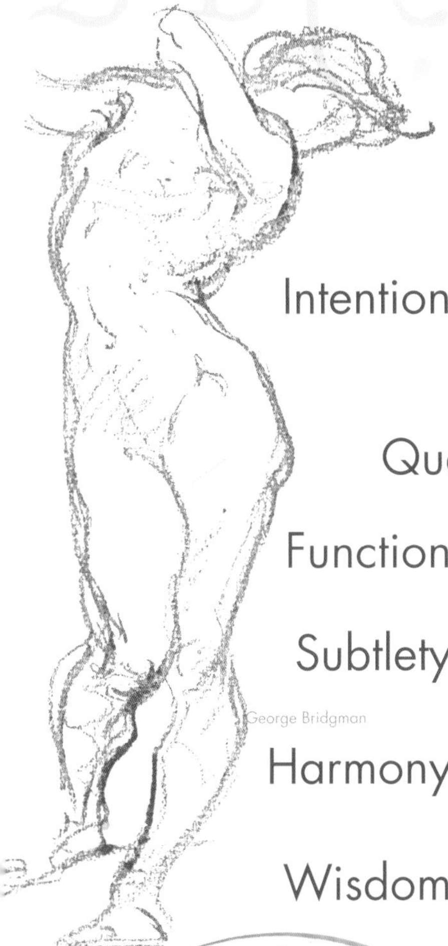

George Bridgman

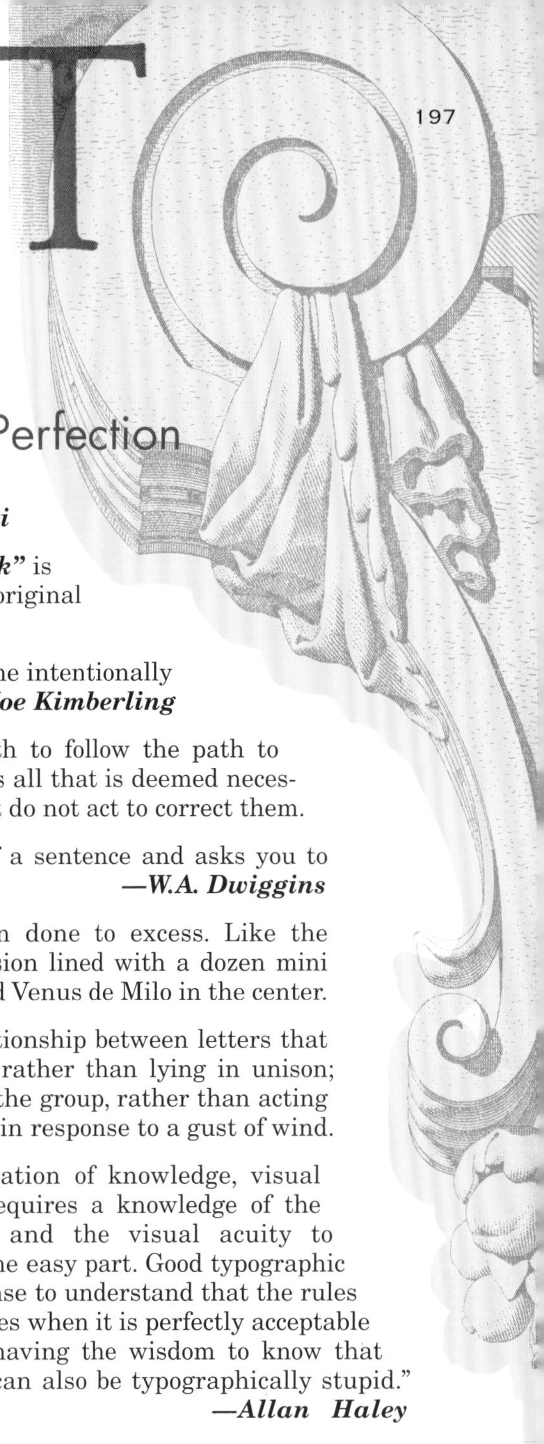

Louis XIII–style bracket from the church of St. Germain des Pres, César Daly, architect

Perfection

"A good artist ought never to allow impatience to overcome his sense of the main end of art, perfection…the one unpardonable fault is bad work."
—Michelangelo Buonarotti

Intention

The only true definition of "good work" is that it absolutely fulfills the vision and original intention of its creator.

"Bad taste becomes good taste when done intentionally —and with good taste." ***—Joe Kimberling***

Quality

Many who know better are loath to follow the path to quality because the quick solution is all that is deemed necessary, so they recognize the faults but do not act to correct them.

Function

"A type that stops you in the middle of a sentence and asks you to admire its smartness is a bad type." ***—W.A. Dwiggins***

Subtlety

Good taste becomes bad taste when done to excess. Like the crescent driveway of a Los Angeles mansion lined with a dozen mini Michelangelo *Davids* upon pedestals—and Venus de Milo in the center.

Harmony

In bad lettering, there is a lack of relationship between letters that comes when shapes oppose one another rather than lying in unison; when a few letters disturb the rhythm of the group, rather than acting in accord as blades of grass lean together in response to a gust of wind.

Wisdom

"Good typographic taste is a combination of knowledge, visual acuity, common sense and wisdom. It requires a knowledge of the tenets of typographic communication and the visual acuity to determine if they are adhered to. That's the easy part. Good typographic taste is also about having the common sense to understand that the rules are only guidelines and that there are times when it is perfectly acceptable to break them. And finally, it is about having the wisdom to know that sometimes, what is typographically hip can also be typographically stupid."
—Allan Haley

Various Alphabets,

Dean's Analytical Guide to the Art of Penmanship

Artistry

"Fine letters were, in the first place, copies of fine written letters. Fine written letters were fine because they were produced in the most direct and simple way by a tool in the hands of a person expert in its use—by a person, moreover, who was an artist."
—W.A. Dwiggins

In truth,

the laws regarding lettering are none; they are wide open to individual interpretation and predilection. Except that certain choices meet certain requirements, and these have been posed variously as being: legibility, fineness and good taste, ***all of which, unfortunately, are Subjective.***

Overshoot
Cap height
Counter
x-height
Overshoot
Diagonal stem or stroke
Counter
Thick vertical stem
Eye
Bar
Baseline
Overshoot
Tail
Apex
Link
Ligature
Full bracket serif terminal
Spur
Inclined stress
Ear
Descender
Loop
Accent (umlaut)
Finial or ball terminal
Ascender
Release
Spur
Spine
arm
July 24. D. M. EATON, No. 63, State-street.
NEW-YORK,
VICTORY, being a
GEORGE A. LUCE, master—
the 29th inst. having one
half of her Freight and Passage, apply
to the master on board, No. 13, LONG-WHARF.
July 24, 1802.
July 24.
Just Received,
TWENTY thousand of Sea-
of superior quality
Also, for an a
PORK, &c.
At No. 17 Greene's
CLEAN HEMP, IRON, CORDAGE,
and a few bales SHEETINGS and DIAPERS—being
the Cargo of the brig Alert, just arrived from St. Petersburg.
July 24, 1802.
Quousque
tientia
ror iste
se effren
nocturnu
bis vigili
ABCD
Quousque
nostra? qu
quem ad
nihilne te
urbis vigili
sus bonoru
ABCDE
Melium,
At nos vigesim
esse, Catilina,
dam, sed ad c
esse clementem
The ART
SERIF Styles
Sans Serif (without serif)
Bracketed serif
Hairline slab serif
Bracketed concave serif
Rolling se

Part 3

TS– of MAKING FACES

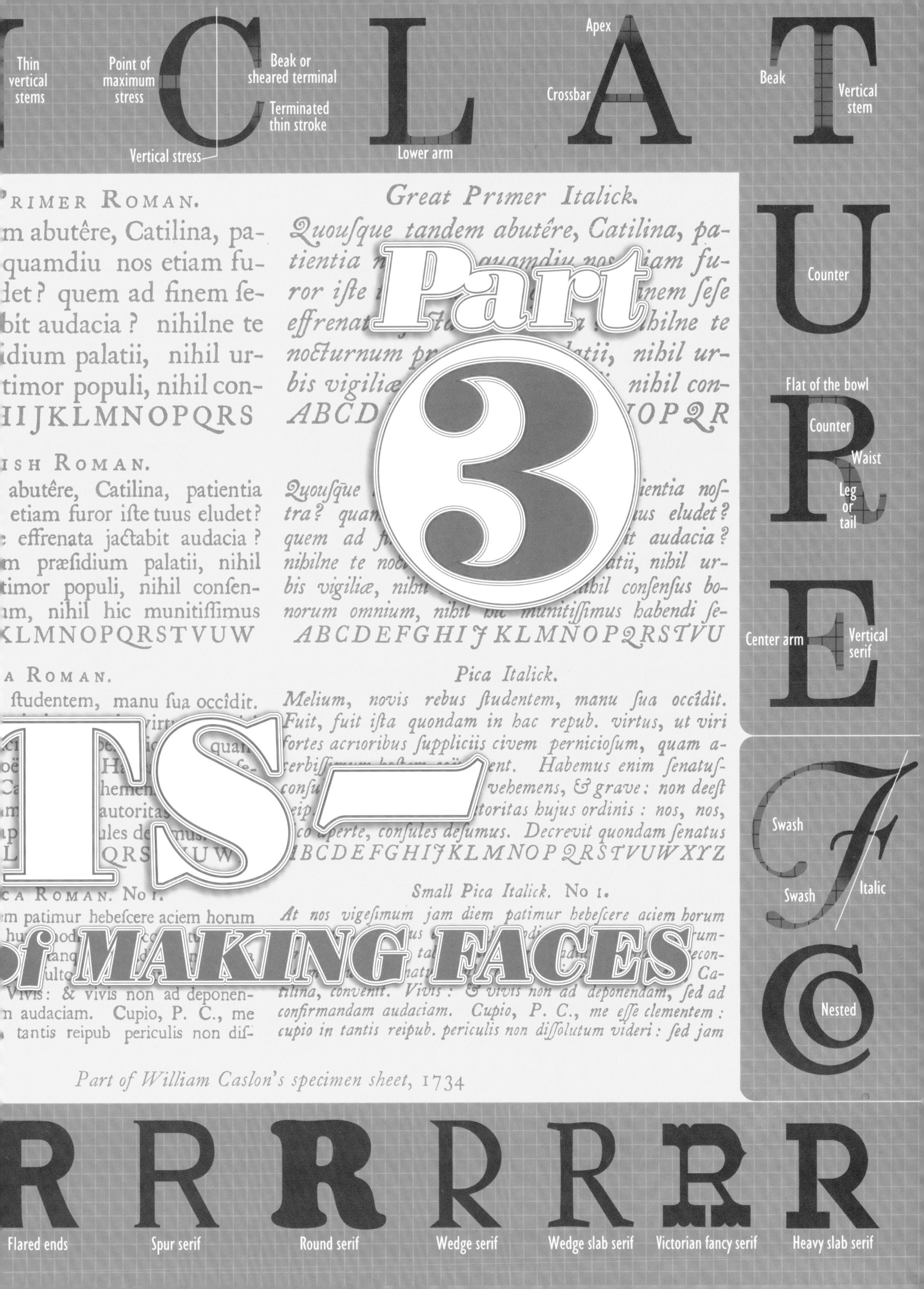
Thin vertical stems
Point of maximum stress
Beak or sheared terminal
Terminated thin stroke
Vertical stress
Lower arm
Apex
Crossbar
Beak
Vertical stem
Counter
Flat of the bowl
Counter
Waist
Leg or tail
Center arm
Vertical serif
Swash
Swash
Italic
Nested
Flared ends
Spur serif
Round serif
Wedge serif
Wedge slab serif
Victorian fancy serif
Heavy slab serif

Part of William Caslon's specimen sheet, 1734

TYPE: Beauty in Abstract Forms

"Good type design may be practiced only by an artist with peculiar capabilities. The most essential of these is the ability to discover beauty in abstract forms." —Frederic Goudy, 1938

"After four thousand years the alphabet has not reached the end of its journey, and from all indications, it never will." —George Salter, 1954

Do we really need another font? Some designers, content with Times Roman, Arial and Brush Script, would answer no. On the other hand, many people—designers, as well as normal people—"collect" fonts and can never have too many. It may certainly be argued that over the centuries almost every conceivable variation on the alphabetic characters has already been thought up. However, two forces conspire to ensure the continuation of font designs for the future. The first is market forces and the need by foundries always to refresh the stock on their shelves. The second is the mania for adding one's own contribution to the tradition of type design. There is something unquestionably marvelous in seeing words typed into a design program in a font of one's own. I've said that it makes me feel, somehow, like God.

If font we must, then what? Searching for the unusual, the obscure, the rare overlooked letter style is one approach. But the results often are too weird for popular acceptance and sustained usage. Most people won't buy products that are too outlandish, which is why the coolest automotive designs never make it past the prototype stage.

Of course, there are many wacky display fonts that have become wildly popular, but one commercially viable option for font designers is to revive and/or tweak the classics—and include free T-shirts and trance music CDs with every font! It's astonishing to me, though, how a basic-style font with a few subtle shape variations can thrill us with its apparent uniqueness. Christian Schwartz's Amplitude, for example, seems at once familiar, yet brand-new. The thirty-five-font family (two styles

BOLD FACE LYRE
Latest Quirky Sans

shown above) is suitable in all contexts and brings both designer and foundry a nice price.

Question: When isn't Caslon Caslon? Answer: When it was digitized sans sensitivity. Today, virtually every historically popular typeface is available as a computer font, but

An Exercise in Versatility

Matthew Carter on lettering and type

"There are significant differences between designing lettering and designing type. With lettering—for a logo, an inscription in stone, or a piece of calligraphy—you know ahead of time the letters and their order. If a letter occurs more than once, you can vary its form according to how it combines with other letters.

"With type design, on the other hand, you don't have the luxury of knowing the order. Typographic letters have a single form and must be randomly combinable. And it's only in combination that letters become type. Sometimes a student who is working on a typeface will show me a single letter, a lowercase *h* for instance, and ask me if it's a good *h*. I say that I cannot judge it in isolation; it is only good or bad as it relates to the other characters in the font. If the student sets the *h* next to *o, p, v* and so on, then we can begin to see how it performs in context, and whether it is good or bad, therefore.

"As the saying goes, type is a beautiful group of letters, not a group of beautiful letters. Of course, many typefaces have had their origins in lettering. A classic example is Herb Lubalin's Avant Garde Gothic, which started life as a logo. The letters had to be adapted from the particular state of a logo to the general state of a typeface, an exercise in versatility."

—Matthew Carter

buyer beware: There are vast differences in quality! At the beginning of the Mac era, fonts were desperately needed and many classics were digitized hastily. Close inspection of such fonts frequently reveals shocking flaws. If you choose to revive a classic, try to copy it without ego, or make something different enough that it becomes not a copy but your own.

The issue of legibility has been debated since the beginning of type history. In *Fred Farrar's Type Book*, 1927, the author writes, "Since the origin of movable types, their principle function has been to express in simple, readable type, the message of the writer, whether it is a book or an advertisement."

Designer George Salter wrote, "In weighing the merits of graphically inspired deviation from assumed norms we must carefully avoid arbitrary impairment of the act of reading for the benefit of the joy of seeing. We must not let the spice become the food, nor the accent obscure the substance."

Fortunately, readers of today are said to have become accustomed to a greater number of fonts than in the past, and therefore a wider variety of font styles is now legible to us. Legibility is still important, since we designers tend to emphasize form over function. The designers of the 1960s psychedelic rock concert posters weren't especially concerned about it, but the man who had something to sell, promoter Bill Graham, was reportedly always yelling at them about legibility.

Ken Barber, type director of House Industries, beautifully expresses the current view. He says, "Lettering can do much more than simply communicate the message of an author or a client who's trying to sell something. The lettering itself can provide a kind of artistic or aesthetic entry point for the viewer; it's capable of eliciting an emotional response. I think traditionally, the message is considered the content and the lettering the vehicle to express the content. However, lettering can be part of the content and can also *be* the content—they become one and the same thing."

a
ABCDEF
aabcdegh
b
ABCDEF
abcdefgh
c
ABCDEF
abcdefgh

Top left at a, enlarged from the specimen sheet shown in the background of page 199, are some of William Caslon's early letters, several printing generations later. Their murkiness poses a real challenge to a designer seeking to reinterpret the original style. At b, a modern, perfunctory Caslon font, awkward and graceless. In contrast, at c, Matthew Carter's Big Caslon (meant to be set at larger point sizes) is so scrumptious, I want to lick it. Witness the top of *g*'s lower loop. One can almost see traces of the tool that engraved the original letterpunch. The alphabet's pen drawn origins are also evident. This is no mere revival of a Caslon font. To me, this is Carter channeling the spirit of Caslon himself.

The laws of typography were made to be broken. But bear in mind that however different and imaginative your fonts may be, the underlying laws of balance, composition and symmetry seem to be eternal. Look at Dada, Deconstructivism, Bauhaus, Psychedelia, Grunge, and Post Thisandthatism: The best of the weirdest stuff still follows the basic laws, just applying them in ways that become harder to recognize. The only ones who think these trends are new are either lacking in historical perspective or are simply too young to have experienced them the first time around.

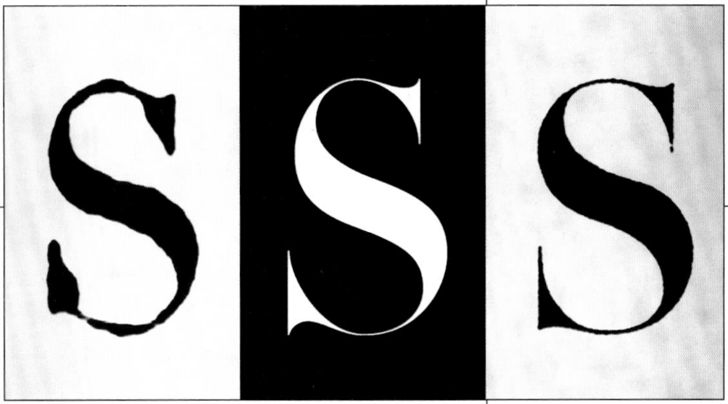

a b c

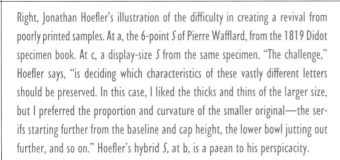

Right, Jonathan Hoefler's illustration of the difficulty in creating a revival from poorly printed samples. At a, the 6-point *S* of Pierre Wafflard, from the 1819 Didot specimen book. At c, a display-size *S* from the same specimen. "The challenge," Hoefler says, "is deciding which characteristics of these vastly different letters should be preserved. In this case, I liked the thicks and thins of the larger size, but I preferred the proportion and curvature of the smaller original—the serifs starting further from the baseline and cap height, the lower bowl jutting out further, and so on." Hoefler's hybrid *S*, at b, is a paean to his perspicacity.

IMPCAESA
TRAIANOAV
MAXIMOTRIB
ADDECLARAND

Paul Shaw and Garrett Boge's font Ghiberti, right, is "a contemporary interpretation of the bold Florentine lettering style of the fourteenth and fifteenth centuries." Donatello, below right, is "a classically proportioned design inspired by the lettering on the fifteenth century cantoria by Luca Della Robbia." Shaw and Boge don't sit around browsing through old *National Geographics* for inspiration. No, the peripatetic pair spends time in museums and libraries and makes photos and rubbings of period inscriptions.

ARS LONGA VITA
BREVIS EST.COM

LATINA EX
MANHATTAN EST

INSPIRATION

F*ew ideas are entirely lacking in antecedents.* Looking backwards, whether thousands of years or to yesterday, becomes the vehicle through which seemingly new ideas spring into being. Think of it as recycling. When it comes to type design, with its necessary adherence to conventionalized letterforms and the need for some degree of legibility as its guiding constraint, mining the past for viable models is often seen as a necessary, if not proud tradition.

That's not to say none of us ever come up with entirely original font concepts from out of our own heads. Absolute originality in all our design work might be the highest goal, providing the results are commercially viable. The designer's eternal dilemma—whether to adhere to accepted norms, or to create something so new and different that it might not be accepted—is explored in the sidebar, next spread, reprinting Will Dwiggins's famous dialogue with his type muse.

Ideas for new fonts, as this section shows, can come from such obvious sources as vintage signage, mosaic inscriptions, old print matter such as magazine ads and book covers, and even from automobile and machinery nameplates. But type inspiration can also come from such intangible sources as a dream, a comment or music.

Whenever we base a font that we intend to sell on someone else's design, we must ask ourselves: Is the designer dead and could his heirs sue? The very question reveals why so many fonts are based on obscure sources in the public domain. Hopefully, we inject our own style and personalities into every font we, uh, emulate, and this personal spin (which is usually just a failure to emulate *correctly*) helps us justify the theft: the highest compliment a designer can pay to a dead one. Designers steal mainly for two reasons: We fear we cannot think up good enough font ideas on our own, and we can't resist copying great old letterforms that inspire and excite us.

AMNPR

Every book on type must mention ancient Rome's famous inscription (c. A.D. 114) at the base of the Trajan Column, and this one is no exception. The letters of the Trajan inscription, believed to have been painted in brush before being incised, have been praised through the years as the finest example of classic Roman lettering. And after that, the praisers try to fix it. Frederic Goudy fixed its flaws in his font Trajan, and so did Carol Twombley—though not quite as much—in her digital version for Adobe. That's because the letters are very inconsistent, and they lean every which way. It's like the stonecutter had his eyes on the sundial, going chip, chip, "When's it gonna be five o'clock?" Look at the stem widths of *N*, above, compared with *R*. The *P* is different again. The late Father Edward M. Catich, noted Catholic typophile who made extensive tracings of the inscription (from which come the five letters above), pointed out in his 1961 book, *The Trajan Inscription in Rome*, that few of the fonts based on the Trajan capitals—actually referenced from a spurious cast of the tablet in the British Museum—accurately reflected the original. But all my nitpicking aside, the Trajan letterforms are piss-elegant and remain inspirational to this day.

Who'd have believed that one of the most startling revolutions in modern-day lettering design, the psychedelic concert poster lettering of the 1960s, was actually a throwback to the Vienna Secession art movement of one hundred years ago? May I present Exhibit A, right, a detail from a poster by Alfred Roller, 1902. Preeminent Fillmore poster designer Wes Wilson spotted it at a gallery exhibit in the mid-sixties and adopted Roller's lettering style, adding his own unique "spin." The rest is history.

16. AUSSTELLUNG
D. VEREINIGUNG
BILD. KÜNSTLER
ÖSTERREICHS

©1997 WES WILSON - ALPHABET

Left, in 1997 Wes Wilson revisited his poster alphabet in this typically undulating portrait commissioned by the author.

Below, the fonts Love Stoned and Love Solid with assorted dingbats from my Peace and Love suite. In creating the fonts, I looked at Wes Wilson's posters as well as at Roller's example above. People always tell me they can't read psychedelic lettering and I just look at them pityingly.

LOVE,
PEACE
AND
LEAFY
GREENS

W.A. DWIGGINS seeks font inspiration from the beyond

It would not surprise me if, in addition to all his other abilities, Dwiggins channeled lettering spirits. I imagine he thought the following "Comment," written for a 1938 prospectus of his font Electra, quite amusing—as indeed it is. Dwiggins reveals the same ethical conundrum with which we modern designers still struggle in swiping from old lettering samples while secretly wishing we could initiate our own original type ideas of equal merit. The question as to upon which planes of existence this conversation between Dwiggins and his honorable muse purportedly took place—or whether it actually took place at all—must remain unanswered until one of us can get up there and ask Dwiggins himself.

"But now look," I said, "take that Fell type. That's got a quality that I'd like to get into a face—kind of warm, human, personal quality—full of warm animal blood. How are you going to get that kind of feeling into a type that looks like a power lathe? We are still human, you know. And if you don't get your type warm, it will be just a smooth, commonplace, third-rate piece of good machine technique—no use at all for setting down warm human ideas—just a box full of rivets... By jickity, I'd like to make a type that fitted 1935 all right enough, but I'd like to make it warm—so full of blood and personality that it would jump at you."

"All right," he says, "all right. All the personality you want. The more the better. All I'm saying is that the personality of Jenson or Caslon isn't the personality you want. You want the personality of an individual living in A.D. 1935. Take yourself, for instance. You're a student of letterforms. What would your personality be, expressed in a type?"

Of course, this pretty much put it up to me, and I didn't know what to say. "I'll show you," he went on. "I'll show you..." and he showed me these letters.

Good design is always practical design.

Enlarged from a 14-point hot-metal specimen of Electra

"Whose design is that?" I asked.

"It's your design. It's a design that you are going to make. And it gets pretty close to your idea of what a modern roman type letter is like." He grinned at me. I had to admit that it was more or less the kind of letter I would make if I weren't trying to please somebody else—if I were just making letters to please myself. "What's it called?" I asked.

"It's called ELECTRA. The Greeks spelled it Elektra—but the Greeks had nothing to do with it, so ECT goes. Now notice how you are going to get the 'personality' you mention out of the unusual shapes of some of the characters—and see how the letters ramp along the line—and, more than anything else, notice how they fuse and melt together, into words. What about it?"....

Well... I don't know... it looked the way Kobodaishi said, when he showed it to me. But when I look at it now, cut, cast and printed—I have a feeling that the Saint knew more about his lotus ponds than he did about power lathes. Maybe I didn't keep my own hand out of it enough—changed his design here and there... It's active. It moves along the line nicely. But I can't quite see the metal shavings part, the high-tension power lines and those things...

There are a couple of touches that I'd like to point out, though. The weighted top serifs of the straight letters of the lowercase: that is a thing that occurs when you are making formal letters with a pen, writing quickly. And the flat way the curves get away from the straight stems: that is a speed product. Things like that were what Kobodaishi meant, no doubt...

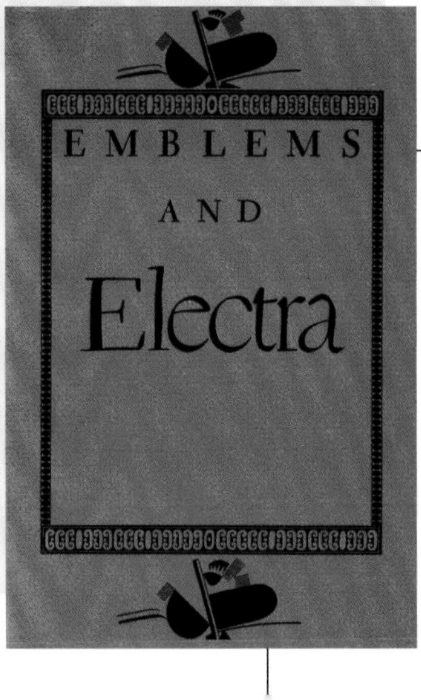
EMBLEMS
AND
Electra

Got in touch with Kobodaishi and had a long talk with him. You will remember him as the Patron Saint of the lettering art—great Buddhist missionary in old Japan.

I told him what I was doing with you people, and said that it would help us a lot if he could give us a kind of idea what the type style was going to be in the next ten years—what was to be the fashionable thing, etc., etc.

He wouldn't say directly. He said: "The trouble with all you people is that you are always trying to reproduce Jenson's letters, or John de Spira or some of those Venetian people. You are always going back three or four hundred years and trying to do over again what they did then. What's the idea?"

"Well," I said, "we think those types were pretty good—about the best that anybody ever made and we'd like to make some like them."

"But why *like* them?" he said. "You don't live in Venice in 1500. This is 1935. Why don't you do what they did: take letter shapes and see if you can't work them up into something that stands for 1935? Why doll yourself up in Venetian fancy-dress costume and go dodging around in airplanes and automobiles dressed up *that* way?"

"I know," I said. "But you can't play tricks with the shapes of letters. If you do, people can't read 'em. People are used to type that looks like that, and you have got to keep mighty close to the old designs."

"Used to 1500 types? Don't you believe it. People are used to newspaper types, and typewriter types. Your Venice types are just about as queer-looking to your friends in Hingham as Greek letters. What people are used to in your time... *That's* no argument."

I didn't say anything for a little while and just let him smoke, and then tried to get him back to giving me an idea of what the trend in typeface fashion was going to be.

"Electricity," he said, "sparks, energy—high-speed steel—metal shavings coming off a lathe—precise, positive—say it with a snap." I waited to see if he would get closer to something I could use. "Take your curves and streamline 'em. Make a line of letters so full of energy that it can't wait to get to the end of the measure. My God—these Lino machines that you tell me about—what kind of letters would they spit out if you left it to *them*? 1500 Venetian? Not!"

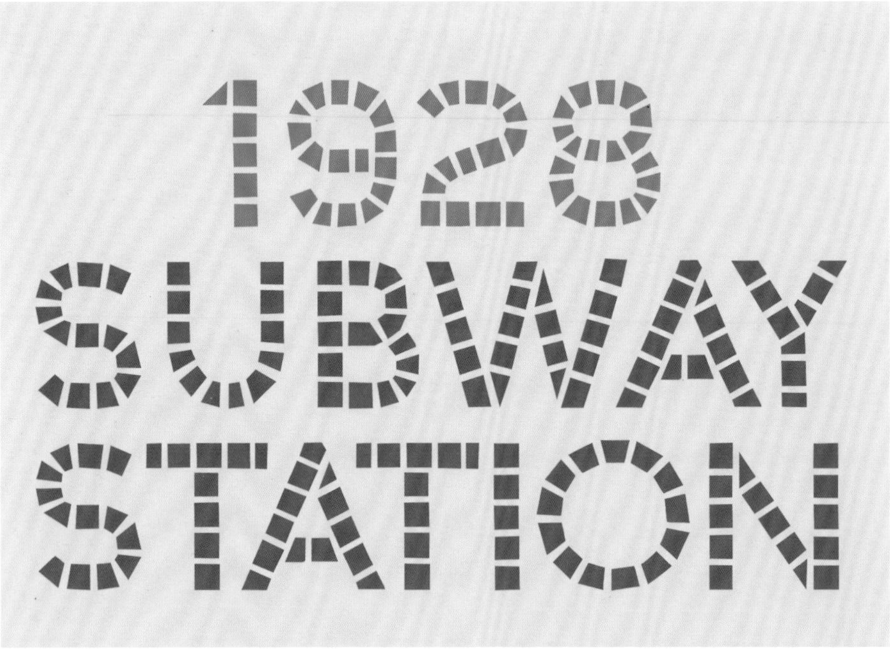
1928
SUBWAY
STATION

Right, in the words of Pablo Medina, the creator of the font Union Square, "Four years ago I consciously noticed for the first time the mosaic typography used in numerous stations in the New York City subway system. The letterforms that I was particularly drawn to were the sans-serif mosaics. The typeface is based on squares which emulate small, broken pieces of tile." Below, crayon rubbing by the author, 1982, of a serif-style mosaic, also from the Union Square subway station.

UPTOWN

GRAND
UPTOWN
EXPRESS

Right, Tobias Frere-Jones worked from historic photos of hand-lettered wall signs in New York City's Grand Central Station to create the font Grand Central Bold. He feels this style of lettering evolved over several generations from roman inscriptional lettering through the 1846 titling caps of Louis Perrin to the c. 1925 station signage, which Frere-Jones affectionately describes as "willfully gawky." Most of the historic, original signs around the station have been removed and "I'm still upset about that," he says. [Font illustration by the author.]

STATION

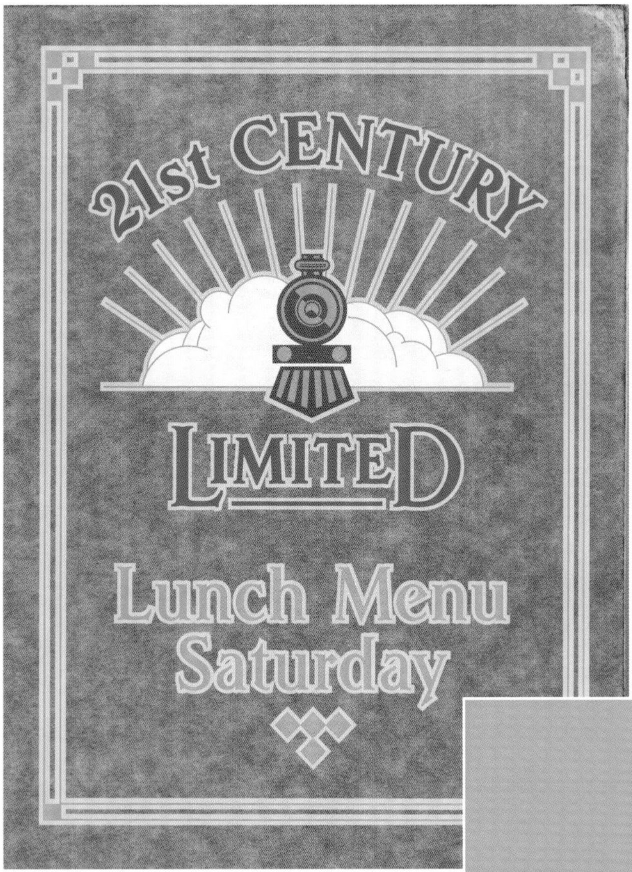
21st CENTURY
LIMITED
Lunch Menu
Saturday

Top, an architect's sketches for a set of capitals used in signage around the historic 1939 Los Angeles Union Station. Architects, not being letterers, usually imbue their alphabets with a certain charming naïveté that makes them appear "gawky," as Frere-Jones noted. Several years ago, I was commissioned to produce two fonts—a regular and a bold—based on these sketches and to expand the alphabet to include a lowercase. Above, I created a faux mosaic treatment to showcase the font, which I named Central Station Regular. Every tile was hand-drawn and colored in Illustrator before applying a Glass filter in Photoshop. Left, another sample of the font. The train graphic is a dingbat, and the background is a scan of an old book cover. In keeping with my belief that enlarged caps, such as the *L* and *D* in *LimiteD*, should appear to have been drawn with the same size "brush," I set the large caps in regular weight and used the bold font for the smaller letters.

1902
KAFFE
WIENER

Left, Kolo, by Paul Shaw and Garrett Boge, is based upon the posters of Koloman Moser, and other Vienna Secession designers such as Gustav Klimt and Josef Maria Olbrich. "We changed proportions and added numbers, punctuation and ligatures that did not exist," says Shaw. "We named the face after Moser because we liked his nickname." So the practice of referencing older lettering is hardly uncreative; more like a challenging puzzle.

THEATER TUSCHINSKI

Above, I would love to base a font on the exotic and historic Theater Tuschinsky logo I photographed in Amsterdam, but it wouldn't sell. It's too exotic, which would limit its usability. Right, you don't necessarily have to travel to Europe to find wonderful alphabetic reference material, though. I found this old wall sign containing about six different lettering styles in Detroit, Michigan.

WALL PAPER
Window Shades
PAINTS OILS AND VARNISHES
PAPERHANGING
AND
DECORATING

Latteria

Left, this sign for Latteria, found in Barcelona, is no longer even there, but its grimy silhouette is a ghostly invitation for fonts to come. Below, you won't be able to go bungee jumping at this Dutch Bunge-Huis (a shipping company), but you might jump on its signage for a font idea, or consider the great Art Deco building itself as inspiration for a border design.

BUNGE-HUIS

Esquire

Left, a clothing store in Italy for lawyers, I guess, done up with a neat steel and neon script. Although not seen in this neon sign, in Europe, neon tubes are sometimes actually cut and welded to create sharp mitered corners, something no American sign shop has ever had the patience to do.

DE-BERNARDI
CASA MUSICALE

Middle left, you can pick up everything at De Bernardi's House of Music, from a flügelhorn to a Humanatone. And if your brain is automatically set, like mine is, to "font-find mode," you might pick up a type idea, as well.

EL
MANISERO,
PEANUTS!
25
CENTAVOS

Left, I am really impressed with this font by Pablo Medina of Cubanica because it speaks "truth" to me. He lifted it off a Cuban restaurant sign in deepest New Jersey, but it could have come straight out of Havana, a place where time—enchantingly—stands still. Look past the Photoshop treatment I cooked up to really see Pablo's font.

Below, this was one of several sources for my font BadTyp. In addition, through the years I kept a running catalog in my head of absolutely atrocious amateur lettering that I finally put together as a font.

P & J
FARM FRESH

happiness waits for you in
Haiti
Unique in the Caribbean...and all the World

1962
RHYTHM
SECTION

Above, Brian Bonislawsky, factotum of the Astigmatic One Eye Typographic Institute, discovered this bit of lettering in an old magazine and from it he built the font Mardi Party, sample left. The trick to creating such fonts is in reconstructing an entire alphabet from only fragmentary clues. The original lettering, in red with yellow inlines, had no outlines, something we cannot yet accomplish in Postscript output. Bonislawsky's ingenious solution was to outline the inline.

HUSSMANN

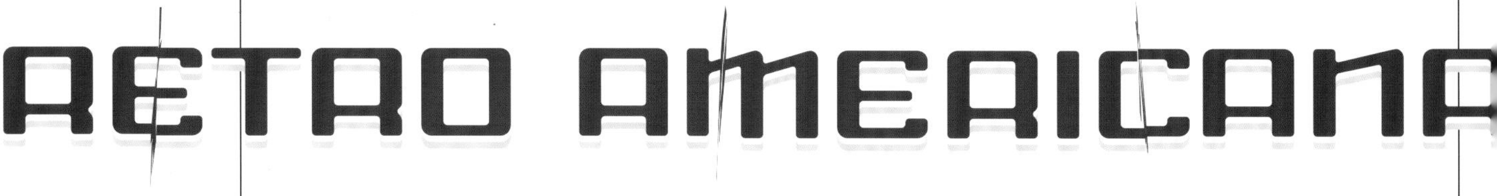
RETRO AMERICANA

Above, cool old logos beware! Font Diner's Stuart Sandler will hunt you down, take your picture, then composite you and turn you into a font. Sandler specializes in retro fonts from the 1950s and 1960s celebrating the best of Americana. From a venerable cooler plaque in the composited digi-pic above, he created the font American Highway. The font sets clean and straight, by the way; slashes and two-step drop shadow were added by the author.

Right, photos such as this one taken at an antique car show by Stuart Sandler cause all of us letterers to salivate and wonder how we might possibly make a font from such a thing. . . before somebody else does! The problem with scripts is working out one or two universal connecting strokes capable of hitching every letter up to every other letter. This has become easier to do in computer fonts, where we can design kerning to overlap, but this connection issue is why, historically, there has been a dearth of true script fonts. Classic hot-metal fonts like Gillies Gothic, below, were half-script attempts to circumvent the problem.

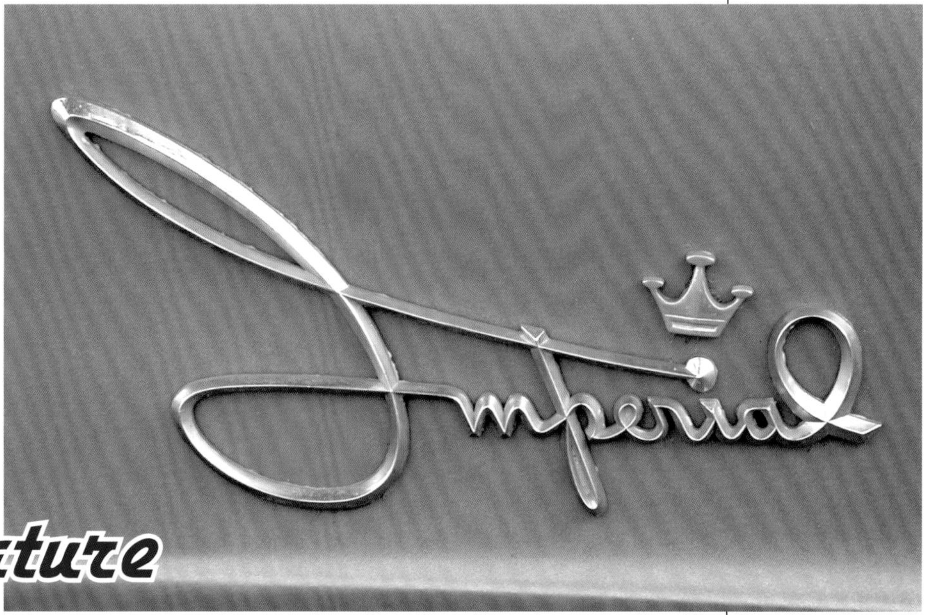
Imperial

Cheat Ligature

Inspiration for a font can come from a mere comment. Patrick Giasson says, "My inspiration for the Royal Family was a statement by Zuzana Licko [the Emigre cofounder] that 'We read best what we read most,' and that in its time, the black letter was a standard of legibility like the linear sans serif is today. I then created a hybrid font that blended letter shapes typical of both eras. It is interesting to see that the end result still has a strong 'gothic' flavor, since we register less the linear features of each character than their black letter counterparts, since only the former now feel neutral." Got that, everybody? Giasson's fonts thrill me because of their technical perfection and absolute adherence to style.

By
Special
Appointment
to {QUEEN FONTA}

1992-2002
techno
music
rears
font...

Or how about music being the inspiration for a font? Here's an earlier Patrick Giasson tour de force. In his words, "I designed Proton1 in 1992, the year I got into techno music and went to the first 'rave' parties in Montreal. I wanted to create a typeface which in print echoed this type of music, hence the mechanical modularity, and the aesthetic reference to the space age and early atomic models. But I also integrated a secondary, more disruptive subsystem to the typeface, to countereffect the usual rigidity of such fonts. While all the characters are based on a modular pattern of dots, their joining stokes are not always positioned where they would be expected." This is a difficult font to draw. Giasson has done it flawlessly.

FONT INSPIRATION:

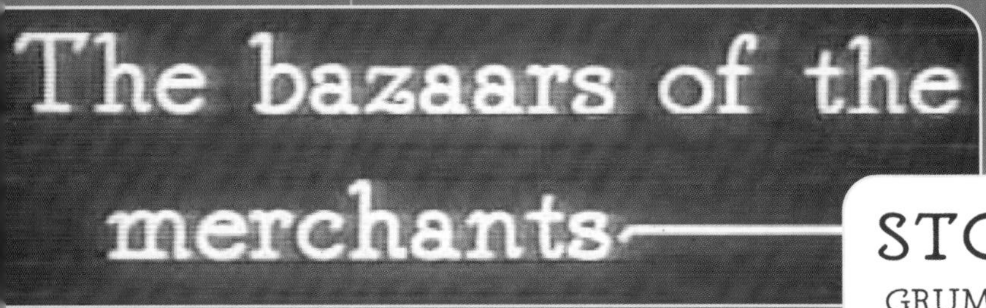
The bazaars of the
merchants

David Berlow designs a (kinder and gentler) family of e-mail fonts

STONE Hearths welcome col
GRUMPY WIZARDS MATCH TOXIC BREW FOR EVIL
The madder boxer shot another quick, gloved jab to the jaw
ABCDEFGHIJKLMNOPQRSTUVWXYZ abcdefghij

"***The original inspiration*** came from film titles for the movie *The Thief of Bagdad*, a silent classic. After a hard day of work in September 1999, this movie came on TV and I started shooting digital pictures off the screen. The next day I digitized a few characters. Then I forgot about it until 2000. Actually, I didn't forget, I got busy with other jobs, built a house and a new studio, and then I returned to complete Tobagdad shown above, right.

Tobagdad vs. Romantina

ABCDEFG abcdefg
ABCDEFG abcdefg

Below: top, initial comparison of three faces. Middle, early version of Italicata. Bottom, the very first version of the Handwriting style, which was drawn—*by hand!*—with a digital tablet.

STONE Hearths welco
STONE Hearths welco
STONE Hearths welco

STONE Hearths welc
GRUMPY WIZARDS MATCH TOXIC B
The madder boxer shot another quick, glov
ABCDEFGHIJKLMNOPQRSTUVW

STONE Hearths welc
GRUMPY WIZARDS MATCH TOXIC
he madder boxer shot another quick, glov
ABCDEFGHIJKLMNOPQRSTUVW

With the film title to go by, Berlow began drawing stroke letters in Illustrator, "but I very shortly move out of that; maybe after *h*." Then he cut and pasted parts together to fill out the rest of the style. He uses the same method with most of his fonts, composing them from what he calls "chunks." Berlow claims that despite all the styles and the variations on the letterforms, no further reference was used. "It's always just a fragment that you have to start with."

Then another year passed, and in mid-2001 I started thinking about how to make better, more expressive e-mail fonts. Despite the fact that technology—in the form of low-resolution screens, lowbrow e-mail applications and the limits of HTML—conspires to hinder type visually; and the sharing of property over the Internet hinders the financial rewards of developing such a face, I figured, what the heck.

So, I thought about how low-contrast faces are what good-legibility fonts end up looking like in print, and how I prefer reading serif fonts. This brought me back to the simplicity and clarity of the titling fonts used on the silent screen. And also, how well the face I had drawn could function for certain kinds of e-mail—like between lovers. With that as a basis, I began removing most of the frills and emotion from the Tobagdad face, and thinking of an appropriate font for business e-mail, I pushed it toward a typewriter face. This effort yielded Biznicina pretty quickly. The serifs are plain, the body widths are relatively uniform and narrower, and the forms are simple, but otherwise it is a cousin of Tobagdad in immediate appearance.

Romantina DouglasFairbanks@THIEFOFBAGDAD

Casualita DouglasFairbanks@THIEFOFBAGDAD

Biznicina DouglasFairbanks@THIEFOFBAGDAD

Bisnizlena *DouglasFairbanks@THIEFOFBAGDAD*

Italicata *DouglasFairbanks@THIEFOFBAGDAD*

Handwriting *DouglasFairbanks@THIEFOFBAGDAD*

Then, I felt I should add a face for casual e-mail, like interfamily, and between friends. This took a couple of tries, as there is little design space available in the low resolutions of e-mail between the business and romance faces. Eventually, I settled on a Cheltenhamesque set of terminals, relaxation of the horizontal strokes, a less geometric pattern of round shapes and freer formed diagonals. During the process, I went back and forth between the three styles, widening and narrowing bodies, tuning shapes and spaces to arrive at the three styles [shown diagonally opposite]. And then, with a light heart at having left three years of on/off work on the romans, I started working on italic faces for emphasis…and more.

The Italicata was drawn to work with all three roman styles. The swash and other experimental characters led me to conclude I needed a handwriting face for signatures and personal messages in otherwise nonpersonal e-mails, and finally I saw the need for an oblique version of the business face for really urgent business.

Once all the outlines have been finished (the handwriting face is far from there), the six styles will be converted to TrueType, hinted and tested at all sizes from 9 pixels per em to 67 pixels per em to make sure they behave properly on all screens. While the design process continues, however, I check to make sure the outlines are going to produce significantly different text. Above and right are tests of the three main roman faces down to 12 pixels per em, where the smallest differences can be seen. ”

David Berlow entered the type industry in 1978 as a letter designer for Mergenthaler, Linotype, Stempel and Haas type foundries. He joined the newly formed digital type supplier Bitstream, Inc., in 1982. In 1989, he founded the Font Bureau, Inc., with Roger Black. Font Bureau has developed new and revised type designs for *The Chicago Tribune, The Wall Street Journal, Newsweek, Esquire, Rolling Stone,* Hewlett Packard, Apple Computer, and Microsoft. The Font Bureau Retail Library consists mostly of original designs and includes over five hundred typefaces.

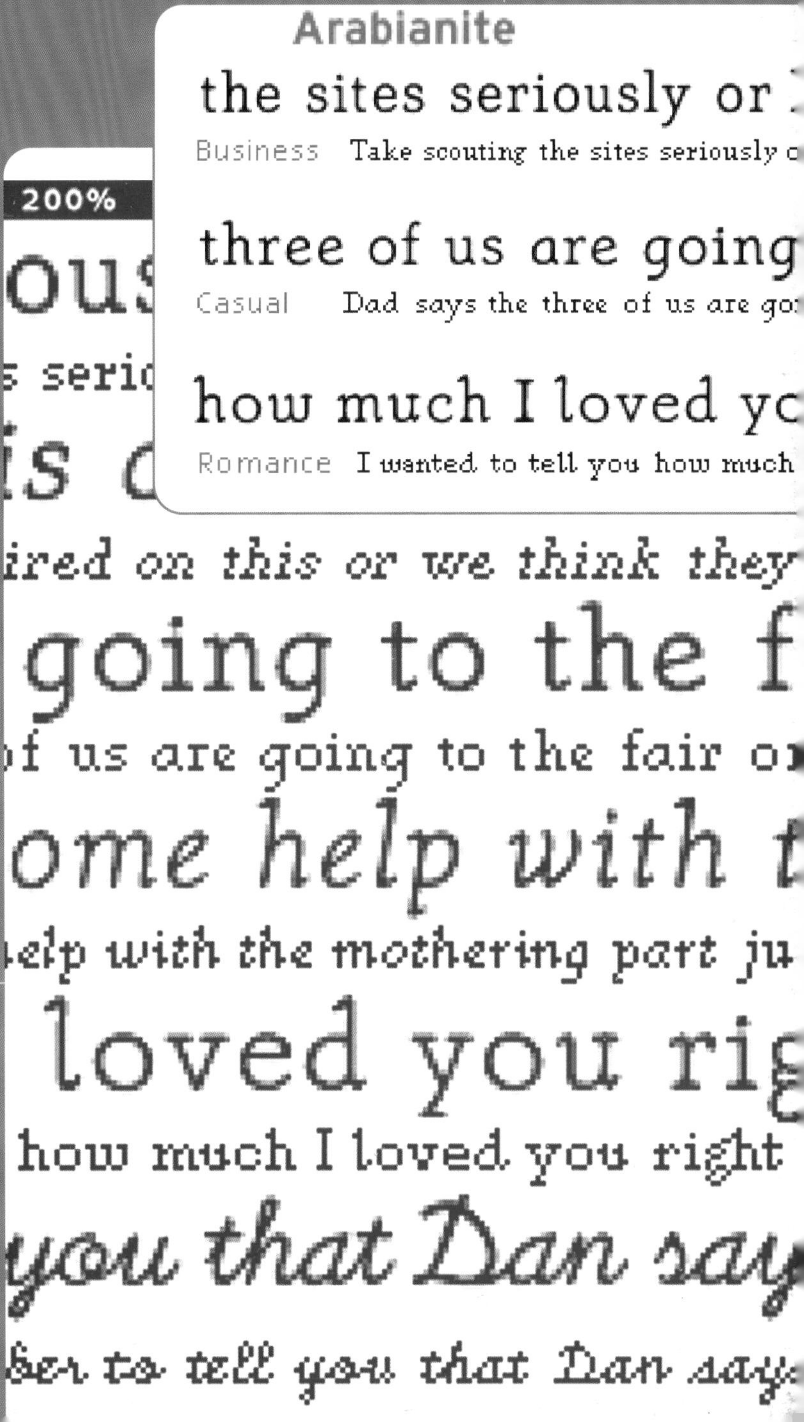
Arabianite
the sites seriously or
Business Take scouting the sites seriously o
three of us are going
Casual Dad says the three of us are go
how much I loved yo
Romance I wanted to tell you how much
200%
ous
s seri
is
ired on this or we think they
going to the f
f us are going to the fair o
ome help with t
elp with the mothering part ju
loved you rig
how much I loved you right
you that Dan say
ber to tell you that Dan say

C-@	C-a Đ Cap Eth Alt-0208	C-b ð lc Eth Alt-0240	C-c Ł L Slash	C-d ł l Slash	C-e Š S Caron Alt-0138	C-f š s Caron Alt-0154	C-g Ý Y Acute Alt-0221	C-h ý y Acute Alt-0253	C-i	C-j	C-k Þ Cap Thorn Alt-0222	C-l þ lc Thorn Alt-0254	C-m Open	C-n Ž Z Caron	C-o Ž z Caro
Space	! ! Exclamation Point	" " Inch Mark (Ditto)	# # Number Sign (Pound Sign)	$ $ Dollar	% % Per cent	& & Ampersand	' ' Foot Mark	((Left Parenthesis	)) Right Parenthesis	* * Asterisk	+ + Plus	, , Comma	- - Hyphen	. . Period	/ / Forwar Slash
@ @ At cost	A A A	B B B	C C C	D D D	E E E	F F F	G G G	H H H	I I I	J J J	K K K	L L L	M M M	N N N	O C O
` ` Grave	a a a	b b b	c c c	d d d	e e e	f f f	g g g	h h h	i i i	j j j	k k k	l l l	m m m	n n n	o o o
Opt-u-A Ä A Umlaut Alt-0196	Sh-Opt-A Å A Ring Alt-0197	Sh-Opt-c Ç C Cedilla Alt-0199	Opt-e-E É E Acute Alt-0201	Opt-n-N Ñ N Tilde Alt-0209	Opt-u-O Ö O Umlaut Alt-0214	Opt-u-U Ü U Umlaut Alt-0220	Opt-e-a á a Acute Alt-0225	Opt-`-a à a Grave Alt-0224	Opt-i-a â a Circumflex Alt-0226	Opt-u-a ä a Umlaut Alt-0228	Opt-n-a ã a Tilde Alt-0227	Opt-a å a Ring Alt-0229	Opt-c ç c Cedilla Alt-0231	Opt-e-e é e Acute Alt-0233	Opt-`- è e Grav Alt-023
Opt-t † Dagger Alt-0134	Sh-Opt-8 ° Degree Alt-0176	Opt-4 ¢ Cent Alt-0162	Opt-3 £ Pound Alt-0163	Opt-6 § Section Alt-0167	Opt-8 • Bullet Alt-0149	Opt-7 ¶ Paragraph Alt-0182	Opt-s ß German Eszett Alt-0223	Opt-r ® Registered Alt-0174	Opt-g © Copyright Alt-0169	Opt-2 ™ Trademark Alt-0153	Sh-Opt-e ´ Acute Alt-0180	Sh-Opt-u ¨ Umlaut Alt-0168	Opt-= Open	Sh-Opt-' Æ AE Dipthong Alt-0198	Sh-Op Ø O Slas Alt-021
Sh-Opt-/ ¿ Invert Question Alt-0191	Opt-1 ¡ Invert Exclamation Alt-0161	Opt-l ¬ Logical Not	Opt-v √ Check	Opt-f ƒ Florin (Guilder) Alt-0131	Opt-x Open	Opt-j Open	Op-\ « L Dbl Guillemet Alt-0171	Sh-Opt-\ » R Dbl Guillemet Alt-0187	Opt-; … Ellipses Alt-0133	Opt-blk	Opt-`-A À A Grave Alt-0192	Opt-n-A Ã A Tilde Alt-0195	Opt-n-O Õ O Tilde Alt-0213	Sh-Opt-q Œ OE Dipthong Alt-0140	Opt-q œ oe Dipth Alt-015
Sh-Opt-7 ‡ Double Dagger Alt-0135	Sh-Opt-9 · Period Centered Alt-0183	Sh-Opt-0 ‚ Sgl Base Quote Alt-0130	Sh-Opt-w „ Dbl Base Quote Alt-0132	Sh-Opt-r ‰ Per mill Alt-0137	Sh-Opt-m Â A Circumflex Alt-0194	Opt-i-E Ê E Circumflex Alt-0202	Sh-Opt-y Á A Acute Alt-0193	Opt-u-E Ë E Umlaut Alt-0203	Opt-`-E È E Grave Alt-0200	Sh-Opt-s Í I Acute Alt-0205	Sh-Opt-d Î I Circumflex Alt-0206	Sh-Opt-f Ï I Umlaut Alt-0207	Opt-`-I Ì I Grave Alt-0204	Sh-Opt-h Ó O Acute Alt-0211	Sh-Op Ô O Circum Alt-021

The ABÇs of FONT DESIGN: It Takes More Than 26 Letters

The chart above shows the character layout for a standard roman font as it appears in Fontographer and FontLab (set to "Macintosh Roman"). I've added color coding to define character subsets such as "accents" or "English punctuation" that are not grouped in one single area. • The chart gives names of characters and in which category each belongs. It also is a tool to help us define those character subsets that may not be necessary to include in certain fonts, or to ensure that no characters within a subset are left out of a complete font. • The definition of "complete character set" will vary with each foundry. If you are not a font designer, the chart provides key combinations for accessing hidden characters on your keyboard. Windows encoding, such as Alt-0183, for applicable characters appears in red. • Note: "Sh" stands for Shift key; "Opt" means Option key. Don't type hypens (as in Sh-Opt-k). An initially tricky two-step process is required when typing composited accent characters such as *ë*. First press Option together with *u*. Let up and then quickly press *e*. The key combination "Opt-u-U" implies that after pressing Option and letter *u*, we must then press Shift *plus u* (though the Shift key isn't listed) to turn lowercase *ü* into cap *Ü*.

KEY TO TYPE CHART:

A complete font will require all categories below. A "basic font," as referred below, indicates an incomplete font that omits certain character categories.

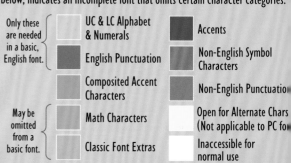

Only these are needed in a basic, English font.
- UC & LC Alphabet & Numerals
- English Punctuation

- Composited Accent Characters

May be omitted from a basic font.
- Math Characters
- Classic Font Extras

- Accents
- Non-English Symbol Characters
- Non-English Punctuatio
- Open for Alternate Chars (Not applicable to PC fo
- Inaccessible for normal use

	C-q	C-r	C-s	C-t	C-u	C-v	C-w	C-x	C-y	C-z	C-[	Opt--	C-]	C-"	C--
					½	¼	1	¾	3	2	¦	–	×		
					One-Half Alt-0198	One-Quarter Alt-0188	1 Superior Alt-0185	Three-Quarters Alt-0190	3 Superior Alt-0179	2 Superior Alt-0178	Broken bar Alt-0166	Minus Alt-0173	Multiply		

	1	2	3	4	5	6	7	8	9	:	;	<	=	>	?
0	1	2	3	4	5	6	7	8	9	:	;	<	=	>	?
0	1	2	3	4	5	6	7	8	9	Colon	Semicolon	Less Than	Equals	Greater Than	Question Mark

	Q	R	S	T	U	V	W	X	Y	Z	[	\	]	^	_
P	Q	R	S	T	U	V	W	X	Y	Z	[	\	]	^	_
P	Q	R	S	T	U	V	W	X	Y	Z	Left Bracket	Slash Backward	Right Bracket	ASCII Circumflex	Under Score

	q	r	s	t	u	v	w	x	y	z	{	|	}	~	**
p	q	r	s	t	u	v	w	x	y	z	{	|	}	~	
o	q	r	s	t	u	v	w	x	y	z	Left Curly Bracket	Vertical Bar	Right Curly Bracket	ASCII Tilde	

-i-e	Opt-u-e	Opt-e-i	Opt-`-i	Opt-i-i	Opt-u-i	Opt-n-n	Opt-e-o	Opt-`-o	Opt-i-o	Opt-u-o	Opt-n-o	Opt-e-u	Opt-`-u	Opt-i-u	Opt-u-u
ê	ë	í	ì	î	ï	ñ	ó	ò	ô	ö	õ	ú	ù	û	ü
cumflex -0234	e Umlaut Alt-0235	i Acute Alt-0237	i Grave Alt-0236	i Circumflex Alt-0238	i Umlaut Alt-0239	n Tilde Alt-0241	o Acute Alt-0243	o Grave Alt-0242	o Circumflex Alt-0244	o Umlaut Alt-0246	o Tilde Alt-0245	u Acute Alt-0250	u Grave Alt-0249	u Circumflex Alt-0251	u Umlaut Alt-0252

-5	Sh-Opt-=	Opt-,	Opt-.	Opt-y	Opt-m	Opt-d	Opt-w	Sh-Opt-p	Opt-p	Opt-b	Opt-9	Opt-0	Opt-z	Opt-'	Opt-o
	±			¥	µ						ª	º		æ	ø
pen	Plus Minus Alt-0177	Open	Open	Yen Alt-0165	Mu (Micro) Alt-0181	Open	Open	Open	SOpen	Open	Ord Feminine Alt-0170	Ord Masculine Alt-0186	Open	ae Dipthong Alt-0230	o Slash Alt-0248

--	Sh-Opt--	Opt-[	Sh-Opt-[	Opt-]	Sh-Opt-]	Opt-/	Sh-Opt-v	Opt-u-y	Opt-u-Y	Sh-Opt-1	Sh-Opt-2	Sh-Opt-3	Sh-Opt-4	Sh-Opt-5	Sh-Opt-6
–	—	“	”	‘	’	÷		ÿ	Ÿ	⁄	€	‹	›	ﬁ	ﬂ
Dash	Em Dash Alt-0151	L Dbl Quote Alt-0147	R Dbl Quote Alt-0148	L Sgl Quote Alt-0145	R Sgl Quote Alt-0146	Divide Alt-0247	Open	y Umlaut Alt-0255	Y Umlaut Alt-0159	Fraction Bar	Euro Alt-0164	L Sgl Guillemet	RSgl Guillemet	f-i ligature	f-l ligature

)pt-k	Sh-Opt-l	Sh-Opt-;	Opt-i-U	Opt-`-U	Sh-Opt-b	Sh-Opt-i	Sh-Opt-n	Sh-Opt-,	Sh-Opt-.	Opt-h	Opt-k	Sh-Opt-z	Sh-Opt-g	Sh-Opt-x	Sh-Opt-t
	Ò	Ú	Û	Ù	ı	ˆ	˜	¯	˘	˙	˚	¸	˝	˛	ˇ
pen	O Grave Alt-0210	U Acute Alt-0218	U Circumflex Alt-0219	U Grav Alt-0217	Dotless	Circumflex Alt-0136	Tild Alt-0152	Macron Alt-0175	Breve	Over Dot	Over Dot	Cedilla Alt-0184	Double Acute	Ogonek	Hachek

HAPE GROUPS

Drawing fonts is mplified by building ke-shaped letters in groups from similar arts. Use the chart at ht as a general guide o the order in which tters may be drawn. me letters admittedly l between categories. s chart will not apply o all styles of font.

Sans Serif: Straight-Vertical-Side Group · Straight-Diagonal Group · Straight-Bowl Group · Round Group · Numbers (shown in parts building order)

ILTEFHMNK AVWXYZ BPRJU OQGCDS 1740869235

LC Vertical Group · LC Diagonal Stem Group · LC Round Group · LC Bowl Group · LC Round-over Group · LC Misc. · LC Ascender Group · LC Descender Group

lkijft vwxyz oceg bdpq hnumr as lbdfhkt gjpqy

Serif: Straight-Vertical Side Group · Straight-Diagonal Group · Straight-Bowl Group · Round Group · Numbers (shown in parts building order)

ILTEFHMNK AVWXYZ BPRJU OQGCDS 1740869235

LC Vertical Group · LC Diagonal Stem Group · LC Round Group · LC Bowl Group · LC Round-over Group · LC Misc. · LC Ascender Group · LC Descender Group

lkijft vwxyz oce bdpq hnumr ags lbdfhkt gjpqy

LIKE G*E*NES, EVERY LETTER CARRIES THE CODE to the *Entire Alphabet*

Pick a letter, any letter—well, perhaps not *I-J-L*—but most other letters, or choose a single logo, or a fragment of antique lettering: Any of these will contain virtually all the information we need to reconstruct the rest of the alphabet. For example, the letter *G* provides sufficient clues, provided we will observe them, upon which to base an entire font. All the defining aspects of the *G* below are described here. These are the sorts of issues that designers look at in determining how to follow through consistently when designing an alphabet. For instance, the letter is sans serif, despite the spur at lower right. Its axis is entirely upright, not slanted as in an italic. The *G*'s thick/thin strokes define it as being roman in nature. The construction of the letter is basically geometric. The tool that drew it is neither pen nor brush. It has been created of "built-up" shapes comprising ellipses and rectangles. Furthermore...

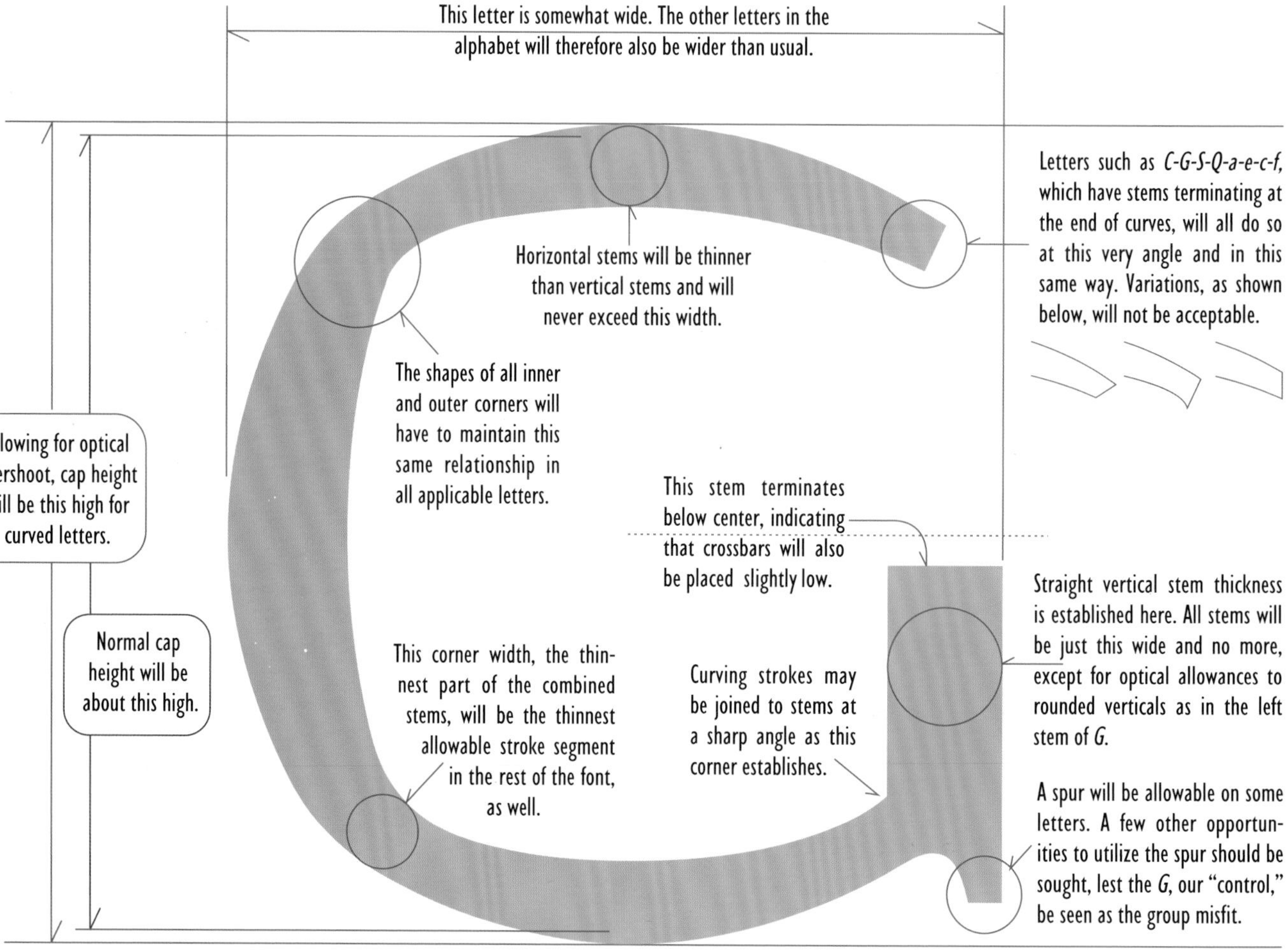
This letter is somewhat wide. The other letters in the alphabet will therefore also be wider than usual.
Horizontal stems will be thinner than vertical stems and will never exceed this width.
Letters such as *C-G-S-Q-a-e-c-f*, which have stems terminating at the end of curves, will all do so at this very angle and in this same way. Variations, as shown below, will not be acceptable.
The shapes of all inner and outer corners will have to maintain this same relationship in all applicable letters.
Allowing for optical overshoot, cap height will be this high for curved letters.
This stem terminates below center, indicating that crossbars will also be placed slightly low.
Straight vertical stem thickness is established here. All stems will be just this wide and no more, except for optical allowances to rounded verticals as in the left stem of *G*.
Normal cap height will be about this high.
This corner width, the thinnest part of the combined stems, will be the thinnest allowable stroke segment in the rest of the font, as well.
Curving strokes may be joined to stems at a sharp angle as this corner establishes.
A spur will be allowable on some letters. A few other opportunities to utilize the spur should be sought, lest the *G*, our "control," be seen as the group misfit.

a
Two points were added to the circle above, then it was turned inside out so a part of it, a, could be used to round the inner corners.

The overall shape of this *G* is not a perfect circle, but a combination of three different arcs, below, that merge at the corners. The outer shape, in relationship to the inner shape, will have to be applied consistently to every other letter employing a round lobe or bowl in its design. Right, only c, among these three outline shapes, will be appropriate for this font.

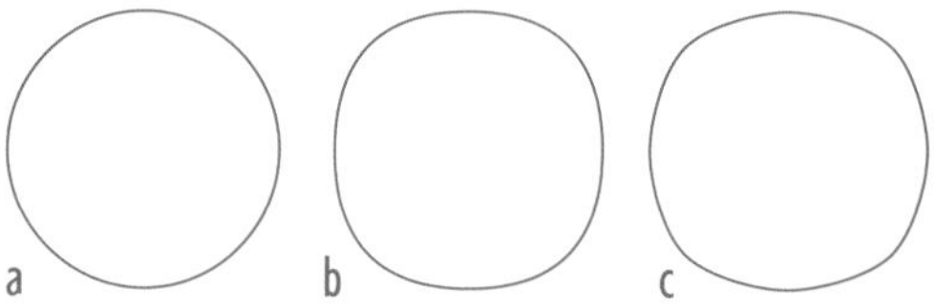
a
b
c

EXERCISE: Finish this alphabet based upon this letter *G*, according to the parameters given. If you are brave, include a lowercase.

Creating Fonts In FONTOGRAPHER

The most difficult aspect of creating a font is drawing the actual letters and characters. The rest, though labor-intensive, is not especially difficult. I've cut the following instructions down to the very basics to enable you, all the more quickly, to join the elite ranks of the digital typographer. Refer to the manual for further info.

Open Fontographer (FOG) application. Go to FILE>New Font (⌘-N). This window, right, opens with empty slots ready to be filled with our characters. If we click the expand button in the upper right corner of the window, it expands to show us all the open slots for potential characters.

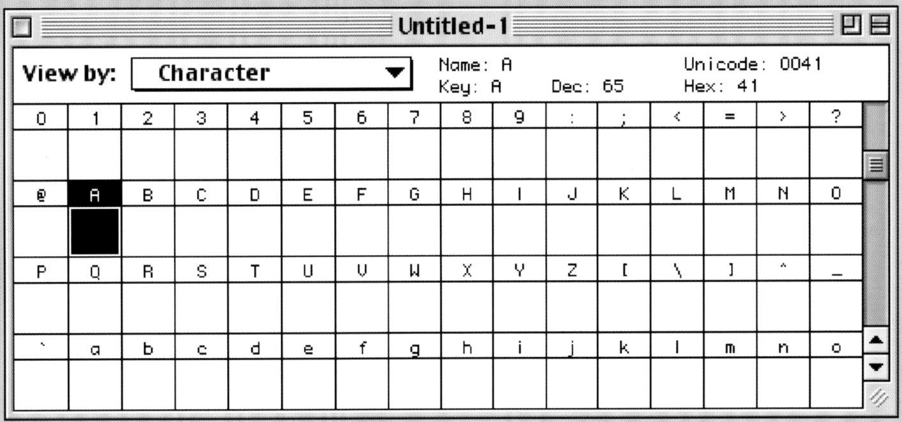
Untitled-1
View by: Character
Name: A
Key: A
Dec: 65
Unicode: 0041
Hex: 41

A Character Edit Window, like the one below for letter *A*, will open when we double-click any character slot. Here's where we'll draw our characters. The Tool and Layers pallets should open with the Character Edit window. If not, go to WINDOWS>Show Tool Pallet, then WINDOWS>Show Layers Pallet. These are sticky pallets that can be dragged to any location and will still follow the Character Edit window when *it* is dragged somewhere.

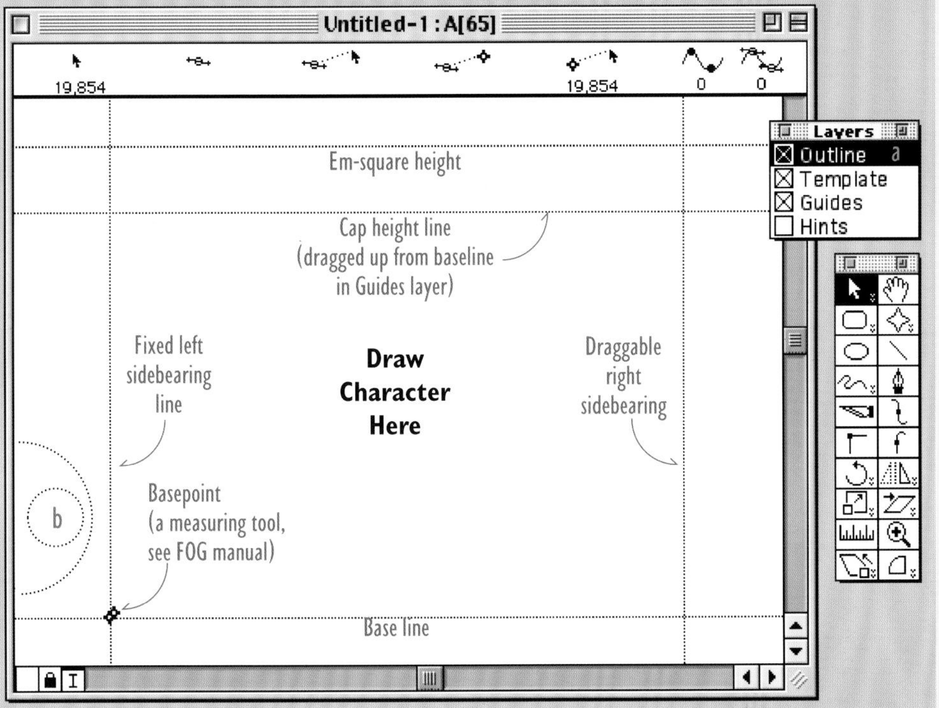
Untitled-1 : A[65]
19,854
19,854
Em-square height
Cap height line
(dragged up from baseline
in Guides layer)
Fixed left
sidebearing
line
Draw
Character
Here
Draggable
right
sidebearing
b
Basepoint
(a measuring tool,
see FOG manual)
Base line
Layers
Outline
a
Template
Guides
Hints

Descent Limit. When we reduce our view of the page, right, the fixed descent guideline is revealed, c. This is the bottom limit for descender characters such as *g, p* and *Q*. We *can* draw below the limit, but when the font is set at 0 points leading, the descender characters may touch the caps and accented characters on the lines below.

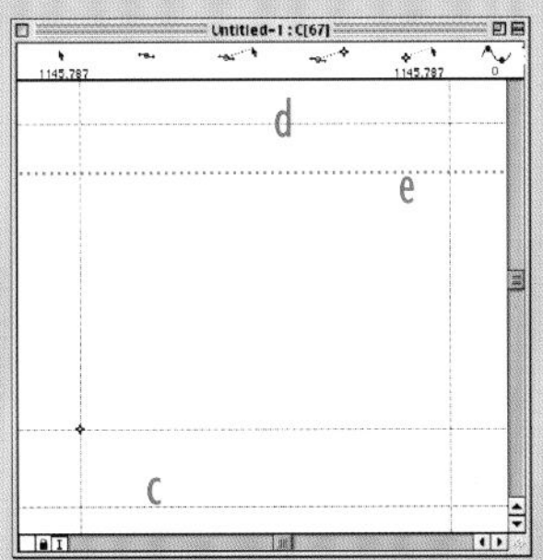
d
e
c

Cap Height. Think of the fixed cap-height guide, d, as the upper drawing limit. Actual cap height should be a bit lower, e, to leave space for accents placed above characters. Go to ELEMENT>Font Info to change the "fixed" ascent and descent lines, but I've never felt the need to change these standards.

The LAYERS PALLET

Outline is the top layer where character drawings are done. It is seen highlighted at a, left, which means we are currently working in Outline layer. The content in layers with x-ed boxes is visible to us unless we click to uncheck them.

Template is the middle layer where scans will automatically be placed when pasted into a character slot. We can also paste our character drawings into the Template layer, either to save earlier versions of a letter we've altered, or to use as reference while making changes in the Outline layer.

Guides is the bottom layer. The basic horizontal guides that give us a standard working height are set by default and can't be moved manually. We *can* drag horizontal guidelines up from the baseline to give us cap height, x-height and overshoot lines. We can also paste art, like a standard stem width, into this layer. But unlike the Template layer, whose contents are visible only within one character's slot, anything pasted into the Guides layer is visible in every character slot. I often place gauge balls, b, off to the side in the Guides layer, then copy and paste them into the Outline layer whenever I need to make sure my stem widths are consistent.

Hints is not a relevant layer unless we want to adjust hinting of our font for a slightly improved appearance on computer monitors and the web. Many designers just go along with FOG's invisible, automatic hinting, as do I.

Paste a Scan into the Template Layer

Open a 300 dpi (or higher resolution) gray-scale scan in Photoshop. Straighten and fix it (see page 158). Create a selection marquee that is about 25 percent taller than cap height, and wide enough to include three or four letters, a (Paste a string of letters at once to save time). Hit Copy in Photoshop, then click on any character window to bring it up, and hit Paste. FOG always pastes to the height of the em square, b. That's why we made the Photoshop marquee higher than the letters, to allow for accent character clearance. Keep the Photoshop marquee alive for the next time we Copy.

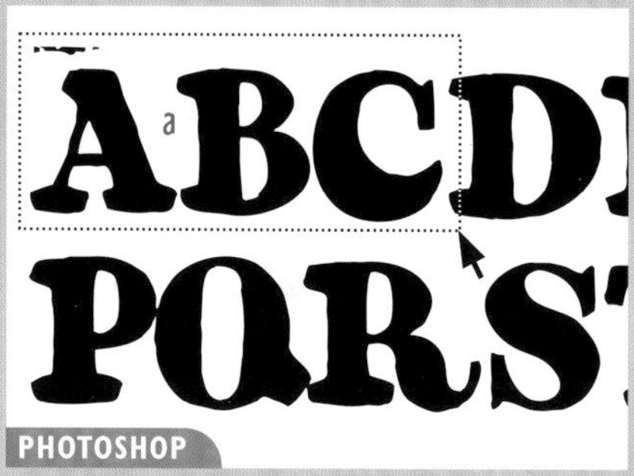

ABCD
a
PQRS
PHOTOSHOP

Above, characters scanned from an old lettering book. Some designers paste just a few letters into FOG to establish a font's trends, then they wing it from there.

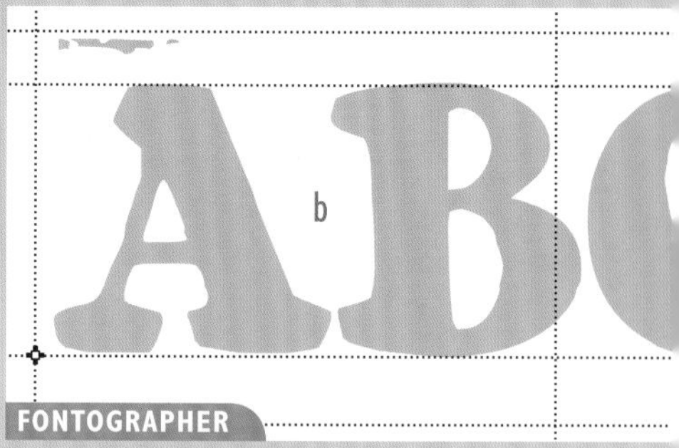

b
FONTOGRAPHER

Above, pasting several characters into one slot helps us to relate one character to another as they are drawn. Later, we Cut and Paste each outline into its own slot.

Paste Illustrator EPS Art into FOG

Because FOG has not been updated in years, it now takes more than Copy to get bezier art from newer versions of Illustrator into FOG. If you've drawn an alphabet in Illustrator, fill the characters 100% black only (no strokes, but compound paths OK), copy them into a new Illustrator document. Save this doc as an EPS file in Illustrator version 3.0/3.2. In Fontographer, double-click a character slot so its window opens, go to FILE>Import>EPS and locate the 3.0/3.2 file. The vector art in the EPS file will appear in the FOG window. If we've imported many characters at once into a character window, they'll need to be individually Cut and Pasted into their own slots.

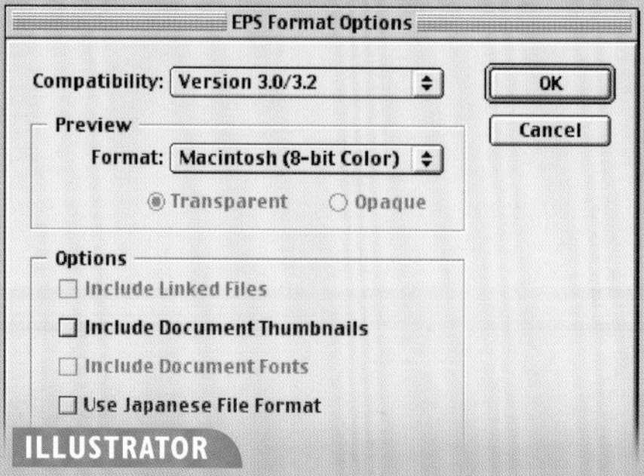

EPS Format Options
Compatibility: Version 3.0/3.2
OK
Cancel
Preview
Format: Macintosh (8-bit Color)
Transparent
Opaque
Options
Include Linked Files
Include Document Thumbnails
Include Document Fonts
Use Japanese File Format
ILLUSTRATOR

Above, the EPS Format Options window where we will select an early version of Illustrator to be compatible with antiquated Fontographer. A message will come up warning, "Saving in an older version may disable... blah, blah, blah..." Click the "So What" (OK) button.

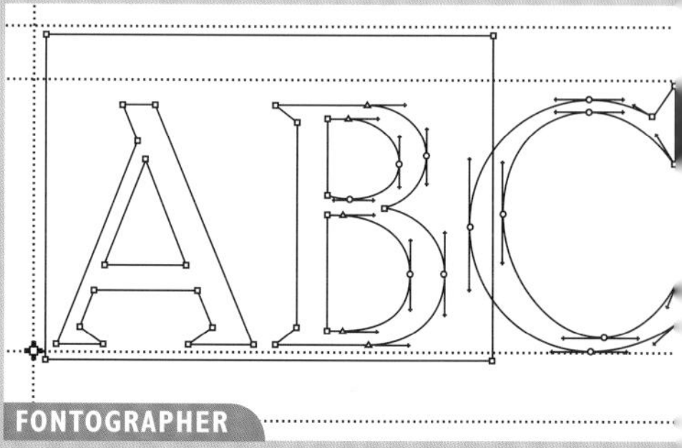

FONTOGRAPHER

A rectangle, 25 percent or so taller than cap height (like the larger marquee we made to paste from Photoshop), should accompany Illustrator EPS Imports so subsequent Imports (with same rectangle) will appear in FOG at same scale. Once in FOG, delete rectangles.

Draw Straight Ahead in FOG

Many of us have become able to draw on computers, our brains visualizing letter shapes a blip ahead of our mouse clicks, just as we'd done with pencils in years past. As an option to importing scans or Illustrator art, we may also draw directly in FOG with its drawing tools that are uniquely suited to making letters. (See the program features comparison chart on page 224.)

SAVE the Font!

As soon as—or perhaps before—we've installed a bit of content, it is about time to save the font. First, hit ⌘-S, which brings up the usual Save dialogue box. Type in the name of the font, leaving the .fog suffix to identify the file as the master and not the actual font you will generate later. Second, go to ELEMENT>Font Info and there type the name of the font again, adding if you wish, a Style Name like *Regular, Bold* or *UltraLightOblique*. Only after this second step does FOG display the font name in our character windows. Fontographer makes Saves fast, so there's no reason not to hit ⌘-S often as we work.

Consulting the Metrics Window

Hit ⌘-K (*K* for kern) to bring up the Metrics window. It's helpful to have this open to check the progress of our characters (especially in relation to one another) as we work in a Character window. The Metrics window updates our changes immediately, showing us a solid black-filled character while at the same time we can be drawing in outline mode. However, the Metrics window renders characters at lower resolution than it should, which can be annoying, unless we make that aspect work for us. This slightly stairstepped, pixelated screen rendering can make the positions of the hills and valleys in our curves more obvious. This is, in a sense, a *higher*-res version of the essential, bottom-line shape information we get when doing hinting.

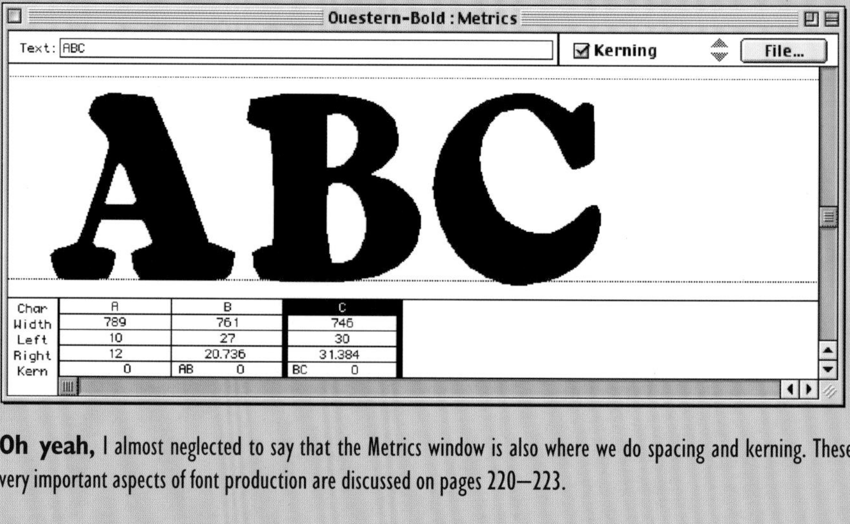

Ouestern-Bold : Metrics
Text: ABC
Kerning
File...
ABC
Char A B C
Width 789 761 746
Left 10 27 30
Right 12 20.736 31.384
Kern 0 AB 0 BC 0

Oh yeah, I almost neglected to say that the Metrics window is also where we do spacing and kerning. These very important aspects of font production are discussed on pages 220–223.

Complete the Character Set

Techniques for drawing letters have been covered primarily in Part 2 of this book. Now you are ready to complete the entire character set for your font. Refer to the chart on page 214 to learn the generic forms of any international characters with whose shapes you are unfamiliar.

Keep All Characters in Character

One indicator of a high-quality font is that all characters maintain style. The sheer labor of having to draw 256 matching characters in a font sometimes causes designers to try to avoid doing so. In example a, right, it is obvious that the numerals and @ symbol are inconsistent with the alphabet. In b and c, all characters were designed just for those fonts.

a
123@ABCabc?!£
b
123@ABCabc?!£
c
123@ABCabc?!£

Alternate Characters

These are characters that populate unused slots in the Option/Shift-Option bowels of a font, sometimes replacing math characters (see chart on page 214 to locate available slots). Alternates can have various functions, such as:

1. Letters that solve setting problems. Right, callouts a point to letters best used midword. At b, alternates for beginnings of words have been substituted. At c, another alternate *s* for when preceding letter's connector is high.

2. Versions of letters that the designer wanted to provide as options, d, or fun stuff like the underlining swash at e.

3. Letters that completely change the look of a font. Kobalt Bold, f, is radically changed by a large set of alternates, g.

4. Dingbats for fun. At h, the keys Shift-Option-K will yield these dingbats from my fonts. I've learned, though, that users rarely discover or make use of our alternates, nor do they read our teach texts to learn of these characters' existence.

real strong abs
real strong abs
f The HAGERCROMSIE
g The HAGERCROMSIE
h
Kobalt Bold
Kobalt Black
Peace Solid
Kobalt Kartoon
Rocket Regular
Ojaio
Magneto

Working Order: A Suggestion for Creating Fonts

The order in which we create characters to fill out the font window can drastically affect our working time and efficiency. I have found it best to work on the various sections of a font in the following order.

1. Uppercase and Lowercase Alphabets. The decisions, stylistic trends, and the actual drawings emerging from this key section of the font will be Copy and Pastable, or at least adaptable, to most other characters to come. Resist the urge to work on the rest of the characters until you feel 99 percent satisfied with the alphabet or you may waste time going back and forth with changes. For example, if you reuse uppercase *S* to make the dollar sign, and later decide you hate the shape of your *S*, you'll have to go back and also fix the dollar sign.

2. Spacing of the Alphabet. Rough centering and letter spacing should really be done at the time letter drawings are created. See page 220 for info on spacing. Finalize spacing, and your spacing plan, before going on to make other characters. That way, the rest of the characters can be correctly spaced as they are created. Another reason for early spacing will be given in point 5, following.

3. Numerals, Punctuation and Math Characters. Many of these characters can be built from parts and pieces of alphabetic characters.

4. Accents. Like every other aspect of a font, the accents should relate overall to the design of the font, and to each other as to general size and weight.

5. Accent Characters. FOG's Copy Reference feature (⌘-G, for "Get Part") allows us to copy a letter like *A* and Paste a noneditable, auto-updating copy into every slot with an accented *A* such as *Ä*, *Â*, *Ã* and so on. Accents can also be Copy Referenced and Pasted to make what are called *composite characters*. While changes to the original *A* will be reflected in all the copies, *A*'s spacing, which Pastes into the accent character slots with the letter, will not update if we later change *A*'s width. *That's* why I urged you to finalize the alphabet design and space it *before* pasting accent characters.

6. All Other Characters. At this point, I usually just start at the top of the font window and start filling in all the characters that haven't been drawn.

7. Kerning. This is, for me, the least enjoyable aspect of making a font. If a font is carefully spaced, excessive kerning can be avoided. Kerning, which is the individual fitting of every letter to every other letter, is covered on page 222.

8. Generating the Font. Before the font is finalized, we should already have generated it several times as a working font in order to make test prints and to see how it looks in design applications like Adobe Illustrator or Quark XPress.

SPACING

Careless letter spacing may impede, or divert our attention from, the act of reading, while spacing that is well executed usually goes unnoticed. Careful and systematic spacing can save us work later by reducing the number of kerning pairs that a font requires. And a well-spaced font is better suited to applications, like the web, that may not recognize kerning at all. Following are some details on spacing.

The Metrics Window, right, is where we do spacing and kerning. Hit ⌘-K to open it. Letters typed into the field at a will appear below. The letters *H* and *O* are traditionally used as the "control characters" to establish sidebearing values that will apply to most other characters. Each letter's right and left values are the same, b and c, because they are both symmetrical in design. The straight left side of *E* will obviously have the same value as the left side of *H*, but the right side, d, had to be eyeballed, or individually assessed.

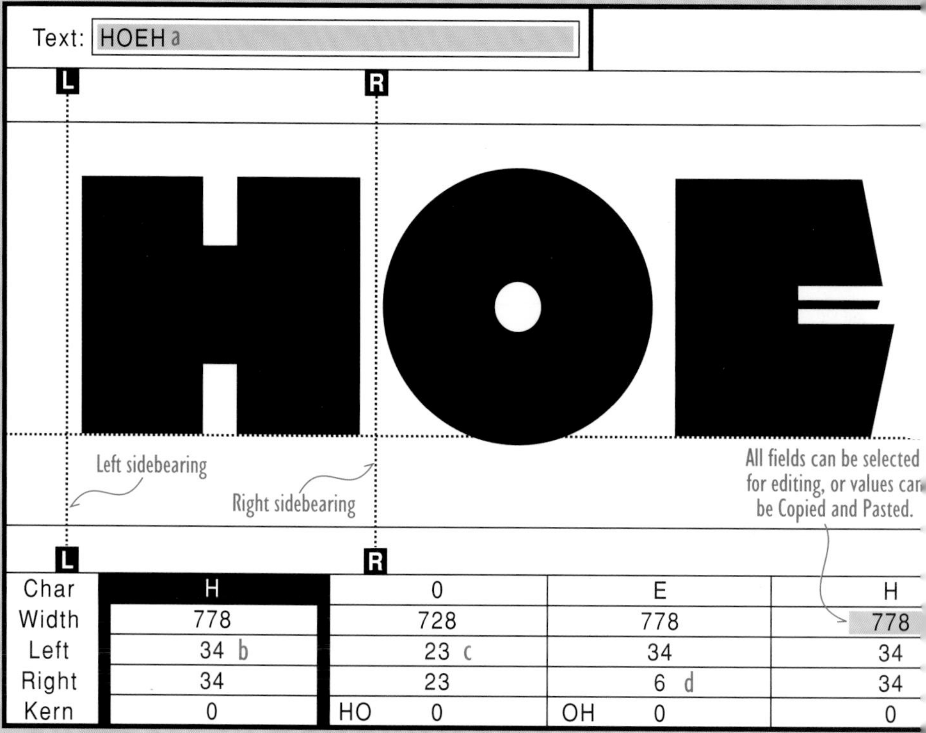
Text: HOEH a
L
R
Left sidebearing
Right sidebearing
All fields can be selected for editing, or values can be Copied and Pasted.
L
R

Char	H	O	E	H
Width	778	728	778	778
Left	34 b	23 c	34	34
Right	34	23	6 d	34
Kern	0	HO 0	OH 0	0

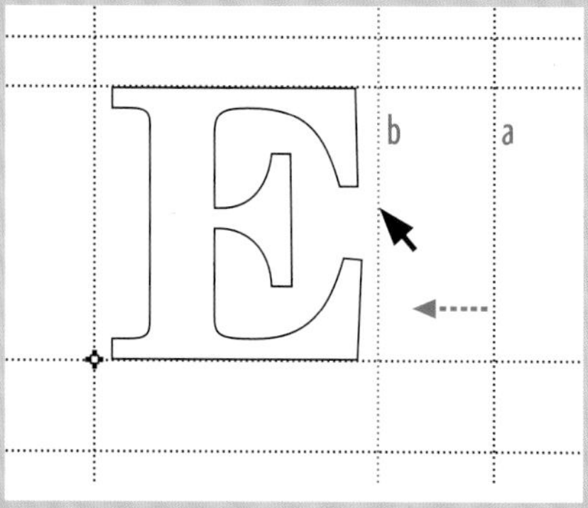
b
a

Initial Spacing

FOG's default character slot width of 1000 units is usually too wide. So, after drawing a letter, drag the right sidebearing, a, closer in to the character, b, and do basic centering by eye. Or METRICS>Equalize Sidebearings will center the character for us. However, mechanical centering based on a letter's edge-to-edge width is often inferior to optical centering where we can take a letter's weight distribution into account.

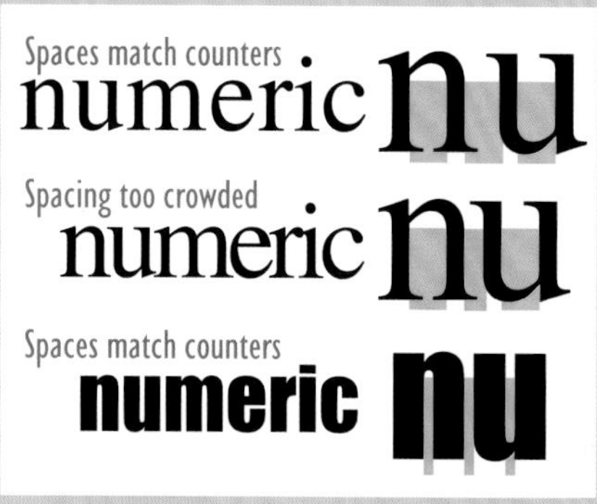
Spaces match counters
numeric nu
Spacing too crowded
numeric nu
Spaces match counters
numeric nu

About Space

Spacing between letters is traditionally related to counter width, thereby not only setting up a pattern of consistent space widths between letters, but within them as well. It follows then that the larger a font's counters, the more open will be the spacing between letters. Heavier-weighted fonts, therefore, will naturally have smaller counters and tighter letter spacing.

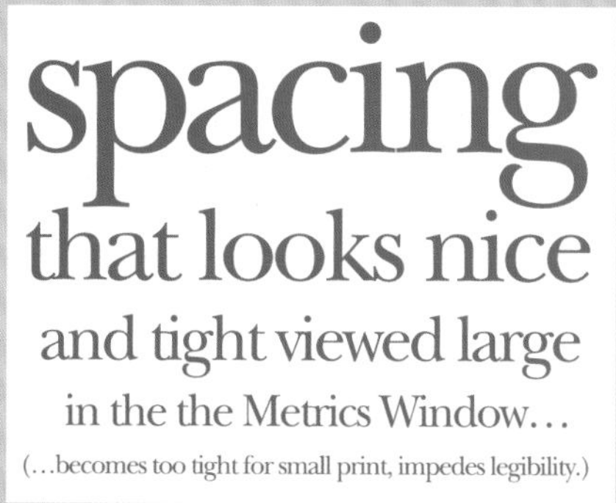
spacing
that looks nice
and tight viewed large
in the the Metrics Window...
(...becomes too tight for small print, impedes legibility.)

General Spacing

Don't space a font too closely—give it some air—so it will be suitable for the largest number of users and uses. Fonts designed mainly for small text should have wider spaces so that at 10-point size, the letters don't visually collide. Fonts for larger, display headlines can have tighter spacing. Most fonts, though, will be used large *and* small, so spacing should be a happy medium.

HIHOHIHO, A-Spacing We Will Go

Here's how to establish sidebearing standards. Open your font, then open a Metrics window. Type *H-H-H* and drag one right sidebearing guide until you like the spacing. Add a letter *I* to the string, or perhaps an *N*. Adjust spacing if needed. Make sure these letters are centered in their slots and that left and right sidebearing values are identical. Copy and Paste that numeric value into the sidebearing fields of all other straight stem letters (see chart, page 221). Next, type *H-O-H-O-O-H* to establish side values for round letters next to straight letters. Then space lowercase letters, using strings such as *i-n-h-n-i* and *n-o-n-o-o-n*. Make sure, despite their different shapes, that spacing ends up looking even from letter to letter. Use the same values for all similar letters.

HHIHNHMIB
Start by comparing various straight-side letters to decide on the best spacing width.
HHOHOOHDHG
Round letters always space closer to straight-side letters, and even closer to each other.
inhni nonoon ecd
The rule applies to lowercases, and to all letter styles: Set standards for all similar letters.

Systematic Spacing

Right, depending upon the type style, a spacing system can often be devised that applies to a majority of a font's characters. In the first three categories, all straight-sided letters should get the same sidebearing value. Letters with similar right sides, such as *B-P-R*, should have the same right sidebearing values. But in every font, there will always be "special needs" characters, requiring individual spacing that must be done by eye.

Symmetrical Characters (& Quasi-Symmetrical)

HIMOQSUZ80! ATVWXY ilmnosu vwxz

Straight Left-Side Characters

BDEFHIKLMNPRU bhiklmnpru 5!

Straight Right-Side Characters

HIJMN adghijlmnqu

Some Special-Needs Characters

BCEFJKLPRfjkrty47

a
ABCD!
b
ABCDEFGHIJKL
c
ABCDE

Mono- and Uniformly Spaced Fonts

Spacing would be a breeze if the widths of all character slots were identical, as in monospaced Courier Bold, a, or if both left and right sidebearing values could be kept the same for all characters. But this usually applies only to geometric sans serifs, or novelty fonts like Mekanik, b, and the author's DotCom, c.

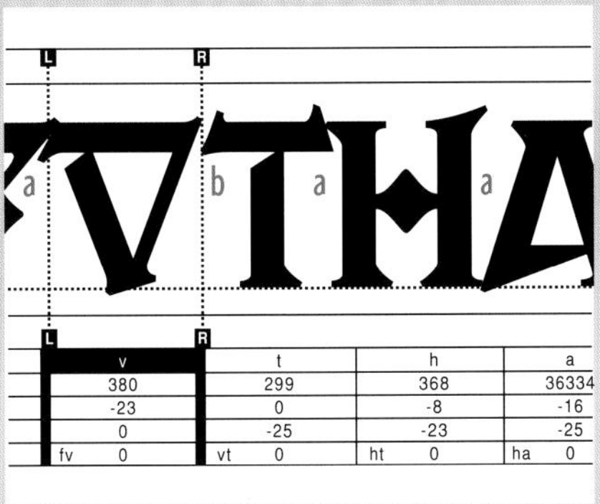
L R
VTHA
a b a a
L R
v t h a
380 299 368 36334
-23 0 -8 -16
0 -25 -23 -25
fv 0 vt 0 ht 0 ha 0

Crash Clearance

Avoid giving negative-value (e.g., -23) sidebearings to letters like *W-A-V-Y-T*, in an attempt to close spacing gaps. Allow some clearance, b, so such letters don't crash with quotes and other wide characters, as at a, above. We can kern away some crashing, but first, spacing should be designed to deal with it. Also, avoid extreme negative-value left sidebearings. In Quark XPress, such letters at the start of a column will appear as though their left edges are chopped off.

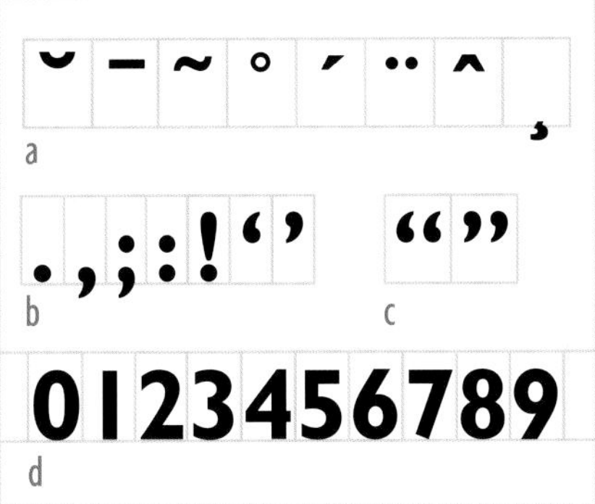
a
b
c
0123456789
d

Spacing Character Groups

Larger foundries often monospace certain groups of characters within set widths to obviate kerning. Accent characters, a; narrow punctuation, b; wide punctuation, c; and numerals, d will be centered within a given set width for each group. This simplifies spacing and makes an orderly font. I prefer to give number *1* a narrower width of its own, however, so it doesn't float in space. Also, accented composite characters are typically spaced, but not given kerning.

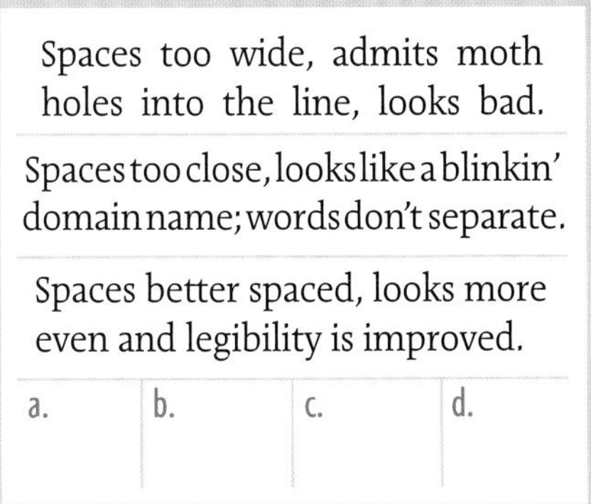
Spaces too wide, admits moth holes into the line, looks bad.
Spaces too close, looks like a blinkin' domain name; words don't separate.
Spaces better spaced, looks more even and legibility is improved.
a. b. c. d.

Spacing the Space

Don't forget to reduce the Space character's overwide default width of 1000 em units. Reassess this width in context by typing several words into the Metrics window, reducing viewing size and adjusting as appropriate. Some say the best Space width is about that of lowercase *i*. Above, a comparison of spaces from a, Palatino; b, Helvetica; c, Bermuda Squiggle; and d, Souvenir (only the pure of heart can see them).

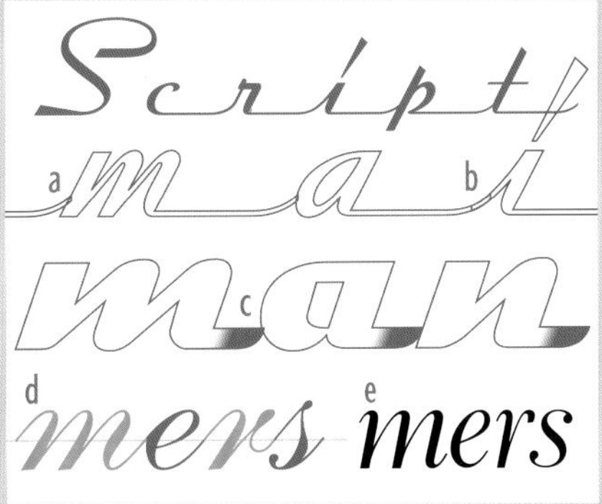
Script
a b
c
man
d e
mers mers

Universal Spacing for Scripts

Above, at a, right sidebearings for Streamline's lowercase are set at 0. Left sidebearings are all negative so preceding letters will overlap, b. Magneto's right-side connecting strokes, c, are all identical and set at 0. Precision is the key to designing ligatures for scripts like Shelley Allegro, d. Easy option: The letter shapes of Dorchester Script, e, suggest a script font, but don't connect. Script fonts require only minimal kerning.

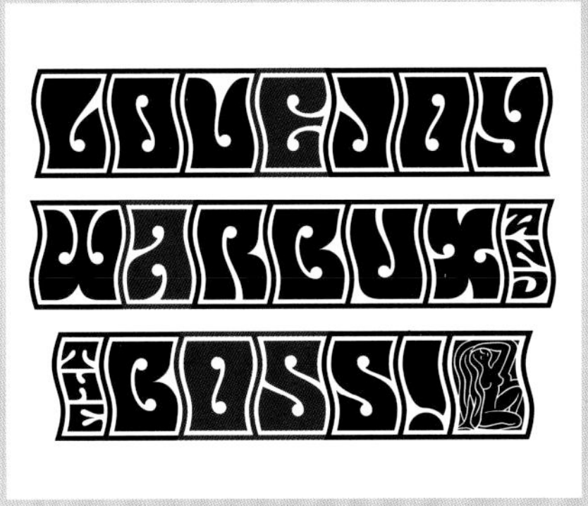

Spaced-Out Spacing

All the left-leaning uppercase characters in my font Peace Outline can transition to right-leaning lowercase by inserting one of eight symmetrical "turn" characters (highlighted). Font uses no kerning; all spaces are slightly negative (alphabetic characters are all right side -36, left side -64), which allows letters to snuggle up. This is just one example of a custom spacing concept that is intrinsic to the font design.

KERNING

An obscure process that many otherwise erudite persons have never even heard of is that of kerning letters to ensure that they fit together snugly and without gaps that would ruin a font's even spacing.

The goal, as already stressed, is to first space our letters evenly and methodically to avoid too much kerning, then to kern all remaining incorrigible pairs. The most particularly troublesome characters—those with parts that slope or stick out—vary according to the style of font. The following are the usual culprits:

AJLPTVWY47fjrtvwy

Right, at a, after establishing ideal letter spacing based on straight-sided *H*, as demonstrated in the preceding pages, we proceed to place every other letter, one at a time, in between *H-H* and space them. Letters *T* and *A*, which pose no special challenges in the *H* string, present a classic case for kerning when paired together.

At b, letters *T-A-T-A* are shown in Fontographer's Metrics window without any kerning. Note that the values in the Kern fields (bottom row at c) are all set at 0 for no kerning. Obviously, the spacing between these letters is way too wide.

At d, kerning has been done (perhaps too tightly) by clicking in the center of *A* and dragging the Kern bar to the left until *A* tucked under *T*. The same kerning value must be used for both sides of symmetrically shaped letters so that spacing is even. Imagine how crummy such combinations would look if there were more space on one side than the other, as below.

TATAVAWAWOAO

a
HHTHHAHH

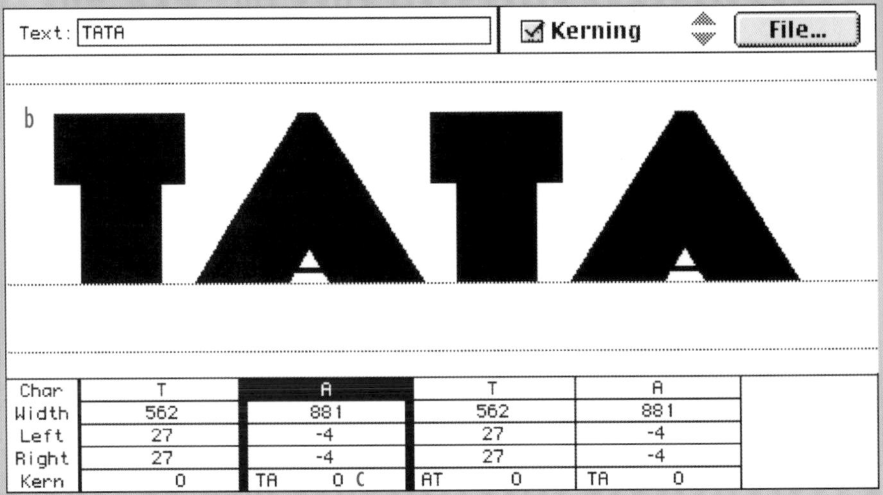
Text: TATA
Kerning
File...
b
TATA
Char T A T A
Width 562 881 562 881
Left 27 -4 27 -4
Right 27 -4 27 -4
Kern 0 TA 0 C AT 0 TA 0

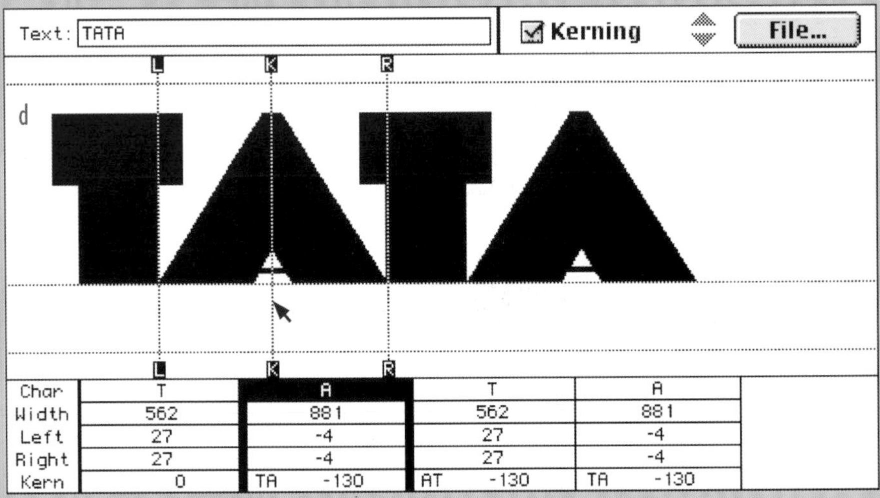
Text: TATA
Kerning
File...
L K R
d
TATA
Char T A T A
Width 562 881 562 881
Left 27 -4 27 -4
Right 27 -4 27 -4
Kern 0 TA -130 AT -130 TA -130

Kerning: Long Form

When I made my first fonts, I assumed that the best way to kern was to start with *AA*, move on to *AB, AC*, and so on to *AZ*, then go back and start again with *BA, BB, BC, BD*, etc. This approach, aside from taking a really long time, is not a good one for at least three reasons: (1) If spacing is done correctly, 75 percent of kerning is not required, (2) Too many kerning pairs bogs a font down, making it weigh more, and load and print more slowly. A font does seem quite light on the kilobyte scale these days, compared with the ongoing growth of the rest of our files, but still, economy is good, (3) Kerning the long way does not allow us to compare kerning values on similar letters. So each kern pair we create depends on our memories to visually gauge values and apply them evenly with each drag of the kern bar. For example, the kerned space between *U* and *N* should be exactly the same as between *U* and *M*, but it may not be if we're just eyeballing the kerning of each pair.

Frequently Fussy Kerning Pairs

The number of kerning pairs a font requires is entirely based on the style of characters. Some of the following commonly called-for kerning pairs may not pertain at all to our fonts. And other pairs, not included in this brief listing, may present themselves as eyesores needing kerning to correct.

AC AG AO AQ AS AT AU AV AW AY A' A" Ac Ad Ae Ag Ao Aq As At Au Av Aw Ay BV BW BY CT CV CW CY DA DJ DV DW DY FA FG FJ FO FT FV FW FY Fa Fc Fb Fe Fo Fr Fs Ff Fu Fy GY KO Ka Ko Ku Ky LO LT LV LW LY L' L" Lo Lv Lw Ly OA OT OV OW OX OY PA PT PV PW PY Pa Pc Pd Pe Po Ps P. P, RA RT RV RW RY Ra Rc Rd Re Ro Rs Ry SS ST SY SV SW Sy Sv Sw TA TO TT Ta Te Ti To Tr Ts Tu Tw Ty T. T, T: T; T- VA VO Va Ve Vi Vm Vn Vo Vp Vr Vs Vu Vy V. V, V: V; V- WA WO Wa We Wi Wo Wr Wu Wy W. W, W: W; W- YA YC YG YO Ya Ye Yi Yo Yp Yr Yu Yv Y. Y. Y: Y; Y- XO xo ew ey ev ff fg f' f ij 's 't of ot ov ow oy ox qu qa ra rc rd re rf rh ro rq rr rt ru rv rw rx ry rz r. r, r- ve vo v. v, w. w, y. y,

a b
SHNOOKS
c
AVARICE
d
ABETTING

Fancy Kerning

When kerning a font, avoid "editorializing" by imposing cool, custom kerning. Leave such touches, as the ever-popular shared stems, a; overlapping *O*s, b; mirror-mirror effect, c; and touching *T*s, d, to the customer who purchases the font. As with spacing, we kern for the average user and usage. By the way, I always feel that it looks better to give the exact same angle to the sloping sides of *A-V-W*, unlike at c, so they will appear parallel when paired.

a
b
c

Sans Kerning

Elsewhere in this book it has been pointed out that certain fonts with extravagant caps, such as scripts and gothics, should never be set all caps. Therefore, we need not kern caps to caps except in this regard: The worst cap collisions should be corrected through kerning, just in case somebody who didn't read this book sets our script font all in caps. Also, it is good practice to type an upper and lower alphabet string into the metrics window and kern all pairs in order from *A* to *Z* and *a* to *z*, just to be sure that the letters won't crash if the font is displayed as an alphabet in a catalog. Above, at a, Gigi Plain, a casual script, without kerning of swash caps. At b, Raceway, a streamlined script with the alphabet kerned. At c, Engravers Old English simply utilizes generous sidebearings for all caps, so kerning is not an issue, although the looseness of the set could be for a user who might just have to decrease tracking.

Auto Spacing and Kerning

Authorities agree that, whereas FOG's Auto Spacing and Auto Kerning features are helpful, they are not to be completely relied upon. Here are some ways in which these features may be used to good measure:

1. Use Auto Spacing initially, with the knowledge that tweaking will be required afterwards. Remember, edge-to-edge centering will not correctly space those letters whose weight distribution is off-balance, as below.

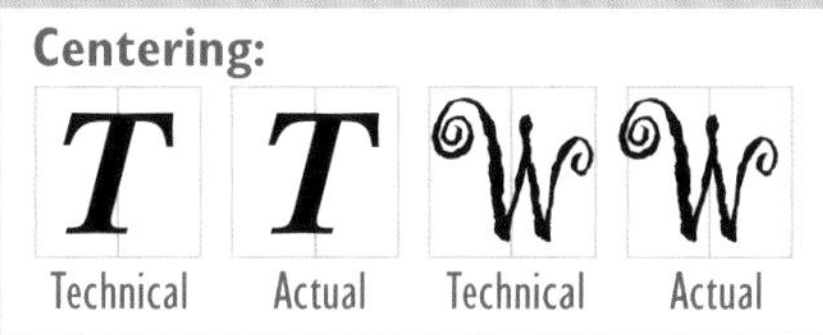
Centering:
T T W W
Technical
Actual
Technical
Actual

2. Use Auto Kerning, but first back up a copy of the font in case you become mired in results you don't like. Be prepared to make lots of manual tweaks after using Auto Kerning.

3. Some suggest doing Auto Spacing once, selecting all characters in the font window, applying the Equalize Sidebearings command, then Auto Spacing a second time before moving on to Auto Kerning.

4. If we've Auto or manually spaced a font and later decide we want to universally increase or decrease space between letters, go to METRICS>Set Metrics (⌥-⌘-M) and type in the characters requiring change and the degree of change to be made to right, left, or both sidebearings.

Forget the Quick Brown Fox

Spacing and kerning, like letters themselves, are best judged within the context of words set in lines of type. Our eyes take in letters better as words than as random strings of characters. To facilitate this process, I compiled the following collection of words that I call "Kern King." It contains virtually every alphabetic kerning pair. The list includes names, English and non-English words, highly obscure words, and several that I had to make up. There are many redundant pairs, of course, and the list could be methodically truncated by some smart designer with time on his or her hands (hint!).

How to Use Kern King

First, complete the spacing of your font in progress, but before adding kerning, generate a font and load it into your fonts folder. Copy Kern King from my web site, www.logofontandlettering.com, paste it into a word processing or layout program document, look at the words in lowercase, then as all caps, and see how they set. Make a list of all the problem pairs: those that are too far apart, and those that are too close together. Open up the font again in Fontographer or FontLab, make corrections to spacing and add kerning. Generate the font a second time. Check again. Repeat process until kerning is perfect.

KERN KING: lynx tuft frogs, dolphins abduct by proxy the ever awkward klutz, dud, dummkopf, jinx snubnose filmgoer, orphan sgt. renfruw grudgek reyfus, md. sikh psych if halt tympany jewelry sri heh! twyer vs jojo pneu fylfot alcaaba son of nonplussed halfbreed bubbly playboy guggenheim daddy coccyx sgraffito effect, vacuum dirndle impossible attempt to disvalue, muzzle the afghan czech czar and exninja, bob bixby dvorak wood dhurrie savvy, dizzy eye aeon circumcision uvula scrungy picnic luxurious special type carbohydrate ovoid adzuki kumquat bomb? afterglows gold girl pygmy gnome lb. ankhs acme aggroupment akmed brouhha tv wt. ujjain ms. oz abacus mnemonics bhikku khaki bwana aorta embolism vivid owls often kvetch otherwise, wysiwyg densfort wright you've absorbed rhythm, put obstacle kyaks krieg kern wurst subject enmity equity coquet quorum pique tzetse hepzibah sulfhydryl briefcase ajax ehler kafka fjord elfship halfdressed jugful eggcup hummingbirds swingdevil bagpipe legwork reproachful hunchback archknave baghdad wejh rijswijk rajbansi rajput ajdir okay weekday obfuscate subpoena liebknecht marcgravia ecbolic arcticward dickcissel pincpinc boldface maidkin adjective adcraft adman dwarfness applejack darkbrown kiln palzy always farmland flimflam unbossy nonlineal stepbrother lapdog stopgap sx countdown basketball beaujolais vb. flowchart aztec lazy bozo syrup tarzan annoying dyke yucky hawg gagzhukz cuzco squire when hiho mayhem nietzsche szasz gumdrop milk emplotment ambidextrously lacquer byway ecclesiastes stubchen hobgoblins crabmill aqua hawaii blvd. subquality byzantine empire debt obvious cervantes jekabzeel anecdote flicflac mechanicville bedbug couldn't i've it's they'll they'd dpt. headquarter burkhardt xerxes atkins govt. ebenezer lg. lhama amtrak amway fixity axmen quumbabda upjohn hrumpf

COMPARISON

I created this chart to compare more-or-less equivalent letter-drawing features in old standby Fontographer (FOG) with the newest font creation software, FontLab (FL), and in Adobe Illustrator (AI), which is still used by many font designers to generate their initial character drawings.

FONTOGRAPHER	FONTLAB	ILLUSTRATOR
Clean Up Paths This feature (⌥-⌘-C) places points in extrema, removes unneeded points, and at lower settings it preserves the original character shape well, even improving it (but tangent points may be converted).	TOOLS>Outline>Optimize (⌘-E) cleans up points, and can even be set to straighten crooked lines. But degree of Optimization can't be adjusted by user. Optimize was designed not as a drawing aid, but to fix point errors that might impede font generation.	Offers no way to automatically place points in extrema or clean up extraneous points. OBJECT> Paths>Simplify does such a poor job of preserving contour—despite offering user tweakable parameters— that its use is not even worth considering.
Three Point Styles Has Corner, Curve and Tangent point styles. The latter transitions from straight to curved paths. The Tangent point's outgoing handle stays constrained to the straight angle assuring smoother transitions.	Has three point styles, like FOG, but FL's can be set to appear in black or in colors. Add points to a contour by clicking with a point tool. Or, with the Edit Tool (arrow tool), hold Control-Option and click anywhere on a contour.	Two point styles handle all bezier functions. The Convert Anchor Point Tool changes smooth points to corner points, but there is no curve-to-smooth or "tangent" transition point style making the liklihood of bumpy transitions very high.
Constrains Handles at Any Angle By holding Shift-Option keys, FOG constrains angle of bezier point. So as we adjust one handle, the opposite handle's position is maintained, whatever its angle. This is an important drawing aid.	Hold the Shift-Option keys to constrain handles to any angle while adjusting them. This works the same as FOG. Also, when drawing with the Pen Tool, Shift will constrain bezier handles to horizontal, vertical or 45°. FOG and AI also do this.	Holding Shift will constrain angle of bezier handles to 0°, 45°, and 90°, but if the handles are at any other degree of angle, we are forced to edit one handle while manually attempting to maintain the opposite handle's angle, which can be frustrating.
Curves Thrust Outward When a bezier point or points are removed from a curve (⌘-M), it tends to spring outward from its center, like a tensed steel band. See page 226 to learn how this feature can benefit our drawings.	Thrust of curves works similarly to Fontographer, making possible a similar approach to editing character contours.	When a point is removed from a curved path, the path collapses inward toward the center of the object. Usually, we want the curve to stay the same except without the extraneous point(s), but now we are forced to completely restore the curve.
Straighten Paths Paths that should be straight vertical or horizontal have a habit of becoming askew. Select the two points bordering a path and hit ⌘-E to straighten them. Works with any number of points at once.	Select two or more points, click on one of them while holding Control>Align Points. Also, the Edit Tool displays crosshair guides as a point is being moved and can help us to visually align the point with another point, or its bezier handle.	To align two or more crooked points, hit ⌥-⌘-J. In the Average window, click a radio button for Vertical or Horizontal. Problem is, one hand then has to leave "keyboard position" or mouse to hit Okay. And radio buttons don't default to last pressed. Sucks.
Minus Points To remove one or more points from a path or paths (FOG calls it merging points) without breaking the paths themselves, hit Merge Points (⌘-M). It's easy and hand stays on keyboard; no tool necessary.	The Delete key removes points without breaking the path, providing that this option is *unchecked* in TOOLS>Preferences>Glyph Window>Edit/Delete Command Breaks Contour. If the box is checked, Deleting a point *will* break the path or contour.	Removing points without breaking the path (Delete key breaks path) requires changing to the Delete Anchor Point Tool. Although this tool becomes the Add Anchor Point Tool when Option key is held, it's a drag to have to change tools just for point removal.
Three Arrow Key Distance Settings Hitting an Arrow key moves any selected object ten units. Option-Arrow moves a tenth unit, and Shift-Arrow moves one-hundred units. The initial distance setting is editable in the Preferences window.	Has one arrow key distance setting of one unit. An object can be moved a distance of ten units by holding Shift and hitting an Arrow key.	Has one Arrow key distance setting. Initial setting can be specified at EDIT>Preferences>General> Keyboard Increment. Holding the Shift key increases the increment x10.
Compound Paths Correct Path Direction (⌥-⌘-K) turns overlapping objects, such as a circle within a circle, into a compound path. Or, select one path, and click the Path Direction Indicator box in a character window.	Control>Transform>Contour>Reverse Contour will create compound paths. Control>Reverse Contour will also do the trick. Many features not found in the upper menu bar are accessible in copious Control key-activated pop-up menus.	Make Compound Path (⌘-8) works fine with newly-created objects. Otherwise, sometimes it works, sometimes partially, and sometimes not at all. If not, try Subtract from Shape. Or use Divide and manually select and delete counters from a letter or object.
Retract Bezier Handles Bezier handles—one or many—may be retracted (removed) from points with ⌘-R. Length of handles can also be numerically altered or retracted in the Point Information window (⌘-I).	Click on the point, press Control>Retract BCPs (Bezier Control Points). Can also be done in the Node Properties Panel, which has special buttons to retract BCPs. As in any program, bezier handles can also be manually dragged into the point.	Retracting handles requires changing tools to the Convert Anchor Point Tool. Or we can drag a handle into its point, but it may twist, ruining the curve on the opposite side of the point. The Straight Lines option in the Simplify window will retract *all* handles.
Unite Shapes/Remove Overlap Several shapes can be united into one (⌘-O), but results can be dicey *even if* Correct Path Direction (⌘-K) was done first. FOG can't knock one shape out of another, it lacks Pathfinder tools.	TOOLS>Outline>Merge Contours unites one or more shapes as one. >Get Intersection deletes all but the overlapped area, so it could be used to knock out a shape. >Delete Intersection removes the overlapped area. Will make a compound path.	Pathfinder Pallet allows uniting of shapes, subtracting of shapes from others, and Divide functions, all of which are essential tools in letter drawing. In Illustrator 9.0, the Pathfinders had intuitive names. In version 10.0, pallet was remodeled, infuriatingly.

FONTOGRAPHER	FONTLAB	ILLUSTRATOR
Import Vector Paths Originally, the Option Copy (⌥-⌘-C) would import Illustrator art into FOG as bezier paths. Now, we must save Illustrator art as early version EPS files and go to FILE>Import EPS. I miss Copy and Paste.	To Paste AI vector art into FL requires first going to Illustrator's Preferences> Files & Clipboard>AICB, then choosing Preserve Paths. Now characters drawn in AI can be Copied and Pasted directly into FL (see additional details below).	Not applicable
Vector Art Pastes to Cap Height When vector art is imported into FOG, it always scales to cap height. This is good, provided we include a larger rectangular envelope with the characters to be pasted (see page 218).	To paste to cap height between FL and AI, create a cap-height rectangle in FL, Copy and Paste it into AI. Then resize all characters drawn in illustrator to the rectangle height and Paste them into FL. This is a funny reversal of the FOG technique.	Not applicable
Special Effects Type effects like drop shadows and outlines can be manually made, but not automatically; several steps will be required. Global transformation to every character at once can be done to save time.	Has Effects features that curve and make outlines and/or drop shadows in a few styles (see page 195) but most will require tweaking. Has an Envelope distort feature that, as with Illustrator, create shapes that usually emerge too weird for everyday usage.	Version 10 finally provided Envelope Distort warp tools that produce very clean and sharp results (see page 194). Some common, important shape maps are missing, however. Disregarding the automation of effects, we can still hand draw any effect in AI.
Equalize Sidebearings This feature centers a letter between sidebearings. It will also center selected points only. For example, select only the top of an *A and* use Equalize Sidebearings to center it between its diagonal side stems.	Characters can be centered within the character slot with Control>Transform>Metrics>Center Glyph. Won't center just selected points, as in FOG. Specifying sidebearing units of equal measure can also be done in this dialogue window.	Horizontal Align Center in the Align pallet will center multiple objects over one another but won't center just the selected points in a drawing in relation to its overall shape. However, the Align pallet also has handy Align Left and Right features absent from FOG.
Expand Stroke For making outline letters, FOG does a good job although expanded outlines are not always precisely parallel to original strokes and therefore may require some spot tweaking.	Has two ways to do this: Make Parallel Path gives square corners, keeps most curves parallel but, like FOG, not perfectly. Expand Strokes offers swelling strokes, won't allow square corners, and results need much tweaking. Both filters offer many options.	Has various brush styles and sizes that can be applied to paths, and of course, paths can be stroked to any width. Use OBJECT>Expand to release brush effects or OBJECT>Path>Outline Stroke to make stroked paths into filled objects.
Arrow Tool With the lock showing in the character window, Arrow Tool can be changed to other tools by hitting keys 0 through 9. Holding the Command key temporarly toggles any tool back to Arrow Tool.	The Edit Tool (arrow tool) can be accessed through any other tool with a short tap of the Command key. Another tap turns returns to the original tool. This is cool because Command needn't be indefinitely held. Keys 1 through 8 will toggle to various tools.	Has three Arrow Tools. When working in any other tool, the last selected Arrow Tool can be temporarily accessed while the Command key is held.
Generating Font Files Prior to FontLab's emergence, all of us used FOG to generate Mac and Windows fonts as TrueType and Post Script 1, and then it all seemed fine.	All users seem to agree that font generation is far more reliably done in FontLab than in FOG. And of course, FOG can't make Open Type fonts or provide encodings such as WinEncoding-Greek or many of the zillions of other international font encodings.	Not applicable

CONCLUSIONS

FONTOGRAPHER As of this writing, the fate of FOG is unknown. An update seems unlikely. Yet it is a program that evolved to a very satisfactory state—many designers adore its simplicity—making an update necessary mainly to keep current and compatible with evolving technology. Should Macromedia update FOG, I fear the code will be completely rewritten (by insouciant programmers who've never created fonts), FL will be badly copied and much of what is positive about FOG will be lost.

FONTLAB This complex program may force font designers to stop designing and go back to school—if only for a week or two—once again. Many of FL's wild features, such as digital point information readouts and matrices of colorful gridlines take some getting used to after FOG. Tal Leming at House Industries makes his position on FontLab clear: "I now do all my drawing in FontLab," he says. "I like the drawing tools a lot more than other tools that I've used, not to mention the way FL generates fonts and handles other production tasks." Importantly, FL is compatibile with Mac's OS 10, which FOG is not. Font designer Cyrus Highsmith says, "Between not having a Mac OSX version and not being able to make Open Type fonts, FOG is rapidly becoming very useless. So far I have been very impressed by Fontlab. I actually had to read large parts of the manual to figure it out. But a big part of the reason it is difficult to use is because it is a very sophisticated program—you can do a lot more with it than you can with Fontographer." Mark Record of The Font Bureau lauds FL's open Python scripting, "I can't stress Python enough. When I'm faced with 20-50 fonts that need to be modified in some little way, I thank the heavens for scripting. It takes a while to learn—and you really have to be a geek to want to learn it—but once you do...Wow!" The makers of FontLab display a refreshing openness to user input which will undoubtedly result in an ironing out of kinks and further improvements in future releases.

ILLUSTRATOR As makers of the premiere vector drawing program, Adobe, In my opinion, must work on enhancing the accuracy and efficiency of its drawing tools with extrema/clean-up settings, and other features contained in FOG and FL, as noted in the chart above. Illustrator should offer us the option of replacing fonts that are no longer in our system folders when we reopen an old file, and should simply delete "offending operands" for us instead of refusing to open damaged files. AI must remove all the "Can't do" warnings to let us perform operations as we wish to! AI is a great program but it could be improved if it sought the advice of high-level, professional illustrators who use the program complexly. AI is not a font creation tool, so if used to draw letters, these drawings must be imported into FL or FOG.

BEZIER COMPARISON

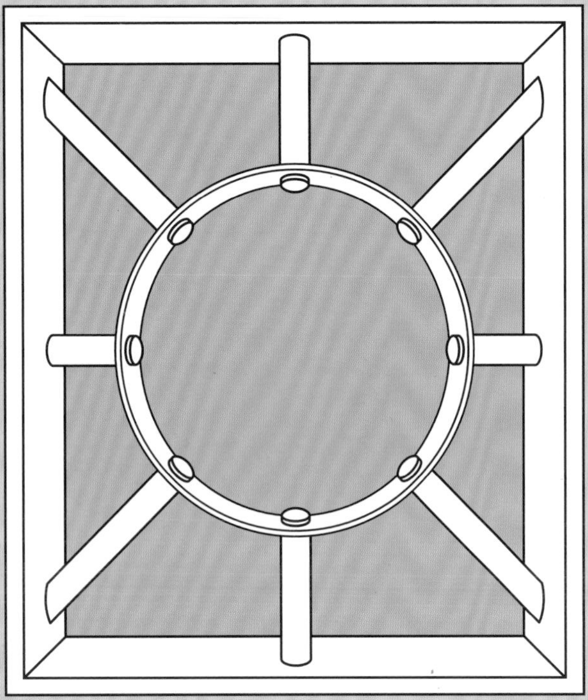

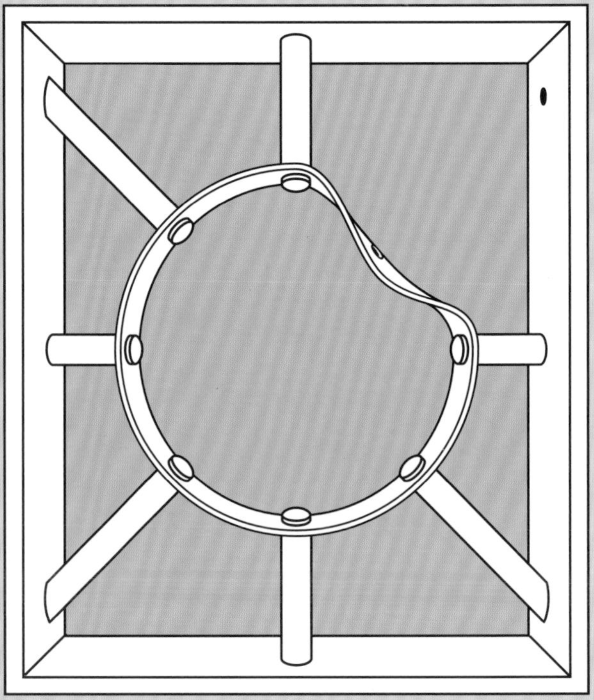

Adobe ILLUSTRATOR In the diagrams above, the bolts holding the steel band into shape represent Bezier points. Only four points are needed to define a circle, but I've added more for this demo. When a point in an Illustrator drawing is removed with the Delete Anchor Point tool, the shape collapses, as in the diagram above right. It's as though the tension is toward the center of the shape, so removing a point causes that segment of the path to draw inward. This sucks, because major tweaks must be done to the surrounding points to get the shape back where we wanted it, minus the extraneous point.

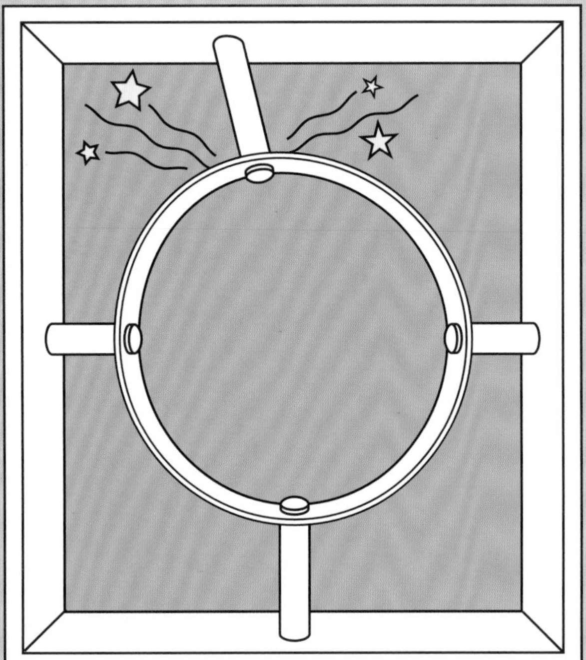

BOING!

Macromedia FONTOGRAPHER Bezier points in Fontographer function differently than in Illustrator. It's a difference that is of enormous benefit to those working in the program. Fontographer's paths are indeed like steel bands, but held in tension. Here, the direction of force is outward, and the tendency of a path is always to self-correct when forced by us into awkward curves by a misplaced bezier point. I allow Fontographer to improve my letterforms by routinely removing certain points of which I am unsure, as in the diagram above right, to let the path spring back into its own natural shape. In most cases, I am pleased with Fontographer's "choices." This natural shape correction also tends to occur when we use Fontographer's Clean Up Paths.

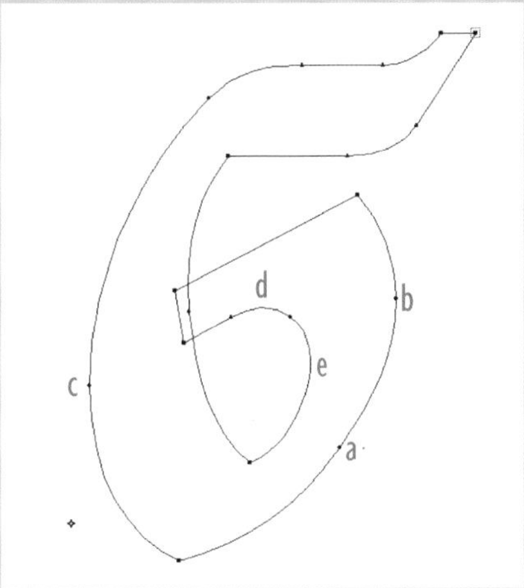
d
b
c
e
a

Relaxing the Curve in Fontographer
Above, the number *6* from my font Margarete began life with bumpy, forced curves at a, b, c, d and e.

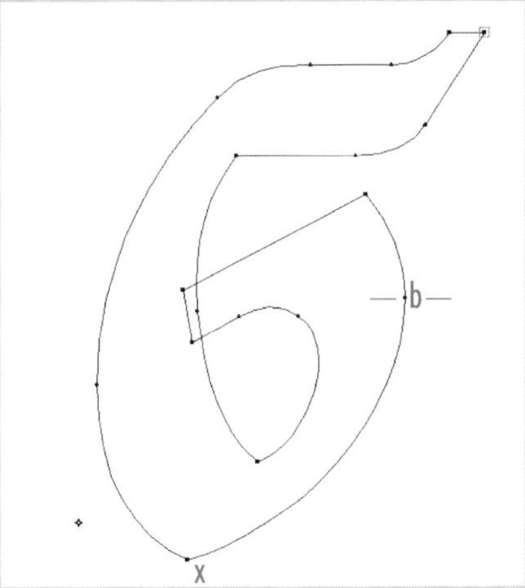
b
x

1. Point a was removed by selecting it and hitting ⌘-M (*M* for Merge Points). The curve between x and b is relaxed, but point b still forces the shape unnaturally.

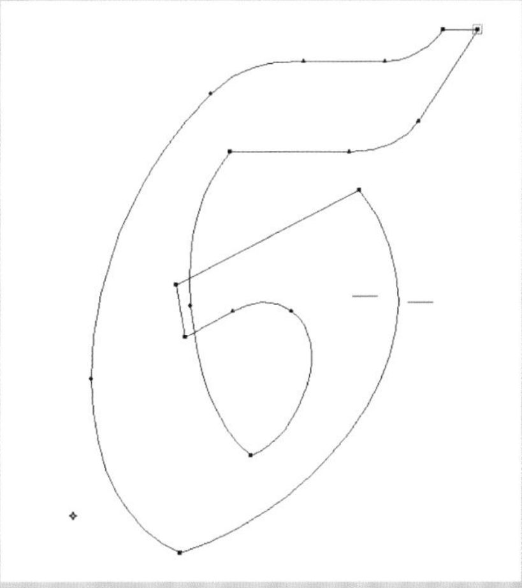

2. Point b was removed by selecting it and hitting ⌘-M. Entire curve is relaxed, extrema position has lowered slightly, softening what before had been a bulge.

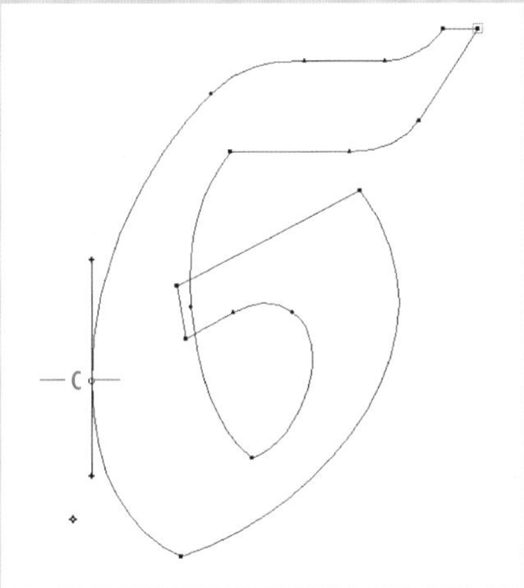
c

3. I don't like point c, either. It seems to be restricting the potential exuberance of this part of the curve. Let's remove it.

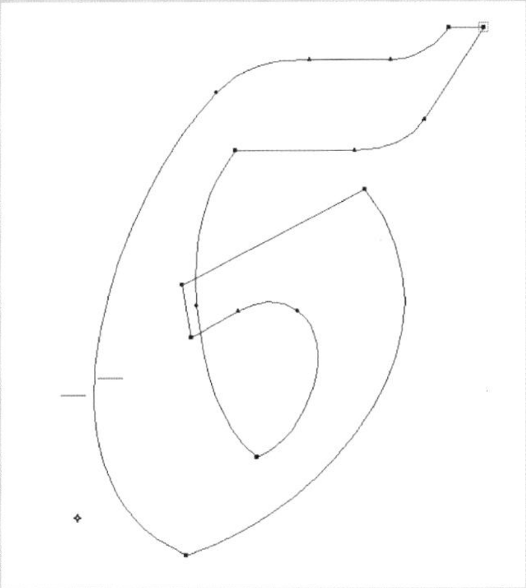

4. Oops, not good. The extrema position has dropped and bulged outward. This technique doesn't always work. Sometimes, removing a point ruins the curve.

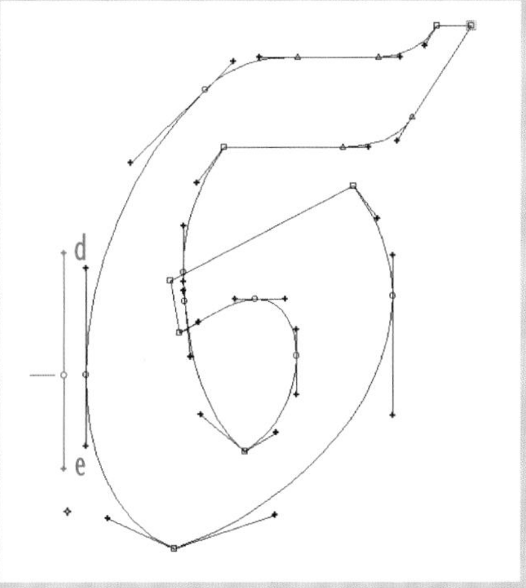
d
e

5. So, I replaced the point and shortened the bezier handles, d and e, to improve the curve. Finally, I let Clean Up Paths (⌥-⌘-C) place my points in extrema.

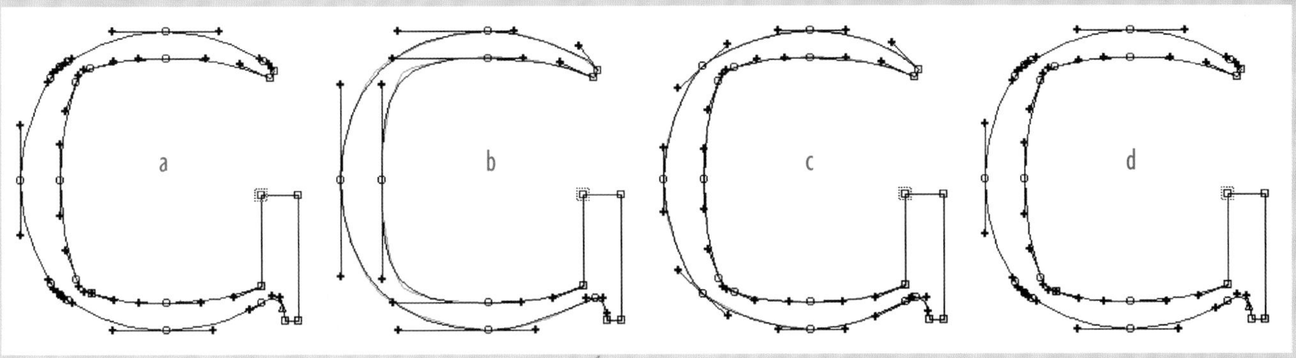
a
b
c
d

CLEAN UP PATHS This is my favorite feature in Fontographer. I often import nonalphabetic Adobe Illustrator drawings into FOG just to Clean Up Paths (CUP). As explained opposite, and above, by removing unneeded points along a path and placing points in extrema, FOG usually smooths out curves. Hit ⌥-⌘-C to open the CUP dialogue window to choose a cleanup level from 1–5. My process goes like this: I will move a bezier point off extrema or tilt the handles out of square to try to get the shape I want. I then use CUP to put points back in extrema, and I tweak again, and repeat CUP until I'm happy with the outcome. Above, a, the original letter shape imported from Illustrator. At b, CUP level 4 was too much and the shape was lost (as proven by the original outline in red). At c, level 3 was perfect: my shape was retained, excess points were removed, and remaining points are well positioned. At d, level 1, cleanup was almost nil, so no improvement was seen. **Tip 1:** If CUP places two points close together, instead of one at extrema, that's usually a sign that the curve was badly shaped. **Tip 2:** If CUP changes your curves too much, check them carefully to decide if they might have become better than before. **Tip 3:** If CUP replaces Tangent points with Curve points, decrease the cleanup level to 1 or 2.

Part 4 BUSINESS SECTION

So what if your design and lettering are the world's best, if you lack the skills to sell them. On the other hand, even if your lettering is the world's worst, if you have dynamite selling skills, you'll succeed over the better technician. We've shown you how to draw logos, fonts and lettering. Here's how to sell 'em.

FINDING BUSINESS

Getting freelance work as a beginner can be tough. As with anything you do, keep trying! I suggest finding a friend or relative who has a business of any kind and offering your services—free, if need be—to build up your portfolio with real, not hypothetical design school assignments. The experience of working with real clients is different than doing class assignments. Often the classwork is resented—precisely because it isn't real—and rushed just to get a grade. But as you will no doubt find, paying assignments are no different than school ones in the sense that you will often have to put your heart and soul into a project you have absolutely no interest in. Recognize this fact when doing classwork—exult in each new challenge, and adopt a professional attitude now!

Try to avoid doing hypothetical assignments. If possible, find a real live client to work for, even if that client is yourself.

Advertising our wares, in one way or another, is still the only way to get work. Michael Schwab once said to me, "The job of the designer, when no other job is available, should be the job of self-promotion." There are passive and proactive approaches to this. A combination of both will be helpful.

PASSIVE APPROACH

•***Design a web site*** to showcase your portfolio. Include meta tags that carry descriptive terms, including references to your locality like "Palo Alto logos." Search engines will eventually find you and so, hopefully, will potential clients.

•***Do a few great jobs,*** hope someone notices, seeks you out (hopefully they are able to find you) and hires you.

•***Work for a design studio*** and let the owners worry about finding clients.

•***Join a professional organization*** like the Graphic Artist's Guild (www.gag.org) for tips, advice, camaraderie and for their jobline. Local user groups, for instance for Flash or Photoshop, are also helpful for forming strategic alliances.

PROACTIVE APPROACH

•***Place ads in creative directories*** like American Showcase, RSVP, and Workbook. Artists such as photographers, illustrators, handletterers and logo designers (though not general-category designers) can purchase pages on which to display samples. These directories are distributed free to thousands of art buyers who may hire you if they like your style. Be aware that a page can cost from $2500 to $4000. Never use hypothetical work in such ads, especially if you've used the logo of a company that never hired you. Be aware that many of these directories have become so heavy with competition that a poorly focused page can yield few or no responses.

•***Buy a mailing list*** of design studios, publication art directors, ad agencies and the like. Lists can be gotten from the aforementioned creative directories or by doing an Internet search for lists. Print up and mail to the list a sample sheet or postcard displaying some of your work and directing recipients to your web site where your web portfolio can be seen. Considering the costs of purchasing the list, postage and printing, each piece mailed could total more than $1.00. A slightly cheaper (though cheaper looking!) approach would be to print the mailers on your own desktop laser printer on card stock, if your printer will handle it.

On two occasions I bought mailing lists. The first time yielded a great response. The second time, the list (from a different source) was badly outdated and 20% of my mailers were returned "addressee unknown," which was tragic. Be careful whose lists you buy.

Start by accepting no job for less than $100. As we progress in experience, our minimums should rise accordingly.

• ***Copy names and addresses*** of magazine art directors and assistant art directors from the mastheads of publications you'd like to work for. Get additional names of art directors and agencies from the credits and indexes in design annuals like HOW and Print. Send packets of printed samples and tear sheets, if you can spare them, of your work. This is a cheaper approach—but much more laborious—than buying lists, though your names will be more up-to-date and definitely more targeted.

• ***Send seasonal self-promo*** greeting cards and novelties such as die-cut pop-ups, or silkscreened drinking glasses. Using this method, some designers have for years kept themselves in the eyes of art directors and art buyers. The truth is, for any given assignment, there are 500 artists who could do the job equally well. The one who gets the job will often be the one whose name most recently passed through the AD's awareness. Keep meticulously updated card files (or backed-up computer files) of clients and potential clients.

• ***Buy lists of email addresses*** and send out bulk emails directing people to your site and your design services. You could get some results, but most people will hate getting spammed, even by you.

• ***Walk into local businesses*** and restaurants with your card or larger printed "leave behind" samples, ask them if they need a logo or a web site. Network, talk to people, leave your cards up on bulletin boards all over the place. Leave your studio purposely to go meet people and hobnob. Friends tend to hire friends, so make friends!

• ***Call up art directors*** and ask to show them your portfolio. This used to be the way it was done, but by the mid-1980s it all changed. Very few ADs will see you nowadays because there are far too many of us running around looking for work and it wastes their time to meet you. After all, your work might totally suck. Some agencies have a portfolio drop off policy. You leave the portfolio overnight and pick it up the next day (hoping that someone actually looked at it). I don't know, but I imagine that in smaller towns than New York, there might still be art directors who would let you make an appointment to show your "book."

When showing a portfolio, always tailor it to that client. Don't include your rave flyers when you see a childrens magazine art director. It is better to show fewer samples that are good, than many that are so-so. Never show a portfolio of all school work. No one buys life class drawings, so omit them. You may assume that the variety of school assignments will show your versatility, but the client is focusing only on those aspects of your work that may apply to his needs. He needs to see that you've already done the kind of work he buys so he can trust you to finish an assignment. If the portfolio you build in art school does not include professional-looking hypothetical work that you can bluff as having been real

Below, self-promotional materials show a range of possibilities. Clockwise from top: Michael Doret's page from the *Workbook* directory; Planet Propaganda's impressive tabloid-sized logo portfolio; Tom Nikosey's 48-page, square-bound booklet lavishly showcases his logos and design in full color; Font Diner sells a set of smart, silkscreened glasses like these but also gives them away to choice clients; Leslie Cabarga's four-page mailer announcing new psychedelic fonts; JHI's 17x22-inch conceptual piece in color on newsprint introduces clients to the firm's design aesthetic; a full color, 16-page booklet designed to showcase Leslie Cabarga's fonts; the Font Bureau's 200-page, hard-cover catalog evokes the grand, type foundry catalog of earlier times.

Michael Doret
The Art of Letterform & Image Design
www.MichaelDoret.com
Introducing
Orion
A New Font
Designed by Michael Doret
Available Now for Purchase
Call for Details
Hollywood and Vine
Montana Red
Big Pines Produce Co.
Future Thought
CSS
NIKOSEY
Font Diner
Psychedelic Typography
differen
Font Bureau
Type Specimens
Third Edition
Leslie Cabarga

jobs, you'll need to start doing work that looks or is real as soon as you leave school.

• ***Submit your work to design annuals*** such as Communication Arts, HOW, Print, AIGA, Type Directors Club, Art Directors Club, Creativity and others. This can cost a fair amount of money and often your work will not be selected and you will end up paying for the printing of the winners' work. Still, submitting work to certain annuals is an absolute ritual for many designers and design firms.

• ***Respond when Leslie Cabarga calls you up*** and asks you to submit work to a book he's doing. You'd be surprised that many designers, from whom I requested work, never got it together to respond. True, we're all busy. But it is no accident that certain names in this industry show up time and time again in design annuals and books like this one. They are ones who understand the value of such free publicity.

• ***Link to other designers*** on your site so they will reciprocate. This might seem counterproductive—potential clients could choose a designer you linked to, instead of you. But the reverse is also possible, and it's good karma. Be helpful to anyone who asks for advice. You don't have to feel jealously competitive of other designers. Such insecurity is generally indicative of bad artists, not good ones. I believe the universe rewards us for being generous.

• ***Initiate projects*** of your own. Seymour Chwast once told me, "You can't make money by sitting around waiting for the phone to ring." Chwast's Push Pin Studios for a time issued a magazine and even marketed candy in beautifully designed tins. Type foundries House Industries and Emigré both publish magazines. One of the reasons I've authored over two dozen books during my career is to initiate work for myself, and not have to take orders from a stupid client—other than myself.

• ***Issue press releases*** to design, font and typography magazines and websites to announce any new fonts you've developed or major logo or design commissions you've bagged.

Designers seeking freelance work, or on-staff positions, are frequently so hungry for a bite, we take any job or client who'll accept us and neglect to consider whether we will be happy doing the work. John Homs explained how JHI, his design firm, holds potential clients up to scrutiny. "We believe in looking for companies we want to work with, that seem to share our creative and strategic values. We look for a good fit: not everyone can be your client. Then we politely and persistently pursue those we're interested in. We design a strategy and tactics for the pursuit process, and we've created promotional materials that we can customize. Our one-on-one approach allows the client to really get to know us and vice versa. That's the way great working relationships get started.

The check-is-in-the-mail paradox: The speed with which a check reaches us is in inverse relationship to how badly we need for it to arrive.

THE PRICE IS...DIFFICULT

Pricing is one of the most difficult issues for graphic designers. Unlike at Sears, where the refrigerator price tag reads $499.99, it is much harder to affix an exact price on our work because there are so many more variables to consider, the least of which is that we are selling an intangible commodity: creativity.

There are a handful of refrigerator manufacturers, but we are, perhaps, 200,000 independent contractors with varying levels of skill and experience, from student to old pro. And we're all competing for the same jobs and for clients who often can't recognize any difference in our quality.

To get a basis for pricing, see the *Graphic Artists Guild Handbook: Pricing & Ethical Guidelines,* which is an excellent, well-researched reference book, currently in its 10th edition. The problem then becomes selling clients on these prices. We constantly find ourselves faced with clients who think of designers as hobbyists and dilettantes whose work has no real value because it is not hard goods like bolts or a tractor trailor. "In this case," suggests illustrator Laura Smith, "I would copy pricing info from the *Guild Handbook* and fax it to the client to convince him."

Following is my procedure for negotiating price. These guidelines apply to any piece of design, whether a logo, an advertisement, or a web site.

1. ***Get information before quoting.*** Find out who the client is, or the end client, if you were asked to quote by another designer or by an advertising agency. Ask how extensively the piece will be used and for how long. What will be the extent of its distribution? Ask how many additional uses the piece will have beyond the initial use. Ask how large it is to appear in print. This is the same basis upon which stock photo and art companies determine pricing.

2. ***Get the client to speak first.*** In the pricing game, as has oft been said, the loser is the one who speaks first. Ask the client what he's budgeted for the project. Hopefully, he won't respond, "I dunno, what would *you* charge for it?" Actually, he does know what he wants to spend, but he also knows this pricing rule, and he hopes you'll tip your hand first. If the client tells you his budget is $1000, he's really giving you his low end. So you put on an injured tone and say, well I was really thinking of $2500 Then you both can compromise on $2000 But if you speak first, telling him that the job is worth $2500, He'll assume that's your high mark and *he'll* sound wounded, start moaning, and tell you his hands are tied, that his budget is $825 but maybe he could squeeze $1200 out *just for you.*

When a client names his price, always ask for more. Perhaps the most important reason to make the client speak first is that he may offer a price far higher than you would have asked. This has happened to me several times. And when it happens, regain your composure and then... ask for more. Remember, the client always starts out on his low end. Many times, just by having the guts to say, "Well, I'd really like to get $____ for this," I have upped a price by as much as 50%.

Sometimes, of course, the price a client throws out really is his budget and there's no negotiating. So then you have to find a way of gracefully accepting, or refusing the offer. Pricing is just like dating: Both parties accept that there's going to be some initial awkwardness, but you have to be willing to work through it to consummate the deal.

3. ***Give a pricing range.*** Sometimes it's better to provide an estimate, for example, of between $2000 and $3000, rather than name a fixed price. This covers you in case of unexpected changes or addi-

tions. It may also sound less scary to the client because it lets him know you have some flexibility. Years ago a client called and asked me how much I'd charge to do a certain logo. I told him $1000. He said, "$1000?" I said, "Yes, $1000." So he said, "I'll call you back." Of course, he never did. This is why some designers never give a price quote on the first phone call.

What I should have done was engage him in conversation about the project and perhaps even discuss ideas in order to begin building a relationship, getting him feeling comfortable with me, finding out we both love cocker-spaniels, etc. After finally naming my price and listening to him swallow hard on the other end of the line, I might have added, "Is that within your budget?" or "I usually charge $1500. for something like this, but I'm really *excited* [bored] about your *project* [really stupid] and would *love* [not!] to work with *you* [or whoever!] on this [to get paid], so I will accept $1000." (It's okay to think, but don't actually say, the stuff I put in brackets.) Now the client sees that you are honest, thrifty, kind, reverent, an animal lover, and willing to work with him to meet his needs because you *really understand where he's coming from* [yawn!].

4. ***Explain your terms up front.*** You'll require a fee for initial sketches or comps, so that if the job is killed at this stage, you will have been compensated for your efforts. There'll be the fee for the execution of the job itself. There will be additional charges if the client changes his mind after you've done the job according to approved sketches, or if he wants additions not called for in the initial job description. And, there'll be a "kill fee" if the job is cancelled, for some reason, before completion. If you finish a job to the client's satisfaction, but he later decides not to use it, you should still receive the agreed-upon fee because you never agreed to work for free and if he doesn't use your work that's his problem. After terms are discussed, e-mail your understanding of the verbal agreement to the client just to make sure his understanding is the same as yours.

We always make our worst decisions—whether in business or in love—when we feel in need. Never work for a client, or date someone, whom your instincts tell you is bad news.

PRICE ACCORDING TO USAGE

It disturbs me to see fixed prices on designers' websites, such as, "Logo: $250; Web site design: $500," not only because those prices are usually too low, but because prices must vary according to the type of client and the extent of usage of our work. Some may say it is unfair to charge one client more than another is charged for the same type and amount of work, just because the first client is more affluent. Isn't that taking advantage? Isn't that price gouging?

No, here's why designers charge AT&T more than Giuseppi's Deli. Giuseppi may use our work for a few ads in the neighborhood newspaper. He may print up 1000 two-color business cards and put some flyers in car windows.

AT&T, or a company of similar size, may spend millions of dollars just to place the logo or ad design they purchase from us in billboards, TV spots and advertisements in high-circulation magazines, nationwide. The usage is greater, so the fee is higher. Moreover, all is fair in the pricing game because everything is negotiable and there is really no way to attach an accurate valuation upon design, except, maybe, to the extent that we can gauge the response to our work in terms of actual sales, although designers are rarely privy to the client's account books.

I used to assume that fees for freelance editorial illustration, which was my main meat for many years, were set according to fixed rates a magazine established for a full page illustration, a half page, or a "spot" (small illustration). Then I discovered that certain artists were demanding higher prices and getting them, so I started doing it too, and getting results.

The capriciousness of art budgets became clear when I found out that if a magazine paid $1100 for a full page illustration, but then decided to use photography instead, it would willingly pay ten times more to fill the same space because, "Photographers have assistants and overhead, they have to hire models, and create sets." After hearing that a few times I realized that there was no such thing as an actual budget. Pricing is based on how little the client can get away with paying us, and in how little regard he holds us.

Designer Gerard Huerta put things in perspective for me when he pointed out, "Time magazine pays us $3000 for cover artwork. The back cover—the same sheet of paper—can cost the magazine's advertisers up to $280,000." We need to remember that the paltry few hundreds or thousands we receive for a logo, product or web site design is usually grossly disproportionate to the profits a client may reap from our work.

In Hollywood, pricing gets down to the level of a Middle Eastern bazaar. It's an ego thing; It makes film people happy if they can cheat someone out of decent pay. Beware, especially, of the entertainment, music, and garment industries, and political campaign work. Such clients seem to pride themselves on cheating people whenever possible. Ask for initial pay up front and make them pay you for the final work C.O.D. I wouldn't worry about getting paid by Warner Brothers, Sony or BMG, for instance, but I would worry about smaller, independent companies in the named fields.

PLUMBING, CONTRACTS AND WFH

When you work on salary for a design firm or agency, you will usually not make as much money as working freelance out of your home or small office. This is because a designer, working alone, gets paid in large chunks and can keep all the money she makes on a job and list itemized deductions on her income tax (it seems to work out better when the IRS doesn't get to automatically grab it from your paycheck). An employee may only get the same amount each week, minus taxes, even if the company has a boom year.

However, many designers can't stomach entrepreneurship and prefer the security of a steady paycheck. The hardest part, of course, is locating clients and attracting work for which one cannot remain cloistered in a studio (at least not at first) but must be proactive, going to meetings, networking, writing proposals, sending out self promotional mailers, and so on. The employee may simply be told what to do and may feel relief at not being required to express much initiative.

Admittedly, as a freelance all my life, I've weathered many lean times, but the flip side is having been able to accumulate enough at times to take an eight-week vacation whenever I wanted to, or take a nap, go to the movies or do laundry in the middle of the day.

It is usually better to charge a flat fee for design, than to charge by the hour. I always think of plumbers, when I think of hourly rates, and—nothing against plumbers—the practice of charging by the hour really denigrates our work in the eyes of clients. Most clients would not feel right about paying us as much per hour as they do their lawyers, and if our work doesn't take us long to complete (the computer has cut my work time in half on an average piece of lettering or illustration), we won't make much money.

From the standpoint of the client's psychology, it's better for us to charge a flat fee, but break it down, if they ask us to, into bite-sized chunks such as Discovery phase, Execution phase, Deployment phase, and silly labels like that. You'll make more money charging flat fees, but explain up front that client additions or alterations cost extra, and these can always be charged at an hourly rate!

Aside from talent, an artist will benefit most from being able to self criticize, to be honestly introspective...and to accept sincere criticism from others without knee-jerk defensiveness.

Advertising agencies and design firms always make clients sign contracts, which usually include something like one-third payment up front before any work begins. Although I have rarely used contracts, my advice to you is to use them, in most cases. When working for large corporations, publishers and ad agencies, they will usually hand you the contract. Remember that in every contract, the writer will try to covertly gain legal and financial advantage over whomever is expected to sign it. Not when we write the contract, of course. I mean the ones *they* want *us* to sign.

I don't use contracts when I'm working with small clients whom I sense are trustworthy and seem to understand concepts like kill fees. I have occasionally judged poorly, but still I've only been burned a few times. If you present a client with a contract and he won't sign it, even one he gets to negotiate on a little bit, I wouldn't deal with him at all. The biggest problem you'll ever have is working with what I call the "amateur client" who has no experience working with artists.

"Work for Hire" (WFH) is a corporate plague upon artists everywhere. Clients get away with making us agree to it because too many of us realize that a job, even with a WFH attached, is better than no job at all, which is a situation freelancers often experience. WFH means that we are signing away our work and all rights to it, forever, to our client. Should our work, say a cartoon character we created, or a logo we designed, go on to have a greater and more illustrious life than we, or even the client, initially envisioned, we have no right to demand further compensation for the additional usage. Many designers make substantial money selling secondary rights to their work. I've resold one image, originally done for a magazine cover, three additional times to other clients. Had I signed a WFH contract I would no longer have owned the art to sell.

There are designers who will not do WFH and insist on placing their © on every piece they do. If they can afford it, I salute them. If I were designing a logo or doing an illustration for some product where the nature of the work was so specific to that company, leaving little possibility for resale, and if the initial compensation was acceptable, I'd have no problem with WFH. Some designers, as an alternative to WFH, will offer to sell the copyright to their work (which normally reverts back to the artist) outright to the client for an additional fee.

When you work as a company employee, all that you produce is generally owned by the company. I know a guy who conceived the idea for a product that went on to become phenomenally successful, netting millions for his employer. At least they gave him a small raise, *but he had to go to them and ask for it!* Another guy, the creator of one of the most successful cartoon series on cable, that has reaped 100 million dollars in merchandising alone, has to content himself with "doing what he loves" (but not sharing in the full rewards) because he created the product under a WFH contract. Just imagine the glee of the network execs as they consider their high profits and "low overhead."

In addition to wanting to keep all the money, corporations increasingly are trying to keep all the credit, too. There's a growing reluctance by corporations to acknowledge creators (or they might have to pay them). Film credits, except for the biggest names, seem to be moving to the ends of movies, authors' bylines are getting smaller and smaller on book covers and clients are increasingly reluctant to let illustrators and designers sign their work. Corporations seem to feel that an artist's signature competes with the company's logo or the product itself. The corporate entity itself wants to be known as the sole creator. In the current hostile corporate environment, we all may end up like the graffiti artists, signing our names on walls in 5184-point letters.

WORKING ON SPEC

"On spec" means working for free, or speculatively, in the hopes that you will please the client and land the account. On spec is often cloaked as a competition. It's really a way for a client to get many designers to work for free and be able to choose from perhaps dozens of submissions. I once received ¥ 1,000,000 from a Japanese firm by submitting the winning design of a trademark character. I agreed to produce rough sketches on spec because I felt the job was so "me." My gambit paid off, the client agreed.

You may wish to accept an on-spec assignment if you are just starting out, have no other work, or need to build up your portfolio. We can always show other clients this work, even if rejected, and claim it was used.

THE AMATEUR CLIENT

He may know widgets in and out—that's how he made his fortune—but God help us when we work for this amateur client who understands nothing about what we designers do. With entrepreneurship on the rise and the explosion in publishing, it has become increasingly likely that you will find yourself working with amateur clients. The first rule is to get some money up front, before you begin working. Tell him it's because, "I haven't worked with you before." And make sure that, in the negotiating stage, he understands all about sketch fees, change charges and kill fees. If he won't sign a contract for your services, that's a good sign that maybe you shouldn't work for him.

Although all clients can be guilty of the following gaucheries, you may be able to spot an amateur client by these signs.

You know you're in trouble when a client tells you…

1. *"I can only afford to pay you $150 bucks for a logo because I still gotta pay the printer, the billboard guy and the fabricator who'll stamp your logo in gold on the stainless steel case."*

Obviously, the client values everybody's work except yours and he's willing to invest perhaps $50,000 in a product based on a logo he claims is only worth $150 to him. Not only is this insulting to us, it marks the client as an idiot.

2. *"I just need a simple logo. That shouldn't take you too long, right?"*

Sometimes the simplest logos take the most time. The client is trying to say (a.) he doesn't want to pay us, and (b.) he doesn't value our time or our process.

3. *"Look, if you'll do this job cheap for me, next time, when I've got a better budget, you're the one I'll call."*

The client is trying to con us. Again. The way this actually works is that by accepting a job for less money than the job is worth, the client loses respect for us and next time, when he has a better budget, he calls another artist whom he respects; who would never have taken a job that paid as poorly as the one we accepted.

4. *"But this job'll be a great portfolio piece for you."*

Translation: I don't want to pay you. Sometimes, it may be worthwhile doing a job that will have great exposure and enhance your portfolio—even for free. But again, this is just another client ploy to pay us less than we deserve.

5. *"I can't afford to pay you anything up front, but I'll pay you a percentage once the product takes off."*

Forget it. You'll never see a cent. If the product does become successful, will you ever be sure you're receiving a proper accounting? Certainly, there are cases where an honest client lived up to his word in full, but such clients are rare. This is another con.

6. *"That printer was an *ssh*le, he screwed me and I won't pay him."*

I worked for the owner of a small record company who always found supposed flaws in whatever typesetting or printing services he contracted for and used these as excuses not to pay anyone. Should I have been surprised when later he refused to pay me for some reason or another? Some clients will agree to pay the designer COD until we become comfortable with him. Then when our usefulness to him ends, he hesitates to pay a few bills and finally skips out on us.

7. *"One-thousand bucks for a logo?! Say, I've got a guy who'll do it for $100."*

"So let him do it," I told the client who called me up a month later willing to pay the thousand for the same logo. "What happened to the $100 logo?" I asked. "It wasn't good enough," he admitted. Well, you get what you pay for!

8. *"I'm not paying for this logo because I can't use it."*

This is a tough one. The guy's business venture collapses, or he simply changes his mind, after you've done the finished logo according to all his idiotic demands. Legally, he has to pay you, and his own circumstances are irrelevant. If you'd been paid one-third up front and one-third upon approval of comps, you'd only be out one-third of the dough. If you had made him sign a contract, you could take him to court.

9. *"I've got this million-dollar idea, see, but you'll have to sign an NDA before I can show it you."*

Every time some smart amateur client has called me up needing a logo and insisting I sign a non-disclosure-agreement (NDA) to legally prevent me from revealing his brainstorm to anyone else, the idea when finally unveiled, has been an insipid one. Ideas, for books or products, are usually not very stealable (although there have been notable exceptions!) because an idea is nothing without its creator's energy behind it. Conversely, even a silly idea can become a mega-hit when someone who believes in it strongly enough puts all his energy behind it. Publishers will generally not steal a book idea because they'd have to hire someone else to write and/or design it, so why not just let you do it in the first place?

10. *"I don't want the logo to be too slick or it'll scare away my working class customers."*

Every night in their living rooms, the poorest and least sophisticated among us (along with the rest of us) watch the most expensive and technologically advanced, state-of-the-art television shows and commercials created by the highest-paid designers on earth. But your client wants you to dumb down his logo. Well, okay…if he's paying!

URLS BEFORE SWINE

Rough sketches can be so tight and quick to produce when drawn on computer, that we are tempted to provide the client with dozens of them in the hope that if fifteen sketches fail to please, the sixteenth might. But unless the client has requested, and is willing to pay for, dozens of rough concepts, it's best to limit him to four or six. Otherwise, the client gets confused and can't choose, or he thinks it must be so easy for us to whip out sketches, he might as well see a dozen more to be sure no concept has been overlooked. This just reinforces the idea in most clients' minds that design is not as valuable as the "real work" of a printer or a lawyer.

Clients can be agonizingly literal. Writer and artist Mark Clarkson explains, "I always want to start the dialogue as soon as possible, lest I go a long way [making sketches] in the wrong direction. But then the…um…client always takes rough sketches at greater than face value. It's like if you were discussing a design at a restaurant and you grabbed a napkin and did a sketch. But the client kept fixating on the wrong issues like the color of the ink in your pen, say, or the texture of the napkin:

What a basic BILLFORM looks like:

Your Personal Logo or Name Here
Your address/phone/fax/email/web site underneath

Date:
Bill to: Client's name
and address here

P.O. #: Your Job number—just make something up.
Client's Job #: If they give you one

Job Description: Leave space here to fully describe the services you will provide in return for…

Total: The amount you want to be paid

Your Signature__________________
Your S.S.# or tax ID#: Don't volunteer unless requested.

Thank You! *Please pay within 30 days of receipt.*

'But I want my book cover in lots of colors, not just blue, and I don't want these curly flowers on the paper, either.' So remember, when it comes to rough comps, think of them as sketches on a napkin."

Because computer roughs are so finished-looking, we must explain to the client that he is looking at roughs that may not be used as final art. One designer submitted logo roughs on paper to a client who decided to use one of them for final art and assumed no further compensation to the designer was required since she was being saved the "extra work" of finishing the logo.

This client didn't realize that if a designer spits on a piece of paper and that spit is used by the client, the designer must be paid in full. If a company goes ahead and uses an artist's work inappropriately, the artist can almost write her own ticket as to the final billing for the illegal use (unless the work was done under a WFH contract). But do everything possible to avoid misunderstandings. Almost nobody wins in court, except lawyers.

MY CLIENT, MY TEACHER

Clients can be really annoying. Either they have no idea what they want, or they'll be so specific about every dumb detail that you'll feel like asking them, "Then what do you need me for?" And the answer is, they don't. Only they don't know how to use Illustrator and Photoshop, so they really just want you to be their hands.

It is true that most clients—like all the drivers on the road ahead of us—are dummköpfe, but every so often, those seemingly ridiculous, annoying little changes have ended up improving the piece. Often, the client's input actually makes us look good. Countless times, after I'd gotten past my resentment over being forced to make a change I didn't agree with, I'd realize that I'd lost objectivity and the client *was* right! After all, even though the client isn't a designer, he may possess basic judgment.

But then again, clients often make our lives a living hell by changing everything good that we've done, leaving us too embarrassed to even want to sign the piece. Jobs like that you just let go. You write them off and deposit the check. The *next* job you do can go into your portfolio.

PROFESSIONAL CONDUCT

It's fun to demonize clients, but remember, they have to deal with *us*, too! Are you the kind of designer who really listens and takes notes on what the client wants, does preliminary research, delivers sketches by the agreed upon date, cheerfully makes changes and finally delivers the finish by deadline? Or are you the kind of designer who treats assignments like school homework, gets flustered and frustrated, procrastinates, calls the client with excuses, makes sketches without heeding instructions, complains or becomes belligerent about changes, and makes the client leave messages for you while you avoid him because you were partying instead of working?

If you disagree with a client, try to give him what he should have, rather than what he thinks he wants.

The fact is, many deadlines are frivolous or false—the client may actually have extra time—but we cannot operate on that basis. Deadlines, especially for publications, can be very tight and dead serious. Many times, art directors confided that we artists are notoriously unreliable. I was also told, on several occasions, that the fact that I respected their deadlines and got my work in on time was one reason why they often hired *me*, rather than someone else.

GETTING THE JOB DONE

Here's a typical scenario: you've just negotiated the price and landed a logo assignment from a small company. Submit a bill for one-third the price of the job. If the client seems reasonable and trustworthy you can agree to bill the total job at the end. Sometimes it's better to show faith in the client to build a relationship, but it's still a gamble on your part. Basically, the more expensive and extensive the job, the more important it is to get up-front money: A web site or brochure design, definitely; a logo or small illustration, not necessarily.

After listening carefully, and taking notes as to what the client wants, begin throwing out some ideas to see if you're both on the same page. If the client is set on an idea that you hate (clients notoriously come up with undrawable, nongraphic concepts), sketch it for him along with some better ideas of your own. He may be smart enough to recognize your superior approach over his preconceived idea. Also, at this time, find out what size and dimensions the finished job must be and if there are printing specifications such as two-colors only, or six PMS spot colors plus blind embossing.

Steep yourself in research to discover the approaches taken by similar companies, or study comparable products, then make your roughs. Invariably you will love one or two of them and present the rest as filler to bulk up the presentation. Invariably the client will like your least-favorite sketch, but she'll ask you to change the colors or to combine the type from one logo with the graphic from another sketch.

Should the client hate all your sketches, but send you away to try again, ask lots of questions first to get her to explain in greater detail what she wants using your rejected sketches as a jumping off point. My policy (though we all hate when this happens) is to do one or two more rounds of sketches until the client is pleased. Otherwise we may lose the job altogether. If after that she is unpleasable, both parties will usually decide to call it quits.

But let's say that the client likes your next sketches and tells you to finish one of them, which you do. Now submit your second bill for the sketches (which usually represents three-quarters of your actual labor on any job). Finally, you hand in the finish. The client looks at it and says, "Great! Just what I wanted… except…whattaya think if instead of two cows as we agreed, make it two mules."

We must now decide whether to bill for the change or to accept it graciously and not be petty. Whether we do so or not will depend upon the complexity of the change (I usually do the first change for free), whether the client has been a pain in the behind, how many other changes have been asked for during the process, and whether or not we feel it worthwhile absorbing the loss of time in order to build a relationship with the client that might lead to further work.

Let's make clear that there are two types of changes: those the client asks for *before* "signing off" (giving official approval) on a sketch, and those changes the client asks for when he changes his mind after we've done the job precisely according to his wishes. In the first case, we are obliged to make changes or we may lose the job. In the second case, the client should pay for our wasted time when he can't make up his mind. Yet, between the sketch and the finish there can be a world of differences and the client should have the right to tweak the finish to his satisfaction—up to a point. Unfortunately, the client can withhold payment if he's not satisfied with the final, so it's best to make nice-nice and try to keep him happy because, in the end, the customer—even when he's a moron—is always right. Once the job is finished and billed don't neglect to request printed samples of the job for your portfolio.

MARKETING FONTS

After we've designed a font, what then? Most larger foundries accept outside submissions and have differing submission guidelines that can be found on their web sites, or by e-mailing them. Most foundries will want fonts with full character sets, though your first submitted version won't need to be complete.

Some foundries pay advances although that has become rare. Most often, you'll receive a royalty the amounts of which can vary widely, from 10 percent to 50 percent according to foundry. Online font foundries seem to distribute fonts according to one of three principles: Sell high-quality fonts at high prices, low-quality fonts at low prices, or give 'em away free.

I have taken many pot shots at free font foundries because those of us who sell our fonts, naturally don't like the idea that our prices—and some customers' senses of value—are being undermined by fonts that are free. If Pontiacs were given away free on the web, many people would not want to pay for a Lexus, even though the difference in quality might be considerable. This analogy is well applied to fonts. Not always, but in general, the quality of free fonts can't compare to that of professional fonts sold by the larger foundries. For one thing, assuming most designers need to eat, how many of us can afford to work for free? Thus, the free fonts are often those produced by students, retirees or others who often don't spend enough quality time with their products to tweak them to a professional level.

Regardless of whether you sell or give away fonts, if you intend to do it yourself, you'll need a web site. Ideally you'll be able to include features like automatic credit card billing and automatic downloading so that font lovers in Australia will not have to wait until you wake up to receive their fonts. The best way to plan your font site is to type "fonts" in a search engine and research font sites as well as font prices.

I, DESIGNAHOLIC

The Latin phrase "ars longa, vita brevis" (art is long, life is short) sums up my feeling that there's just too much to accomplish and too little time to do it in. When I was a boy, my mother used to say to me, "Why don't you go outside and play?" I'd answer, "What do you mean—there's no pencil and paper out there!" Or she'd say, "You're always working!" And I'd say, "I'm not working, I'm playing." And that's how my life has gone, ever since.

Author James Michener wrote, "A master in the art of living draws no distinction between work and play. He hardly knows which is which. He simply pursues his vision of excellence through whatever he is doing and leaves others to determine whether he is working or playing."

So I began to wonder if workaholism is a prerequisite to greatness, if other designers were like me, and if I should tell my readers that you have to work hard to get good at this. I sent a short survey to the contributors of this book. I asked for percentages of time spent working, as opposed to time with family and other activities. The following averages, the result of twenty professionals surveyed, are revealing (see above). But more interesting were the comments that invariably accompanied the surveys some of which I've included, without identifying the writers:

What percentage of waking hours do you spend:

Working	With spouse /family	Hobbies	Recreation	On the internet
71%	11%	2%	9%	7%

"There is never enough time to get the work done. It always seems barely enough, so any time that isn't specifically set aside for the rest of life tends to be converted to 'guilt time': I really should be working. Because, for some reason, I think my work is important."

"Your survey really shows me how much my life sucks! I need to make some significant changes, however, my mind seems to need to remain consumed with problems to solve and information to absorb."

"Even while doing other stuff, I'm always thinking about design/illustration. Ideas will come to me from all kinds of experiences and feed in."

"When I'm working, all I think about is sex, and when I'm having sex, all I think about is work."

"If the word 'working' includes designing as well as thinking, or 'pre-designing,' dreaming up projects, talking to potential clients, seeking inspiration and other such nebulous activities, mental and otherwise, then 80–90 percent of my time is spent this way."

"I have sacrificed much 'fun' time in my life since I started working at a young age. [Your survey results] really make me wonder if I should take more time for myself, because my bank account certainly isn't growing."

"If work paid about three times as well, I'd be happy to do a little less of it. I can't afford not to be insanely busy"

"Ahh, what a sad, sad life we type designers live, all for the love of letters. I wish I had time for hobbies."

"It is quite shocking to actually tally the hours spent on work versus the rest of life that includes family, friends, socializing, etc."

"I'm not sure anyone who isn't born with this affliction called 'creativity' can really understand what it means to live with the 'sweet & sour.' One day art schools will require all prospective graduates to complete a course called 'Insatiable Appetite 101' or 'The Unscratchable Itch.' I've had the disease since birth...The blank page forever challenges my pencil."

For myself, I have learned that there is an ironic agony that follows an artist's progression. The further we are able to advance along the artistic path, the greater becomes our ability to see just how much farther the road extends. Designer Michelangelo Buonarotti must have felt this. On his death bed he uttered, "I regret that...I am dying just as I am beginning to learn the alphabet of my profession."

DIRECTORY

Contributors

Adcrobatics, ***20, 22***
Jonathan Macagba,
New York, New York
tel: (212) 260-1785
info@adcrobatics.com
www.adcrobatics.com

Lalo Alcaraz, ***173***
Los Angeles, California
pocho@pocho.com
www.lacucaracha.com

Astigmatic One Eye
Typographic Institute, ***210***
Brian J. Bonislawsky
North Miami, Florida
astigma@astigmatic.com
www.astigmatic.com

Jill Bell, ***31, 85, 90***
Los Angeles, California
tel: (310) 322-5542
jill@jillbell.com
www.jillbell.com

Black Dog, ***21, 30, 163***
Mark Fox
San Anselmo, California
tel: (415) 258-9663
mfox@blackdogma.com
www.blackdogma.com

Keith Campbell, ***20***
New York, NY
fax: (201) 569-2510

Michael Clark ***84***
Richmond, Virgina
tel: (804) 261-4965
typerror@aol.com
www.ideabook.com/michaelclark

Mark Clarkson, ***171***
Wichita, Kansas
tel: 316.688.5071
mark@markclarkson.com
www.markclarkson.com

Chris Costello, ***20, 31***
Watertown, Massachusetts
tel: (617) 926-4251
chriscostello@grolen.com
www.costelloart.com

David Coulson
Pittsburg, Pennsylvania
tel: (412) 243-7064
david@davidcoulson.com
www.davidcoulson.com

Cubanica, ***206, 209***
Pablo A. Medina
New York, New York
tel: (800) 615-3533
info@cubanica.com
www.cubanica.com

Rick Cusick, ***84, 125***
Overland Park, Kansas
tel: (913) 648-6405
rickcusick@mac.com

Device, ***101, 111, 162***
Rian Hughes
London, United Kingdom
FAX (44) 0207 575 3055
RianHughes@aol.com
www.devicefonts.co.uk

Tony DiSpigna, ***51, 81***
Brooklyn New York
tel: (718) 837-2204
Dispigna1@aol.com

Michael Doret, ***30, 47, 229***
Los Angeles, California
tel: (323) 467-1900
michael@michaeldoret.com
www.michaeldoret.com

Stan Endo, ***25, 182***
Los Angeles, California
tel: (323) 856-9027
sendo@earthlink.net
www.endodesign.com

Shepard Fairey, ***7***
Los Angeles, California
tel: (213) 383-9299
amanda@obeygiant.com
www.obeygiant.com

Louise Fili Ltd., ***27***
Louise Fili
New York, New York
tel: (212) 989-9153
louise@louisefili.com
www.louisefili.com

Mark S. Fisher, ***28, 101, 163***
Lowell, Massachusetts
tel: (978) 452-0977
marksfisher@bigplanet.com
www.marksfisher.com

FlashFonts, ***21, 23, 28, 31, 48, 50***
Leslie Cabarga
Los Angeles, California
tel: (323) 549-0700
fax: (323) 549-0202
lescab@flashfonts.com
www.flashfonts.com
www.logofontandlettering.com
www.lesliecabarga.com

Font Diner, ***210, 211, 228***
Stuart Sandler
Blaine, Minneapolis
diner@fontdiner.com
www.fontdiner.com

The Font Bureau, ***228***
David Berlow
Harry Parker
Boston, Massachusetts
tel: (617) 423-8770
fax: (617) 423-8771
info@fontbureau.com
www.fontbureau.com

Form Function & Finesse, ***23***
Seth Bernstein
St. Louis, Missouri
fax: (314) 647-6444
sbernstn@swbell.net

Patrick Giasson, ***211***
London, United Kingdom
Tel: +44 207 713 1039
patrickgiasson@hotmail.com

Shane Glines, ***145***
Eugene, Oregon
tel: (541) 221-8811
sglines@earthlink.net
www.shaneglines.net

Hoefler & Frere-Jones Typography,
146, 206
Jonathan Hoefler
Tobias Frere-Jones
New York, New York
Tel: (212) 777-6640
info@typography.com
www.typography.com

Nigel Holmes, ***162***
Explanation Graphics
Westport, Connecticut
tel: (203) 226-2313
fax: (203) 222-9545
www.nigelholmes.com
nigel@nigelholmes.com

Gerard Huerta Design, ***26***
Southport, Connecticut
tel: (203) 256-1625
gerardhuerta@earthlink.net
www.gerardhuerta.com

JHI, ***20, 26, 228***
John Homs
Richmond, Virginia
tel: (804) 340-5200
fax: (804) 340-5201
info@jhigoodidea.com
www.jhigoodidea.com

Viktor Kaganovich, ***172***
Hamburg, Germany
tel: +49 40 22748030
mail@ viktorkaganovich.com
www.viktorkaganovich.com

Larabie Fonts/ Typodermic
Ray Larabie
Mississauga, Ontario
ray@typodermic.com
www.typodermic.com

Christian Lavigne, ***147***
Paris, France
tel: 33 (0)1 43 26 45 85
lavigne@toile-metisse.org
www.toile-metisse.org/cl

Tom Nikosey, ***174, 228***
Encino, California
tel: (818) 704-9993
Logoten@aol.com
www.tomnikosey.com

Mitch O'Connell, ***110, 145***
Chicago, Illinois
tel: (773) 588-8797
info@mitchoconnell.com
www.mitchoconnell.com

Jim Parkinson, ***19, 146***
Parkinson Type Design
Oakland California
tel: (510) 547-3100
parkinson@typedesign.com
www.typedesign.com

Daniel Pelavin, ***19, 43, 163, 175***
New York, New York
tel: 212 941-7418
daniel@pelavin.com
www.pelavin.com

Planet Propaganda, ***20, 29, 30, 228***
Madison, Wisconsin
tel: (608) 256-0000
travis@planetpropaganda.com
www.planetpropaganda.com

Pushpin Group, Inc., ***29, 230***
Seymour Chwast
New York, New York
tel: (212) 529-7590
fax: (212) 529-7631
info@pushpininc.com
www.pushpininc.com

Ross Culbert & Lavery, Inc., ***30***
Michael Aron
New York, New York
tel: (212)206.0044
maron@rclnyc.com
www.rclnyc.com

Michael Samuel, ***23, 169***
Michael Samuel Graphics
New York, New York
tel: (212) 722-8125
logosam@earthlink.net
www.samuelgraphics.biz

Wolfgang Schindler, ***165***
Hamburg, Germany
tel: +49 40 51 26 50
schindler@invisiblecircle.de
www.invisiblecircle.de/schindler

Michael Schwab, ***27***
San Anselmo, California
tel: (415)-257-5792
fax: (415) 257-5793
michael@michaelschwab.com
www.michaelschwab.com

Paul Shaw, ***83, 202***
New York, New York
Tel: (212) 666-3738
Fax: (212) 666-2163;
paulshaw@aol.com
www.letterspace.com

SignalGrau Design, ***22, 23, 26***
Dirk Uhlenbrock
Essen, Germany
tel: +49.201.730511
fax: +49.201.730521
du@signalgrau.com
www.signalgrau.com

Mark Simonson, ***31***
St. Paul, Minnesota
tel: (651) 649-0553
mark@ms-studio.com
www.ms-studio.com

Smiling Otis Studio, ***21, 31***
Russ Cox
Lancaster, Pennsylvania
tel: (717) 291-0597
fax: (717) 291-0598
russ@smilingotis.com
www.smilingotis.com

TreePeople, ***20***
Maryrose Hopke
Beverly Hills, CA
tel: (818) 753-4600
info@treepeople.org
www.treepeople.org

Doyald Young Design, ***84***
Doyald Young
Sherman Oaks, California
tel: (818) 788-5562
doyald@pacbell.net
www.delphipress.com

Foundries Represented:

astigmatic.com
devicefonts.co.uk
fontbureau.com
fonts.com
P22.com
fontdiner.com
flashfonts.com
typography.com
logofontandlettering.com
jillbell.com
letterspace.com
ms-studio.com
typedesign.com
girlswhowearglasses.com
costelloart.com
adobe.com/type/main.jhtml
comicraft.com
itcfonts.com
emigre.com
burodestruct.net
regleszero.com

Resources:

Identifont.com (locate fonts)

regleszero.com (online type magazine)

typographer.com (type news)

typographi.ca (type news)

typophile.com (type forums)

fontlover.com (type news)

Oswald Cooper (web movie)
www.cheshiredave.com/movies

Jim Gallagher (Fontographer guru)
supportandmore.com

typesociety.org (The Society of Typographic Aficionados)

fontlab.com (font creation software)

Despite every effort to ensure the thoroughness and accuracy of the information and tutorials in this book, I know that many readers will have suggestions for, and perhaps objections to, parts of the content.With the intention of making this the very best book that it can be, I invite your comments, criticisms, corrections, tips and tricks and will attempt to incorporate all that have merit into future editions of the book. However, I will not be able to comment on readers' personal work or offer tech support on issues covered or not covered in this book (even with 240 pages, I was regretfully unable to include all the information I had hoped to). Please contact me through my web sites, logofontandlettering.com, and flashfonts.com.

INDEX